Mexico and Its Diaspora in the United States
Policies of Emigration since 1848

In the past two decades, changes in the Mexican government's policies toward the 30 million Mexican migrants living in the United States highlight the importance of the Mexican diaspora in both countries, given its size, its economic power, and its growing political participation across borders. This work examines how the Mexican government's assessment of the possibilities and consequences of implementing emigration policies to protect and promote the rights of this population, and engage migrant organizations from 1848 to 2010, has been tied to changes in the bilateral relationship. Understanding this dynamic gives an insight into the stated and unstated objectives of Mexico's recent activism in defending migrants' rights and engaging the diaspora, the continuing linkage between Mexican migration policies and shifts in the United States–Mexico relationship, and the limits and possibilities for expanding shared mechanisms for the management of migration within the framework of the North American Free Trade Agreement.

Dr. Alexandra Délano is Assistant Professor of Global Studies at The New School in New York City. Her research focuses on Mexican migration, immigrant integration in the United States, and diaspora engagement policies. She received her doctorate in International Relations from Oxford University and has been a Post-Doctoral Fellow in Politics at The New School for Social Research and a Fellow at Yale University. Her articles have appeared in *International Migration Review, The Journal of Ethnic and Migration Studies, International Migration, Social Research, Foro Internacional, Americas Quarterly,* and *Migración y Desarrollo.*

Mexico and Its Diaspora in the United States

Policies of Emigration since 1848

ALEXANDRA DÉLANO
The New School, New York

 CAMBRIDGE
UNIVERSITY PRESS

CAMBRIDGE UNIVERSITY PRESS
Cambridge, New York, Melbourne, Madrid, Cape Town,
Singapore, São Paulo, Delhi, Tokyo, Mexico City

Cambridge University Press
32 Avenue of the Americas, New York, NY 10013-2473, USA

www.cambridge.org
Information on this title: www.cambridge.org/9781107011267

First published 2011

Printed in the United States of America

A catalog record for this publication is available from the British Library.

Library of Congress Cataloging in Publication data

Délano, Alexandra, 1979–
Mexico and its diaspora in the United States : policies of emigration since 1848 /
Alexandra Délano.
    p. cm.
Includes bibliographical references and index.
ISBN 978-1-107-01126-7 (hardback)
1. Mexico – Emigration and immigration – Government policy – History.
2. Foreign workers, Mexican – United States.   I. Title.
JV7401.D45   2011
325′.2720973–dc22   2011002260

ISBN 978-1-107-01126-7 Hardback

To all those who work to promote and protect the rights of Mexican migrants, aquí y allá

Contents

Acknowledgments

This journey began in the summer of 2000 when I first witnessed the realities of the Mexico–United States border in field trips to Calexico and multiple crossings of *la línea* as part of the Summer Seminar in U.S. Studies at the University of California, San Diego (UCSD). As a Mexican citizen standing on the U.S. side of the border, smelling the New River and the stinking waters that the Border Patrol will not touch for fear of infections but that migrants submerge themselves in, and talking to migrants who had been detained, my indignation was mostly about what was happening on the other side. What made these men and women so desperate to try to cross again and again even if this meant undergoing painful and humiliating experiences? Why were they more afraid of the Mexican police waiting for them on the other side than of the U.S. Border Patrol as they munched through the snacks they were given at the detention center? How could the Mexican government and so many Mexican citizens remain passive and continue to see this process and its consequences as a "natural phenomenon," a "rite of passage," a "necessary evil?"

Much has been written about U.S. immigration policy, its contradictions, and its unintended consequences. Similarly, there is a wide bibliography on Mexican migration, its history and, more recently, Mexico's policies. However, few studies look at both policies side by side and at the ways in which migration flows and policies are linked to variations in the United States–Mexico relationship. This became the focus of my work, first because I wanted to understand the evolution of both countries' policies and the ways in which they have influenced each other. Second, and most importantly, I wanted to uncover the generally unchallenged acceptance of Mexico as the weaker actor in this relationship and its implications in terms of the government's "inability" to control migration flows and address their causes and effects. This view was greatly influenced by my studies in International Relations at El Colegio de México and the work of many of my professors there who have disputed the assumption of Mexico as a defenseless actor vis-à-vis the United States. I am forever indebted to El Colegio for the opportunity to be a part of such a rich community of scholars and students; this community largely shaped my views not just on the issues that we studied but on education and the role of academia in policy and advocacy. I am particularly grateful to Ana Covarrubias Jorge Domínguez and Sergio Aguayo for their mentorship and support.

Throughout these ten years of work on Mexico–United States migration, I have been privileged to have the opportunity to learn from and have the support of experts in the field. Gilbert Joseph and Patricia Pessar at Yale University helped me gain confidence in the work I was doing and provided the unforgettable opportunity to give my first lecture. Andrew Hurrell, my advisor at Oxford University, has taught me as much about the ways to unpack and make a compelling argument as he has about the importance and value of having a mentor; he has been an example to follow as a scholar, a professor, and a friend. His support and his belief in this project from its early stages have been essential and have motivated me to continue challenging myself in this field.

My arrival at The New School has been one of the most important steps in my professional life and I am deeply grateful to Vicky Hattam, David Plotke, Jonathan Bach, and Ary Zolberg for trusting me and giving me a place as a colleague. Teaching at The New School is a unique experience, every day, and I thank every single one of my students for all that I have learned from them and with them.

Los caminos de la vida have brought me to live in New York City for almost five years now, but a part of me is and always will be on the other side of the border and I would not be able to be at peace "here" if I weren't somehow connected to "there." Thanks to Carlos González Gutiérrez, former Executive Director of the Institute of Mexicans Abroad (IME), I have had invaluable opportunities to work on a number of projects related to research about the institute and to teach a course about Mexican communities abroad through the diplomatic academy, *Instituto Matías Romero*. This connection to members of the Mexican foreign service, and the people who work for the IME in Mexico, the

United States, and Canada, inspires me to continue working in this field
and focus on projects that may help create awareness and inform better
policies in Mexico and the United States.

The field research that I refer to in this work would not have been
possible without Carlos's support as Executive Director of the IME and
his staff. I also thank Arturo Sarukhan for the opportunity to work and
do research at the Mexican Consulate in New York. This experience was
definitive in helping me develop a better understanding of the work that
is done through the consulates, and it also provided access to primary
sources that are quoted in this work. Many current and former Mexican
government officials and specialists on migration issues were also kind to
offer their time for interviews that were of great value for my research.

As part of this research, I had the unique opportunity to meet and
formally or informally interview a number of people who work with the
Mexican communities in the United States and Canada, either as consular
employees, community leaders, teachers, or advocates, and to personally
interview more than 400 Mexican migrants at five Mexican consulates.
Each one of their experiences and stories moves me; even though their
names are not quoted here, they are the voices that need to be heard
and that I hope to reflect in some form through my continuing work on
migration.

A number of people have been kind readers of my work and have
helped me improve it through their constructive criticism and suggestions.
I am deeply grateful to the two anonymous readers selected by Cambridge
University Press for their insightful and detailed comments, which were
incredibly helpful in my process of rethinking, revising, and improving
the manuscript. Stephen Castles, Julián Escutia, Alan Gamlen, Carlos
González Gutiérrez, Andrew Hurrell, Kevin Middlebrook, Vicky Hattam,
and David Plotke also provided helpful comments on previous versions
of this manuscript or parts of it. I also thank my editor, Eric Crahan, for
supporting this project and for making the editorial process an enjoyable
experience with his patience, precision, and good nature. The book would
not have been possible without his effort, or the careful work of Susan
Zinninger, copyeditor, and Peter Katsirubas, project manager.

Portions of this work have appeared in the following publications
and are published with permission: "Immigrant Integration vs. Transnational Ties? The Role of the Sending State," *Social Research* (Vol. 77,
No. 1, Spring 2010, pp. 237–268); "From Limited To Active Engagement:
Mexico's Emigration Policies from a Foreign Policy Perspective (2000–
2006)," *International Migration Review* (Vol. 43, No. 4, Winter 2009,

pp. 764–814); "From 'Shared Responsibility' to a Migration Agreement? The Limits for Cooperation in the Mexico–United States Case (2000–2008)," *International Migration* (September 2009); and "The Mexican Government and Organised Mexican Immigrants in The United States: A Historical Analysis of Political Transnationalism (1848–2005)," co-authored with Gustavo Cano, *Journal of Ethnic and Migration Studies* (Vol. 33, No. 5, July 2007, pp. 695–725).

This work has been part of a process of crossing many borders, both physical and personal. It would not have been possible without my partner on this journey, my best friend, and greatest motivation every day, Paul. Thank you.

New York, April 2011

Mexican Foreign-Born Population and Mexican Consulates by State

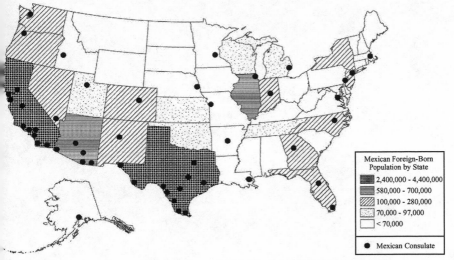

Mexican Foreign-Born
Population by State
- ▓ 2,400,000 - 4,400,000
- ■ 580,000 - 700,000
- ▨ 100,000 - 280,000
- ░ 70,000 - 97,000
- ☐ < 70,000

● Mexican Consulate

Sources: US Census Bureau, American Community Survey 2009; Secretaría de Relaciones Exteriores 2010

Mexican-origin population in the United States 1900–2009

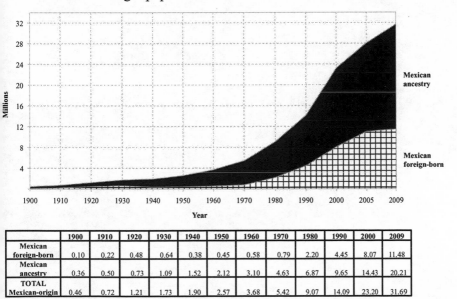

	1900	1910	1920	1930	1940	1950	1960	1970	1980	1990	2000	2009
Mexican foreign-born	0.10	0.22	0.48	0.64	0.38	0.45	0.58	0.79	2.20	4.45	8.07	11.48
Mexican ancestry	0.36	0.50	0.73	1.09	1.52	2.12	3.10	4.63	6.87	9.65	14.43	20.21
TOTAL Mexican-origin	0.46	0.72	1.21	1.73	1.90	2.57	3.68	5.42	9.07	14.09	23.20	31.69

Source: CONAPO (2008), "Población de origen mexicano residente en Estados Unidos, 1900-2007"; US Census Bureau, American Community Survey 2009.

Introduction

Engaging the Mexican Diaspora

On May 27, 2009, Mixteca Organization, a community-based organization in Sunset Park, Brooklyn, offered its first Mixteca Diaspora Awards to four "courageous leaders" that have "worked to create a lasting foundation for the success and growth of the Mexican Latin American immigrant community."[1] Although the word "diaspora" is rarely used by Mexican migrants and community organizations, or by the Mexican government, which normally favors the term "Mexican communities abroad," for Dr. Gabriel Rincón, founder and president of Mixteca Organization, this is a "real term" that describes the suffering of Mexican migrants and the reasons behind this "forced migration" (personal interview, 2009). In his view, the use of the term "diaspora" in the Mexican case reflects the experience of traditional diasporas: "Even if Mexican migration is explained more by economic than political causes, these are just as meaningful as the Jewish experience in the sense that there is a great deal of suffering in the process of crossing the border, in leaving their families behind, in the conditions of poverty that exist in Mexico and force them to leave, and in their inability to go back home" (personal interview, 2009). Dr. Rincón, a first-generation Mexican immigrant, recognizes that the Mexican community in general does not identify with the term "diaspora" and in most cases its members do not understand what

---

[1] The honorees were Ambassador Rubén Beltrán, Consul General of Mexico in New York; Vice Chancellor Jay Hershenson of the City University of New York (CUNY); Jaime Lucero, President of Casa Puebla New York; and Adriana Rocha, Practice Director of CompassPoint Nonprofit Services (information obtained from Mixteca Diaspora Awards flyer, May 27, 2009).

it means. Still, he argues, for those who do know what the term means, it makes sense.

Whether or not the approximately 31 million Mexicans and Mexican Americans currently in the United States, or some groups among them, can be considered part of a diaspora is still a matter of debate, given the diversity within the community and its varying relationships with the home country. In the academic literature the use of the term in reference to Mexican emigration varies, with some authors favoring its broader use and others making a point about not using it for this case.[2] Even though some government officials and the Institute of Mexicans Abroad (IME, in Spanish) do refer to the "Mexican diaspora" as such, in the Mexican government's discourse, the term "Mexican communities abroad" prevails. This can be explained as an explicit resistance to using the term "diaspora" because of its historical and political roots in relation to the Jewish or Armenian experiences, or the idea that "diaspora" might imply a more permanent migration, which until the late 1980s was not considered to be characteristic of Mexican migration. It could also be explained simply as a general preference for continuing to use the term "Mexican communities abroad," which can be more easily understood and create a broader identification for Mexican migrants.

For example, Jorge G. Castañeda, former Secretary of Foreign Affairs (2000–2003), describes the IME, designed under his administration, as "the latest in a series of programs or institutions created by the Mexican government as a link with the diaspora, or what it likes to think of as a diaspora" (Castañeda, 2007: 157). In a personal interview he explained in greater detail that he does not agree with using this term: "I do not believe in the diaspora or in the idea of a Mexican lobby similar to the Jewish lobby. Rather, we should equip Mexican migrants with the tools

---

[2] From an academic perspective the use of the term "diaspora" to describe the Mexican experience corresponds with the criteria set by authors such as Sheffer (1986), Shain and Barth (2003), and Cohen (2008), among others, in an attempt to widen this notion and provide a more nuanced understanding of migrants' relationships with their homeland. In response to critiques that the term is now too broad and risks being devoid of any real meaning (Brubaker, 2005), a number of authors have established certain criteria to establish whether a group can be designated as a diaspora, mostly coinciding with the premise that a dispersed population's identification with a real or imagined homeland and maintenance of emotional or social ties with it is a key feature of a diaspora. Reflecting the variety of experiences within the diaspora, the divisions within it, and the fact that not all members are active in the same way, the use of the term even in these broader terms recognizes that "not all migrants will cohere into communities and not all migrant communities will imagine themselves as transnational." Thus the term "diaspora" is not a synonym for all migrants (Cohen, 2008: 13).

to organize on their own to defend their rights, to have an institution of their own – the Institute of Mexicans Abroad – but not necessarily to be a political influence in the U.S. on Mexico's behalf" (personal interview, 2009). There is a sense in these statements that by using the term "diaspora" there is a negative implication that the Mexican government is influencing the development of a lobby group and that the lack of clarity in the use of concepts such as this can lead to misperceptions of the Mexican government's activities in the United States.

In contrast to this view, the Mexican Ambassador to the United States, Arturo Sarukhan, favors the use of the term "diaspora," arguing that it represents a move away from the clientelist relationship that existed through the so-called *Comunidades* approach of the 1990s. From his perspective, the use of the term "diaspora" embodies the idea of building a mutually beneficial relationship (personal interview, 2009). Ambassador Enrique Berruga, former Undersecretary for North America (2000–2003), disagrees with the use of the term "diaspora" in the Mexican case, given its connotations with regard to situations of repression, but his explanation for the rationale behind the government's establishment of the IME and its Advisory Council reinforces this idea of the government's interest in developing new types of relationships with Mexican migrants in the United States and changing the language and symbols that inform this relationship: "We needed a more updated institution. We needed to interact with migrant leaders in a non-paternalistic way. They are the ones who know how things work over there.... And in a context of democratization in Mexico we also needed to democratize our institutions and provide a space for a more active and participatory society" (personal interview, 2010).

The use of the term "diaspora" might seem to be a minor and petty detail in the bigger picture of Mexican migrants' needs in the United States and the government's efforts to respond to them. However, the choice of terms and the language used in the definition of objectives and interactions with Mexican migrants is important because it reflects the continuing struggle within the Mexican state to define its position on emigration. It shows the legacies of a historical ambivalence and in some cases indifference with regard to emigration in the Mexican government's recent attempts to respond to the growth and development of Mexican migration and Mexican migrant organizations in the United States. The language of "Mexican communities abroad" as opposed to "Mexican diaspora" also captures the diversity of Mexican migrants and their organizations in terms of their legal status, their interest in maintaining ties with Mexico, their transnational activities, their state or region of origin, and the fact that until very recently they have not acted as a unified bloc with common goals, either in relation to their political objectives in Mexico or the United States. This book shows how the Mexican government has changed its discourse and policy in relation to Mexican emigrants since the late 1980s, and has since then played a key role in providing services to promote the rights of this population beyond consular protection activities and developing relationships with migrant leaders and their organizations, all within the context of perceived or real limits and opportunities offered by the bilateral relationship with the United States.

In this work I choose to use the term "Mexican diaspora" to reflect characteristics of the Mexican experience that are sometimes overlooked, including the historical roots of this migration and the complex transnational identities and relationships that migrants and their organizations have developed with their home country. The discussion of the term "diaspora" in the Mexican case is also useful as a window into the government's process of redefinition of what Mexican emigration represents for the country and how it engages with this population. Finally, the reference to Mexican migrants as being part of a diaspora also places this discussion within the larger framework of the debate about diasporas and development. In the Mexican case, the influence of migrants in the country's development, through remittances and investments in communities of origin, is one of the factors that has influenced a change in the government's discourse and response to the needs and demands of this population, as has been the case in a number of migrant-sending states[3] and in the international community.

This book analyzes how the Mexican state has shaped its objectives and interests regarding emigration and its relationship with the diaspora, and how transformations in the dynamic of the United States–Mexico bilateral relationship since the 1980s have influenced changes in this policy

---

[3] Barry (2006: 13–14, n. 5) argues that the terms "sending state" and "host state" are misleading "and reflect and reinforce policy positions in the North that developed *receiving* countries neither generate nor facilitate migrant flows." She also claims that these terms imply that sending states are passive and host states are active. Gamlen (2006) has also pointed out the need to debunk the myths of sending states as poor, disinterested, southern states: Sending states are not necessarily "responding to inferior positions in the asymmetrical world system" and neither are receiving states solely developed countries. Without disregarding these nuances, in this study, I use the common terminology of "sending state," "homeland," and "country of origin," as well as "host state," "country of destination," or "receiving state."

area.[4] I focus particularly on the evolution of Mexican emigration policies from a position of limited engagement to a more active relationship with Mexican nationals in the United States and more direct responses to U.S. policies and legislation, as well as closer contacts with the U.S. government regarding the management of migratory flows, particularly since the 1990s.

I argue that these changes are not only a result of the growth of the Mexican migrant population and its increasing political and economic influence in Mexico in a context of democratization, as most studies have suggested (Sherman, 1999; Shain, 1999–2000; Martínez Saldaña, 2003; Smith, 2003b). Rather, these developments and policy shifts also need to be understood as a result of closer economic integration between the countries, which gave way to a new interpretation of Mexico's relations with the United States and a reevaluation of the scope and limits of the foreign policy principle of nonintervention and the strategy of "delinkage"[5] in this issue area, an aspect that has not been thoroughly explored in the existing literature and continues to shape Mexico's emigration policies.[6] The process of economic liberalization beginning in the 1980s and the

---

[4] By emphasizing the study of Mexico's emigration policies I focus on policies involving the Mexican population living abroad, including the state's position on emigration flows – whether it promotes them, restricts them, or is indifferent – and its policies regarding the protection of migrants and promotion of relations with the diaspora. With limited exceptions, this study excludes the analysis of Mexican policies and legislation on immigration to the country, and its management of flows in its southern border; this is a topic of increasing concern addressed in works such as Castillo (2006); Castillo and Toussaint (2009, 2010); and Amnesty International (2010).

[5] Given the complexity and disparity of interests on each issue, both Mexico and the United States have generally been reluctant to link issues in the bilateral agenda. For Mexico, linking issues is generally perceived as a bargaining game in which it would end up as the loser or produce adverse effects in other areas. An example of this is Mexico's reluctance to use oil resources as a bargaining instrument. Thus, Mexico usually prefers maintaining the "disadvantageous but nonetheless familiar" status quo. For both countries, "preserving the relationship [takes] precedence over resolving the issues" (Ronfeldt and Sereseres, 1983: 88–89).

[6] Hernández-López (2008) recently published a legal analysis of the changes in Mexico's interpretation of the principle of nonintervention in migration issues. The author's argument differs from mine in its claim that the transnational impact of migration has been the main factor influencing changes in Mexico's conception of sovereignty and therefore its interpretation of the constitutional foreign policy principles. Although I recognize the importance of the transnational impact of migration as well as domestic factors that have influenced this process of change, I argue that the developments in the bilateral relationship are key in the gradual transformation of Mexico's perception of limits and possibilities regarding emigration policies, which is tied to a reinterpretation of the non-intervention principle.

institutionalization of Mexico–United States cooperation on commercial and financial issues, particularly through the North American Free Trade Agreement (NAFTA), implied a learning process that resulted in key changes in Mexico's approach to the bilateral relationship. In many cases, this led to more proactive policies for promoting Mexico's interests in the United States and to the development of new mechanisms for collaboration with the U.S. government rather than using the discourse of vulnerability in the asymmetrical relationship as an excuse for limited action on sensitive issues, such as migration.

I explore the significance of the United States–Mexico bilateral relationship not only as part of the context in which policies are designed, but as a key factor that has shaped the sending state's responses to emigration and has varied over time. Through a historical review it is clear that Mexico's emigration policies have developed not only in response to political and economic changes at the domestic and transnational levels but also in relation to foreign policy principles and interests, mainly in relation to the United States. Thus, the Mexican state's consideration of the limits and possibilities for developing activities related to emigrants are not only determined by pressures and interests inside the state, but also by how it measures the consequences of a certain policy (or nonpolicy) with regard to a potential reaction from the U.S. government. This analysis shows that the sending state's activities vis-à-vis the diaspora and its responses to the host state's policies are not predetermined by a structure of power asymmetry such as the one present in the United States–Mexico relationship; the perceptions of what is acceptable or not within this structure have varied as a result of changes at the domestic, transnational, and bilateral levels.

SENDING STATES' INTERESTS

Conventional wisdom is that most sending states are disinterested in establishing relationships with their diasporas, that states concerned with emigration are abnormal, or that sending states are unable to pursue their objectives and interests regarding emigration as a result of their generally weaker position in the international system (Schmitter-Heisler, 1985; Gamlen, 2006). However, there is increasingly solid evidence that a growing number of sending states, in both the developed and developing world, have established more forms of contact with their diasporas and have gradually sought to engage them in domestic economic and political life (Østergaard-Nielsen, 2003; Koslowski, 2005; Brand, 2006; Gamlen, 2006; González Gutiérrez, 2006c, 2006d; Brinkerhoff, 2008; Agunias, 2009; Iskander, 2010). To varying degrees, many sending states implement policies to control emigration, offer consular protection and services for their emigrants in the host country, or grant political rights and economic incentives in their country of origin.

In part, the rising interest of states in managing emigration and engaging with their diasporas is due to the growth of emigration as well as the increasing impact of transnational relations between emigrants and their homelands, facilitated by the technological revolution in communication and transportation systems.[7] Many sending states are increasingly dependent on emigration as an economic or political safety valve or as a generator of foreign currency and political support abroad (Guarnizo, 1998: 46). Some countries also see emigrants as potential ambassadors for promoting economic and political relations with other countries (Levitt and de la Dehesa, 2003: 599). In addition, in a context of globalization, economic integration, and the proliferation of a human rights regime, international and domestic pressures are building up on liberal states to find new and creative ways to manage emigration, both through national policies and through cooperation with other countries.[8] As Hollifield

[7] The technological revolution in communications and transportation systems in recent decades is considered one of the main factors that has strengthened transnational social networks created by migrants by facilitating "faster, more frequent, and more intensive interaction" between the home community and the host state. However, as Fitzgerald (2006b: n. 35) points out, some skeptics argue that previously existing technologies already enabled long-distance ties. The main difference is that the current technological innovations have considerably reduced the costs of these services, leading to widespread access. Nonetheless, Fitzgerald signals that a quantitative shift does not necessarily have a qualitative effect. He raises the question of "the *extent* to which a basket of communication and transportation technologies alters migrants' ties between source and destination countries," and emphasizes the need for a systematic historical approach to research in this issue area.

[8] It is worth noting that there have been recent efforts to encourage the development of common rules and practices regarding international migration, such as the United Nations' (UN) International Convention on the Protection of the Rights of All Migrant Workers and Members of their Families, adopted by the General Assembly on December 18, 1990 (A/RES/45/158) and entered into force on July 1, 2003. However, by November 2010, this convention only had thirty-one signatories and forty-four parties, which are mainly migrant sending countries (see http://treaties.un.org/Pages/ViewDetails.aspx?src=TREATY&mtdsg_no=IV-13&chapter=4&lang=en, last viewed on November 27, 2010). Another example of these efforts is the report issued in 2005 by the Global Commission on International Migration (2005; see Bhagwati, 2005 and Newland, 2005 for responses to the report). In September of 2006, the UN hosted the

(2004: 901–902) states, "if rights are ignored or trampled upon, then the liberal state risks undermining its own legitimacy and *raison d'être*."

As evidence of sending states' growing interest in managing emigration and their relationships with the diaspora, one of the main innovations in their approach to the issue is the development of formal mechanisms, such as constitutional reforms and institutions to manage state–diaspora relations and to respond to the causes and consequences of emigration (Guarnizo, 1998; Itzigsohn, 2000; Fitzgerald, 2006b; Agunias, 2009). This is due, in part, to the fact that sending states increasingly realize that they cannot extract obligations from the diaspora without extending rights (Gamlen, 2006: 13).

In general, states are more willing to extend economic rights than political rights because of the conflicting interests regarding the political influence of emigrants in their home country. For example, in the case of voting rights, some political actors may consider it more costly than others, given the size or the political orientation of the émigré community, although most agree on the benefits of providing economic incentives for emigrants' investments in the home country or of facilitating the transfer of remittances. Comparative analyses across different countries, such as those by Agunias (2009), Levitt and de la Dehesa (2003), and Gamlen (2006), provide evidence to support the view that "emigrant–state relations are not new, but nor are they inevitable" and just as some states may be interested in controlling emigrants or giving them incentives to maintain a relationship with the home state, others may denounce them and cut any ties with them (Barry, 2006: 14, n. 7).[9]

High-Level Dialogue on International Migration and Development during the 61st Session of the General Assembly. The meeting brought together representatives of 130 countries, as well as UN and IOM (International Organization for Migration) officials to discuss these issues; it also included a previous period of consultations (in July of 2006) with NGOs, civil society, and the private sector. The main result of this meeting was the organization of the Global Forum on Migration and Development, which was held in Brussels in 2007, in the Philippines in 2008, in Athens in 2009, and in Mexico in 2010. Still, these efforts toward multilateral cooperation are considered by some as "all talk and no action," because few formal agreements, particularly involving host countries, result from existing dialogue (Migration Information Source, 2006).

9 Levitt and Glick-Schiller (2004: 1023–1024) identify three different types of sending states on the basis of their relationship with their emigrants: transnational nation-states, strategically selective states, and disinterested and denouncing states. Gamlen (2006: 21) suggests a similar typology of states that use diaspora engagement policies based on three preliminary categories: exploitative states, which extract obligations without extending rights; generous states, which extend rights without extracting obligations; and engaged states, which both extract obligations and extend rights.

Emigration policies and relationships between states and diasporas are dynamic and vary across time according to a wide range of factors involving the sending state, the host state, and the diaspora. Evidence from comparative studies supports the observation made by Gamlen (2006: 4) that diaspora engagement policies are not part of a "unitary, coordinated state strategy" but "form a constellation of institutional and legislative arrangements and programs that come into being at different times, for different reasons, and operate across different timescales at different levels within home-states." This furthers the argument made by Shain (1999–2000: 662) that states' positions on these issues are in constant flux, depending on the characteristics of the diaspora and its general attitude toward the home regime, the political nature of this regime, official and societal perceptions of emigration, reliance on the economic investments of diaspora members and emigrant remittances, the political role assigned by the government (or its opposition) to the voice of the diaspora in domestic or international affairs of the country, and citizenship laws, among other factors.

In this sense, Fitzgerald (2006a: 286) emphasizes the need to examine migration policies from a neopluralist perspective, given the "multiplicity of interests that are subject to contestation within the institutional arena of the state." In his view, it is necessary to take into account inputs from domestic and foreign actors as well as "the multiple outputs that can take the form of various and even contradictory policies at different levels of government and across localities." In support of this argument, he presents evidence about local governments' opposition to the Mexican state's federal policies to control emigration in different periods (Fitzgerald, 2009). Thus, he argues that realist assumptions of sending states following "their" interests are inadequate frames for studying policies related to the management of migration.

Notwithstanding the importance of the study of varying and diverging interests within the state regarding emigration, as noted by Calavita (1992) and Boswell (2007), particularly regarding the *liberal* state, in my analysis of the Mexican case I identify the interests of the government elite at the federal level as key factors determining state policies. Despite some local authorities' opposition to the federal government's stated objective of controlling emigration and providing incentives for emigrants to return to the country (particularly during the first half of the twentieth century), which Fitzgerald (2006a, 2009) documents, the Mexican state still generally achieved its overarching implicit objective of maintaining a safety valve to economic and political problems in the country, as well as

preventing disputes with the United States. Although more actors within
Mexico are now involved in the debate over policies in this issue area
at the federal, state, and local levels, particularly in a context of democratization and decentralization since the late 1980s, Mexico's policies
toward emigrants are still mainly decided by the government elite, particularly the Executive and the Foreign Ministry. In the Mexican case,
the history of centralism and presidentialism that characterized Mexican
politics for many decades continues to be a key explanatory factor of
Mexico's foreign policies, including emigration: "Mexico's new foreign
policy continues to be guided by state interests and is still molded by the
presidents' preferences and will" (Domínguez, 2000: 322).

A MULTILEVEL ANALYSIS

The reasons why states vary with respect to the degree to which they
extend rights, the kind of ideology and rhetoric used in relation to emigrants, and the policies or programs that they pursue to control or manage
emigration can be explained by domestic, transnational, and international
factors. At the domestic level, states have economic and political interests
with regard to their emigrant population. Emigrants may be considered
a safety valve to economic problems such as unemployment, which may
lead to lax control of the borders and limited promotion of their return.
In some cases, they may also benefit from emigration as a safety valve
to political opposition at home. The characteristics of the regime (democratic or authoritarian) and ideological factors such as nationalism also
influence the type of engagement with diasporas and emigration policies.

At the transnational level, states may develop certain types of relationships with the diaspora to control political dissidence abroad, to legitimize
the government, or to promote the government's image abroad. States
may be interested in engaging with diasporas to guarantee the flows of
remittances, promote the transfer of technology and skills that emigrants
acquire abroad, or promote their investments in the home country. Other
nonstate actors, such as political parties, may also establish relationships
with the diaspora to obtain their financial or political support. Finally,
the size and organizational capacity of the emigrant community may
determine the state's interests in responding to its needs or demands.

At the international level, states' policies may be influenced by
their geopolitical position and their relationship with the host state
or states. For example, Østergaard-Nielsen (2003: 25) emphasizes the
need to explore whether "former colonial/metropolitan links or current

asymmetric power relations with receiving countries influence sending country attitudes to emigration and relations with overseas nationals." Some states design and implement certain emigration policies to gain legitimacy or establish a position in the international system or vis-à-vis a particular country (Guarnizo, 1998: 60). States may also be interested in mobilizing the diaspora in favor of their interests in the host country. In some cases, foreign policy traditions and ideology can determine the state's interests and capabilities regarding emigration and the relationship with the diaspora (González Gutiérrez, 1997; Shain and Barth, 2003; Østergaard-Nielsen, 2003).

One of the main challenges in the analysis of why states pursue certain migration policies, and what their interests are, is that they have "stated and unstated" objectives (Castles, 2004c: 854). As Castles (2004a: 223) explains, "politicians and officials may be reluctant to declare their true objectives for fear of arousing opposition... driven both by the need to maintain legitimacy and the unwillingness to face up to past policy failures." Thus, when examining states' policies in this issue area it is necessary to look beyond the stated objectives for hidden agendas, at the domestic, transnational, and international levels. In different periods, developments at one level may take precedence over others in terms of influencing states' decisions to pursue certain strategies regarding emigration; however, explanations based on only one of these factors have limited explanatory value, especially in cases in which the sending and receiving states are closely linked in other policy areas. The Mexico–United States bilateral relationship is an example of this dynamic.

THE MEXICAN CASE

In the past twenty years, and more emphatically since 2000, Mexico reversed a long history in which its migration policy consisted of softly promoting migrants' return, helping them maintain their ties to the home country through contacts between community organizations and consulates, and providing protection as well as support in crisis situations. By defending migrants' rights more consistently and energetically, and establishing direct links between Mexican institutions and migrant communities, the government adopted a proactive attitude that not only transcended government changes since the end of the 1980s but was consolidated and extended as more channels for migrants' participation in the home country opened through consular activities and the creation of programs and institutions dedicated exclusively to this population.

At the same time, the general stability in the United States–Mexico relationship, despite economic, diplomatic, or political crises, strengthened the view that "the costs of disagreeing with the U.S. are manageable" and sharing a border with the United States is not an obstacle but rather an opportunity that can be used to Mexico's advantage, as was the case with NAFTA (Aguayo, 2003). Thus, Mexico has been more active in promoting a specific migration agenda at the bilateral level and formally reacting to U.S. policies that affect Mexican migrants. From the late 1980s, the Mexican government has also participated actively in the development of bilateral mechanisms for the management of migration.

Notwithstanding these developments, the nonintervention principle is still prominent in the Mexican government's discourse and the potential linkage between issues in the bilateral agenda is still addressed with caution, a characteristic that leads to questions concerning the limits and potential of sending states' activism vis-à-vis the host state. This analysis also raises key issues regarding the challenges that host and sending states face in terms of managing migration as part of their bilateral agenda, the implications for regional integration, the consequences and potential of closer relations between sending states and their diaspora, and the possibilities and limits of the home country's diplomatic activity in relation to the receiving country's migration agenda (Aguayo, 2004; Meyer, 2005a).

The Mexican government's new attitude since the late 1980s is explained as a result of various domestic, transnational, and international factors, which are analyzed in detail in Chapter 1. At the domestic level, the liberalization of the Mexican economy, the configuration of a new political elite and its interest in closer integration with the United States, and the democratization of Mexico's political system in a context of the regime's legitimacy crisis gave way to new domestic pressures – from public opinion, nongovernmental organizations (NGOs), and media – regarding the need to address the causes and consequences of migration. It is also related to the gradual abandonment of a nationalist, anti-American rhetoric in general but it is significant to note similar changes in the discourse on emigration (García y Griego and Verea, 1998; González Gutiérrez, 1999; Sherman, 1999; Martinez-Saldaña, 2003; Smith, 2003b). The influence of the changes in Mexico's political system as factors that determined shifts in its migration policies provides evidence to support the argument that governmental obligations toward migrant populations are shaped by the nature of the political system of each nation (Castles and Miller, 2003).

At the transnational level, closer relations between migrants and their sending communities as a result of the development of new technologies, attempts to participate more actively in Mexican and U.S. politics through binational political organizations, the internationalization of competition between Mexican political parties, the growing economic influence of migrants in Mexico through remittances, and the diversification of contacts between the civil societies of the two countries led the Mexican government to seek a closer relationship with the communities abroad. Some have argued that this was a way to try to "co-opt and control" them and use them as a possible influence in the United States favoring Mexico's interests (Goldring, 2002; Smith, 2003b), whereas others explain it as a response to their demands for services and support from their home government (González Gutiérrez, 1999; Rivera-Salgado, 2000; Martínez-Saldaña, 2003).

Notwithstanding this debate, the main idea to emphasize here is that the Mexican state's interest in developing closer links to migrant organizations and Mexican-American leadership as well as the creation of specific programs to develop links with this population were not only a process that developed from above, but also a result of pressures from below stemming from "transnational migrants – that is, from relatively large groups of people whose economic, political, cultural and social lives take place across national borders and involve more than one nation-state" (Guarnizo, 1998: 47).

At the international level, the development of a closer relationship with the United States through economic liberalization policies and NAFTA integration "prompted a new attitude among Mexican officials to institutionalize bilateral affairs, that is, to engage the U.S. government, formalize bilateral dialogues, and create mechanisms to manage bilateral affairs" (Domínguez and Fernández de Castro, 2001: 154). The fact that Mexico abandoned its nationalist discourse regarding the relationship with the United States also made it possible to "redefine its relationship with Mexicans and Mexican Americans in the U.S. and to revise concepts and practices of membership and citizenship" (Smith, 2003b: 308–309). In turn, this change also led to greater activism in Mexico's defense of migrants' rights and a repositioning of migration issues as a priority in the bilateral agenda. From the analysis of the correlation between changes in Mexico's migration policies and the evolution of the bilateral relationship, it is evident that "the asymmetrical nature of the U.S.–Mexican bilateral relationship establishes the broader context in which migration occurs and national governments find the latitude to develop and implement desired policies" (Martínez-Saldaña, 2003: 34).[10]

Moving beyond this argument, I provide evidence to support the claim that the interpretation of the asymmetrical nature of the relationship varies over time, as does the sending state's perception of the possibilities and limits of action within this power structure. This assessment is determined by the context of the bilateral relationship, which in this case is significantly influenced by the process of economic integration. Although the main focus of this work is to explore the linkages between changes in the bilateral relationship and changes in Mexico's migration policies, they cannot be understood without taking into account the developments at the domestic and transnational levels, such as changes in the sending state's political system and in the extent and type of emigrants' activity in relation to the home country. Thus, I examine the recent changes and continuities in the Mexican government's discourse and activities regarding migration, its relationship with Mexican migrants in the United States, and the priority given to migration issues in the bilateral agenda.

A FOREIGN POLICY PERSPECTIVE

The study of migration from the perspective of political science and international relations is very recent, especially compared to the development of the literature in the fields of sociology, demography, economics, international law, anthropology, and history (Schmitter-Heisler, 1992; Portes, 1997; Brettell and Hollifield, 2000). One of the explanations for the lack of attention to the international causes and consequences of migration in international relations is the fact that a realist, state-centric approach generally dominated the discipline, particularly during the Cold War period. Therefore, unless migration was considered a problem that affected the core interests of states, changed the balance of power, or created conflict between countries, it was not addressed as a priority and remained on the agenda of "low politics" (Hollifield, 2000: 152).

As the causes and consequences of migration have become more directly linked to patterns of conflict and cooperation between states, security, processes of regional integration, and notions of sovereignty and citizenship, it has increasingly become part of the agenda of "high

[10] This argument is also developed in the following works: Alba (1993, 2000, 2003, 2004), García y Griego and Verea (1998), Guarnizo (1998), Smith (2003b), Levitt and de la Dehesa (2003), and Fitzgerald (2006a).

politics." It has also attracted the attention of scholars in international relations and political science that aim to "bring the state back in" and understand how migration impacts relations between countries as well as domestic and foreign policy agendas (Kritz, 1983; Mitchell, 1989, 1992; Massey, 1999; Hollifield, 2000; Brand, 2006).

However, the general focus of political science and international relations studies regarding international migration has been on host states – particularly concerning issues such as border controls, security interests, and questions of citizenship and national identity (Koslowski, 2005: 7). Meanwhile, the policies of sending states aimed at regulating migration flows, addressing their causes, or developing relationships with the diaspora have been the object of few studies within these fields.

Existing works generally explain sending-country emigration policies (specifically with regard to labor migration) as a result of a structural dependence on migrant remittances or determined by the need of a safety valve to unemployment or political pressures (Castles, 2004a: 213). However, there is growing evidence about the capacity and interest that countries of emigration – both in the developed and in the developing world – have in controlling population movements, establishing closer ties with their diaspora, extending political and economic rights for emigrants, and exercising pressure in host countries for the benefit of the migrant population (Guarnizo, 1998; Shain, 1999–2000; Itzigsohn, 2000; Levitt and de la Dehesa, 2003; Østergaard-Nielsen, 2003; Smith, 2003a; Levitt and Glick-Schiller, 2004; Barry, 2006; Brand, 2006; Fitzgerald, 2006a, 2006b; Gamlen, 2006). Thus, there is a recognized need to reconsider the role of sending states in developing transnational relationships with their communities abroad and to examine the domestic, transnational, and international causes and consequences of their emigration policies as well as the implications of these policies in bilateral relations and their linkage with other economic and political processes such as regional integration and democratization.

Most of the literature on sending countries is based on transnational studies from sociological, anthropological, or political perspectives, concentrating mainly on the ties between migrant communities and their countries of origin and their organization or empowerment in the host country. In the field of international relations, as García y Griego (1989: 8) points out, "one can search in vain for a single reference to international migration in texts that present realism as an International Relations theory." Although in the final Cold War years new theoretical approaches such as neoliberal institutionalism became more popular, they concentrated mainly on the study of international security and economic issues and "migration did not make it onto the agenda of International Relations theorists" (Hollifield, 2000: 153).

As the causes and consequences of migration have become more pressing issues, there has been a "virtual explosion of theory and research" on this topic over the past fifteen years (Schmitter-Heisler, 2000: 77). There has also been considerable progress in the development of studies within the field of international relations and some attempts to apply concepts from international relations theories to explain migration policies (Meyers, 2000, 2002, 2004; García y Griego, 1990, 2008; Rosenblum, 2004; Rudolph, 2004; Betts, 2009, 2011; Paoletti, 2010).[11] However, there are few systematic studies about the factors that determine the policies of sending countries and their impact in relations with the receiving country: "sending country policies are hardly given a prominent place in analyses of migration management or protection of migrant workers' rights" (Østergaard-Nielsen, 2003: 14).

Authors such as Rico (1992), Haus (1995), Guarnizo (1998), Martínez-Saldaña (2003), and Rosenblum (2004) have studied migration policies as "intermestic" issues. Similarly to Putnam's two-level games (1988), they examine the domestic sources of sending countries' migration policies and their linkage with international or transnational factors as well as the importance of the home state in shaping migrants' modes of integration and participation in the home and host countries. These studies reveal that as the characteristics of migration change and the issue becomes a greater concern for governments and civil society, the linkage between foreign policy and domestic policy objectives grows.

---

[11] One of the few works that analyzes migration policies and outcomes by applying an international relations theoretical framework is García y Griego's (1990) study of bilateral state bargaining and conflicts in the Mexico–United States case using Keohane and Nye's theory of complex interdependence. Another rare example of the use of theory to explain patterns of cooperation in migration issues is Rudolph's (2004) study of the prospects for a regional migration regime in North America based on realist, neoliberal, and constructivist approaches to regime theory. Meyers (2000, 2004) also uses various theories of regime formation (structural and game-theoretic approaches) and theories of integration (supranationalism and intergovernmentalism) to explain multilateral cooperation with regard to the free movement of labor. He argues that none of these are useful and proposes an alternative framework based on bargaining and cross-issue linkages between countries of origin and destination. More recently, Betts (2009) develops a theoretical framework grounded in international relations theory to explain international cooperation in the refugee regime. Paoletti (2010) uses interdependence theory as well as some aspects of realist and neo-Marxist theories in her analysis of Libyan–Italian bilateral agreements on migration.

Both receiving and sending states face "constraints and vulnerabilities in handling migration as a political issue" or linking it with foreign policy objectives; "these limits are usually derived from the social 'rootedness' of the migration process," the complex domestic politics involved in the design and implementation of migration policy, and "weaknesses in the administration or political ability of states to control international population movements" – particularly in the case of sending states (Mitchell, 1992: 288). For example, to avoid conflict at the domestic level, sending states generally resist reform of migration laws and rarely focus on economic development policies as a way to control emigration (Teitelbaum, 1984: 447–448). Sending states that are in a situation of dependency or asymmetry with regard to the receiving state face additional pressures in deciding how to develop their relationship with the migrant community and their capacity to protect their rights (Fitzgerald, 2005: 3). However, authors such as Weiner (1995: 34) claim that countries of emigration have more control over international population flows than is widely believed and that apparently spontaneous population movements may actually represent deliberate government policies. This supports the claim by Itzigsohn (2000: 1127) about the need to examine the new forms of intervention by the states of origin in the politics of the country of reception, the systematic forms of intervention by immigrants in their country of origin, and the high degree of institutionalization of these transnational linkages.

Recently, studies by Martínez-Saldaña (2003), Østergaard-Nielsen (2003), Levitt and de la Dehesa (2003), and Fitzgerald (2005) recognize that sending states' structural positions in the international system and the asymmetry of power between sending and receiving countries are key factors that define the policy options of sending countries. As Østergaard-Nielsen (2003: 220) explains, "sending countries are not unaware that too much overt pressure on their nationals in another country may not be welcome by the host country authorities.... In order not to strain bilateral relations or, indeed, put their nationals abroad in a vulnerable position, sending countries may hold back on their mobilizing efforts." However, none of these studies has systematically examined the relationship between asymmetry of power and sending-state policies, or the linkage between shifts in sending-state policies and changes in bilateral relations, which could be due to conflict, to changes in the international context, to closer integration in other policy areas, or to growing transnational activity in the countries involved. Moreover, within this discussion it is essential to make a distinction between less developed and developed sending countries, as their capabilities and interests will vary considerably with regard to the receiving state, which may or may not be a more developed country.

In the Mexican case, most studies focus on the domestic or transnational factors that have influenced changes in the government's stance on migration issues (e.g., Sherman, 1999; Rivera-Salgado, 2000; Shain, 1999–2000; Goldring, 2002; Smith, 2003b). The relationship with the United States is considered a significant element in the design and implementation of migration policies in terms of the asymmetry of power between the countries. However, there is a gap in the study of the international considerations that historically constrained Mexico's migration policies and their linkage with the other factors – such as changes in the political system and transnational relations between migrants and their home country – that influenced a change in Mexico's traditional position of limited engagement in the management of migration into a more proactive stance toward these issues since the late 1980s. How do the domestic, transnational, and international political processes influence the development of its emigration policies? How do the Mexican state's emigration policies relate to foreign policy principles and objectives? Has economic integration through NAFTA influenced Mexican migration policies? To what extent do changes in Mexico's emigration policies have an effect in the United States–Mexico bilateral relationship? These are some of the questions that are explored in this book.

INTERNATIONAL RELATIONS THEORY AND EMIGRATION POLICIES

My analysis of the Mexican case emphasizes the international dimension of emigration policies both as an independent factor and also in relation to transnational and domestic factors, following a model of complex interdependence. I examine the context of asymmetry of power, the way in which Mexico perceives its vulnerability in this context and therefore defines its foreign policy and its position on emigration, and how this perception has changed over time partly as a result of the process of economic and regional integration and growing interdependence between the countries. These changes are also linked with the process of democratization in Mexico and the growing transnational impact of migrants, both political and economic, which have led to growing domestic pressures for the Mexican government to adjust its migration policies.

Given the numerous elements involved in migration policy design and implementation, and the multidisciplinary methodologies and theories to study migration, efforts to develop a general theoretical framework have been considered futile or impractical (Portes, 1997). Nonetheless, there have been serious attempts to develop cross-disciplinary and multilevel approaches that take into account how the various factors that shape migration and migration policies interact (Brettel and Hollifield, 2000: 2; Meyers, 2004). In addition to providing more comprehensive explanations of these issues within the social sciences, this type of approach can also lead to developing "more balanced and realistic polices" (Castles (2004a: 222). Following Moravcsik (1997: 542), even if this means taking an eclectic approach, existing international relations theories should not be seen as substitutes but as complements that can provide different elements depending on each case and each issue.

In the specific case of international relations theory, it has been argued that the dominant schools are not suited to the task of understanding the dynamics of migration because they do not consider the domestic, social, political, and cultural facets of state actors in world politics, which is where the dynamics of migration are played out (Heisler, 1992: 599). Notwithstanding the limitations of any single theory to explain the complex and multiple factors involved in migration policies, this study shows how an international relations perspective focused on the state but that also accounts for the interactions between domestic, transnational, and international factors and actors, as well as ideology and perceptions, can contribute to our understanding of some of the dynamics of migration policy making, particularly in the case of sending states in an asymmetrical relationship with the host state. Beyond a realist, neorealist, or neoliberal institutionalist perspective focused on the state and the structural limitations of the distribution of power in an anarchic international system, Keohane and Nye's (1977) model of complex interdependence,[12] and more recent developments such as Putnam's two-level games are useful in the case of migration because they do account for the interplay between domestic, transnational, and international factors and also consider the influence of ideology and perceptions in these interactions.

Keohane and Nye's premise for developing the model of complex interdependence was that the nature of the international system had

---

[12] Krasner (1990) and García y Griego (1990) have also analyzed specific aspects of United States–Mexico migration based on this model, particularly with regard to bilateral cooperation on these issues. Paoletti (2010) also employs this framework to analyze the Libya–Italy case.

changed and it was necessary to complement realist explanations with
new accounts of state behavior in a world of increasing dependence between states and mutual sensitivity and vulnerability to new levels of interactions and changes in transactions (including flows of money, goods,
people, and messages across international boundaries). In this context,
policy becomes the outcome of a wide range of forces that interact at the
domestic, international, and transnational levels where states no longer
have absolute control over outcomes. Interdependence in world politics
refers to situations characterized by reciprocal effects among countries or
actors in different countries.

Unequal sensitivity and vulnerability to changes in one country's position within a situation of mutual dependence are described as a situation
of asymmetrical interdependence. States' perceptions of the costs of these
asymmetries will determine their interest in creating common arrangements to regulate interdependence. The key word to emphasize here is
"perceptions." Although there are strong hypotheses derived from the
structural asymmetry of power explanations, Keohane and Nye (1977:
19) claim that inequality between countries in terms of resources and
power is not enough for us to understand bargaining outcomes and that
it is necessary to take into account the domestic context and how it influences states' positions. They argue that, in conditions of interdependence,
states have to take into account both the domestic and international
dimensions of the issues and transactions involved. However, at the same
time, actors other than states can change perceptions of "national interests," which are not calculated in terms of power relative to other states,
as realists claim. Rather, "national interests will be defined differently
on different issues at different times and by different government units"
(Keohane and Nye, 1977: 35). Transactions among societies – economic,
political, and social – represent different sets of costs and opportunities
for domestic actors. These groups will affect patterns of political action
based on their perceptions of costs and benefits of particular interactions at different times. These multiple channels connecting societies at
interstate and transnational levels make the distinction between domestic
and foreign policy blurry and influence outcomes of political bargaining.
Thus, it is necessary to take into account changes in perceptions and their
effect in domestic, transnational, and international politics rather than
considering the state a unitary and self-interested actor (Keohane and
Nye, 1977: 34–35).

Furthermore, against structuralist explanations that anticipate similar
political behavior in all areas, interdependence theory argues that states

can cooperate on one issue but this does not entail a change in the power distribution of the relationship or the calculation of vulnerabilities and sensitivities in other issue areas; "goals, outcomes and political processes are likely to vary by issue area" and are affected by government interests but also by domestic groups, coalitions, and international agendas (Keohane and Nye, 1977: 30–31). In a context of interdependence where more issues acquire importance and become affected by international and domestic problems, states have greater difficulty in controlling the agenda and formulating coherent and consistent policies. Thus, "opportunities for delay, . . . inconsistency and incoherence abound when international politics requires aligning the domestic policies of pluralist democratic countries" (Keohane and Nye, 1977: 27). Adding to this idea, Putnam (1988: 460) makes a distinction between issue areas on which domestic interests are homogeneous and those in which there is more heterogeneity, such as migration, thus affecting policy design and implementation as well as prospects for cooperation with other actors or states.

From a nonrealist perspective, the impact of social forces (i.e., public opinion, interest groups, political parties, or parliamentary processes) is considered key in determining state preferences (Risse-Kappen, 1991: 179). The "national interest" is not considered a closed category; rather, domestic influences intervene in determining the payoffs of a negotiation. Axelrod and Keohane (1985: 229) agree with the idea that payoff structures are not simply based on objective factors but are grounded on actors' perceptions of their own interests: "[B]eliefs, not realities, can govern conduct." This means that it is necessary to understand the processes through which interests are perceived and preferences determined, an analysis that is closely related to constructivist arguments. Thus, in this study I place a particular emphasis on the construction of Mexico's foreign policy discourse with regard to migration in the United States–Mexico bilateral agenda and the use of the principle of nonintervention and the strategy of delinkage in part as a reflection of its *perceptions* of limits and possibilities for action within the structure of the relationship with the United States but also in ways that in some cases justified inaction or limited response to issues of emigration.

Changes in the bilateral relationship, as well as in domestic politics in a context of democratization and in the transnational relationships between migrants and the home country, have led the Mexican state to adapt these strategies and principles to new realities. I argue that this process of "learning," as described by Keohane and Nye (1984: 264–266), within a context of increased economic interdependence post-NAFTA is key to understanding the shifts in Mexico's emigration policies since the mid-1990s. This book examines the reasons for these changes in policy and the processes through which they took place, and it analyzes the extent to which discourse and policy actually reflect a different view of emigration as opposed to the Mexican government's traditional indifference or limited responses to this issue.

Various works focused on migration within the fields of political science and international relations take into account the particularity of each country's history as well as the ideology and the perceptions of immigration and emigration as factors that influence discourses about migration and their effects on policy (see Russell, 1989; Rosenblum, 2004; Brand, 2006). As Brettell and Hollifield (2000: 19) argue, "getting to the roots of anti-immigrant sentiments and their connection to the way nationals of the receiving society construct their own identities in relation to immigrants should be a prime research agenda for scholars of international migration." In the same way, in the case of the sending state and civil society's perceptions of emigrants and their construction and reconstruction in the national discourse as members of the nation, "heroes of the nation," or as those who betrayed it or are no longer a part of it, is revealing in terms of the priority given to the issue, the timing of policies to reach out to the migrant population, the resources that are devoted to engaging the diaspora, and the extent to which political or economic rights are extended to this population.

METHODOLOGY

To explain the linkage between changes and continuities in Mexico's migration policies and the dynamic of the United States–Mexico relationship, the book provides a historical background, based mainly on secondary literature, from Mexican and U.S. sources.[13] Chapters 2 and 3 broadly cover the period from 1848 to 1982, taking the signing of the Treaty of Guadalupe-Hidalgo (1848) and the Treaty of La Mesilla (1853) as the starting point of Mexican migration to the United States, given that the current border between the countries was formally established then. The historical review ends in 1982, with the Mexican economic crisis that eventually led the government to liberalize its economic policies and to develop a closer relationship with the United States.

---

[13] It must be noted that all translations of sources, quotes, and interviews in Spanish are my own.

Having established the historical elements of Mexico's migration policies and their relation to the structure of the bilateral relationship and to foreign policy considerations, in the second section of the book (Chapters 4, 5, and 6) I examine the transformations in this dynamic from 1982 until 2006, with the end of Vicente Fox's administration. Drawing from primary sources, including interviews, Mexican government documents, and press articles, I identify the changes and continuities in the use of nonintervention and delinkage strategies in the management of the relationship with Mexican migrants and the priority given to migration issues in the bilateral agenda. To understand the breadth and the implications of these changes, in this section I also examine reactions from the U.S. government, public opinion, and migrant organizations to Mexico's policies.

The primary sources used in Chapters 4, 5, and 6 include fifteen in-depth interviews with Mexican government officials, U.S. representatives of organizations dedicated to immigration issues, and Mexican migrant community leaders conducted between December 2004 and April 2010; fifty interviews with members of the IME's Advisory Council (CCIME, in Spanish) conducted between June 2009 and February 2010; informal conversations with Mexican government officials working at U.S. consulates and at the Embassy in Washington, D.C.; internal documents obtained through research at the Mexican Foreign Ministry, the IME, and the Mexican Consulate in New York[14]; participation as an observer or speaker at a number of meetings and events sponsored by the IME in Mexico City and in New York City; field research at eight Mexican consulates in the United States and Canada (including Los Angeles, Chicago, New York City, Portland, Atlanta, New Orleans, Houston, and

---

[14] The interviews with government officials were conducted in person (except for four done by telephone as noted in the bibliography) in Mexico City, Washington D.C., and New York City. The interviews with members of the IME Advisory Council and other community leaders were conducted in person (except for nine done by telephone) in New York City, Houston, Los Angeles, Atlanta, Toronto, New Orleans, and Chicago; to protect the interviewees' confidentiality, their names are not disclosed. The internal documents from the Mexican Foreign Ministry and the Institute of Mexicans Abroad were obtained in Mexico City between April and August 2003, July and September 2004, and July 2006 and March 2008. Internal documents were also obtained with permission at the Mexican Consulate in New York between July 2005 and April 2007. Some of the primary documents used in reference to the U.S. position, such as joint declarations by U.S. and Mexican presidents, press conferences, and testimonials, were accessed through electronic sources.

Toronto)[15]; as well as press articles based on U.S. and Mexican newspapers, mostly accessed through electronic archives.

The relevance of these findings in relation to broader theoretical debates in political science and international relations regarding developments in state–diaspora relations and the changing role of sending states, international cooperation over migration management, and the linkages between economic integration, interdependence, and migration policies is explored in Chapter 1 and in the Conclusions.

OVERVIEW

The book is organized in six main chapters. Chapter 1 seeks to explain and categorize the factors that influence Mexico's emigration policies and their variation over time. Drawing from the existing literature and evidence from the United States–Mexico case, I divide these into domestic, transnational, and international factors. I analyze some of the limits of explanations that focus on only one of these levels and argue that international factors (particularly the evolution of the Mexico–United States bilateral relationship) should be considered one of the key variables determining the evolution of Mexico's policies. This chapter establishes the main categories for the analysis of the historical development of Mexico's emigration policies and the changes taking place since the mid-1980s, which are discussed in the following chapters.

The historical background includes Chapters 2 and 3, which examine four periods between 1848 and 1982. In these chapters I discuss how the need for a safety valve to economic and political pressures faced by the Mexican state as well as the government's foreign policy considerations regarding the stability in the relationship with the United States determined its decision to limit its response to emigration control and protection of nationals abroad. As a point for comparison with the changes in the 1980s, I examine specifically how the Mexican government considered its responsibility toward Mexican migrants, the domestic pressures

[15] These visits were conducted between June 2009 and February 2010 as part of an independent evaluation of the IME conducted by the author with the support of the Inter-American Development Bank and the Fundación para la Productividad en el Campo, A.C. and with the assistance of Samantha Morales at The New School. They included a total of 950 interviews with the Mexican population awaiting documentation at the consulates, informal conversation with personnel and partner agencies collaborating in IME projects, evaluation of the offices and materials available with regard to the IME's programs, and visits to thirty Plazas Comunitarias in these consular districts (see Délano, 2010).

it faced with regard to this issue, and the policies it established to provide consular protection or administer the population flows more effectively; the type of transnational ties it developed with the Mexican community through migrant organizations or contacts with community leadership; and its diplomatic response to U.S. migration policies.

Chapters 4, 5, and 6 analyze the evolution of Mexican migration policies since the mid-1980s, from limited engagement to a more active protection of Mexican nationals in the United States through consulates and specific programs and institutions created for this purpose. Chapter 4 focuses on the period between 1982 and 2000 and Chapters 5 and 6 examine the developments during Vicente Fox's administration (2000–2006). I highlight the importance of the process of economic integration and the rapprochement between the U.S. and Mexican elites as a key factor that influenced the reinterpretation of Mexico's relations with the United States, which in turn changed perceptions of the limits of the delinkage strategy and the principle of nonintervention on migration issues. I also explain the process through which the Mexican government developed a stronger relationship with the Mexican and Mexican-American communities in the United States and responded more actively to U.S. legislation and policies affecting Mexican migrants. These developments are key to understanding Mexico's recent moves from delinkage of migration from other issues in the bilateral agenda and maintaining a distant relationship from the United States, to introducing the current idea of shared responsibility in the management of the flows, proposing a United States–Mexico migration agreement in 2001, and participating more actively in lobbying activities and other campaigns to promote comprehensive immigration reform in the United States.

In Chapters 5 and 6 I examine how the Mexican government changed course in terms of the traditional role assigned to migration issues in the national and bilateral agendas and in its limited interpretation of consular protection and diaspora engagement strategies. Based on in-depth interviews and primary sources, I examine the process whereby Mexico moved away from a passive and reactive attitude to U.S. migration policies by proposing an agenda for bilateral cooperation on these issues and by strengthening and institutionalizing the relationship with the Mexican-origin communities in the United States. By promoting an agenda that implicitly and explicitly gave migrants access to channels for direct political participation in Mexico and tools for empowering and strengthening their organizations in the United States (i.e., through the IME, the promotion of consular IDs, and the passage of legislation allowing for absentee voting), the Mexican government also moved toward a broader interpretation of its consular activities and to an active defense and protection of migrants' rights.

These policies represent a significant departure from Mexico's tradition of limited engagement on migration issues, but as I explain in this chapter there is still a lack of consensus among different factions of the Mexican government and Mexican public opinion regarding whether a more active position on these issues is convenient both in terms of its efficacy and in terms of the negative reactions it can produce in the United States. The Mexican government's actions and the debate over their impact and limitations reveal that concerns regarding the principle of nonintervention and the strategy of delinkage are still present and have a determining influence in how the Mexican government interprets the scope and limitations of promoting a migration agenda in the bilateral context and engaging the Mexican communities in the United States.

Finally, the Conclusions discuss current developments in Mexico's migration policies during the Felipe Calderón administration, up to July of 2010. I examine recent evidence about the durability and extent of changes in Mexico's position on emigration and diaspora engagement policies, as well as the pressures currently faced by the Mexican government given the linkage between migration and security issues and the increased violence in Mexican border towns.

I also examine the implications of these findings for the analysis of the United States–Mexico relationship and the future of integration in the NAFTA region. In the context of studies of the United States–Mexico relationship, these findings support claims regarding the idea that the concept or asymmetry of power has been used selectively by Mexican governments, in some cases as an excuse for inaction. The structure of power asymmetry does imply that Mexico is more vulnerable to changes in the dynamic of migration flows and to potential reactions from the United States that could affect this and other areas of the relationship. However, Mexican governments have gradually learned that the use of foreign policy strategies and tools such as lobbying for policies and legislation that favor Mexico's interests, expressing official opinions on U.S. immigration policies, appealing to multilateral forums in defense of Mexican emigrants, and engaging the diaspora in activities related to their homeland do not necessarily lead to conflict with the U.S. government or have negative effects in other areas of the relationship.

I

The Mexican State's Interests

A Multilevel Analysis

> The idea that we can't have a mature relationship with the United States, that they will always take advantage of us, that it cannot be a win–win relationship means that we assume a defeatist position and make no progress. We continue to belittle ourselves despite being one of the most important countries in terms of our size, resources and economy. As long as we continue feeding taboos and focusing on immediate political goals, we won't make any progress on issues such as migration.
>
> – Enrique Berruga, Former Mexican Foreign Ministry Undersecretary for North America (2000–2003), personal interview, Mexico City, April 27, 2010

The 2,000-mile shared border between Mexico and the United States has determined the existence of an exceptional bilateral relationship between these nations. The two countries are linked through trade and investment, tourism, migration, common problems such as drug traffic and environmental concerns, as well as cultural, social, and family ties. In 2009, Mexico was the third most important trading partner for the United States after Canada and China, and the United States is Mexico's main market for exports and supplier of imports, with an estimated total turnover trade of $305 billion dollars in 2009.[1]

The largest American population living abroad is in Mexico (estimates range from 600,000 to 1 million), and 98 percent of Mexican migrants are in the United States. This includes 11.4 million first-generation Mexican migrants, of which an estimated 6.6 million are undocumented; they

---

[1] See U.S. Census Bureau, Foreign Trade Statistics (available at http://www.census.gov/foreign-trade/balance/#top; last viewed June 4, 2010).

represent more than half of the total number of undocumented migrants in the United States (U.S. Census, 2010; Hoefer et al., 2011). Including the population of Mexican ancestry, the 31.7 million Mexican-origin population living in the United States constitutes 64 percent of the growing Hispanic population of 46.9 million in the country (U.S. Census, 2009, 2010; see also Consejo Nacional de Población [CONAPO], 2008a, 2008c). Part of what makes this a unique case compared to other migrations is the size of the migrant population, the extent and dynamic of the shared border, and the fact that there is a history of Mexican migration to the United States dating back at least 160 years.

The Mexico–United States bilateral relationship has generally been described as a "special relationship," although each country's concept of "special treatment" is different and has evolved according to different contexts (Meyer, 1985: 15). In general, the idea of a special relationship means that despite the vast asymmetry between the countries, given Mexico's strategic geographical location and economic and political importance to the United States, it is able to maintain a "relative autonomy" from Washington. As long as Mexico's actions do not affect U.S. core objectives and as long as Mexico supports the United States on issues that are central to its definition of vital interests, it has been able to maintain a certain level of independence in foreign and domestic policies (Ojeda, 1976a; Ronfeldt and Sereseres, 1983: 68). Historically, the United States understood that this autonomy was important for Mexico to help the Mexican leadership "reaffirm its internal legitimacy through a nationalistic discourse" (Meyer, 2003a: 11). Thus, the United States generally supported the Mexican governments that came to power – even if this was through undemocratic channels – and maintained a cordial relationship with the PRI (*Partido Revolucionario Institucional* or Institutional Revolutionary Party) regime from 1929 to 2000 without questioning its authoritarian practices. This relative autonomy and noninterference in Mexican domestic affairs was guaranteed, provided that the Mexican governments maintained economic and political stability in the country as the United States did not want an unstable, violent, or unfriendly neighbor (Chabat, 1996: 152; Kaufman Purcell, 1997).

Although the levels of conflict and cooperation, dependence and interdependence between Mexico and the United States have varied across different periods, the asymmetry of power between the countries has been considered a determining factor in establishing the limits and possibilities for Mexican foreign policy. Many American and Mexican scholars disagree on "the extent to which the asymmetries between the countries translate into effective power by the U.S. over the Mexican government" and the way in which it has varied over time (Vásquez and García y Griego, 1983: 9). For example, Ronfeldt and Sereseres (1983: 85) explain that "dependency is not entirely a myth, but in policy terms it is limited and negotiable," given that it is not in the interest of the United States to damage Mexico, as this would also mean harming itself.[2]

This idea is also expressed by Rico through the concept of the precipice paradox, which suggests that the United States will exercise pressure over Mexico to benefit its own interests but will never push Mexico "over the precipice" into a critical economic or political situation, as this would also affect U.S. interests, given the high level of interdependence and the great number of governmental and nongovernmental links between the countries and societies (Rico, 1986: 62). Thus, although there is consensus about the fact that the United States has considerable leverage over Mexico given the power structure, there can be variations in the way this asymmetry is expressed according to the bilateral and international context or to each particular issue.

Notwithstanding these caveats, Mexico's dependence on U.S. foreign investment, trade, tourism, and technology has translated into certain foreign policy strategies through which the Mexican government has historically tried to protect its vulnerable position vis-à-vis the United States. Traditionally, this included the advocacy of the foreign policy principle of nonintervention in dealing with the U.S. political system; delinkage or compartmentalization of issues in the bilateral agenda; and negotiations with the Executive rather than lobbying or working with the U.S. Congress or the relevant departments.

UNITED STATES–MEXICO RELATIONS AND MEXICAN EMIGRATION POLICIES

In the specific case of migration, throughout the history of migration flows between Mexico and the United States, the asymmetry of economic and political power between the countries has determined the fact that the

---

[2] An example of this situation is Operation Intercept in 1969, when the United States decided to close the border to pressure Mexico to agree on a joint anti-narcotics campaign. Although the United States achieved its final objective, this operation aroused "irate opposition among businessmen on the U.S. side of the border, who suffered from the disruption of Mexican tourism and commerce" (Ronfeldt and Sereseres, 1983: 87). A more recent example was the closing of the border in 2001 after the September 11 terrorist attacks, which implied high costs in terms of commerce and tourism on the border areas (Andreas, 2003: 9–11). Other examples are the opposition to ideas about a possible deportation of undocumented workers, which affect the interests of U.S. agricultural, manufacturing, construction, and service industries.

United States has been able to obtain low-wage Mexican labor, recruiting and disposing of it according to economic and demographic conditions, without assuming high costs when there are changes in the flows and without having to guarantee these flows through formal channels. Moreover, the United States has more resources and capabilities to adjust to these changes and achieve its objectives through unilateral policies. When there have been formal agreements, the United States has been able renegotiate, violate the rules, or pull out without serious consequences, as exemplified by the evolution of the Bracero Program from 1942 to 1964 (see García y Griego, 1983a, 1990; Krasner, 1990).

Mexico has been highly dependent on the continuation of migration flows – through formal or informal channels – as a safety valve[3] for economic and political pressures and, more recently, as a key source of income for remittance recipients (1.8 million Mexican families were remittance recipients in 2006; CONAPO, 2009). As a result, Mexico is vulnerable and sensitive to changes in the flows and to the impact of U.S. restrictive policies. Therefore, in general, Mexican governments have tried to maintain a relatively disadvantageous but stable status quo to guarantee the continuation of the flows and avoid entering into negotiations that could increase the state's vulnerability in the long term or lead to conflict with the United States. This has been translated into the strategy of delinkage and the use of the nonintervention discourse in relation to migration management in the bilateral agenda and relations with the Mexican population in the United States.

The delinkage strategy means that Mexico has generally preferred to deal with issues separately in the bilateral agenda, considering that linking them would affect (or "contaminate") other priority areas in the bilateral relationship, particularly regarding economic cooperation or political support; or that it would compromise Mexico's interests in other areas,

[3] In mechanical terms, an escape valve or safety valve operates as a regulating system to channel the excess of internal pressure and prevent an explosion. Durand (1994: 67) argues that this metaphor is inadequate to explain United States–Mexico migration because it implies that the causes of migration are solely determined by pressures existing in the country of origin (it does not take into account the demand for workers in the host country or the existence of family networks that promote these flows); that the flows go in one direction only (rather than being circular and temporary); that the liberation of excess pressure can be done freely and with no difficulties; and that the sending country is in charge of its regulation. He explains that this metaphor does not reflect the reality of migration or its historical development, and it can only be used to describe certain periods and some of the causes and consequences of migration. Nevertheless, the idea of a safety valve has been widely used to describe the causes for United States–Mexico migration and the Mexican government's position regarding the issue.

such as a possible linkage with negotiations over oil (as was the case when Mexico rejected a possible negotiation for a guest worker program in 1974) or cooperation on priority issues (for example, when Mexico agreed to exclude migration from the NAFTA negotiations to facilitate passage of the agreement). Moreover, as a result of failed bilateral attempts to manage migration, such as the Bracero Agreements, Mexico considered that any negotiation would turn out to be disadvantageous to its position and would not necessarily guarantee better protection for migrant workers. As long as the flows continued uninterrupted, Mexico had few incentives to attempt a negotiation with the United States by linking it to other issues.

This situation is explained because, generally, the actor that cannot manage migration when such control is important to its negotiating position is the most vulnerable actor in this issue area (García y Griego, 1989: 36). In this case, the sending state is rarely in a strong negotiating position, unless migration is linked with another issue that the receiving state considers more important, as was the case at the beginning of the Bracero Program in 1942.[4] However, this linkage is not always considered convenient; as Rico (1992: 270) argues, "sending countries may be expected to be interested in linking foreign policy as a moderator of immigration policy," but they "are not always comfortable with the notion that there is a connection between the two realms."

Theories of cooperation generally argue that the use of bargaining chips and issue linkage are favorable for the weaker partner in a negotiation and that once a regime is established in one area, it is easier to link issues and extend the original agreement into new areas. According to these hypotheses, it would be expected that Mexico and the United States would cooperate more extensively on migration issues after the signing of NAFTA. However, even in cases where states cooperate extensively on some issues, there is little evidence of their willingness to make linkages in sensitive areas such as migration, energy, or security in order to obtain concessions in others. Moreover, there are cases where linkage between the issues can hinder further cooperation (George, 1988). For example, in the end, the linkage of negotiations over a temporary worker program and cooperation on other economic and military issues during the Second World War increased Mexico's dependence on the United States.

---

4 Evidence of such situations is described thoroughly by Mitchell (1992) and his collaborators in their analysis of U.S. foreign policy and migration from Central America, Mexico, and the Caribbean.

It also made it more vulnerable to changes in the U.S. position on the issue (Craig, 1971). As I discuss in Chapter 5, one of the main criticisms in relation to the failure of the 2001 negotiations between Mexico and the United States for a migration agreement is that Mexico tried to link the entire bilateral agenda to immigration (Baer, 2004). Although there have been variations in Mexico's position, and attempts to link issues, the idea that delinkage is a better strategy to protect an issue from being "contaminated" by problematic areas is still prominent in its foreign policy strategies, particularly regarding migration.

Another reason for Mexico's traditional lack of initiative on the management of migration at the bilateral level is related to the government's considerations regarding "the dangers associated with *intervening* in U.S. domestic politics" (Rico, 1992: 268–269). The principle of nonintervention has been one of the main axes of Mexican foreign policy since the late nineteenth century.[5] Formally introduced by President Venustiano Carranza in 1918, this policy was based on the idea that every country should respect the principle of self-determination and not interfere in the domestic affairs of others. This position reflected part of the lessons of Mexico's nineteenth-century history, which was characterized by a number of foreign interventions that hindered the consolidation of the Mexican independent state and led to significant territorial losses. However, as Ojeda explains, this was not just a policy based on legalistic terms to defend the Mexican state or to support other countries "romantic[ally] and philanthropically," but a way in which Mexico achieved its own domestic interests (Ojeda, 1974: 477).[6] Thus, the principle has been interpreted and implemented with flexibility, according to different circumstances and to international and domestic contexts (Ojeda, 1976a; Chabat, 1986: 91; Heller, 2002; Covarrubias, 2006).

On the one hand, in terms of emigration policies, this was reflected in Mexico's relationship to the Mexican community in the United States and consular protection activities, at least until the late 1980s. While Mexico fostered relations with migrant community organizations and supported their activities since the mid-nineteenth century, consulates worked under

---

[5] For further discussion on Mexican foreign policy principles, see Sepúlveda Amor (1984, 1994, 1998).
[6] An example of this was Mexico's noninterventionist position regarding the 1959 Cuban Revolution, which not only served the purpose of preserving Mexico's traditional foreign policy but also had a legitimating purpose given the support of Mexican leftist groups to the Cuban Revolution and the comparison between the Cuban process and Mexico's unfulfilled revolutionary promises (Ojeda, 1974; Pellicer, 1968, 1972).

the specific mandate of noninterference in U.S. domestic politics. Their activities included issuing travel documents, performing notary and civic registry functions, carrying out orders by Mexican judges, informing the Mexican government about the political situation in the country or region assigned, promoting the image of Mexico, and generally defending the interests of nationals abroad (González Gutiérrez, 1997: 49–50). In terms of consular protection, these activities were "limited by the principle that the consulates should not question the legal norms – nor the local political authorities of a particular jurisdiction" and should "admonish *braceros* to avoid confrontations with the police, courts and local citizens" (Zazueta, 1983: 449). Thus, they were traditionally "done silently," as a "conscious attempt to avoid unnecessary publicity concerning protection services" (González Gutiérrez, 1993: 227).

On the other hand, nonintervention in migration issues was interpreted in terms of "respecting the sovereign right of the U.S. to pass legislation on this question without attempting to influence the domestic policy-making process" (Rico, 1992: 268–269). For example, during some of the most important debates regarding immigration reform, particularly in the 1970s and 1980s, including the Immigration Reform and Control Act (IRCA) of 1986, although Mexican authorities were presumably invited to participate and comment on the issues, they refused to become actively involved; Mexican authorities argued that these were unilateral initiatives and Mexican opinions would not make a difference. They also considered that just as a "positive change in the status quo was not a possibility, a negative one was seen as not likely" (Rico, 1992: 267). Moreover, as was the case in other areas of the bilateral relationship, Mexico had little experience and expertise regarding lobbying on these issues and there was little hope about what it could achieve as well as fear about the consequences that a more active position on this issue could bring to other more important areas of the relationship, such as trade and investment (Rico, 1992: 268–269).

Until the 1990s, Mexico held on to the principle of nonintervention as a justification to avoid lobbying with the United States and dealt only with the Executive branch (mainly with the White House and the Department of State) in its bilateral negotiations. This resulted in a "closet diplomacy" based on "quiet, informal, loosely structured personal consultations focused on specific issues rather than on the broader relationship or issue linkages" (Ronfeldt and Sereseres, 1983: 79–80). This logic rested on the idea that by abstaining from using mechanisms to interfere in U.S. domestic affairs, Mexico would leave the United States with no

justification to interfere in Mexico (Eisenstadt, 2000b: 73). However, this
was considered naïve reasoning given that the United States would have
interfered in Mexico's domestic affairs if it considered it in its interest
regardless of whether Mexico did so or not. Furthermore, the U.S. political system is organized in a way in which lobbying from other countries is
not considered a violation of sovereignty (Ronfeldt and Sereseres, 1983;
Eisenstadt, 2000a, 2000b). One of the consequences of this position was
that, in general, Mexico was not well organized for understanding the
U.S. government processes and representing its interests with the administration and its agencies on a daily basis.[7]

CHANGES IN FOREIGN POLICY AND EMIGRATION POLICIES
FROM THE 1980S

From the end of the Second World War until the 1980s, Mexico's foreign
relations were generally "distant and defensive" (Chabat, 1996), "stable
and relatively free from conflict" (Bagley, 1988). This was facilitated by
the existence of a closed economic model that inhibited contacts with the
outside; a closed political model based on a strong nationalist rhetoric;
and an external environment generally indifferent to Mexican domestic
politics (Chabat, 1996: 152). However, as Mexico's economic and political systems showed signs of exhaustion, Mexican foreign policy began to
change. By the end of the 1960s, the Mexican economic model based on
import substitution showed its weaknesses – namely high rates of unemployment and underemployment, excessive concentration of wealth, and
a growing commercial deficit – and the regime's legitimacy was called
into question, particularly among the middle classes (Zoraida Vázquez
and Meyer, 1994: 213). At the same time, the content of the "special
relationship" with the United States seemed obsolete as Washington's
priorities focused on Cold War efforts (Ojeda, 1977: 9).

When Mexico's economic problems reached crisis levels, particularly
in 1982, the nationalist justification for a distant relationship from the
United States was transformed, as direct and indirect support of the U.S.
government became crucial to avoid a deepening crisis and the default of
Mexico's international obligations (Meyer, 2003a: 12). From the 1982
crisis, Mexico's foreign policy regarding the bilateral relationship was

7 Ronfeldt and Sereseres (1983: 80–1) point out that, until the 1980s, Mexico's repre-
  sentational capabilities did not compare favorably with those of other Latin American
  countries, which used their UN missions and hired lobbyists and U.S. law firms to provide
  background analyses for their diplomats.

"very different, almost opposed to the one that had prevailed for the past 100 years" as a new technocratic political elite – mostly educated in the United States – implemented measures to liberalize the economy and seek closer integration with the United States in the context of the end of the Cold War and bipolarity, the collapse of communist regimes, and regional tendencies toward economic integration (Meyer, 2000: 126–127, 137–138).

From the late 1980s through the 1990s, the Mexican government gradually shifted "from its position of deliberate non-engagement on migration matters to a stance of increasing dialogue with its U.S. counterpart" and from a limited relationship with Mexican migrants and Mexican Americans to an active pursuit of contacts with these groups and the development of programs and institutions involving this population (Domínguez and Fernández de Castro, 2001: 33). In contrast to its traditional position, in the mid-1990s the Mexican government communicated its views clearly to the United States concerning local initiatives affecting migrants, such as Proposition 187,[8] and migration legislation then under discussion in the U.S. Congress (García y Griego and Verea, 1998; Domínguez and Fernández de Castro, 2001: 33). Mexico also pursued a closer relationship with the Mexican and Mexican-American communities in the United States through the Program for Mexican Communities Abroad (*Programa para las Comunidades Mexicanas en el Exterior*, also known as *Comunidades* or *PCME*), which included cultural, education, health, business, and tourism initiatives; it supported the creation of hometown associations; and it pursued lobbying activities that directly involved the Mexican-American community in support of NAFTA.

Mexico–United States cooperation was facilitated by the opening of Mexico's economic and political system as Mexico adopted a "less ideologically oriented and more pragmatic foreign policy" and promoted the institutionalization of the bilateral relationship with the United States (González González, 2000: 18). The turning point of this change was the signing of NAFTA in 1993, which represented a break with the nationalist doctrine and persistent anti-Americanism in the country. One of

---

[8] Proposition 187, also known as Save Our State (SOS), was a citizen initiative introduced in California in 1994. It proposed to eliminate migrants' rights to access public education, welfare, and nonemergency health services and increase controls against them at the local level. Student groups, labor unions, and human rights activists held protests in Mexico in support of Mexican migrants and against Proposition 187. The context in which the citizen initiative was introduced and the reactions to it are explained in detail in Chapter 4.

the consequences of this openness and closer relationship to the United States was Mexico's decision to change its foreign policy strategies and interpretations of the constitutional principles on which they were based. This included intense lobbying campaigns in the United States (through Congress, business, political and social leaders of the Mexican-American community, and think tanks – see Eisenstadt, 2000a, 2000b; Velasco, 2000); using public relations tools to promote Mexico's image in the United States (through cultural programs, the expansion of relations with the foreign press, strengthening the consular networks with new personnel, resources, and improving relations with local authorities and communities); and decentralizing Mexican foreign policy-making processes by giving a more prominent role to some ministries and departments rather than controlling it solely through the Executive and the Foreign Ministry (González González, 2000: 16–20).

As a result of this closer relationship with the United States, a significant development was the creation of new mechanisms for consultation and cooperation between Mexico and the United States and a strengthening of the existing commissions, such as the annual cabinet-level Binational Commission meetings. This included periodic presidential meetings dedicated to specific issues; annual meetings for congressional delegations in Interparliamentary Group Conferences; NAFTA-related trilateral meetings; conferences for border governors (created in 1980) and conferences for attorney generals on border states (created in 1986); the Working Group Regarding Migration and Consular Affairs created in 1987 as part of the United States–Mexico Binational Commission; the establishment of border commissions – Border Liaison Mechanisms – in 1992; the Interior Consultation Mechanisms on INS Functions and Consular Protection; the Safe and Orderly Repatriation Agreements; the signing of numerous Memoranda of Understanding since 1996; the Binational Study on Migration (1995–1997); and the joint training programs between the U.S. Border Patrol and the Mexican *Grupos Beta*,[9] as well as other less formal agreements and information exchanges, particularly

---

[9] The Beta Groups for the Protection of Migrants (*Grupos Beta de Protección a Migrantes*), established in 1990 by Mexico's National Migration Institute, are unarmed agents that provide assistance to migrants in their journey to the United States and inform them of their rights and the dangers they might face. There are currently sixteen *Grupos Beta* with a total of 144 agents operating in Mexico's northern and southern borders (Amnesty International, 2010; Instituto Nacional de Migración: http://www.inm.gob .mx/index.php/page/Grupo_Beta; last viewed November 9, 2010).

regarding the protection of migrants and border controls (Fernández de Castro, 1997: 63–64; Storrs, 2006).

From the late 1980s, the so-called intermestic nature of some of the most important issues in the bilateral agenda triggered a debate not only about the country's foreign policy principles, but also about the notion of sovereignty (Rico, interview with Thelen, 1999: 473). The needs of a growing and more politically and economically active migrant population put the Mexican government in a position in which it was "caught between, on the one hand, wanting to preserve the principle of nonintervention and, on the other, protecting them [the migrant population]" (Rico, interview with Thelen, 1999: 474). This situation led Mexican authorities to examine more thoroughly which type of activities were acceptable within the U.S. legal and political framework and develop a more flexible interpretation of the principle of nonintervention in relation to these issues.

As suggested by Keohane and Nye's 1984 afterword on *Power and Interdependence*, some of the reasons why state interests change are partly a result of political changes at the domestic level. In the Mexican case these include the transformations in the composition and objectives of the political elite since the 1980s, the liberalization of the economy, and the democratization of the political system. As well, Keohane and Nye argue (1984: 264) that new knowledge may be used to redefine the content of the national interest. In the Mexican case, political changes at the domestic level occurred parallel to a process of learning in the bilateral relationship that included more transparent and open contacts between U.S. and Mexican authorities; a broader information exchange between the governments at local, state, and federal levels; better knowledge about their respective political systems; and deeper, institutionalized mechanisms for collaboration between both countries as part of the process of economic integration since NAFTA. Finally, to fully explain these changes in Mexico's emigration policies it is also necessary to examine changes at the transnational level, including the growth of the Mexican migrant population in the United States and their economic and political impact in Mexico and in the United States.

THE MEXICAN STATE'S INTERESTS

Since the first periods of emigration, these flows have been implicitly accepted as a safety valve to economic and political pressures in Mexico. This has been a constant element determining the government's decision to maintain the status quo – as long as it implies a continuous flow of emigrants – and to limit its own control over emigration, with some exceptions in the early twentieth century. In general, when referring to institutions, programs, legislation, or policies related to emigrants, Mexican officials have argued that their objective is to contribute to improve their quality of life and assume the constitutional responsibility to protect the rights of all Mexican nationals while respecting host states' – mainly the United States' – sovereignty. Although in the past this was mostly done through conventional consular protection activities and diplomatic channels, since the 1990s the Mexican government has gone beyond traditional definitions of "consular protection" in its efforts to establish stronger relationships with the Mexican and Mexican-American communities and their leaders and organizations in the United States through programs and institutions dedicated to building liaisons and providing services to these groups, such as the PCME, created in 1990, and the Institute of Mexicans Abroad (IME), established in 2003 (González Gutiérrez, 1993, 1997, 2006b). Since the 1990s, Mexico has also been more proactive in its responses to U.S. policies and legislation by expressing its position on U.S. immigration policies, promoting bilateral cooperation mechanisms – including the proposal for a comprehensive migration agreement in 2001 – and appealing to multilateral forums in favor of Mexican emigrants' rights. This represents a key transformation of Mexico's traditional interpretation of the foreign policy principle of nonintervention and a more flexible use of the strategy of delinkage in the bilateral agenda.

Changes in Mexico's emigration policies from a limited engagement to a more active relationship with emigrants and a proactive response to U.S. policies and legislation are the result of converging domestic, transnational, and international factors. Although most studies recognize the importance of various factors at these three levels (Shain, 1999–2000; Smith, 2003b; Martínez-Saldaña, 2003), the evidence analyzed generally has to do with economic and political developments at the domestic and transnational levels. In this book I argue that the context of the United States–Mexico relationship is a crucial factor that has determined the Mexican government's assessment of the possibilities and consequences of implementing certain emigration policies in different periods. Changes at the foreign policy level are certainly linked with transformations in domestic and transnational politics, but the historical developments in the United States–Mexico bilateral relationship should also be examined as an independent factor that has influenced Mexico's emigration policies.

In the following sections I discuss the factors operating at the domestic, transnational, and international levels that have influenced the changes in Mexico's emigration policies. The different categories obtained from this analysis are useful to identify historical changes and continuities in the Mexican government's position, and the periods when each of these factors had an impact on policy, as discussed in the following chapters.

Domestic Factors

Regime Change. Mexican civil society has generally been considered "indifferent to migration" in the sense that it has not organized efforts to impose costs on the government for the lack of attention to the causes of migration and the plight of migrants in the United States (Bustamante, 2001, 2002b, 2002c; Durand, 2004). This may also have to do with the context of authoritarianism in Mexico, which limited the ability of civil society to mobilize around such issues. However, in a context of political opening and democratization in Mexico, particularly since the mid-1990s and with a climactic point in 2000 when the PAN (*Partido Acción Nacional* or National Action Party) won the election after seventy years of PRI rule, the media, public opinion, scholars, and human rights organizations acquired a stronger voice, domestically and internationally, and represented growing pressures for the Mexican government to respond more actively to protect emigrants' rights and prevent abuses against them.

At the same time, in the mid-1990s, anti-immigrant sentiments became stronger in the United States, stricter policies were put in place to control the border and limit services for emigrants, and the number of Mexican migrant deaths at the border soared; an estimated 5,300 persons have died in their attempts to cross the border illegally between 1994 and 2009 (Tuirán and Ávila, 2010: 122). These situations were widely reported by Mexican and international media, which led to increasing concern within various sectors of Mexican society and public opinion regarding emigration, as exemplified by demonstrations in Mexico against Proposition 187 in 1994. In turn, this led the Mexican government to react and attempt to develop a stronger position on emigration, not only through services and programs directed toward the protection of emigrants and the extension of political rights (such as dual nationality and absentee voting rights), but also through stronger responses to U.S. policies, which are described in the sections that follow.

Perceptions of Emigrants in the Home Country. Conventional wisdom is
that sending states' main interests in developing relationships with labor
emigrants are economic, driven by their dependence on remittances and
the need to promote emigrants' investment in the home country (Barry,
2006: 28). It has also been noted that "diaspora investment and remittances are particularly strong forces in changing the home country perception of its diaspora" (Shain, 1999–2000: 667). In the Mexican case,
there is a definite shift in Mexican society's perception of migrants, from
pochos[10] and traitors to "national heroes" that invest in development
projects in Mexico through programs such as the so-called 3 × 1 Matching Funds Program.[11] More significantly, remittances are now the second
most important source of foreign currency in Mexico (after oil exports),
currently amounting to an estimated $24 billion dollars per year (Interna-
tional Fund for Agricultural Development [IFAD], 2007). As Barry (2006:
14) notes, "the increasing importance to Mexico of its emigrants' capital contributions has driven a sea change in the national identity toward
one that more readily locates emigrant citizens well within the *imagined
nation* of Mexican citizens."

Remittances have certainly become a key element of Mexico's emigration policies and have been recognized by the government as one of the
main reasons why it should extend rights and strengthen its ties with emigrants, particularly during the Vicente Fox administration (2000–2006).
In the mid-1990s and again in 2000 the central bank (Banco de México)
improved its methods to calculate the amount of remittances sent to the
country and made them public (Lozano Asencio, 2004; Banco de México,
2007). As well, the 3 × 1 Program grew significantly in the mid-1990s,
extending to almost every state in the country, with wider coverage in
the media. This influenced a change in the Mexican public's perception

---

[10] *Pocho* is a derogatory term used to refer to Mexican emigrants in the United States.
The word is normally used to describe a fruit that is rotten. When used in relation to
emigrants, it refers to Mexicans who have adopted the American way of life. For a
detailed analysis of the term see Shain (1999–2000: 677–679).

[11] Originally established in 1992 between the Zacatecas State Federation in California and
the government of that state (as the 2 × 1 Program), the 3 × 1 is a scheme by which federal, state, and local authorities match funds sent by hometown associations and state
federations for development projects in their communities in Mexico. New initiatives
for promoting emigrants' investments in Mexico have been developed through the IME,
such as Mi Casa en México, which helps emigrants obtain mortgages and identify
opportunities to buy a home in Mexico (details are available at http://www.ime.gob.mx
"Vivienda"; last viewed February 11, 2011). More details about the 3 × 1 Program are
discussed in Chapter 4.

of emigrants and led the government to respond through more active policies.

However, as Sherman notes (1999: 866–867), an explanation for Mexican emigration policies based on the interest in guaranteeing a continuing inflow of remittances is insufficient:

> If the existence of policy were explained by settlement or the desire for remittances, Mexican governments since 1965 would have increased their attention to Mexicans abroad, while the fact is the attention they did pay was almost exclusively to Mexican-Americans. . . . Maintaining the influx of remittances is undoubtedly one objective of Mexican policy, as they are the third most important source[12] of foreign exchange. But this has long been assumed to be the primary motivation for policy, when in fact more complex elements of a long-term integrationist strategy are present here.

Emigrants' contributions through social and economic remittances have long been recognized by the Mexican government as one of the positive aspects of emigration. For example, in 1942, a commission named by President Ávila Camacho to study whether Mexico should accept negotiating the Bracero Agreements with the United States argued that Mexican agriculture would benefit from the techniques acquired by braceros and that the economy would grow with the flow of dollars from their salaries (García y Griego, 1990: 103). However, it was mainly the interest in negotiating other pending bilateral issues with the United States and obtaining its support for Mexico's industrialization program that finally led to the decision to establish the Bracero Program, as the government assumed that emigration and its economic benefits would continue regardless of the agreement.

The amount of remittances sent to Mexico has increased significantly in recent decades (from $1.8 billion dollars in 1980 to $2.5 billion in 1990, $10 billion in 2000, and $24 billion in 2007 – see Lozano Asencio, 1992, 2004; Banco de México, 2007), partly as a result of the growth of the emigrant community but also as a result of the new information provided by the Banco de México. The importance of remittances as a source for development and the fact they are the main source of income for millions of families in Mexico has certainly led to a greater interest from the federal and local governments as well as other groups, such as the financial community, to reach out to emigrants. Remittances currently represent about 3 percent of Mexico's national gross domestic product

---

[12] Note: It is now the second most important source of foreign exchange.

(GDP),[13] but in major sending states such as in Michoacán they amount to 13.2 percent of the state's GDP, and in Zacatecas 9.5 percent (Banco de México, 2007).

Since the 1990s, the Mexican state modified its discourse and outreach programs toward emigrants as a reaction to greater domestic and external pressures arising from the publicity given to emigrants' contributions to the economy as well as to the problems the emigrants faced in the United States. However, there are multiple interests involved in this outreach beyond the economic motivations. A telling fact is that it was not until the year 2000 that the Mexican government launched programs and instrumented policies to facilitate and lower the costs for sending remittances (such as Directo a Mexico and the issuance of secure *matrículas consulares*[14]), which may be considered a more obvious indication of the Mexican government's interest in guaranteeing the flow of remittances (Goldring, 2005; Lozano Asencio, 2005).[15]

Transnational Factors

Promoting Mexico's Economic Interests in the United States through the Diaspora. The economic support of Mexican Americans in the United States and the promotion of their links with Mexican businesses in

[13] This percentage varies between 2 and 3 percent, depending on the source. For a comparative analysis about remittances as a percentage of the GDP and remittances per capita, see Knerr (2005: 167–168). According to IFAD (2007), Mexico is well below Honduras, where remittances represent 24.8 percent of the GDP, as well as Haiti (21.1 percent), El Salvador (18.2 percent), Nicaragua (14.9 percent), Bolivia (8.7 percent), and Ecuador (7.8 percent), among other countries in Latin America and other regions. In addition to IFAD (2007), for comparative maps and data see "Snapshot: Global Migration," *The New York Times*, June 22, 2007 and "The Global Remittances Guide," Migration Policy Institute (http://www.migrationinformation.org/datahub/remittances.cfm; last viewed December 20, 2007).

[14] Since 2002, many financial institutions in the United States began to accept *matrículas consulares* (consular IDs) as a valid form of identification for opening a bank account; by 2006 more than 400 institutions accepted them (IME, 2006b). Among other things, this allows immigrants to transfer money to Mexico, in many cases at a lower cost than through money transfer services. The Mexican government has led an intense campaign for the acceptance of consular IDs by banks and other institutions. This is discussed in greater detail in Chapter 5.

[15] A similar conclusion is presented by Brand (2006: 91) in her analysis of the Moroccan case where she argues that, without denying the key importance of the remittance factor, a unidimensional analysis focusing only on the state's interest in foreign exchange overlooks other important elements that influence the state's response to emigration; in this case, the emphasis placed by the Moroccan state on identity preservation as well as emigrants' desires to remain affiliated to the home country.

Mexico was also a motivation for developing policies of rapprochement with the émigré community in the late 1960s and 1970s. However, similar to the argument about remittances, this is also an insufficient explanation for the government's activities because its interest in maintaining or developing these contacts has not been constant and the results have not always met the expectations. As I discuss in Chapter 3, in the context of a greater mobilization of Mexican Americans through the Chicano movement and their growing political influence in the United States, Presidents Luis Echeverría (1970–1976) and José López Portillo (1976–1982) developed closer ties to Mexican-American business groups and leaders, "hoping to utilize the increasing empowerment of the Mexican-American community economically and politically" (Shain, 1999–2000: 671). Nevertheless, Bernardo Sepúlveda, Mexican Secretary of Foreign Affairs during the de la Madrid administration (1982–1988), argues that even though the government maintained contacts with Mexican and Mexican-American community leaders during this period, some Mexican Americans came to be considered untrustworthy as they were taking advantage of contacts with Mexican officials for their personal benefit (personal interview, 2006).

Carlos Salinas de Gortari's government (1988–1994) reactivated contacts with them in the 1990s in the interest of garnering their support for NAFTA and promoting business relationships between Mexicans and Mexican Americans. However, the small number of Mexican-American businesses and congressmen that lobbied in favor of NAFTA was not a determining factor in the passage of the agreement (Eisenstadt, 2000b: 95; de la Garza, 2000: 146). As well, the development of business ties during the 1990s through the government's efforts did not render the expected results, because Mexican-American businesses preferred to develop their own networks independently (de la Garza, 2000: 145).

The Mexican-American community's response to the Mexican government's efforts has not been consistent either; there is an element of mistrust and suspicion, as well as fear of accusations of dual loyalty that have "inhibited their relations with official Mexico" (Shain, 1999–2000: 672).[16] Thus, the relationship between Mexican Americans and the

---

[16] Shain (1999–2000) notes that, at times, some members of the Mexican-American community have expressed their interest in developing closer political cooperation with the Mexican government and promoting its interests in the United States and also in achieving a stronger voice inside Mexico. However, as de la Garza (2000) and others have argued, these attitudes are neither generalized nor continuous.

Mexican government has been ambivalent and the government's active promotion of relationships with them in pursuit of economic objectives has varied over time. This cannot be explained solely as a result of the government's varying interest in their investments or their promotion of Mexican economic objectives in the United States. Neither this factor nor the Mexican state's reliance on emigrants' contributions (through investments or remittances) to the home country provides sufficient evidence to explain, on their own, the type of changes in emigration policies taking place since the 1990s.

Emigrants as a Political Force at Home and Abroad. If the argument holds that dependence on the economic contributions that emigrants make to the sending country does not necessarily drive emigration policies (Itzigsohn, 2000: 1143), other factors such as political incentives need to be taken into account. In this case, the interest in mobilizing the support of emigrants as a lobby group in the host country, the need to control political opposition abroad and domestic criticism regarding emigration, or political parties' interest in emigrants' financial or electoral support may explain why or why not sending countries develop certain types of emigration policies.

In the Mexican case, the initial change in the approach to emigrants in terms of political interests had to do with the growth of the Mexican and Mexican-American population in the United States and its increasing political power. Since the 1986 IRCA, the number of Mexican migrants with legal status in the United States had grown significantly and had also spurred a new wave of emigration. Furthermore, the patterns of emigration changed from temporary and circular to longer or permanent stays, and settlement in new areas beyond traditional immigration states. This made the Mexican government realize the need for a long-term strategy with regard to emigration policies and to the diaspora (González Gutiérrez, 1993). Gradually, the Mexican migrant and Mexican-American community acquired a stronger political voice in the United States and in Mexico. Given that more than 2 million Mexican migrants benefited from the 1986 amnesty and were no longer inhibited or limited by their undocumented status, they had better opportunities for creating organizations and participating in political and economic processes in Mexico and in the United States, as reflected by the growth of hometown associations and state federations. Meanwhile, the number of Mexican-American voters had increased significantly after the National

Voting Rights Act of 1965 was passed,[17] and many Mexican Americans were elected to local and federal positions, where they "[took] advantage of their newfound power and... used their positions to defend community interests, resulting in a reduction in discrimination and the expansion of educational, employment, and political opportunities" (Shain, 1999–2000: 680).

Participation of U.S.-Based Emigrant Organizations in Mexican Politics. The importance of the Mexican emigrant community in Mexican politics was made evident during the 1988 Mexican presidential campaign. The front-runners, Salinas de Gortari (PRI) and Cuauhtémoc Cárdenas (*Frente Democrático Nacional* – National Democratic Front[18]), both sought the political support of Mexican emigrants in the United States, particularly in California and Texas, "hoping that their clout would influence Mexican voter behavior" (Shain, 1999–2000: 682). The PRI's controversial victory led to protests from Mexican migrant organizations in the United States. These groups also criticized the Mexican government's emigration policies and demanded voting rights, the end of corruption by immigration officials in Mexico, better consular services, and a more active defense of their rights (Alarcón, 2006: 159–160; Martínez-Saldaña, 2003).

Salinas de Gortari responded by creating the Program for Mexican Communities Abroad (PCME), the *Grupos Beta*, and the Paisano Program, and by strengthening Mexican consulates in the United States. These initiatives, which are explained in detail in Chapter 4, were all directed toward protecting migrants leaving or returning to Mexico, providing better services for Mexicans in the United States, and promoting relationships with Mexican-American leaders and organizations (Shain, 1999–2000: 685). With these activities, the government tried to show "concern for the fate of Mexican migrants" to improve its image at home and abroad, and ameliorate "the collective frustration of being unable

---

[17] The Voting Rights Act outlawed any discrimination in voting, particularly with a view toward protecting the rights of ethnic minorities. It established that literacy tests would no longer be a requirement to qualify for voting; it eliminated poll taxes; and it provided for federal registration of voters in areas that had less than 50 percent of eligible minority voters registered.

[18] The FDN was founded by former leftist members of the PRI and was later transformed into the PRD – *Partido de la Revolución Democrática* or Party of the Democratic Revolution, the current leftist party in Mexico.

to produce enough jobs for the population" (González Gutiérrez, 1993: 228).

Controlling Political Dissidence Abroad. It is in reference to the creation of the PCME that Smith (2003b) and Goldring (2002) argue that the Mexican government was trying to "co-opt and control" Mexican emigrants and their organizations in the United States to promote its own interests and prevent political dissidence: "co-opting and channeling the disaffection of U.S.-residing Mexicans through the Program helped control the image of Mexico presented to the U.S. media and, more importantly, helped legitimize the regime at home through its good works abroad" (Smith, 2003b: 309). Previous efforts at controlling the type of organization of Mexican emigrants can be exemplified by the promotion of organizations such as *Brigadas de la Cruz Azul* and *Comisiones Honoríficas* during the 1920s, which the government sponsored partly in response to the politicization of the emigrant community and the proliferation of dissident groups in the United States, as described in Chapter 2. However, in the past, the absence of real competition among political parties in Mexico and the PRI's capacity to subdue opposition meant that the government was able to control dissidents abroad more effectively, and that the need to legitimize the government through more active and continuous engagement with emigrants and their organizations did not lead to institutionalizing this type of activity. This contrasts with the establishment of the PCME in 1990 and the expansion of its agenda through the IME in 2003, an institutional effort that has lasted more than two decades.

Emigrants as a Lobbying Group. Another key motivation for the Mexican government to improve its relationship with Mexican Americans and develop more active policies to engage with them and offer them services was the awareness "of their potential in pressuring for NAFTA" (Guarnizo, 1998: 62). The Mexican government led one of the most expensive lobbying campaigns to influence business groups, congressmen, Mexican-American leaders, and the Mexican-American community in general to pressure Congress to vote in favor of the fast-track passage of NAFTA. This included hiring various lobbying agencies, holding a great number of meetings between Mexican officials with key personalities, and placing television advertisements targeting the Mexican-American community. However, there is no evidence of the key importance of this group in the passage of NAFTA or any other economic initiative related to Mexico. As Domínguez (2000: 311) notes, "the Mexican government would undoubtedly desire to have the support of Mexican Americans in order to persuade the U.S. government, but generally, this is not the case." Nonetheless, the Mexican government has continued developing strategic relationships with these groups given the growth of the Mexican-American community, its increasing influence in U.S. politics as part of the Hispanic population (the largest minority in the country since 2003), the growing number of Mexican Americans in elected positions, and the importance of Mexican-American organizations such as MALDEF (Mexican American Legal Defense and Educational Fund), LULAC (League of United Latin American Citizens), and NCLR (National Council of La Raza) in the immigration debate and issues affecting Mexican emigrants. In fact, the current Felipe Calderón administration sees relationships with these groups and other grassroots organizations as the most effective way to have a positive influence in the immigration debate in the United States without antagonizing certain groups that react negatively to Mexico's activism on these issues (Sarukhan, personal interview, 2009).

An example of Mexico's political interests was the constitutional reform to grant dual nationality during Ernesto Zedillo's government (1994–2000). This was framed mainly as a response to Proposition 187 and the need to provide Mexican emigrants with opportunities to become U.S. citizens and participate in political decisions such as this. Although Mexico has been cautious in terms of handling the idea of a potential lobby because of the fear that such an activity would be perceived as interference in U.S. domestic politics, at that time President Zedillo declared that he hoped this would help Mexicans defend their rights and also create an ethnic lobby with political influence (Dillon, 1995). This was a rare kind of statement for the Mexican government and has not been repeated publicly in such terms, particularly by the Executive. Nonetheless, this provides evidence to sustain the argument that there is ambiguity in the Mexican government's position as well as stated and hidden objectives, given the complexity of the issue and the reactions that could arise, domestically, transnationally, and bilaterally, if the interests behind its position at different times were publicly expressed.

Although the Mexican government's approach to recognizing emigrants and developing a closer relationship with them has mostly been top down (Guarnizo, 1998), these policies have encouraged more political organization of emigrants vis-à-vis the homeland, leading to demands for more political rights, such as absentee voting (Barry, 2006: 15). This right was exercised for the first time in 2006 but participation rates were disappointingly low, leading to questions about migrants' real interest in participating in Mexican politics.[19]

The influence of Mexican emigrants in their home country has been enhanced by developments in communication and transportation technologies that facilitate contacts between migrant hometown associations or state federations with their communities of origin and their participation in local events and politics. This was also possible as a result of the gradual process of democratization taking place in Mexico, which allowed new actors to voice their concerns and participate more actively in Mexican politics. Thus, the change in Mexico's policies was influenced not only by the domestic interests of the governing elite, but also by the transnational activity of Mexican emigrants in a context of political opening and increasing public attention to migration.

International Factors

The United States–Mexico Relationship. The asymmetry of power between Mexico and the United States has been a constant element influencing the Mexican state's decision to implement certain emigration policies or refrain from action regarding the management of migration flows or engaging the diaspora. On the one hand, Mexico's dependence on economic and political support by the United States traditionally "prevented it" from approaching sensitive issues such as migration in the bilateral agenda or pursuing policies that could create tensions in the relationship. On the other hand, Mexico's greater vulnerability to changes in migration flows meant that Mexico generally preferred to maintain the status quo, even if it was disadvantageous to Mexican emigrants, and therefore it avoided taking positions on U.S. policies or legislation as long as the flows continued.

Beyond the traditional justification for these actions, I argue that the state's interpretation of the limits and possibilities regarding migration issues within this power structure has varied over time as a result of the evolution of the bilateral relationship in a context of political changes

---

[19] Although the constitutional reform granting absentee voting rights had been passed since August of 1996 (together with the reform on dual nationality), it contained a clause that required Congress to reform the Mexican Federal Elections secondary regulations (*Código Federal de Instituciones y Procedimientos Electorales*, or COFIPE), which would determine the rules on how this right would be exercised. The passage of the legislation regulating absentee voting in June of 2005 was partly a response to lobbying activities by migrant organizations and the IME's Advisory Council. This is discussed in detail in Chapter 6.

in Mexico as well as significant transformations in the characteristics of Mexico–United States migration. In a context of interdependence, particularly since the mid-1980s and after the passage of NAFTA, Mexican foreign policy discourse and strategies have changed and the collaboration between the United States and Mexico at different levels, including government and nongovernment actors, has expanded. These developments have had an impact on Mexico's approach to emigrants, its reactions to U.S. migration policies and legislation, and its recourse to multilateral forums on issues regarding the defense of migrants' rights. Even though the asymmetry of power is a structural condition of the relationship, it is not an unmovable obstacle; both foreign policy traditions and ideology, and the perceived impact of emigration policies in the relationship with the host country, determine the type of policies that the sending state chooses and the way in which they are promoted at different times.

Securing U.S. Political and Economic Support and Preventing Conflict. Given Mexico's greater vulnerability to changes in the dynamic of migration flows and to potential linkages between conflict in this issue area and the general climate of the relationship, Mexico's general position has been to limit its reactions to U.S. legislation or policies on immigration, compartmentalize or delink issues in the bilateral agenda to prevent "contamination" between conflicting areas, and exercise its responsibilities of consular protection cautiously and with great attention to the principle of nonintervention.

The fact that emigration was generally considered a political and economic safety valve to domestic pressures led to lax emigration policies and a preference for maintaining the status quo. During the first century of U.S. emigration (1848–1942), foreign policy considerations played a role in Mexico's migration policies in terms of the government's interest in guaranteeing consular protection for its nationals and controlling the border areas but being cautious not to create tensions with the United States, given the recent loss of the northern territories and the political and economic instability in Mexico, which made the country more vulnerable to external pressures. Thus, its initial efforts to provide support to the Mexicans who were in the territories that became part of the United States and its claims regarding the protection of their rights through diplomatic channels were limited and easily gave in to U.S. pressures or lack of response to Mexico's concerns (Lajous, 1990).

Even though Mexico initially had an exceptionally advantageous position in negotiating temporary worker agreements during the Second

World War (i.e., the Bracero Program, discussed in Chapter 3), the asymmetry of power in the relationship was obvious in Mexico's limited success in guaranteeing implementation of the rules established in the negotiations and defending Mexican workers. The Mexican government generally accepted the status quo, even if it implied violations of the rules established by the Bracero Program, given its priority interest in maintaining economic and political stability in the country and guaranteeing U.S. support for industrialization and commercial activities.

After failed attempts to renew the Bracero Program, by the mid-1970s Mexico decided to abandon the possibility of negotiating further bilateral agreements with the United States regarding temporary migrant workers. It sought to maintain the convenient status quo by remaining passive on the issue at the bilateral and domestic levels. This policy, known as the "policy of having no policy" (García y Griego, 1988), was thought to prevent conflicts with the United States and to guarantee the continuation of the migration dynamic as a channel for the political and economic tensions in the country. Moreover, given the experience with the Bracero Program, cooperation with the United States and linkage between issues was considered disadvantageous, both in terms of the government's vulnerability in negotiating with the United States and its limited capacity to ensure the implementation of specific conditions for the benefit of migrants.

These examples show that in this type of relationship, in which the United States has greater capacity to implement unilateral initiatives, pull out of existing agreements, and absorb the costs of changes to the status quo, Mexico generally reacted by taking a passive position and prioritizing the stability of the bilateral relationship when considering policy options in response to emigrants' needs and demands. Nevertheless, developments in Mexico's policies since the 1990s show that the perception of the limits implied in the asymmetry of the relationship has changed, particularly in a context of interdependence and economic integration. Shifts in Mexico's emigration policies also signal the importance of foreign policy traditions and ideology in determining the state's interests and objectives in this issue area.

For example, after a historical position of delinkage of sensitive issues such as migration from the bilateral agenda and avoiding positions that could be interpreted as intervention in U.S. domestic issues, in 2001, for the first time, Mexico placed migration issues as a priority in the bilateral agenda by proposing a comprehensive migration agreement. Even though the negotiations stalled after 9/11 and were later abandoned, instead of retreating, the Mexican strategy gradually refocused and moved toward the idea of lobbying in favor of the bills that coincided with Mexico's position and promoting a comprehensive immigration reform, including the five points on which the proposal for the bilateral migration agreement was based (regularization of undocumented workers who were already in the United States; increasing the number of visas for Mexican immigrants; broadening the scope of temporary worker programs; increasing border safety; and targeting development initiatives to areas of high outmigration and strengthening the Mexican economy to reduce emigration pressures). In their statements, President Fox, the Secretary of Foreign Affairs, the Undersecretary for North American Affairs, the Ambassador to the United States, and various consuls strongly emphasized the government's support or concern regarding specific bills.

This represented a fundamental shift from the position maintained in 1986 during the process leading to the passage of IRCA, when the Mexican government chose not to get involved in the debates over the content of the legislation and did not take an explicit position on the issue, considering that this was not in accordance with the principle of nonintervention. It was also a much stronger position than the one assumed in 1996 when the government simply expressed its concern with the IIRIRA (Illegal Immigration Reform and Immigrant Responsibility Act), PRWORA (Personal Responsibility and Work Opportunity Act), and AEDPA (Antiterrorism and Effective Death Penalty Act) laws and their effects on Mexican emigrants once the legislation was passed. This is discussed in greater detail in Chapter 4.

Mexico–United States Economic Integration. In a context of economic liberalization and rapprochement with the United States since the mid-1980s, and particularly since the NAFTA negotiations, the Mexican government began to modify its discourse regarding the United States–Mexico relationship. This implied changes in a traditional discourse of anti-Americanism as part of Mexican nationalism, as well as changes in Mexican foreign policy.

Mainly as a result of the process of the NAFTA negotiations, and the process of economic liberalization leading to it, Mexican officials found a wider space for action in different policy areas in the United States–Mexico relationship as they developed contacts with new actors in the United States, both within the government and outside of it, which implied a "pluralization of contacts between the two societies" (González Gutiérrez, 1993: 225). This encouraged the Mexican government and its representatives in consulates in the United States "to abandon their self-imposed and exaggerated cautiousness, which was based on a rigid interpretation of nonintervention and which failed to take advantage of the opportunities offered by the U.S. political process" (González Gutiérrez, 1997: 52). NAFTA, and the process of economic liberalization in Mexico leading to the agreement, also opened up a series of new channels of communication between the countries and forms of cooperation in areas where they did not exist before. In the case of migration there was a significant development of agreements, working groups, consultation mechanisms, binational studies, and other forms of collaboration that led each country to have a better understanding of the other's position, to common definitions on the issues and joint proposals for solutions.

From the traditional position of nonintervention that implied a limited reaction to U.S. policies and a lack of definition of its own policies, as well as a focus on traditional consular protection activities, Mexico moved toward more proactive policies. This included opposition to U.S. legislation both through official statements and lobbying activities and also the development of a stronger and better defined position on the issue.

In terms of Mexico's definition of responsibility toward emigrants and its consular protection activities, with the creation of the PCME in 1990 and then the IME in 2003, the Mexican government moved toward institutionalizing its relationship with the Mexican communities in the United States, offering a wider range of services for them, developing better channels of communication between emigrant organizations and the government, and providing them with opportunities to participate in these institutions. This was exemplified by the creation of an Advisory Council (CCIME) within the IME structure, which is made up of an average of 125 elected Mexican, Mexican-American, and Mexican-Canadian community leaders. The move toward institutionalizing this relationship also gave the communities an opportunity to exercise their rights in their country of residence (through the passage of the reform on dual nationality) and in their home country (by granting absentee voting rights). These developments are explained in detail in Chapter 6.

Another consequence of the process of political and economic opening in Mexico was that the government became more sensitive to international criticism on human rights issues and democratic governance, which increased the pressures for changing its stance on emigration (Shain, 1994–1995). This is exemplified by the fact that Mexico was one of the early signatories of the UN International Convention on the Protection of the Rights of All Migrant Workers and Members of their Families (in May of 1991, although Congress ratified it in 1999), and the convener of the Regional Conferences on Migration (commonly known as the Puebla Process), begun in 1996.[20] Gradually, Mexico also took advantage of opportunities to participate more actively in international forums related to immigration and make use of multilateral mechanisms to defend emigrants' rights in the United States. A significant example of Mexico's use of multilateral instruments to defend emigrants' rights, even in cases of strong disagreement with the United States, was taking the case of fifty-two Mexican emigrants charged with the death penalty in the United States to the International Court of Justice (ICJ) in 2003. Mexico alleged absence of due process and violation of the Vienna Convention on Consular Relations, because the accused were not allowed to contact their consular representatives and to obtain the corresponding legal assistance. In what is known as the Avena Case, on March 31, 2004 the ICJ ruled in favor of the Mexican nationals, ordering the United States to revise each case and reconsider each verdict.

These developments in Mexico's emigration policies illustrate the fact that foreign policy considerations, in particular the relationship with the host state, influence how the sending state perceives and defines its capabilities and responsibilities toward the émigré community. Nonetheless, just as domestic and transnational factors have changed historically and influenced policies at different times, the weight of foreign policy factors in Mexico's emigration policies has also varied over time. This variance occurs on the basis of the Mexican government's perceptions of the costs of taking a specific stance on these matters with regard to the bilateral relationship with the United States. In this case it is noteworthy that since the late 1980s the process of economic integration and the development of formal mechanisms for cooperation with the United States in various issue areas have allowed for a wider space for action and a redefinition of objectives, interests, and strategies in Mexico's emigration policies.

Mexico's transition from a passive to an active position on these issues provides evidence of the ability of sending states to reinterpret the limits and possibilities for pursuing their interests on migration within a

---

[20] The participating governments are Belize, Guatemala, Honduras, El Salvador, Nicaragua, Costa Rica, Panama, Mexico, the United States, and Canada.

structure of asymmetric power. In a situation of asymmetry, a context of growing interdependence as is the case with NAFTA could imply more pressures for the sending state given its greater sensitivity to changes, but it can also "[raise] the stakes for, and the leverage of, migrant-sending states at the bilateral level, as exemplified by some of Mexico's recent actions regarding emigration" (Rosenblum, 2004: 114). The general stability of the bilateral relationship in a framework of economic integration and the development of new contacts and new agendas at different levels is part of the context in which the Mexican government has decided to expand its activities and become more assertive on certain issues, even if its objectives are not always achieved as a result of the power structure of the relationship.

The reactions from U.S. public opinion or government officials to Mexico's activities and policies are still a matter of concern, and they have an impact in the government's strategies and discourse. This varies, however, according to the specific situation and the context – which is also tied to domestic and transnational developments – rather than leading invariably to an expected limited response, as was the case in the past. From a comparative perspective, a focus on the international level of analysis can help us understand to what extent and in which contexts a state's position in the global system, and particularly the characteristics of its relationship with the host country, influences its emigration policies.

In sum, Mexico's emigration policies are determined by the state's economic, political, and foreign policy interests, which have varied according to transformations taking place at the domestic, transnational, and international levels. These changes began in the late 1980s with the gradual economic and political opening of Mexico, the growth and political and economic influence of the emigrant community, as well as a closer and more integrated relationship between the United States and Mexico. As noted in the broader theoretical framework on sending states, the process of definition of states' emigration policies is variable. In the Mexican case, the definition of interests and objectives in this issue area is strongly influenced by the characteristics of the regime and the interests of the government in turn, the size and type of organization of the diaspora, and the status of the United States–Mexico relationship. Thus, these policies have not always been consistent; "they have not followed a linear process and have not been exempt of contradictions" (González Gutiérrez, 2006b: 211). In many aspects they are still in a process of development.

Drawing from the argument made by Østergaard-Nielsen (2003: 23) that "there are many and multi-level factors to consider in the analysis of the particular sending county's relationship with and policies towards emigrants and citizens abroad," in the following chapters I disaggregate these factors across different periods, based on the domestic, transnational, and international levels of analysis described here.

HISTORICAL BACKGROUND

Variations in Mexico's Emigration Policies
in a Bilateral Context (1848–1982)

2

The Consolidation of the Mexican State and the Safety Valve of Emigration (1848–1942)

With the signing of the Treaty of Guadalupe-Hidalgo (1848) and the Treaty of La Mesilla (1853), the current 1,958-mile (3,152-km) border between Mexico and the United States was officially established. Under these treaties, Mexico lost almost half of its territory to the United States and about 1 percent of its population residing in those areas (Gonzáles, 1999). Mexicans who lived in the territory that now belonged to the United States were given the option of moving south to Mexico or keeping their property and becoming American citizens. Approximately 75,000 out of 100,000 Mexicans in the territory decided to remain in what became the American Southwest (Monto, 1994: 27). Although this population did not actually migrate to the United States, it can be considered the first generation of Mexican immigrants in the country as a consequence of the new territorial division.

With limited exceptions, Mexico's policies toward emigration were generally passive, based on the idea that population movements should not be controlled by the government, and the fact that emigration provided a temporary solution to the economic and political problems in the country. Attempts to manage these movements in certain periods proved unsuccessful. The Mexican government limited most of its activities regarding the population in the United States to consular protection, which varied according to each consulate and to specific situations faced by Mexican migrants.

There were periods of concern about depopulation in some areas of the country and the government attempted to promote development projects to attract the Mexican population in the United States. It also tried to dissuade potential emigrants from leaving the country, as well as provide support in repatriations, but these policies were mostly ineffective. In terms of consular protection, Mexico brought specific complaints to the U.S. government concerning discrimination and abuse against Mexican emigrants, but these were generally unsuccessful demands and were not pursued actively or consistently by the Mexican government as part of a broader well-defined position on emigration or an effective response to U.S. immigration policies. One of Mexico's main concerns throughout this period was to avoid tensions in the bilateral relationship and guarantee the support of the United States in other areas, which meant that issues such as the protection of migrants' rights were not addressed as a priority issue in the bilateral agenda.

The main objective of this historical background, developed in Chapters 2 and 3, is to identify the domestic, transnational, and international context in which Mexico's migration policies were developed and to examine in greater detail how foreign policy considerations regarding the bilateral relationship with the United States affected the sending state's position on the issue. I give particular attention to the development and use of the foreign policy strategies of delinkage and nonintervention as a measure of the variation in Mexico's position on these issues in later periods. This analysis provides a basis for comparison with the changes in Mexico's emigration policies since the 1980s as well as a historical context to understand the significance and implications of these transformations.

1848–1910: TOWARD THE CONSOLIDATION OF THE MEXICAN STATE

Throughout most of the nineteenth century, population flows between Mexico and the United States were mainly local, the border area was loosely demarcated, it had a small population, and the presence of U.S. and Mexican authorities was infrequent. Immigration inspectors paid little attention to migrant workers, casual border visitors, or recruiting agents in border towns, and until the mid-1870s U.S. immigration laws generally stimulated immigration (Corwin, 1978b: 30).[1] Given the flexibility for crossing into U.S. territory, Mexicans who lived in the

---

[1] The first Laws on Immigration and Sedition, passed in 1798, had the objective of expelling dangerous immigrants and admitting only white foreigners into the country. However, from 1819 until 1875, immigration laws promoted the admission of foreigners into the territory with an open-border policy. The first restrictive immigration laws to control

border areas or who had family ties with those living in the United States found it easy to migrate, particularly after the construction of new railways (built between 1880 and 1884) that linked central Mexico to the north. Between 1848 and 1860 most Mexicans migrated to work as miners and ranch workers in California and later on to Nevada, Arizona, and Colorado (Corwin, 1978a: 25–27). In the 1880s the expansion of the railway to El Paso and the pacification of the border in the Texas area increased Mexican migration to the state; by 1900, "Mexicans were working in irrigation agriculture nearly everywhere in the Southwest as pickers, planters, and packers... by then hardly any Anglo rancher or farmer in the borderlands was without his *meskins* [(Mexicans)]" (Corwin, 1978a: 28–29).

As the population along the border began to grow, particularly at the end of the nineteenth century, surveillance increased. The first port-of-entry stations were built in 1894, the U.S. Border Patrol was created in 1924, and the U.S. government implemented restrictive immigration laws against Asians and other "dangerous" foreigners, such as the Chinese Exclusion Act of 1882.[2] However, Mexicans were generally exempt from these restrictions and were welcomed as a crucial element for U.S. economic growth and the population of its territory.

As the influx of Asian immigrants decreased, U.S. employers saw Mexican immigrants as an easy and natural replacement for cheap labor and grew increasingly dependent on it. Thus, they supported measures to facilitate their entry into the country.[3] Mexican smugglers (known at

the admission of immigrants, particularly from Asia, were passed in 1875 (see Zolberg, 2006).

[2] From 1875 to 1929 the U.S. Congress passed various laws that expanded the definition of "dangerous" foreigners, which had been established in the Laws on Immigration and Sedition of 1798. The Chinese Exclusion Act of 1882 imposed limitations on the number of Chinese immigrants allowed to enter the country and imposed a tax on all immigrants. The first laws that prohibited the hiring of migrants were passed in 1885 in response to labor organizations that argued that their presence affected wages and working conditions for the local population. In 1907 the United States established quotas to control the number of Japanese migrants and imposed more restrictions and taxes on immigrants. The Burnett Law of 1917 prohibited emigration from certain Asian countries, and it established more fees and restrictive definitions of eligible migrants. Further restrictions were put in place with the quota system based on national origin established in 1921 and 1924 (Corwin, 1978b: 136–137; Verea, 1982: 15–19; Zolberg, 2006).

[3] Employers even justified the hiring of Mexican workers by arguing that they were a "suitable race" that was "physically constituted" for agricultural work given their "low height." According to the employers, "being closer to the ground" made it easier for Mexicans to pick up the harvest. They also argued that Mexicans had a "gypsy spirit"

that time as *enganchadores* or *enganchistas*, or as *pasadores*), most of whom were railroad agents, created informal networks between employers and workers to facilitate the contracts (*enganches*) and began to make a business out of this exchange (Massey et al., 2002: 27–28). Meanwhile, problems of economic development encouraged those most affected by loss of land as a result of government policies, unemployment, or harsh working conditions to migrate with the certainty that they would find a job in the United States (Corwin and Cardoso, 1978: 38–40). By the beginning of the twentieth century, "Mexico's economy and society had evolved in a manner which met the preconditions for mass labor migration to the U.S." (García y Griego, 1981: 3).

Consular Protection without Confrontation

The Mexican government's position toward the emigrant population was to provide general consular protection in cases of discrimination and employer abuse and to support the cultural activities of grassroots organizations. Its main objectives were to maintain the emigrant communities' cultural ties and loyalties to their home country and to resolve pending border disputes while preventing further confrontations with the United States.

The main issues under discussion regarding the shared border were the problems with the invasion of Mexican border towns by marauding Indian bands, the activities of criminal gangs, and the stealing of cattle (Lajous, 1990: 55; Corwin, 1978a: 27). The United States attributed this situation to the Mexican government's lack of control of the border and on various occasions threatened to send U.S. troops to Mexican territory, using this situation to pressure Mexico with regard to pending border disputes (Lajous, 1990: 45). Finally in 1882, the governments established an agreement for the management of these issues; cooperation between the Mexican and U.S. armies was recognized as a necessity, given the need to secure the border and protect the population in border areas (Lajous, 1990: 55).

Despite the absence of a formal government policy to address the causes and consequences of emigration, Mexican consulates were present

that made them return to their origins and cultural roots, which meant that it was a temporary migration and would not lead to problems of assimilation. These arguments continued to be used until the 1960s, when employers were trying to justify the renewal of the Bracero Program (Bustamante, 1983: 263).

and active in the United States during this time. They offered protection for the Mexican community to prevent exploitation, help with repatriations, and present claims defending their civil and property rights in the United States; they also contributed to the sociocultural activity of the community and kept watch over subversive activities of certain groups along the border[4] (Lajous, 1990: 40; Terrazas y Basante, 2004).

One of the Mexican government's first actions regarding its population in the United States was to provide assistance to those who wanted to return to Mexico after the Treaty of Guadalupe-Hidalgo was signed. As part of this policy, three commissioners were sent to Texas, New Mexico, and California to inform the Mexican population of their right to move to Mexico or become U.S. citizens. Concerned about the possibility that a great number of Mexicans would leave the newly acquired territories, U.S. authorities argued that the right to send commissioners for this purpose had not been contemplated in the Guadalupe-Hidalgo Treaty. Thus, the Mexican government retreated and many Mexicans living in these territories became U.S. citizens against their will as a result of their illiteracy, their limited access to information, and the absence of authorities who could assist them (Zoraida Vázquez, 1990: 154).

Although the Guadalupe-Hidalgo Treaty protected the Mexican population as U.S. citizens, they were discriminated against, their property rights were violated, and they faced obstacles in the enjoyment of their political and economic rights. In 1878, using information gathered by each consulate, the Mexican Foreign Ministry launched an investigation about violations of Mexicans' property rights in the United States. In 1884 there was another investigation regarding abuses of Mexican workers in agricultural labor along the Río Bravo, which was presented to the U.S. Department of State. In 1888 and 1901 the Mexican Foreign Ministry also protested against judicial abuses to Mexicans (Lajous, 1990: 61). However, U.S. authorities generally ignored these complaints and Mexico did not pursue them through other diplomatic channels (Zoraida Vázquez, 1990: 155).

The consuls' commitment to the defense of Mexicans and the success of their efforts were uneven. This success depended partly on the support they obtained from the Mexican government, the number of

---

4 Guerrilla groups such as *Las Gorras Blancas* and *La Mano Negra*, organized by Mexican landowners in New Mexico, destroyed railroads and properties as a way to prevent what was considered an expansion of U.S. domination in Mexico given the fact that the railroads were being built through U.S. investors and represented a closer linkage between Mexico and the United States (Lajous, 1990: 63).

representations, their personnel and resources, and the consuls' personality (González, 1999). Furthermore, all these activities were regulated by the Mexican Consular Law of 1871, which determined that all consular activity for the protection of Mexicans would be conducted with strict respect of other states' sovereignty. This generally meant that Mexico refrained from activities or statements that could be interpreted as an intervention in U.S. domestic affairs.

At the time, the United States and other host states generally opposed intervention by sending states in terms of their relationship with emigrants, fearing that this would hinder their process of integration (Choate, 2007). Whether or not and to what extent Mexico limited its activities as a direct response to the U.S. position on this issue is a topic that requires further archival research. Nevertheless, there is evidence of a cautious response to problems related to emigration, which aroused criticism from certain groups in Mexico. As well, consular relations with Mexican organizations were mostly focused on cultural activities, regardless of emigrants' demands for support in other issues. In contrast, despite U.S. restrictions, countries such as Italy sought alternative channels to reach out to their population by subsidizing schools that would teach them Italian, promoting ties with the home country through religious organizations, and subsidizing remittances and return migration (Choate, 2007).

The First Mexican Migrant Organizations

Mexican migrants' hardships in the United States played an important role in their type of organization as an ethnic group, because these created a sense of solidarity, community, and common purpose among them (Gutiérrez, 1995: 14). Throughout this period, the Mexican community created self-help organizations or *mutualistas* with the objective of defending their civil and human rights and enhancing their Mexican cultural values and ethnic solidarity. The *mutualistas* (mutual-aid organizations) were one of the first efforts by the community to organize social welfare associations for Mexican workers. Generally, *mutualistas* were named after important individuals or events in Mexican history. Some of them restricted membership to Mexican citizens, whereas others were also open to people of Mexican origin and even non-Mexicans. The *mutualistas* mainly provided funeral and illness benefits, collective support, group defense against exclusion from political participation or abuse at the workplace, as well as recreational services. In response to union exclusion experienced by Mexicans, the *mutualista* model usually proved more successful in organizing workers and providing benefits for them (Gómez-Quiñones, 1994). Through the nineteenth century, *mutualistas* remained among the most numerous community-membership organizations, the largest of which was the *Alianza Hispano-Americana*, founded in 1894.[5]

Other types of organizations, such as the *Juntas Patrióticas* (patriotic councils) or *Juárez Clubs*, had a more political purpose related to the homeland and sought to collaborate in support of the Mexican Republic and the defense of the country against foreign interventions, although their impact in Mexican politics was not significant. In the years after 1848, some groups of Mexicans living in the United States were concerned with political instability and conflict in Mexico. To support the Mexican Republic they created the *Juntas* or *Sociedades Patrióticas*, which were active in raising funds, recruiting volunteers, and purchasing weapons for the Mexican army, especially during the French intervention of 1862–1867. According to Gómez-Quiñones (1983), the members of the *Juntas Patrióticas* supported Republican candidates in the U.S. elections because they were generally more favorable to the Juárez government. The *Juntas Patrióticas* were also dedicated to cultural activities; they sponsored festivities such as *Cinco de Mayo* parades, beauty contests, and debates about social and political issues relevant to the community. To promote these events they often worked closely with the Mexican consulates.

The consulates mainly supported cultural activities, although in some cases they assisted *mutualistas* in claims against discrimination or employer abuse. However, the unsatisfactory response from the Mexican consulates and the government to some of these cases led to resentment among this population, which was a favorable environment for the opposition groups from Mexico to develop their campaigns in border areas. Such was the case of the rebellion led by the Flores Magón brothers and the *Partido Liberal Mexicano* in 1906 and, later on, of exiled revolutionary leaders and propagandists. This was a key concern for the Mexican government, which instructed consulates to identify and curtail the sources of support for these groups (Gómez-Quiñones, 1976, 1983; Taylor, 2004: 43).

---

[5] The *mutualistas* also lay the foundations for labor unions, community organizations such as the *clubes de oriundos* (hometown associations), and civil and human rights organizations that proliferated in the twentieth century (Gutiérrez, 1995: 95–99).

Responses to Emigration and Immigration in Mexico

The limited engagement of the Mexican government in most matters related to emigration is also explained by the fact that President Porfirio Díaz's (1876–1911) main concern with the issue had to do more with immigration into Mexico than with emigration into the United States. Díaz sought to attract European, Chinese, and Japanese immigrants to promote the colonization of Mexican territories as a way to develop agriculture in unpopulated areas, take advantage of the exploitation of the countries' natural resources, and have enough labor force for the construction of railroads. He also began a project to repatriate Mexicans in the United States who wanted to return to Mexico (Lajous, 1990: 35–36). Despite these efforts, the colonization project failed.[6] By the beginning of the twentieth century, public opinion was critical of the preferential treatment that Díaz was giving to foreigners and their companies. In response to these pressures, the government's policy toward immigrants became more restrictive and it canceled many of their concessions (Lajous, 1990: 38).

There was a significant increase in Mexican emigration to the United States from the 1890s onward (from 78,000 in 1890 to 103,000 in 1900 and 222,000 in 1910; see Gibson and Jung, 2006: Table 4). This was mainly a result of the land reforms in Mexico affecting many peasants, and the expansion of the railway that made it easier to get to the north. However, Porfirio Díaz's government considered these flows as a natural phenomenon that the government should not prevent or control (Cardoso, 1982: 31). The fact that the United States also saw Mexican migration as beneficial, given the economic expansion and labor shortages in the American Southwest at the beginning of the 1900s, meant that there was no external pressure for the Mexican government to be more proactive in tackling the root causes of emigration or controlling the flows.

Mexican opposition groups and newspapers accused the government of neglecting the underlying problems that led to emigration. They used emigration as evidence to attack Díaz's "failed" policies and the unequal

---

[6] Compared with Brazil, Argentina, and the United States, which received close to 200,000 immigrants a year, in Mexico by 1889 there were nineteen colonies with close to 6,000 inhabitants, two-thirds of which were repatriated Mexicans; by 1892 there were twenty-four colonies with 10,000 inhabitants, and by the end of the colonization program in 1907 there were only 30,000 immigrants (Lajous, 1990: 35).

distribution of benefits in the country. They also criticized the lack of protection for Mexican workers in the United States as the Mexican consulates informed Mexico City of the rising number of complaints received by their offices related to unemployed immigrants, harsh labor conditions, and segregation in schools (Gómez-Quiñones, 1976; García and Maciel, 1986). Nevertheless, domestic pressures regarding these issues did not lead to widespread mobilizations and the Díaz government did not modify its position. Before the outbreak of the Revolution, apparently "disturbed by editorial opinion and consular reports," the Díaz regime was "at the point of undertaking a full-scale investigation of the causes of this out-migration" and a survey to determine the number of Mexicans in the United States (Corwin, 1978c: 177); the lack of resources and the focus on the political situation undermined these efforts.

The 1907 recession in the United States brought migration issues to the fore as large-scale forced repatriations to Mexico increased. However, the Mexican government's response was slow and ineffective. The Díaz government's only contribution was to publish information in the local newspapers about the problems Mexicans faced in the United States in an attempt to dissuade them from leaving the country. It also attempted to begin keeping consistent migration records through the creation of the Migration Service, founded in 1909 (Corwin, 1978a: 30).

Opposition parties and leaders blamed the Díaz government for the problems related to emigration: The Liberal Party accused "a tyrannical dictatorship of depopulating Mexico," and Francisco I. Madero's Anti-Reelection Party blamed the government for expatriation, while Ricardo Flores Magón consistently argued that "the Díaz regime failed to protect Mexican workers in the U.S." (Corwin, 1978c: 177, 213 n. 3). Despite domestic criticisms regarding the drain of labor to the United States, repatriations, and abuses against Mexican emigrants in the United States, in 1909 Díaz agreed to negotiate with President Taft and sign an executive agreement authorizing the migration of 1,000 Mexican workers to Colorado and Nebraska, given the apparent need for sugar beet workers (García y Griego, 1981: 11). This reflects Mexico's main interest in maintaining emigration flows and preserving a good relationship with the United States. To achieve this, the government avoided measures to address the underlying causes of migration, it limited complaints concerning violations of Mexicans' rights to traditional consular channels, and, in this last case, agreed to supply labor to fulfill U.S. needs.

1910–1942: THE REVOLUTIONARY STATE

During the first decades of the twentieth century, the emigrant population grew significantly as a result of the hardships and violence experienced in Mexico during the revolutionary years (1910–1917) and the increase in the demand for workers in the United States during the First World War.[7] By 1910, the Mexican foreign-born population had doubled to 222,000 and it doubled again in 1920 to 486,000 (Lajous, 1990: 60; Gibson and Jung, 2006: Table 4). The flow of new emigrants in the beginning of the twentieth century, and the fact that many of the Mexican families living in the United States decided not to return to the country after the Revolution, resulted in a significant demographic growth of the Mexican population living in the United States. By 1930 it was estimated that there were between 641,000 and 1 million Mexicans in the country (García y Griego, 1981: 3).

Given the decline in the number of European emigrants to the United States as a result of the First World War and the Immigration Act of 1917, the demand for Mexican workers increased: "[A]lthough the law of 1917 for the first time established general immigration restrictions on the Mexican border, employers were quick to ask the Secretary of Labor to exempt Mexican contract workers from literacy tests and the eight-dollar head tax" (Corwin and Cardoso, 1978: 52). From 1917 to 1921 the U.S. government established a unilateral program for the recruitment of Mexican workers in order to guarantee the levels of production during the war. This program, considered by some authors to be the First Bracero[8] Program, involved the hiring of close to 72,000 Mexican workers (Kiser and Kiser, 1979: 3–4; Alanís Enciso, 1999); most of them were repatriated in 1921 because of the economic recession of the immediate postwar period, but the majority returned to the United States during the economic boom of the 1920s.

After the Revolution, emigration was an important concern for Mexican governments; there were labor shortages in many areas as well as high levels of unemployment in others. Nevertheless, the lack of organization

---

[7] Given the growing pressures of U.S. labor unions, employers continued to prefer hiring a foreign labor force rather than satisfying local employees' demands (Corwin and Cardoso, 1978: 52–53).

[8] The word "bracero" is derived from "brazo" (arm), and it refers to Mexican workers hired to offer their labor or "arms," mainly for agricultural work (Samora, 1971).

and clear definition of responsibilities in the agencies in charge of the situation hindered the development of an official and efficient policy on the issue (Alanís Enciso, 1999: 38–39, 64–65). The limited priority of these issues in the national agenda and the lack of resources that were devoted to policies such as repatriations and colonization projects were also due to the ambiguity within the political elite on this issue. Many government officials feared the economic and political consequences of the return of migrants, preferring for them to remain "on the other side" despite a nationalistic rhetoric promoting their return (Alanís Enciso, 2007).

Mexican governments in this period "regarded an open border as an *escape valve* for revolutionary unrest and political enemies," but at the same time they attempted to discourage emigration and protect workers in the United States in response to nationalist groups, labor unions, and Mexican hacienda owners who demanded a solution to the problem (Corwin, 1978c: 178–179). Government officials also tried to use emigration as an element to obtain legitimacy and "defend the new revolutionary order" by arguing that it was a consequence of the development problems inherited from the Porfirio Díaz regime and promising to solve these conditions with socioeconomic reforms (Corwin, 1978c: 182; García y Griego, 1983a: 53). In addition, the Mexican government used a nationalist rhetoric to argue that this situation was a result of the demand from U.S. employers that Mexico could not avoid and the United States was taking advantage of. However, in some cases this was presented as a positive asset, given that emigrants who worked temporarily in the United States generally returned to Mexico with new techniques and training that contributed to the country's development. There were various failed attempts to attract these "highly skilled" migrants back to Mexico, especially those working in agriculture (Alanís Enciso, 2007).

"Mexicanization" and Nonintervention

When President Venustiano Carranza came to power in 1917, he proposed a national strategy for managing emigration based on three points: dissuasion, contract protection, and "Mexicanization" of emigrants. This entailed bringing back Mexicans from an "exile" resulting from the "economic and political necessities of the previous regime," helping them manage their income, preventing their settlement in the United States, and even assisting the development of migrant organizations as a "possible political lever" to favor the Mexican revolutionary government (Corwin,

1978c: 191). Based on Article 11 of the 1917 Constitution, which recognizes Mexican citizens' right to freely enter and exit the country, the government argued that it could not impose restrictions on emigration (Cardoso, 1979: 21).[9] Nonetheless, there were limited attempts to manage these flows through stricter controls on the issuance of passports and requirement of contracts with a U.S. employer in order to cross the border. Even though the government was unwilling to implement additional measures to control emigration, as some nationalist groups and Mexican employers demanded, it promised to strengthen consular protection and "reduce emigrants' hardships while they resided abroad" (Alanís Enciso, 1999: 73).[10] However, these actions would be carefully designed under the specific foreign policy principle of nonintervention, expressed in the 1918 Carranza Doctrine, and "recourse to diplomatic pressure was to be used only as a last resort" (Cardoso, 1979: 25–26).[11]

An example of the Mexican government's cautiousness in its consular activities in order to prevent accusations of intervention in U.S. internal affairs was the failure of the initiative to publish, in 1917, a handbook for Mexican emigrants with guidelines about acceptable contracts from U.S. employers. This was intended to prevent discrimination and violation of migrants' rights at the workplace, which was one of the main problems reported by consular representatives. However, the handbook was not published because the Mexican government considered that it was beyond its jurisdiction and it posed a risk in terms of being interpreted as an intervention in U.S. domestic issues (García and Maciel, 1986: 18). As I discuss in Chapter 6, a similar situation occurred in 2004 with the publication – and subsequent removal – of the *Migrants' Guide* with similar content about migrants' rights as well as the dangers involved in crossing the border. This reveals the historical relevance of the principle of nonintervention in Mexico's emigration policies and its permanence to date.

---

[9] Critics of this position argue that the Mexican government has used this interpretation of the constitution as an excuse for inaction on emigration problems (Corwin, 1978c: 180).

[10] Safeguards for migrant workers were included in Article 123 of the 1917 Mexican Constitution (García y Griego, 1981: 54; Alanís Enciso, 1999: 67).

[11] In 1918, Carranza presented his foreign policy doctrine before the Mexican Congress. This policy was mainly based on the principles of equal sovereignty and nonintervention. As a response to the various foreign interventions experienced by Mexico in the nineteenth century, the proclamation of a noninterventionist foreign policy was considered essential to prevent other countries (mainly the United States) from interfering in Mexico's domestic affairs.

The results of the Mexicanization plan were meager. Most of the effort did not go beyond the nationalist rhetoric and symbolic calls for emigrants to return to Mexico and contribute to the development of the country (González, 1999). Even though the Mexican government protested the ill treatment of Mexican workers in the United States, it accepted the U.S. Department of Labor's campaign to continue bringing Mexican workers to the United States from 1917 until 1921, which was seen as a contradictory position (Kiser and Kiser, 1979: 10–12). Corwin explains this position as a result of the early revolutionary governments' concern about imposing controls on emigration and forcing repatriations because the lack of employment for returning or potential emigrants could call into question the regime's capacity to consolidate or fulfill its objectives: "Mexico had little to offer... except unfulfilled revolutionary promises" (Corwin, 1978c: 178).[12] According to Gilbert González (1999: 28–29), "conceivably, by allowing emigration to take place, Mexico escaped a fundamental social transformation... arguably, emigration provided Mexico's *way out.*"

Although the arguments about how emigration prevented further political and economic problems in Mexico and about the country's capacity to absorb the migrant workforce are subject to debate, the perception that migration functioned as a safety valve has been recognized "even by the highest Mexican and U.S. authorities," which means that regardless of its accuracy, it was an idea that significantly influenced policy in this area (Rico, 1992: 274–275). Alanís Enciso (2007: 17–18) complements this idea in his extensive historical account of government officials' fear of the consequences of a potential return of a large number of Mexican migrants, both in terms of the economic pressures and the political unrest that it could create, because migrants would compete for jobs with the

---

[12] Some of the revolutionary leaders, such as Francisco I. Madero, framed the problem of migration in terms of how it affected development in Mexico, given the need to secure laborers for production in the borderlands. This concern was also raised with regard to the political volatility of the *campesinos* and the need to prevent violent mobilizations. Thus, Madero proposed projects to study the possibility of rooting migrants in certain regions in Mexico, give them land, and strengthen their national roots. However, as Walsh (2000) explains, nothing came out of these plans, mostly because of the instability of the Mexican government and the lack of resources for development projects. In Walsh's view, these types of repatriation and colonization projects, which Presidents Álvaro Obregón and Plutarco Elías Calles also failed to implement in the 1920s and 1930s, show that although the Mexican government viewed migration as an economic necessity and even as a safety valve for potential political threats, it also considered migrants as agents for development (see also Cardoso, 1982).

population living in Mexico; this led to the government's general preference for migrants to remain in the United States (or as Alanís Enciso puts
it, "*que se queden allá*").

An additional consideration that led the Mexican government to accept
the unilateral hiring of Mexican workers in the United States was the
need for diplomatic recognition and political support from the U.S. government. When President Álvaro Obregón (1920–1924) came to power,
President Woodrow Wilson conditioned his diplomatic recognition on
Mexico's resolution of disputes regarding U.S. citizens' property in the
country and other pending disputes. For Mexico, this was not just a
protocol issue because the absence of political relations with the United
States meant that even if the regular economic exchanges continued, the
U.S. government would not support Obregón's efforts to stop Mexican opposition groups' activities in the United States that threatened
his administration or to stop the traffic of weapons to Mexico; moreover, Mexico could not have access to capital markets or receive loans
without the U.S. government's approval (Zoraida Vázquez and Meyer,
1994: 150–151; Águila, 2004: 100–101). Thus, "in spite of a widespread
anti-American sentiment, President Wilson's meddling in revolutionary
affairs, American occupation of Veracruz in 1915, and Pershing's invasion of North Mexico in 1916," in order to gain U.S. recognition, Mexico
succumbed to the American government's pressures (Corwin, 1978c: 179;
Alanís Enciso, 1999). This included allowing the recruitment of labor at
the border during World War I (the program was extended until 1921),
under no Mexican supervision. Although the Mexican government did
protest through diplomatic channels against reported abuses of Mexican
workers, and demanded that U.S. employers should meet contract obligations, these efforts were rarely successful and were not actively pursued
(Corwin, 1978c: 180).

Ambivalent Responses to Emigration

Emerging labor unions in Mexico, dominated by the *Confederación
Regional Obrera Mexicana* (CROM), as well as intellectuals expressed
their concern about growing emigration and labor shortage in Mexico;
they demanded that Mexican authorities do something to stop discrimination and exploitation against Mexicans in the United States (Corwin and
Cardoso, 1978: 57). Some sectors of the Mexican public reacted strongly
against news that their countrymen were victims of racism, violence,
and job abuses in the United States; they argued that emigration was a

symptom of what was wrong with the country and the failure of the revolutionary governments to solve underlying problems. These perceptions had political salience throughout this period. In many cases, such as the repatriation campaigns in 1921–1922 and 1929, the Mexican government reacted with a strong nationalist rhetoric to bring back the *"hijos de la patria"* to prevent domestic criticism (Zazueta, 1983). However, it must be emphasized that Mexican public opinion was ambivalent about the issue and its impact on government policy is not self-evident: Some groups lamented the hardships suffered by emigrants at home and abroad; others saw emigrants (who were negatively referred to as *pochos*) as traitors to the nationalist cause and opportunists who left the nation when they were most needed (Cardoso, 1979: 19–20; Taylor, 2004: 92–93; Alanís Enciso, 2007). Despite the Mexican government's frequent declarations regarding support for the return of migrants as part of this nationalist discourse, in practice few measures were taken in this regard (except in the periods of mass returns caused by economic circumstances in the United States, such as 1908–1909, 1920–1923, and 1929–1932), and Mexican officials recognized the limited amount of resources to finance their return or give them land once they arrived in Mexico (Alanís Enciso, 2007: 44, 48–50).

The Mexican government responded to these pressures through campaigns to advise emigrants on the problems and dangers they would encounter in the United States (arguments that had also been used during the Díaz regime). These efforts also included a nationalist appeal, repatriations, checkpoints to detain potential undocumented emigrants, and administrative controls to prevent farm workers from leaving (Alanís Enciso, 1999: 69–70). One of the administrative measures that the government used was to delegate the responsibility of passport emission to local authorities. The idea was that the pressures of labor scarcity would lead states to take more effective measures to prevent emigration. In the case of Sonora, Plutarco Elías Calles (who was then governor of the state) was successful in promoting drastic measures to prevent recruiters from taking Mexican workers during harvesting seasons, and he conditioned all contracts to the return of Mexican migrants to the state. In 1920, the government also established a workers' protection office in the border towns of Ciudad Juárez and El Paso to regulate labor contracts. In addition, consuls tried to supervise contracting and prevent middlemen exploitation (Cardoso, 1979: 16–23; Corwin, 1978c: 179–180). Despite these efforts, emigration did not stop; financial constraints, lack of bureaucratic machinery, absence of cooperation with U.S. authorities, and unavailability of job opportunities in Mexico limited these efforts (González, 1999).

In addition to the limits of federal policies to control emigration, Fitzgerald (2009) has documented how conflicting interests at the state and local level also hindered efforts in this regard. Using field and archival research in Arandas, a municipality in the state of Jalisco, Fitzgerald offers compelling evidence to show how state and local officials played a role in the failure of some of Mexico's emigration policies as they subverted orders from Mexico City according to their own needs. While the Mexican government attempted to dissuade emigration or control the geographic origin of migrants through propaganda, issuance of travel documents, or later on by establishing hiring centers during the Bracero Program, some local governments saw it as an escape valve to alleviate economic and political crises and quietly avoided these directives. However, there is an underlying question that Fitzgerald does not address about the extent to which the federal government ignored these local challenges to its directives because it also saw emigration as an escape valve to economic and political pressures faced by the state. Furthermore, given that these policies were not actively pursued on the basis of arguments such as the constitutional right to freely enter and exit the country, it could be argued that the calls for dissuading emigration and promoting migrants' return were mostly motivated by a nationalist rhetoric, as Alanís Enciso (2007) documents, and by the need to legitimize the regime.

Expanding Consular Activity

Given the failure of these efforts to limit emigration or promote migrants' return, the Mexican government focused its efforts on protecting emigrants who worked and lived in the United States and developing ties with their organizations.[13] Consuls were successful in protecting Mexican nationals in employer and civil disputes and in problems with government

---

[13] Alanís Enciso (2007: 108) provides evidence of the Mexican government's early attempts to offer services to migrants in the United States, given its recognition of its inability or unwillingness to support their return to Mexico. In 1935 Mexican representative Antonio Nava argued that he would propose the creation of schools and libraries that would offer texts in Spanish to all Mexicans living in the United States. Alanís Enciso points out that this initiative reflected a sense of solidarity toward migrants that existed among some circles in Mexico, but in reality it was difficult to achieve because the Mexican government did not have the resources to support education even in the national territory. This proposal is an interesting precedent in light of the programs developed in the 1990s to provide educational and other services to the Mexican population in the

agencies. For example, Corwin (1978c: 188) points out as a "remarkable dimension of consular activities" the defense of Mexicans from discrimination and segregation in schooling, housing, and social services, and from military drafts during World War I and II, as well as arbitrary arrest, incarceration, or deportation. However, these efforts were limited as a result of fear and distrust from emigrants who did not report cases, the importance given to the principle of nonintervention by the Mexican Foreign Ministry and the consulates, and their lack of funds and personnel (Cardoso, 1979: 25–28; 1982).

In response to repatriations during the 1921–1922 economic crisis in the United States, the Mexican Foreign Ministry had created a special protection division, which was in charge of issues related to Mexicans in the United States, particularly with repatriations. During this period, President Obregón took an active interest in helping the close to 50,000 workers who returned to Mexico. Nevertheless, the resources were limited and many Mexicans took advantage of the program by returning to Mexico with the government's support and then going back to the United States (Carreras de Velasco, 1974: 137–138; Cardoso, 1977: 576–577). The conditions in Mexico had not improved, support from the government was very limited, and the majority of repatriated individuals returned to the United States approximately one year after they had been sent back to Mexico and remained in the United States until they were deported in 1929 (Cardoso, 1977: 590). As the problems regarding protection of emigrants and deportations increased, especially during the repatriations of 1929,[14] the size of the consular corps and the scope of its activities expanded through the 1920s and 1930s. The government was also concerned about the potential impact of the migrant communities in Mexico's political affairs as Mexican opposition parties and leaders (e.g., the *Partido Laborista* and José Vasconcelos) and extremist groups (e.g., the *Unión Nacional Sinarquista*) became increasingly popular among Mexicans in the United States (Gómez-Quiñones, 1983, 1994).

One of the consulates' major influences in Mexican emigrants' activities was their sponsoring of a wide variety of community organizations, from *mutualistas* to political groups such as the *Clubes Liberales* and

United States, such as the donation of Mexican textbooks to libraries and schools and the *Plazas Comunitarias* program.
14 Although there is no official record of the number of repatriations during the Great Depression, it is estimated that between 350,000 and 600,000 Mexicans were sent back to Mexico during this period (see Carreras de Velasco, 1974; Gonzáles, 1999).

the *Juntas Constitucionalistas*. During the 1920s and 1930s, the consuls mostly encouraged the formation and development of *Comisiones Honoríficas* (honorary committees or consulates) and *Brigadas de la Cruz Azul* (Blue Cross brigades), which were community-based groups dedicated to cultural and civil-rights issues with an important role in protective duties, assistance, and repatriation efforts (Carreras de Velasco, 1974: 68; Corwin, 1978c: 189; Cardoso, 1982). Through these associations, the consuls helped develop community leadership and unions; they organized repatriations; and they promoted *Mexicanidad* projects to strengthen Mexican emigrants' ties with their cultural roots (González, 1999). Some consuls occasionally organized fundraisers when resources were not available for the community's projects (e.g., to provide food, shelter, or return transportation for unemployed and indigent Mexicans); this brought them closer to the local population and made the consuls important figures (Zazueta, 1983). Although the consuls' role was sometimes challenged and the response from the community to their influence was ambivalent,[15] they were generally figures around which most members of the Mexican community rallied (Balderrama, 1982).

As part of these community organization efforts, trade unions with Mexican and Mexican-American members began to protest inferior wages and labor conditions. The *Confederación de Sociedades Mexicanas* (CSM), based in Los Angeles and formed in 1927, and the labor union *Confederación de Uniones Obreras Mexicanas* (CUOM), created in 1928, maintained close ties to the consulates and to the CROM in Mexico (Gómez-Quiñones, 1994). Their most important activities concentrated on the Imperial Valley strikes from 1928 through 1934. The consulates followed this situation closely and provided support to the unions (González, 1994, 1999).[16]

By 1930, Mexico had over fifty consular agencies in the United States, including *abogados consultores* (consulting lawyers) and *Comisiones Honoríficas* (Gómez-Quiñones, 1983).[17] Even though the promotion of

[15] Some members of the community resented the consuls' intervention in their affairs, whereas others greatly appreciated that the consulate took an interest in their welfare. There is an ongoing scholarly debate about whether the consulates had a positive, neutral, or negative effect on emigrant communities (González, 2004).
[16] Gilbert González (2004: 176–177) challenges the argument that the consuls played a positive role and protected Mexicans' interests; he claims that they were pursuing their own objectives by controlling these groups for their political gains.
[17] For a detailed list of the *Comisiones Honoríficas* and *Brigadas de la Cruz Azul*, see Secretaría de Relaciones Exteriores (1928).

the development of these groups and the influence of the Mexican government in their formation can be interpreted as a deviation from the traditional interpretation of nonintervention, the Mexican government kept a close watch on these agencies' activities, making sure that their role was limited to improving the situation of Mexican immigrants in the United States and promoting Mexican nationalism "without getting involved in sensitive political issues that could generate international conflicts" (Águila, 2004: 111). In the end, the success of these groups depended largely on each consul's support and their successful choices for the location of these agencies (Águila, 2004: 114–115). In addition, insufficient resources, the high mobility of members, and political factionalism, among other factors, limited their activities (Cardoso, 1982; García, 1996; González, 1999). As opposed to developments in the 1990s, the government's efforts in promoting the creation of Mexican community organizations in the United States and collaborating with them in offering a wider range of services to the community were neither centralized nor institutionalized.

Authors such as Gilbert González (1999) have argued that the objective underlying the Mexican government's actions since the Revolution was to incorporate the *México de Afuera* into a political ideology and social relations consonant with the interests of the ruling upper classes in Mexico. This would explain why the Mexican government tolerated and encouraged more social and organizational proactive efforts that it could lead and control – such as the *Comisiones Honoríficas* and *Brigadas de la Cruz Azul*.[18] In González's (1999) view, another of its goals was to develop emigrant groups as a possible political lever to influence American policy toward revolutionary reforms in Mexico. Although it is true that the Mexican government sponsored and promoted these types of organizations, with a view toward improving consular protection, developing relationships with the community, as well as promoting the state's image abroad, the argument that the Mexican government thought of using these groups as a way to influence U.S. policies requires further investigation. Throughout my research I found no evidence related to lobbying in the United States through these organizations. As explained here, the extent of the consulates' actions in this regard depended on the consuls' own perception of duty and personal political ideology as

[18] David G. Gutiérrez (1999: 493) also argues that the government was aiming to develop "appropriate allegiances" between the Mexican community and the government. See also Corwin (1978c).

well as the limits imposed by the principle that these activities should not be perceived as interference in U.S. domestic affairs (Balderrama, 1982; Águila, 2004).

It is worth mentioning that, during the 1920s and 1930s, the new generations of Mexican Americans also began to mobilize the community against increased discrimination caused by U.S. economic depression, the repatriation campaigns, and the growth of the urban Mexican population. In this context, important organizations emerged in defense of Mexican Americans, such as the League of United Latin American Citizens (LULAC, founded in 1929) and the Mexican American Movement (MAM, founded in the 1930s). Their main objective was to encourage the assimilation of Mexican Americans as American citizens and prevent discrimination by helping them achieve higher levels of education and English proficiency (González, 1994). According to Gutiérrez, the fact that these organizations did not include Mexican immigrants and did not address problems related to them indeed exacerbated differences and resentments between these two groups (Gutiérrez, 1995). The relevance of this separation of agendas, as well as the formation of Mexican-American organizations, is important because it influenced the Mexican government's type of response to its population abroad in the following decades, as well as the formation of Mexican immigrant community organizations.

Repatriations and Bilateral Relations

The Depression of 1929 changed both the Mexican and the U.S. governments' positions toward migration. The economic crisis contributed to the strengthening of anti-immigrant positions within the U.S. government and society. Mexican emigrants were accused of increasing levels of unemployment for the local population and the fall of wages, as well as of living off Americans' taxes. As a response to these political and economic pressures, the U.S. government organized a campaign for massive repatriations to Mexico:

[A]lthough U.S. politicians were at a loss as to how the faltering economy might be revived, there was one decisive action they could take that would address, if only symbolically, the concerns of frightened U.S. workers: a massive roundup and deportation of Mexican immigrants.... Through the massive use of repressive force and police powers, the U.S. government sought to undo in the 1930s what it had actively encouraged over the preceding two decades (Massey et al., 2002: 33–34).

The Mexican government was forced to respond to this situation, but it was evident that the country's economy was not ready to provide opportunities for the repatriated population and meet their expectations (Corwin, 1978c: 194; Alanís Enciso, 2007). Mexican authorities facilitated migrants' return and promoted political and economic measures as well as colonization projects to provide jobs for the returning emigrants in rural areas, with limited success. These measures were criticized both in Mexico and in the United States. Though some supported repatriation as an example of an "economic and social conquest" equivalent to the nationalization of oil, Mexican intellectuals and other groups in Mexico argued that the repatriated population would not be able to readapt or that many who were unemployed or ill would return and become a burden (Alanís Enciso, 2007: 202–204). Meanwhile, in the United States the repatriation campaigns were criticized because of their limitations and their focus on the return of some groups, particularly those working in agriculture, and the fact that those left behind would be more prone to rely on the support of U.S. public services. Some argued that this called into question the state of the bilateral relationship and the idea of good neighbors; they were also aggravated by the Mexican government's choice of the name "March 18 colony" for the main area where migrants were repatriated in the 1930s, in reference to the date of the nationalization of American oil companies (Alanís Enciso, 2007: 274–276). The March 18 colonization project and the campaigns to promote migrants' return ended in 1939 in response to these and other critiques, such as the fact that so much support was given to Spanish refugees in Mexico in contrast to the limited resources offered for the repatriation campaigns.

At the same time as they attempted to support to repatriated emigrants, mainly those in urgent situations, Mexican authorities expressed their opposition to the U.S. unilateral policy: In times of economic growth the U.S. government and many economic sectors had promoted Mexican migration without taking into account the Mexican government's interests; now that there was a crisis they wanted to get rid of emigrants (García y Griego and Verea, 1988: 106). Many nationalist and anti-American groups in Mexico expressed their concern with the U.S. government's actions and demanded that the government should prevent further emigration. Despite these anti-American pressures, in 1929, Mexico decided to make a proposal to the United States for the signing of an agreement for the bilateral management of repatriations, given that the costs were extremely high for Mexico and could not be faced independently. This proposal, as García y Griego (1983a: 54) describes, was "ill timed and not acted upon" in the context of an economic crisis in the United States and tensions in the bilateral relation. However, it is evidence of Mexico's higher vulnerability to changes in migration flows vis-à-vis the United States and the fact that domestic criticism regarding Mexico's inability to defend emigrants' rights in the United States, even in the context of bilateral temporary worker programs, was not considered an obstacle to pursuing further agreements with it when the Mexican government considered it in its interest. This was made clear throughout the duration of the Bracero Program, discussed in the next chapter.

CONCLUSIONS

Through this historical analysis it is possible to identify how domestic, transnational, and international factors affected Mexico's response to emigration control and the protection of nationals abroad in the first periods of emigration. At the domestic level, Mexican emigration policies were determined by the need to consolidate the state and guarantee political and economic stability. The political and economic situation in Mexico, characterized by unemployment, social tensions, and political division, explains the government's implicit acceptance of emigration as a safety valve to prevent political mobilizations and economic pressures. Political opposition and problems of unemployment and displacement of peasants were particularly exacerbated as a result of Díaz's policies of industrialization and modernization in the late nineteenth century. Although some groups in Mexico complained about the situation migrants faced in the United States and associated emigration with the government's failed economic policies, these criticisms did not represent significant domestic pressures that led the government to change its general position on the issue beyond the reinforcement of its dissuasion campaigns and nationalist discourse or its support in repatriation efforts and strengthening of consular activities. Furthermore, the existence of a closed political system, characterized by the use of censorship and the repression of opposition groups, prevented concerns such as emigration from becoming significant issues in the national agenda.

Although the Mexican government launched campaigns to support repatriated workers and dissuade them from leaving the country, the efforts to provide alternatives in their home country were limited in scope and efficacy. The government generally maintained its position regarding the constitutional right of freedom of movement for the population and limited its policies on emigration control. The unsuccessful attempts to impose administrative controls and other campaigns to dissuade emigration lead to the question of whether the federal government's priority was in fact to control population movements or if these policies were just symbolic responses to pressures from some groups within Mexico while the end goal was to maintain the status quo of a migratory movement determined by the forces of supply and demand in Mexico and in the United States as well as to maintain the general stability in the bilateral relationship. Another explanation could be that the federal government simply lacked the capacity and resources to control these movements and create alternatives for its working population.

At the transnational level, from the mid-nineteenth century it is possible to identify a relationship between organized Mexican migrants and the Mexican government, particularly through consulates, but this interaction did not significantly influence Mexican migration policies beyond consular activities and, in some cases, control of dissident groups established in the United States. Given its limited capacity and interest in controlling emigration flows, the Mexican government's main activities regarding Mexican migrants in the United States were based on consular protection. Consuls were present and active in the United States from 1848; they provided aid in cases of discrimination, violation of property rights, labor disputes, and the development of migrant organizations. However, this activity varied according to each consul's preferences and objectives, and to the type of problems experienced by the community in each period, and it was limited in design and implementation by the foreign policy principle of nonintervention. Organized migrants focused most of their activity in protecting their rights, providing mutual aid to community members, and organizing cultural activities. In some cases, migrant organizations participated in political campaigns related to Mexico.

Mexico's policies were significantly influenced by foreign policy considerations mainly concerning the bilateral relationship. The asymmetry of power in the relationship with the United States, the recent loss of the northern territories, and the political and economic instability in Mexico implied that Mexico was more vulnerable to U.S. decisions regarding immigration and had limited capacity to pressure for changes. This was made evident in Mexico's unsuccessful complaints regarding discrimination against migrants during the nineteenth century, and its limited capacity to control emigration and deal with repatriations in the 1920s and 1930s. Mexico's economic and political dependence on the United States was part of the reasoning behind the government's limited consular protection activities and caution in expressing opposition to U.S. policies and legislation affecting emigrants' rights. The government considered that such activities could change the status quo in the bilateral relationship in general and possibly be interpreted as intervention, leading in turn to U.S. interference in Mexican affairs. Thus, in most cases Mexico agreed to the conditions established by the United States regarding migration; it limited its consular role to traditional protection and documentation activities (with some exceptions, including the government's promotion of the formation of specific community-based groups in the 1920s and some consuls' participation in labor disputes in the 1930s); and it avoided linkages between migration and other issues to prevent conflict.

3

From the Bracero Agreements to Delinkage (1942–1982)

From 1942 to 1964, Mexico and the United States established bilateral agreements for the management of labor contracting of Mexican emigrants in the United States. These agreements became known as the Bracero Program or Bracero Agreements. This period is crucial in the history of migration between Mexico and the United States because the structure of the migratory flows was consolidated during these years and the governments' policies for managing the flows began to be defined more clearly. This was also an exceptional period because, for the first time, the U.S. and Mexican governments agreed on the establishment of common rules to administrate the hiring of Mexican workers in the United States through bilateral mechanisms. In previous similar agreements, Mexico had generally accepted the terms established by the United States. The reasons why the rules of the Bracero Agreements worked or not, and the consequences that this program had in the future of migration policies and migration flows in the United States–Mexico case, are significant in terms of variations in the interpretations of the limits and possibilities of action within the asymmetrical relationship as well as the obstacles that the sending state faces in taking a more active position vis-à-vis a more powerful state.

Once the United States canceled the Bracero Program in 1964, the Mexican government spent ten years attempting to renew these agreements with the goal of limiting undocumented migration and the exploitation of Mexican workers. However, by the mid-1970s, as the domestic and bilateral context changed, Mexico decided that linkage between issues made it vulnerable to U.S. pressures and was against its own

interests. In 1974, Luis Echeverría's government rejected a U.S. proposal for a new temporary worker agreement in exchange for oil. Among
various considerations, including nationalism, the past experience with
the Bracero Program, and the fact that the safety valve of immigration
remained open, this position was also a result of Mexico's confidence
in the prospect that its oil exports would guarantee prosperity and limit
its economic dependence on the United States, which seemingly made a
negotiation regarding the management of migration unnecessary. A similar situation occurred in 1979 when Mexico was confident that new data
on oil reserves would give it an economic boost and therefore cooperation with the U.S. on various issues, including migration, was no longer
a priority.

Thus, from the mid-1970s until the late 1980s, the Mexican government's main interest became to preserve the status quo by limiting the
salience of migration issues in the national agenda and avoiding negotiations with the United States that could lead to a negative outcome in this
or other areas of the bilateral relationship, a position which is commonly
known as the "policy of having no policy." This began to change in 1982
as Mexico's dependence on U.S. economic support increased. These are
key examples of how variations in the context of the bilateral relationship
influenced Mexico's position on migration.

1942–1964: THE BRACERO AGREEMENTS

From the beginning of the Second World War in 1939, Mexico had
insisted on maintaining a neutral position and resisted a clear definition
about what it was willing to do to cooperate with the United States
and the Allies. Mexican public opinion, political parties, and other leftist and conservative groups opposed Mexico's participation in the war
with arguments regarding the defense of Mexican sovereignty and the
need to oppose U.S. hegemony (Torres, 1991: 22). However, President
Manuel Ávila Camacho (1940–1946) thought that by giving the United
States proof of its goodwill and guarantees of its support through commercial and military agreements, Mexico would be able to take advantage of the circumstances and obtain U.S. support in the solution of the
pressing economic problems in the country and the development of its
industrialization program. As a result, it was possible for the countries to
establish formal and extensive cooperation in many political, economic,
and military issues under conditions that were exceptionally advantageous for Mexico. The entry of the United States into the Second World

War gave Mexico an unprecedented capacity to negotiate with the United States from a stronger position and "substantially altered the U.S. government's perception of the importance of Mexico for the country's security" (Torres, 1991: 10).

Thus, in June 1942, Mexico declared war on the Axis and met with U.S. officials to discuss the details of Mexico's military cooperation. Part of the U.S. government's demands included an agreement to hire Mexican workers temporarily in order to prevent harvests from being lost. Before the war, U.S. employers had been able to hire Mexican workers without the need for formal agreements. However, the United States' decision to establish a bilateral program with Mexico that would guarantee the supply of workers was a response to pressures from agricultural employers – mainly from the Southwest – who were concerned about the scarcity of workers and the demands for better salaries and work benefits from U.S. labor unions (Craig, 1971; Hawley, 1979; García y Griego; 1990: 102, 105). Even though the U.S. government was at first resistant to the idea of signing an agreement with Mexico, an INS (Immigration and Naturalization Services)[1] Commission, which included representatives from the Departments of Agriculture, State, Labor, and Justice, conducted a study about labor conditions in the United States and concluded that the scarcity of labor was critical and the best and cheapest solution was to import it from Mexico.

Initially, the Mexican government had an ambivalent response to the U.S. proposal because it would imply higher levels of migration and possibly compromise the development of Mexico's industrial sector. The government also feared that this situation would create a greater dependency on the U.S. economy, that the returning braceros would be an explosive force that demanded better salaries and working conditions, and that their work in U.S. agriculture would affect the prices of Mexican products (Craig, 1971: 20–21). In addition, the recent experience of the 1929 repatriations had caused discontent in Mexico and concerns about its effects on Mexico's economic and political stability. Nationalist and religious groups as well as labor unions were against this proposal,

---

[1] The INS was established in 1940 and was based on the preexisting Immigration Office of the Labor Department. Until March of 2003, the INS was an agency associated to the Department of Justice with the mandate of implementing the Immigration and Nationality Law (INA). Its responsibilities included the admission of migrants and nonmigrants, naturalization and deportation processes, and the administration of the Border Patrol. In March of 2003 the INS was absorbed by the Department of Homeland Security, which assumed and expanded the INS's enforcement and services functions.

which had no guarantees against racial and religious discrimination, harsh labor conditions, the separation of families, or any provisions regarding workers' benefits and unionization.

A commission appointed by President Ávila Camacho to study the situation concluded that Mexican emigration could not be controlled and that the absence of legal channels in a context of high demand for labor from U.S. employers would only generate more undocumented migration (García y Griego, 1990: 103). The commission also argued that Mexican agriculture would benefit from the techniques acquired by braceros and that the economy would grow with the flow of dollars from their remittances. Thus, despite nationalist critiques and opposition to any negotiation with the United States, the Mexican government decided it was convenient to establish an agreement to manage migration flows and to provide military cooperation to the United States as a way to obtain its support in other issues (Craig, 1971: 23; Pfeiffer, 1979: 75–77).[2]

The Mexican government linked this negotiation with the solution of pending issues in the bilateral agenda, such as payments to U.S. oil companies affected by the 1938 expropriation, the renegotiation of its foreign debt, and the solution of water disputes along the border, as well as support for economic development through commercial and financial treaties (Torres, 1991: 37–51). As Craig (1971: 52) argues, "crises situations in the international environment may permit weaker nations to diplomatically achieve victories in a short period, which in non-crisis intervals would have been obtainable only over a long period of time, if at all." Nevertheless, what was at first considered a victory for Mexico in the long term led to more dependency on U.S. markets and financial services and created problems that worsened as the United States lost interest in Mexico's cooperation. Krasner's (1990: 48–49) argument that the rules negotiated between states in an asymmetrical relationship can put the weaker state in a more vulnerable position in the long term is exemplified by the breaking of the conditions established in the Bracero Program and its consequences for Mexico. Mexico's vulnerability in negotiating with the United States regarding the Bracero Program had high costs for Mexican emigrants in terms of the protection of their rights because

---

[2] Mexico's military collaboration was based on the participation of Mexican Squadron 201 in the U.S. armed forces, the installation of warning equipment in the Baja California peninsula, an air base in Yucatan, and permits for air transportation of personnel and equipment in Mexican territory. Mexico also negotiated a commercial agreement that allowed the United States to import raw materials for the military industry at a low price (García y Griego, 1990: 102; Torres, 1991: 32–35).

the government's priority was the continuity in emigration flows and co-operation with the United States, regardless of the lack of compliance with the rules of the program.

In the negotiation of the Bracero Program, the Mexican government demanded special guarantees for the Mexican workers: nondiscriminatory treatment, fair working conditions and salaries equivalent to those received by American workers, the establishment of a bilateral commission to supervise the hiring of workers, and direct participation of the U.S. government in the management of the program.[3] The Bracero Agreement was ratified through diplomatic notes on August 4, 1942; on September 29 of that year, the first group of 500 Mexican emigrants arrived in California. Even though this was considered a diplomatic victory for Mexico, paradoxically the conditions it established became some of the main problems in the administration of the Bracero Program and, in the long term, weakened its position vis-à-vis the United States. This situation is accurately described by Craig (1971: 23): "Mexico acquiesced to the Bracero Program because its advantages far outweighed its disadvantages. It was the U.S. who eventually rejected a program that Mexico by necessity accepted."

Compliance and Dispute Resolution: The Sending State's Vulnerability

One of the first disputes related to the Bracero Program was the disagreement over the location of hiring centers for Mexican workers. Mexico had insisted on establishing them away from the border to provide opportunities for the unemployed or underemployed rural population in the center of the country and to alleviate political and economic pressures in these

[3] It was established that employers could only hire Mexican workers through the program, which would be administered by both governments. The contracts would have a duration that could vary between a minimum of forty-five to ninety days to a maximum of one year. The braceros' work was to be guaranteed for at least 75 percent of their time of residency in the United States; it was forbidden to send Mexican workers to zones where Mexico thought that they would be discriminated against, or to recruit them for military services or sectors other than agriculture. The contracts were signed by the workers and the employers, who would pay for their expenses and transportation from the hiring centers in Mexico to the United States. The employers had to guarantee that workers' homes and places of employment met certain sanitary conditions and minimum requirements, that salaries were based on the prevailing wages in the area for U.S. workers, and that hiring braceros would not affect the salaries or working conditions of U.S. native workers. Mexico's 1931 Federal Law for Labor would protect braceros and the Bracero Program would be submitted for annual ratification in both countries (Verea, 1982: 23–24; Morales, 1989: 150–151).

areas (García y Griego, 1981: 30; Verea, 1982: 24–25). This would also prevent the hiring of agricultural workers in the north who were needed for harvesting cotton. The hiring center system proved to be inefficient and in the end produced an alternative flow of workers who sought other ways to get to the United States. At the same time, U.S. employers promoted undocumented migration by hiring "wetbacks"[4] through other means to avoid the payment of transportation and circumvent the administrative difficulties implied in the application for bracero workers through hiring centers and the U.S. bureaucracy (Galarza, 1964). In addition, the concentration of bracero contracts in certain regions began creating problems of labor scarcity and loss of specialized workers in Mexico, particularly in the north and in some states in the center of the country (Torres, 1991: 39).

The second problem was related to the veto that Mexico issued against Texas to prevent the hiring of bracero workers in that state, considering previous cases of discrimination against Mexican migrants. The veto was not effective as a result of both governments' lack of control over migration flows,[5] the high demand for workers and the insufficiency of contracts, and the problems with hiring centers. This resulted in the development of informal hiring networks outside the existing legislation and made it more difficult for the Mexican government to protect undocumented workers in the United States (Verea, 1982: 24–25).[6]

The most salient conflict during the first years of the Bracero Program was a result of the Texan government's decision to open the border to

---

[4] *Mojados* or "wetbacks" was a term used to describe undocumented workers, who arrived in the United States by crossing the Río Bravo. Other undocumented workers called *alambristas* crossed into U.S. territories by jumping fences or cutting barbed wire (*alambres de púas*; see Samora, 1971). Currently the commonly used terms for these migrants are "undocumented," "unauthorized," "irregular," and "illegal immigrants" or "illegal aliens."

[5] Neither government, nor any of their specialized agencies, participated actively in controlling undocumented migration. The INS lacked enough resources to fulfill its obligations efficiently and it had alliances with U.S. employers to facilitate the entry of undocumented workers. As Calavita (1992) explains, this was a precarious but useful alliance because the continuing flow of undocumented migrants was convenient for both; it justified the existence of the INS and the allocation of resources to this office, and it provided cheap labor for employers.

[6] Despite the existence of a flow of undocumented migrants, Texan employers continued to insist that the Mexican government change its position and eliminate the veto. This shows that the lack of formal cooperation had certain costs for Texas, although these were not high enough to force the United States to ask for a compromise at that moment (García y Griego, 1990: 107).

Mexican workers. This was justified under Public Law 45 (used during the First World War), which allowed the unilateral hiring of foreign workers for one year. Mexico protested the U.S. government's refusal to impose sanctions on Texan employers; it only received promises for more surveillance, to no avail. The law was repealed the following year, but the hiring networks established between Texan employers and Mexican migrants helped maintain the flow of undocumented workers. Thus, from the beginning, the Bracero Program was characterized by corruption, problems between government agencies,[7] insufficiency of contracts, and poor administration both from Mexico and the United States.[8] Regardless of the lack of compliance with the rules established through the agreements, the fact that Mexico did not cancel the program or increase pressures on the U.S. government to enforce the rules is significant. This provides evidence of Mexico's inability to control the flows and its growing need to maintain emigration as a safety valve, as well as its caution in terms of straining the bilateral relationship.

After the War: The Bracero Program as a Safety Valve

As the number of braceros and undocumented workers grew, the U.S. population became more aware of the implications and consequences of the Bracero Program. Labor unions began to demonstrate against the

---

[7] In the case of the INS, Calavita (1992: 4–10) explains how immigration authorities used the power obtained by the Bracero Program to interpret and implement laws according to their interests and needs, and how they used their capacity to influence the congressional agenda. Regarding the Border Patrol, Andreas argues that its function was to appear to control the border but at the same time to guarantee the supply of labor for employers. They were the agents responsible for implementing the laws but at the same time they facilitated their breaking (Andreas, 2000: 34). In the Mexican case, Pfeiffer explains how the lack of resources for the authorities and institutions in charge of managing the program promoted and facilitated corruption. The Mexican government's ambivalence regarding the operation of the program made it difficult to rectify the situation (Pfeiffer, 1979: 80–82).

[8] Another example of the violation of the rules of the Bracero Program, which has recently become a controversial issue in Mexico, was the repayment of the braceros' savings funds, which were taken from their salary and in most cases were never returned. Currently, so-called exbraceros are demanding that their employers pay the debts that, as Bustamante (2002d) argues, are also Mexico's responsibility because the government approved the contracts that established these savings funds and promised to guarantee those payments. In 2002, a U.S. court concluded that the exbraceros referred to prescribed debts and therefore would not proceed. Some workers have received these payments from the Mexican government but the exbracero movement is still demanding a complete solution.

importation of foreign labor, particularly at the end of the war when the emergency situation for hiring emigrants was no longer justified. Nevertheless, at that time, their pressures were insufficient to offset the power and influence of employers who relied on migrant labor, even in new sectors of the U.S. economy.[9]

In Mexico, some intellectuals and opposition groups began to talk about the flow of undocumented workers as proof of the postrevolutionary government's failure and its indifference regarding the solution of problems in the countryside. Craig (1971: 22) argues that the Bracero Program was a "national humiliation" because despite the workers' degrading labor conditions, low salaries, and discrimination in the United States, they were still fighting to get a Bracero contract or to emigrate as undocumented workers. Although some authors (Craig, 1971; Torres, 1991) mention critiques from opposition groups, these were not widespread. Thus, at the time they did not represent a high political cost that could force the Mexican government to take a more proactive position regarding development in rural areas, protection of migrants in the United States, or cancellation of the Bracero Program.

On the contrary, by then, the Bracero Program had become a political and economic necessity for Mexico because it released the pressures of unemployment and dissatisfaction with government policies. At first, the Mexican government had considered it a temporary alternative while it waited to reap the benefits from its economic and industrialization programs. The government had anticipated that the import-substitution model and industrialization would create new jobs and allow for the more equal distribution of income, thus reducing the need for emigration. However, these expectations were not fulfilled in the short, medium, or long term and the levels of emigration continued to grow.

In November of 1946, the U.S. government announced that it would not renew the Bracero Program. The Mexican government asked for an extension, arguing that it needed to prepare the country for the return of close to 200,000 Mexican braceros hired between 1942 and 1946. The U.S. Congress passed Public Law 40 to terminate the program on December 31, 1947 after a six-month extension. However, the repatriation pressures were not as high as expected, partly because the

---

[9] Between 1943 and 1946, the United States and Mexico signed an agreement to allow Mexican workers to work on U.S. railroads under the same conditions as braceros. The program was canceled temporarily in August of 1943 because Mexico demanded better salaries for the workers, and in 1946 the United States decided to terminate it.

repatriation process was very slow and "there was no rush for getting rid of Mexican emigrants" (Morales, 1989: 164). Although the return of U.S. soldiers and the slowing down of the U.S. economy after the war seemed to be obvious reasons to end the Bracero Program, Mexican labor had become a key element of U.S. production in various sectors, particularly agriculture. Americans returning from the war did not want to occupy the badly paid and harsh jobs that Mexicans were doing, and employers had adjusted their businesses to the possibility of having abundant and cheap labor.

Despite reports about corruption and violation of Mexican workers' rights in the United States, as well as the experience of the U.S. government's indifference regarding the administration of the program, Mexico asked the United States for a renewal of the Bracero Program. Neither of the two governments nor the employers or the migrants had been completely satisfied by the management of the program, but they all saw advantages in its continuation. In the end, by 1948 the U.S. government was convinced by the employers' demands for more bracero contracts. However, the new rules for the hiring of migrant workers reflected the change in the international context and the new position of both governments: "[T]he Bracero Program evolved from a wartime to a peacetime activity where key interests and power politics were given a freer hand" (García y Griego, 1983a: 63). Mexico "conceded little by little to each of the U.S. requirements for the renewal of the program . . . in exchange for maintaining the flow of unemployed and dissatisfied Mexican labor to the North" (Morales, 1989: 176–77).[10] In the postwar period the bilateral conflicts regarding the administration of the program were more salient, given that the U.S. government lost interest in participating directly in the management of the program and no longer relied on Mexico's military cooperation (García y Griego, 1981; García y Griego and Verea, 1988:

---

[10] Calavita (1992: 42) argues that the new Bracero Program was based on rules made to fit employers' interests. The hiring of Mexican workers would now be managed directly by U.S. employers and not by the government, once the Labor Department certified the scarcity of labor. Employers would also be in charge of transportation costs and the financing of a fund to pay for the workers' return to Mexico. The contracts no longer specified the minimum wage or the mechanisms for investigating and solving disputes, although they allowed for periodic inspections by Mexican consulates and the Employment Service. As a result of the delegation of power from the government to other agencies and employers in the management of the program, there was an increase in corruption, the breaking of contracts, and abuses against Mexican migrants.

107–108).[11] Thus, Mexico's limited capacity to pressure the United States to comply with the agreements became more evident.

Mexico's position was determined, on the one hand, by a growing dependency on commercial relations with the United States, which meant that Mexico wanted to avoid conflicts and maintain good bilateral relations to guarantee the continuation of commercial agreements and support for industrial development. Thus, the government considered that having a formal agreement on migration, even if it was not completely in accordance with Mexico's interests, was a guarantee for preventing bilateral problems and maintaining the same level of migration flows.

On the other hand, demographic growth in Mexico exceeded job creation and created internal migration toward urban centers, where it was harder to control the unsatisfied population and eliminate political pressures against the government. During Miguel Alemán's presidency (1946–1952), the political elite, businessmen, and intellectuals were worried about the relevance of the Revolution's promises of equal distribution of income, "land and liberty," its objectives, and the means to achieve them.[12] Emigration made evident that there were unresolved economic problems dating far back, that Mexicans did not find the life conditions promised by the revolutionary leaders and the PRI, and the fact that other issues had been given priority over the necessities and demands of the groups that had supported the Revolution (Torres, 1991: 67).

In contrast to the first Bracero Program negotiations, issue linkage and demands for conditions favorable for Mexico were no longer an option. Even though Mexico protested against the violation of contracts, it was not able to change the situation or to implement policies to reduce or control emigration, be it through development in emigrants' communities or increasing resources for border control.

[11] Guiraudon's (2001) analysis about the decentralization of border controls is helpful to understand some of the reasons why the U.S. government preferred not to be involved in the administration of the Bracero Program. By delegating these responsibilities to other government institutions and actors, the state can more easily reconcile conflicting interests, calm the population's anxiety, reduce the costs of regulation, and exercise control, even through undemocratic means, without facing political costs, because it does not have formal commitments with any group or any type of measures. Calavita (1992: 40) also argues that Congress prefers to delegate responsibilities to administrative areas to avoid political costs. However, the U.S. government's different levels of involvement during the Bracero Program exemplifies that, in some cases, the state's direct participation in the management of migration is essential to reconcile conflicting interests and provide guarantees of effective border control.

[12] As an example of these concerns, in 1950 the renowned Mexican writer and diplomat Octavio Paz wrote that "the Mexican Revolution has died without resolving our contradictions" (Paz, 1993: 187).

The Mexican government's limited capacity to negotiate and to act unilaterally in favor of its emigrants was made evident during the El Paso incident of 1948. In this case, Mexico complained about Texan employers who did not pay braceros the minimum wage. Mexico threatened to terminate the program and renew the veto against sending Mexican workers to that state. Texan employers showed their capacity to continue hiring Mexican labor despite these complaints as well as Mexico's attempts to prevent the arrival of new workers to Texas. Supported by the INS, Texan employers opened the border to the workers and continued to hire them under the same conditions as before.

In response to this situation, U.S. President Harry Truman (1945–1953) merely offered a formal apology. Mexico accepted and canceled the contracts for a few months until the next renegotiation of the program. In the meantime, undocumented flows continued and the U.S. government argued that the "1948 agreement had failed precisely because of Mexico's veto on Texas, which promoted the traffic of undocumented workers, as well as Mexico's insistence on placing the hiring centers far from the border" (Morales, 1989: 172). Finally, the Mexican government gave in; in 1950 the veto against Texas was revoked and new hiring centers were established in two northern cities (Hermosillo and Monterrey). It was also decided that, in the future, both governments would have to establish a joint determination of blacklisted states (García y Griego, 1981: 32).

In 1949 the United States implemented a policy known as "drying out" to control the flow of undocumented emigrants by legalizing all the Mexican workers who were in the United States until August 1 (close to 87,200 workers were eligible), giving them preference for new contracts over braceros coming in the following years, and deporting undocumented workers who came into the country after that date (Verea, 1982: 28). However, this policy proved to be inefficient in terms of protecting Mexican workers' rights, and U.S. employers took advantage of the fact that they no longer had to pay for the transportation or saving funds of workers who had obtained visas; they also benefited from the wage depression that resulted from the abundance of Mexican labor at the border due to the increase in deportations.

Regaining the Advantage? The Bracero Program and the Korean War

The advent of the Korean War (1950–1953) offered another opportunity for the Mexican government to use an external circumstance as leverage and negotiate favorable conditions for the braceros (Craig, 1971: 70).

As soon as the U.S. economy began to concentrate on military production, it required labor and resources from Mexico.

President Alemán used his capacity for negotiation in this circumstance to his advantage and asked the U.S. government to become directly involved again in the administration of the Bracero Program. Under the pressure of employers that required labor, the United States passed Public Law 78, which guaranteed the fulfillment of contracts and the protection of Mexican workers (see Galarza, 1964: 51–52 and Verea, 1982: 29–30). Mexico also managed to keep its veto power over certain states and establish the hiring centers according to its own preferences. The only issue over which the United States did not give in was Mexico's demand to enforce sanctions on employers who hired undocumented workers; instead, they were protected by the Texas Proviso amendment of 1952 that allowed employers to hire workers without having to verify their migratory status (see Verea, 1982: 30–31). As the international context changed, Mexico gradually lost its bargaining power; discrimination, abuses against emigrants, and violation of contracts continued.

The rules established in 1951 were in force until 1964, although with some amendments and extensions. In 1952 the United States passed the Immigration and Nationality Act (INA, also known as McCarran–Walker Act). This law maintained the quota system established in 1924, with limits for the number of emigrants admitted that were based on ethnic and nationality considerations. This did not affect legal admissions from Mexico because it allowed unlimited immigration from the western hemisphere. The law also facilitated family reunification and added new categories for temporary workers, such as the H-2 visas for agricultural and other workers.

By the end of the Korean War, the problem of undocumented workers became more evident and controversial for U.S. public opinion. Nativist groups' demands for greater control over the border were very strong during McCarthy's racist campaigns in the 1950s. Labor unions gained support from anti-immigrant groups that perceived foreigners as a threat and blamed unemployment on migrant workers. Although a lack of coordination by these groups limited their capacity to oppose the employers' lobby, little by little they gained political clout and became strong enough to promote their agenda (Craig, 1971: 68). Their influence was evident in the U.S. government's new measures for border controls, including the Domestic Security Law (1950), which allowed for the exclusion and deportation of potentially dangerous foreigners, particularly communists.

The Unraveling of the Bracero Program

In 1953, there was another confrontation between the U.S. and Mexican governments regarding the conditions for hiring braceros. The United States pressured Mexico into eliminating or reducing certain labor guarantees and reopening the hiring center that had been closed in Monterrey. Given Mexico's resistance, the United States opened the border to Mexican workers under Public Law 309 until Mexico accepted these conditions. As García y Griego notes (1981: 49), nowadays the situation in 1954 would be considered an anomaly and even ironic, because the United States was promoting an open border against Mexico's will.

Mexican authorities tried to dissuade and prevent the workers' flow into the United States as well as develop programs to employ workers arriving at the border, with limited success. This situation made evident Mexico's inability to control migration flows and the capacity of the United States to hire workers without requiring agreements with Mexico. At the next negotiating round, the United States modified certain rules to favor employers; despite the fact that it had opposed these conditions, Mexico still considered it to be more convenient to maintain the Bracero Program in force.

A few months later, the U.S. government implemented Operation Wetback to deport close to 1 million undocumented workers and facilitate the regularization of legal migrants and braceros (Verea, 1982: 32). This program satisfied most of the groups that were pressuring the U.S. government to control the border (the INS, the Labor Department, labor unions, and anti-immigrant groups; see Massey et al., 2002: 37–38).

As a consequence of the repatriations, there were problems and unrest in the Mexican countryside. The Mexican government's continuing cooperation with the United States was criticized by nationalist groups, but the government's main concern was to keep the safety valve open as a way to muffle problems related to unemployment and social tension in the country, and guarantee the entry of dollars through remittances – close to $205 million dollars were sent to Mexico between 1942 and 1947; $88.2 million dollars between 1948 and 1951; and $200 million between 1954 and 1959 (Verea, 1982: 26, 28). As Verea (1982: 113–116) and García y Griego (1981: 29) interpret it, emigration was seen by the government as a necessary evil.

From 1954 onward, the Mexican government reduced its pressure regarding the Bracero Program, as well as surveillance of Mexican workers and consular activity. From 1955 to 1964 there were no severe disagreements between the governments regarding the Bracero Program and no fundamental changes in its operation (Craig, 1971: 101–149). The Mexican government's loss of bargaining power and passive position is made clear in the following description by García y Griego (1983a: 72):

> [The] Mexican defeat in January 1954 merely laid bare the end-result of a process that had been unfolding for several years. On the one hand, as close observers had known for some time, Mexico lacked either the political will or the policy instruments to withhold the labor of its workers on whose behalf it was negotiating, and its "cooperation" with the U.S. in this and other issue areas was not vital. On the other hand, domestic criticism was forcing Mexico to adopt positions which it could not sustain.

In Mexico, lack of development in rural areas and insufficient land reform led to critiques from workers, middle and lower classes, and labor unions (Torres, 1991: 131–132). By the 1950s, economic and political development in the country had created a new social structure whose members expressed their interests through nontraditional channels. The middle class, represented in different demonstrations by doctors, teachers, railroad workers, telephone workers, oil workers, and electricians, was mobilizing to demand democratization and political rights (Loyo Brambilla, 1975; Loaeza, 1985; Pozas Horcasitas, 1993). The pressures from leftist groups were more salient during the Cuban Revolution, which, for many, provided an example of what the Mexican Revolution had failed to achieve (Pellicer, 1968, 1972).

In the specific case of migration, some critics raised the issue of abuses caused by the direct recruitment of workers by U.S. employers and the government's inability to negotiate better salaries. They also argued that the benefits of remittances were not widespread, given that the money was staying in the United States or in border towns, where many families had migrated. However, as opposed to the United States, the Mexican political system was not structured in such a way that public opinion or organized groups could have a decisive influence in the government's policies regarding migration or any other area. In the context of the Bracero Program, Bustamante (1983: 269) explains that "public opinion was kept in almost complete ignorance with respect to both the content of the negotiations and the complaints that the government was making to the United States in the context of the Bracero Agreements."

From the end of Adolfo Ruiz Cortines' administration (1952–1958) to the beginning of Adolfo López Mateos' government (1958–1964), members of the PRI expressed their dissatisfaction with the neglect of the Revolution's objectives, particularly in terms of land reform and worker organizations. Political leaders feared the explosion of popular sectors that demanded the land and economic benefits that the revolutionary governments had promised but had eschewed in the interest of industrialization and development of urban centers (Torres, 1991: 131). Meanwhile, Mexican labor unions also manifested their concern regarding migrant workers' situation and called for a more forceful policy to control emigration and to protect workers' rights. For example, in 1953 the *Organización Regional Interamericana de Trabajadores* or Regional Inter-American Workers' Organization (ORIT) organized a conference with Mexican and U.S. labor unions, with the objective of discussing the workers' situation in both countries and the problems related to migration, and proposed coordinated solutions (ORIT, 1953).

In the United States, as in many other countries, the growth of social and labor movements characterized the beginning of the 1960s. During Dwight Eisenhower's administration (1953–1961), employer lobbies continued to dominate decisions over migration policy, but the stronger organization of labor unions, religious groups, and the media against discrimination, racism, and undocumented migration created a conflict of interest for the U.S. government (Craig, 1971: 138–147; Andreas, 2000: 34; Massey et al., 2002: 39–40). In 1959 the U.S. government passed the New Wagner Peyser Law, which guaranteed minimum wage and safe working conditions for agricultural workers. It was a response to the fact that undocumented migration, the mechanization of agriculture, and the use of new technologies had depreciated salaries and created more competition for jobs in this sector. Against labor unions' claims – mainly those of the AFL–CIO – that emigrants were responsible for these problems, employers argued that Mexican braceros were efficient workers that filled jobs that Americans did not want to do, and they were not cheap labor, given the fact that employers had to pay for their transportation and insurance (this could have been true if all the employers actually complied with the conditions in the bracero contracts). However, employers also reduced their lobbying for the Bracero Program as a result of the availability of undocumented workers and new techniques for production, as well as the strengthening of controls from the Labor Department and other agencies that made it more difficult to hire braceros.[13]

---

[13] Craig (1971: 163) mentions how at first the Departments of Agriculture, Justice, and State defended the existence of the Bracero Program but as the civil rights movement and labor unions became stronger, they changed their alliances. This reinforces Calavita's (1992: 99–100) argument about the precarious alliances between institutions and groups

In 1960, the civil rights movement criticized the quota system for the admission of migrants as a racist policy; it also demanded the protection of minority rights in the United States and joined labor unions, the Catholic church, and other liberal groups in a coalition demanding immigration reform and the end of the Bracero Program, which was seen as a system for the exploitation of migrant workers. President John F. Kennedy (1961–1963) responded favorably to their demands. In 1963, he rejected the renewal of the Bracero Program.[14] In an attempt to repeal this measure, the Mexican government argued that emigration would continue as a result of structural factors resulting from both countries' situation and it was preferable to administer it bilaterally than let it continue through other channels. Mexico also asked for a gradual repatriation of the workers and a period of grace, which was extended until 1964 through Public Law 78.

Over the next ten years, Mexico insisted unsuccessfully on the renewal of the Bracero Program. Even though the cancellation of the program had immediate costs for U.S. employers given the scarcity of labor in California and Arizona, and the need to reorganize production to adjust to higher wages and less flexible labor, in most cases they were able to solve these problems through new machinery, the hiring of undocumented immigrants, or exceptional contracts of Mexican workers. For a few years, there were minor agreements with Mexico to allow for the employment of some migrant workers and the readmission of braceros in certain sectors. For example, in May 1965 the Mexican Foreign Ministry and the U.S. Department of State exchanged diplomatic notes to establish the conditions under which braceros would be hired as a transition mechanism in regions where there was scarcity of labor. In 1967 a temporary agreement was signed to hire Mexican workers to work for agricultural employers in California and Arizona while they made the

in the United States, as well as the influence of government agencies' interests in the design and implementation of migration policies.

[14] Most authors mention President Kennedy's democratic orientation as a factor that determined his response to these groups' demands. However, party preferences (Democratic or Republican) do not explain why previous Democratic Presidents (i.e., Roosevelt and Truman) or subsequent ones (i.e., Carter and Clinton) did not respond to migration issues with similar policies or projects. Cornelius explains that public opinion's "attitudes, beliefs, and perceptions [constitute] an important constraint on the range of immigration policy options which are likely to be considered seriously by the U.S. president and Congress, *regardless of the political party in power*" (Cornelius, 1983: 392; italics added). Nevertheless, there are few studies about the specific relationship between changes in migration policies and party ideologies. Some useful references are Bustamante (1977) and Gimpel and Edwards (1999).

necessary adjustments to face the suspension of the Bracero Program. Temporary workers were available through the H-2 visas program and other special visas for sectors that could prove the scarcity of local workers. Through these measures and strong controls that included the repatriation of workers, the U.S. government sought to prevent wage depression and low working conditions for U.S. workers. During these years, the Mexican Foreign Ministry also negotiated other contracts directly with some agricultural associations in the United States (Verea, 1982: 36–37; Torres, 1991: 192–193).

These facts show that the United States faced costs as a result of the cancellation of the Bracero Program. However, given that the flow of workers continued through these smaller agreements and mostly through unauthorized channels, these costs were never high enough to lead the U.S. government to reconsider its decision; "if the U.S. had suffered costs that could be attributed to Mexico's refusal to send braceros, these would have been low and probably insignificant" (García y Griego, 1990: 106–107, 110).

Responses to Changes in Migration Patterns

The cancellation of the Bracero Program and the insufficient number of visas to meet the supply and demand of workers, particularly in a period of economic growth for the United States, resulted in an increase of undocumented migration that "effectively substituted braceros" (García y Griego, 1990: 110; Massey et al., 2002: 44–45). Even if migrants were detained many times in one year, they tried crossing as many times as necessary until they were successful.[15] The growth of undocumented migration resulted in the increase of traffic of workers, falsification of documents and corruption of U.S. and Mexican authorities, and frequent violations of migrants' rights.

---

[15] This was convenient for the Border Patrol and the INS as much as for the migrants. For the U.S. agencies, it represented the possibility of reporting a greater number of arrests because migrants crossed a number of times until they were able to escape the Border Patrol, and thus justify the allocation of more resources. At the same time, this situation gave migrants the opportunity to go back to Mexico without delay and try to cross again as soon as possible. The term "revolving door" has been used to refer precisely to this situation in which the migrant enters and exits the United States many times. Ironically, both the migrants and the INS knew and benefited from the fact that one or a few apprehensions did not dissuade migrants from crossing again and that they would continue to try until they succeeded; this situation persists to date (Andreas, 2000: 37; Cornelius, 2001, 2003; Massey et al., 2002: 46–47).

The characteristics of emigrants also changed: Their stay in the United States had increased their quality-of-life expectations, given them social mobility, and made it possible to bring their families to the United States or to stay there on their own for longer periods of time. During the twenty-two years that the Bracero Program lasted, 4.6 million contracts were issued for braceros, 687,139 Mexican emigrants were admitted legally, and approximately 5 million undocumented migrants were apprehended in the United States and deported (Verea, 1982: 48, 162–169). At the beginning of the 1960s, the U.S. Census estimated the Mexican foreign-born population at 576,000; by 1970 it had grown to 760,000 (Gibson and Jung, 2006: Table 4).

Throughout the existence of the Bracero Program, the role of the consulates diminished in terms of defending the interests of Mexican expatriates and providing leadership for the Mexican-American community. Although Mexican consuls "continued as zealous defenders of Mexicans in the United States" after World War II, these activities were developed on a smaller scale and were more selective (Corwin, 1978c: 189–190). Despite complaints about the Bracero Program and reactions in Mexican public opinion against the reports of exploitation of workers in the United States, the consulates' role in defending them was not as prominent as before. This can be partially explained by the fact that some of the problems related to migrants (i.e., employer abuses and the absence of fair working conditions) were channeled through the Bracero Program, which was managed by Mexican officials in Mexico. Although in most cases these renegotiations did not turn out to Mexico's advantage, at the time the Bracero Program was considered the main institutional response to emigration. The low profile of consular activities is explained by the existence of the Bracero Program as a channel for most problems related to emigrant workers and the Mexican government's interest in maintaining the status quo as a safety valve for potential economic and political problems; it was also a way of avoiding tensions with the United States in the management of the flows.[16]

---

[16] Sherman's (1999) explanation for the lack of attention to emigrants during the Bracero Program and through the 1960s is that the Mexican state has tended to manifest interest in emigrants at moments of political and economic instability and crisis. Given that "the 1960s corresponded to the heyday of the Mexican miracle and the dominance of the PRI," Sherman argues that the Mexican state did not consider it necessary to incorporate migrants as a strategy to resolve challenges to its legitimacy. Although I agree that the Mexican government's involvement in issues related to Mexican migrants is related to economic and political circumstances in Mexico, this argument does not consider the fact that governmental attention to migration issues is also influenced by the dynamic of United States–Mexico bilateral relations.

The Second World War opened up new opportunities for Mexicans in the United States by increasing their participation in the armed forces, defense industries, and union jobs; this accelerated their social integration and upward mobility (Gutiérrez, 1999). Some of the first *clubes de oriundos* (hometown associations), which organized migrants based on their community of origin, began to develop in the 1960s. The activities of the *clubes de oriundos* were similar to those of the *mutualistas*, but as they grew and developed in the following decades, their relationship with local governments and their influence in their communities in Mexico gradually increased. Although Mexican officials tried to maintain close contacts with emigrants through the Bracero Agreements, cultural programs, and visits, including the formalization of the celebration of Mexico's Independence in the United States, during this period the relations between the Mexican community-based associations and the consulates were not as close as before (Gómez-Quiñones, 1983). In Zazueta's view (1983: 460), "by the 1950s the political dialogue that had peaked in the 1920s and 1930s seems to have faded." Meanwhile, issues regarding political, economic, and human rights of the second and third generations of Mexican immigrants born in the United States were mostly addressed by the Mexican-American organizations that already existed and those created in the 1960s (Corwin, 1978c). Through their support in education, language, and job training, these organizations facilitated Mexican Americans' integration in the United States.

In 1962, César Chávez and Dolores Huerta organized the National Farm Workers Association (NFWA) later known as United Farm Workers (UFW). The NFWA rallied against the Bracero Program because of the abuses it led to. After the program was canceled, the organization dealt with other problems related to Mexican farm workers in the United States. Through Chávez, the NFWA established contact with agencies and unions from Mexico to help Mexican migrants in their organizational efforts and labor disputes (Gómez-Quiñones, 1983).

Following the lead of the Civil Rights Movement in the United States, the Chicano Movement,[17] formed mainly by Mexican Americans in the Southwest, organized a campaign with the objective of obtaining full recognition of their rights as U.S. citizens and, at the same time, claimed their own ethnic identity based on what they called the "Plan of Aztlán."

---

[17] There is no clear etymology of the word "Chicano" or its origin, but it may be a contraction of "Mexicano." The term is mainly associated with the literary and political movements of the 1960s and 1970s among Mexican Americans, which established "Chicano" as a term of ethnic pride. The term has strong political associations and its usage and acceptance vary by generation as well as by region in the United States.

Cultural nationalism, *indigenismo*, and the romanticizing of the Mexican Revolution became common among activists of the 1960s (Gómez-Quiñones, 1983). Toward the end of the decade, the Chicano Student Movement (*Movimiento Estudiantil Chicano de Aztlán* or MEChA) made great efforts to strengthen ties with the Mexican government and academic institutions, but its activities declined after 1975.

Although the Chicano movement was not representative of the Mexican and Mexican-American communities as a whole, it influenced the creation of some of the most important nonprofit organizations concerned with support of Mexican Americans and other Hispanic-origin populations in the United States (Cano, 1997). For example, the Mexican American Legal Defense and Educational Fund (MALDEF) and the National Council of La Raza (NCLR) were created in 1968. The emergence of the Chicano Movement also gave birth to organizations that began to reassess the relationship between Mexican immigrants, Chicanos, and Mexican Americans.[18] For example, the *Centro de Acción Social Autónoma* (CASA), also established in 1968, sought to provide assistance to undocumented immigrants and integrate Mexican Americans and Mexicans as part of one and the same group (Gutiérrez, 1999). Existing groups such as LULAC, the American G.I. Forum, and the Community Service Organization (CSO) also began to address issues of first-generation immigrants' rights (Gutiérrez, 1999). According to Gutiérrez, "the rhetoric of Chicano militants on both immigration and ethnic politics contributed to [these organizations'] growing awareness of the close relationships that bound Mexican immigrants to American citizens of Mexican descent," although the disagreements between Mexican Americans, Chicanos, and Mexican migrants did not disappear (Gutiérrez, 1995: 203).

Neither the Chicano Movement nor any other issue related to migration motivated widespread support from the Mexican public, except within certain intellectual circles and leftist opposition groups who complained about abuses to Mexican workers related to the Bracero Program and about the consequences of emigration for Mexican development

[18] It is worth mentioning that Mexican Americans had (and continue to have) an ambiguous position regarding migration: Some criticized Mexico for considering migration an "inevitable" phenomenon and for its limited efforts to improve economic conditions in communities of origin; they were also against U.S. laws that promoted the entry of more migrants, given that this would imply more competition in the job market. However, they did support measures for the protection of migrants' rights because many times they were also discriminated against and treated as foreigners or undocumented workers (Rico, 1992: 258).

(Craig, 1971). Moreover, the Chicano Movement and the involvement with Mexican Americans were viewed with apprehension among political circles in Mexico (Gómez-Quiñones, 1983: 433; Iskander, 2010).

Given that the Mexican government's main policy toward emigration during this period had been based on maintaining the Bracero Program, when it ended and the Mexican government realized its inability to reestablish formal cooperation with the United States to manage these flows, it sought other alternatives to control emigration pressures, such as the *Programa Nacional Fronterizo* (National Border Program) of 1965. The objective of this program was to create new job offers in the *maquiladora* sector in the north through the establishment of factories that would produce export goods, promote investment, foster technology transfers, train workers, increase the flow of foreign currency, and improve the income of the population of the region.

However, the program did not fulfill these expectations and some scholars argue that it was counterproductive because it attracted more emigrants to the border and it made it easier for them to cross in search of better salaries and labor conditions in the United States (Bustamante, 1975; Urquidi and Villarreal, 1975; García y Griego and Verea, 1988; Martin, 2002). Given this inability to find effective solutions for emigration or develop bilateral mechanisms to manage migration flows and guarantee the protection of migrants' rights, in the ensuing years the government returned its attention to consular activities and also focused on fostering relations with Mexican Americans.

1965–1982: FROM COOPERATION TO LIMITED ENGAGEMENT

In 1965 the U.S. Immigration and Nationality Act was reformed. Among other things, the new law abolished the quota system based on national and ethnic background and imposed a global limit of 20,000 visas for migrants of almost every country (excluding immediate family members). It also established a system of preferences for the acceptance of migrants according to U.S. needs and taking into account family reunification. The eastern hemisphere had a limit of 170,000 visas – 20,000 per country. From 1968 onward, the western hemisphere had a 120,000-visa quota, which was divided between all countries and had no special limits for any country (Verea, 1982: 76–77; Massey et al., 2002: 40–44).

Despite these limitations, the incentives and possibilities that Mexicans had to migrate to the United States were not reduced. Between 1965 and 1976, the U.S. admitted around 60,000 to 70,000 Mexican immigrants each year. In 1976, Alba argued that the law's influence had not been felt in either the composition or the volume of Mexican emigrants (Alba, 1976: 156). However, the 1977 Eilberg amendment reduced the number of Mexican immigrants to 44,000 (the lowest number of migrants since the Bracero Program).[19] Compared with an average of 200,000 contracts per year during the twenty-two years of the Bracero Program, the 20,000 per year cap (in competition with other countries), plus other work visas available through the H-2 program, was very limited (Verea, 1982: 164–165; Massey et al., 2002: 43–44). Moreover, the procedures to obtain H-2 visas for workers were complicated and costly for employers. As a consequence, work opportunities for undocumented migrants continued to be available and employers' dependency on this labor kept growing.[20]

At the same time, the incentives for emigrating to the United States had grown because of the high levels of unemployment and unequal distribution of income in Mexico. This was partly a result of problems associated with the import-substitution economic model, added to the pressures of demographic growth in Mexico (between 1960 and 1980 the Mexican population grew from 35 to 67 million). The strengthening of family and hiring networks, the existence of more migrant smugglers (*coyotes* or *polleros*), and new job offers in service, construction, and industrial sectors facilitated this continuing process of emigration (Bustamante, del Villar, and Ojeda, 1978: 318). The number of emigrants from nontraditional sending states and urban centers began to grow. Most of the flows were circular: migrants went to the United States for periods of six or eight months, mainly during U.S. harvesting seasons, and returned

[19] In 1977, a claim was presented against the INS because a greater number of visas had been granted to Cuba than the rest of the countries in Latin America. The Supreme Court ruled against the INS because it had reduced the number of visas available for other Latin American countries by including Cuban refugees in the "quota" for the continent. In compensation, the U.S. government offered 149,946 additional visas to the hemispheric quota. From 1977 to 1982, the Silva Program allowed for the legal stay of thousands of migrants in the United States (including 100,000 Mexicans) for a period of two years (Verea, 1982: 159). During this time, the number of visas for Mexicans reached high levels, including 101,000 in 1981, but at the end of the program it fell back down to between 55,000 and 60,000.

[20] Massey et al. (2002: 41) explain that even though employers could have attracted local workers by offering better salaries and working conditions, they refused to do so because it would imply higher prices, inflation, and disadvantages in terms of competitiveness. Moreover, after twenty-two years of what was almost a monopoly of migrants in some sectors, their type of work became socially identified as foreign labor and was considered unacceptable for local workers. Thus, Bustamante (1978: 523) argues that Mexican labor "is not cheap by nature but it has become cheap as a result of structural conditions [in Mexico and the U.S.] that have created a docile work force with no negotiating power."

to Mexico for four to six months until they needed money again. With the growth of migration and commercial flows, the culture of the border permeated both countries by creating free trade zones, increasing industrialization, and offering more job opportunities in these areas (Alba, 1976: 158–159).

From 1965 to 1986, approximately 1.3 million legal migrants, 46,000 migrants with a working visa, and 28 million undocumented Mexicans entered the United States (23.4 million of which were temporary or circular migrants; Massey et al., 2002: 45). The Mexican foreign-born population had almost tripled between 1970 and 1980, reaching an estimated 2.2 million by 1980 (Gibson and Jung, 2006: Table 4). As Mexican immigrants' presence became more salient, many U.S. anti-immigrant groups protested against this so-called silent invasion. In Mexico, the general population did not participate in the debate over the issue, but critics of the government, particularly among intellectual circles, began to talk of emigration as a "silent exodus" (Alba, 1976).

The Policy of Having No Policy

After its failed attempts to renew the Bracero Program and given the restrictive measures adopted by the United States, the Mexican government decided to manage the situation through a policy that is now commonly known as the policy of having no policy, as defined by García y Griego (1988). Although this was not an explicit policy and did not mean that the Mexican government had no policies at the different levels concerning migration policies (i.e., it continued its consular protection activities and relations with the migrant community as well as development programs and demographic policies to manage the flows), this position is interpreted in terms of the government's interest in preserving the status quo by limiting the salience of the issue in the national and bilateral agenda and avoiding negotiations with the United States that could lead to a negative outcome in this or other areas of the relationship (García y Griego, 1988: 145–147). Despite the fact that this was a very limited and noncommittal policy, the government did not face significant domestic criticism or high political costs as a result of it (Verea, 1982: 117–119).

By taking this passive position, the Mexican government implicitly acknowledged that it preferred the status quo to promoting a change that could place the country in a more vulnerable position vis-à-vis the United States or create a domestic problem by closing the door to emigration.

The Mexican government considered that the United States would not make any positive changes but a negative change was also very unlikely (Ronfeldt and Sereseres, 1978: 246; Rico, 1992: 267). Given the fact that undocumented migration continued despite the restrictive measures in the United States and that the safety valve to economic and political pressures in Mexico remained open, Mexico stopped considering the negotiation of a Bracero Program as the best way to pursue its interests regarding migration. As Rico (1992) argues, this situation implied a "silent or tacit cooperation" because there were no formal or explicit rules but both governments agreed on maintaining the current structure, even if the costs were asymmetrical.

By the end of the 1960s, the national and international circumstances that had contributed to the so-called special relationship between the United States and Mexico had changed, because Mexico was no longer considered strategically important to its neighbor. Mexico's political and economic stability had deteriorated at the end of the 1960s, its foreign debt kept growing, and so did its dependency on the U.S. market – which was about 66 percent of Mexico's imports and exports (Pellicer, 1976: 42–43). The lack of confidence over Mexico's economic stability was aggravated by the political tensions that followed the repression of the 1968 student mobilizations and led to a loss of foreign investment (Ojeda, 1977: 34–38). Thus, Mexico became more and more vulnerable to Washington's policies and decisions of U.S. transnational companies in Mexico (Ojeda, 1976b: 1).

At the time, Mexico did not consider it adequate or necessary to try to influence U.S. policy on issues related to its interests through Congress, and most issues were dealt with directly with the Executive (Torres, 1991: 189). The Mexican government did not have the institutional capacity to work on a daily basis with the U.S. political system and, as Ronfeldt and Sereseres explain (1978: 243), it rejected lobbying strategies because they could be considered a form of intervention. This was reflected in Mexico's limited response to changes in U.S. immigration policies, as was the case when the special temporary worker programs created after the Bracero Program were canceled. Despite the favorable position that existed in parliamentary meetings about renegotiating a Bracero Program with Mexico, the U.S. government reacted to pressures from labor unions and in 1968 it canceled the special contracts that had been negotiated after the program had ended (Torres, 1991: 192–193).

Despite Mexico's failed attempts to renegotiate the Bracero Program and its omission of migration from the bilateral agenda, during the

1970s the government's ties with the Mexican-American community were strengthened and the government became very active in developing contacts with Mexican-American leaders, organizations, and businesses in the United States. Although these initiatives were not formalized or pursued systematically, they are relevant because, as I will discuss further on, the government's activism with these groups set the stage for the development of more comprehensive policies of rapprochement with the emigrant community from the 1990s onward.

Echeverría and the Chicano Movement

When President Luis Echeverría came to power (1970–1976), the import-substitution model based on protectionism, industrialization, and exchange rate stability had shown its weaknesses, mainly derived from the decline of agricultural development, the unequal distribution of income, and deficits in the trade balance. In response to domestic and international criticism over the economic and political situation in Mexico, added to the loss of a privileged position vis-à-vis the United States, the government's "solution" was to promote an active foreign policy that emphasized the creation of a third-world coalition and a "new economic order" that would favor developing countries (Green, 1977a). Echeverría sought to diversify Mexico's export markets to reduce the country's economic and political dependency on the United States and play an active international role to recover Mexico's prestige (Pellicer, 1976: 37–38, 50; Green, 1977a: 3; Shapira, 1978: 88–89).

As part of his foreign policy strategy, Echeverría also took an active interest in the population of Mexicans abroad, particularly Mexican Americans (De la Garza, 1983). At the end of the 1960s, interest in the Mexican population abroad was widespread among intellectuals, businessmen, and some government officials, and the ties between Mexico and the Mexicans living in the United States began to grow in cultural, political, social, and economic areas (Gómez-Quiñones, 1983).

Responding to Echeverría's initiative, Mexican consuls renewed their active role in defense of Mexicans' rights and supported the community's organizational efforts. Echeverría also promised more action against smugglers and immigration fraud cases, and he established a fertility program to control population growth and emigration pressures. In 1972, the United States and Mexico set up high-level intersecretarial study groups to examine the migratory problem and to exchange proposals on what could be done through international cooperation (Corwin, 1978c).

The main issue on which Echeverría concentrated the government's efforts regarding the Mexican-origin population in the United States was the support of the Chicano Movement. In an environment of political repression in Mexico, support for the Chicano Movement was seen as convenient for the government because "it could present its benevolent face to the world by declaring itself the natural ally of Chicanos seeking to return to [their] Mexican roots.... While celebrating nationalist ideals for the pleasure of the Chicanos, the regime could display potent historic symbols that incidentally reflected the PRI's nationalist traditions and its political aims" (González, 1999: 213). The government offered assistance to Chicanos, promoted contacts with Mexican-American leaders and activists, created scholarship programs for Mexican Americans interested in studying in Mexico (such as the *Becas de Aztlán*), donated funds for the establishment of cultural centers, and distributed Mexican books for libraries and schools in cities with large Mexican communities (González Gutiérrez, 1993; Iskander, 2010). These educational programs, as well as academic projects in Mexican universities related to the Mexican community in the United States, continued to develop in the following years.[21]

In the early 1970s, the Mexican government organized numerous meetings between Mexican-American leaders and officers in Mexico, including President Echeverría, ambassadors, and other high-ranking officials (González, 1994, 1999). Echeverría's successors continued these exchanges with the objective of finding areas of mutual interest, establishing networks, and sharing information (González Gutiérrez, 1993). The *Comisión Mixta de Enlace* (Binational Outreach Commission), created during the administration of José López Portillo (President Echeverría's successor), formalized contact and managed relations between the Mexican government and several Mexican-American organizations (Gómez-Quiñones, 1983).

Although the Mexican government gave attention to the Chicano Movement and the Mexican-American leaders, the extent of its support throughout this period varied. As Iskander documents, this engagement

---

[21] In 1978 the *Dirección General de Relaciones Internacionales*, a special office within the Ministry for Education, was created to support the education of migrants in the United States. El Colegio de la Frontera Norte, a university specialized in migration and border issues, was founded in Tijuana in 1983. Many academic institutions also organized exchanges with Chicano studies programs. Most recently, the Institute of Mexicans Abroad awarded 300 scholarships through its *IME Becas* program for Mexican migrants going to college in the United States (Instituto de los Mexicanos en el Exterior, 2011).

was "often complicated and delicate, and the conversations fraught with misunderstanding, miscommunication, and confusion" and was characterized by ambiguity (Iskander, 2010: 198). Some authors (González, 1999; Sherman, 1999) have interpreted these variations as a result of the economic situation in Mexico: During the years of economic growth and the oil boom when Mexico had a stronger international position, Mexican authorities seemed to lose interest in ties with the Mexican Americans and their potential support in achieving its foreign policy objectives or improving Mexico's image abroad. During the crises, Mexico again turned toward Mexican Americans and sought stronger ties with them. In contrast to this view, Iskander (2010) identifies these variations mainly as a result of misunderstandings between Mexican-American or Chicano groups and the Mexican government, which led to cautious approaches from both sides regarding potential collaboration. During the López Portillo administration there were attempts to formalize these relationships and take advantage of the connections with Chicano groups "as a source of political leverage," but these efforts to "control the engagement," as Iskander (2010: 205) describes it, "ultimately suffocated it out of existence."

Added to these misunderstandings between the government and the organized Mexican-Americans groups, De la Garza (1983) argues that the government's support regarding Mexican Americans' political activities was always limited because it feared possible negative U.S. reactions to an apparent interventionist position. This was also evident in Mexico's limited responses to Carter's proposal for an amnesty program in 1977. Even though Mexico privately expressed its concern regarding its potential "economic, social and even political effects by closing off an escape valve for unemployed Mexicans," it refused to make its opposition public as it was "apparently unwilling to risk a crisis in relations [with the U.S.] by stirring up a controversy over the issue" (Riding, 1977; see also Iskander, 2010: 205–206).

Responses to the Growth of Mexican Emigration

In 1974, Echeverría began a family planning program to address the issue of demographic growth (Verduzco, 1998: 375–397). The positive effects of this program – and its continuation by succeeding governments – were made evident in the following decades with the reduction of the average number of children per family from 7 in 1965 to 2.5 in 2000. However, the focus on development and job creation in high-emigration

areas was very limited (Tamayo and Lozano, 1991) and most of the
activities related to emigrants concentrated on consular protection. Even
if Mexico preferred a bilateral solution, Echeverría considered that the
political environment was not favorable for a negotiation with the United
States. In presidential meetings, migration was only mentioned in passing.

This was a convenient position for the Mexican government because
the continuing flow of Mexican migrants to the United States and the
strategy of "benign omission," as described by Gómez-Quiñones (1981:
33), prevented a national discussion of emigration as a result of failed
development policies in Mexico (Cornelius, 1978: 422). Demands from
national groups that could pressure the government to modify its policies
regarding emigration were also limited, or at least they were not organized
in a cohesive bloc. This made it easier for the Mexican government to
ignore the issue and avoid taking more proactive measures; sporadically,
the government asked for special protection for migrants in the United
States or suggested a negotiation, but it did not insist too much or follow
up on these proposals.

Undocumented migration grew significantly between 1965 and 1970
but it reached a stable average by 1986. According to Massey et al.
(2002: 71), during this period the de facto structure of migration flows
worked smoothly; it "minimized the negative consequences and max-
imized the gain for both countries." Although the authors recognize
the impact of both countries' policies (or lack thereof) in the transformation of migrants' characteristics and an increase of undocumented
migration, which made the management of migration costlier in the long
term, they argue that it would have been convenient to maintain the "system" that functioned from 1965 to 1986 (Massey et al., 2002: 71–74).
This argument is important because it contrasts the cost of migration
policies instrumented after 1986 with the circularity and limited human
costs of the situation in the previous two decades. That does not mean,
however, that the policies of these years were adequate or desirable,
because they operated in a way in which the actors participating in the
process (the governments and their agencies, employers, smugglers, and
even migrants) were not accountable for the causes or consequences of
undocumented migration and had no incentives to modify the situation.

The growth of the Mexican foreign-born population became the focus
of U.S. anti-immigrant groups in the context of economic recession. These
groups began to express a growing hostility against foreign workers, particularly Mexicans; they blamed them for wage depression, unemployment, high costs of health and education services, high criminality rates,

violence, and corruption, and they accused them of avoiding tax payments and threatening their moral and community values (Pellicer, 1976: 196–197). In their requests for more restrictive measures to control migration flows they referred to Mexican immigration as an "illegal invasion," "hordes of foreigners," "intruders," a "silent invasion," a "nation within the nation," an "army of undocumented immigrants," a "national crisis," a "burden on taxpayers," and "a threat to the state."[22]

The U.S. government responded to these pressures by treating the issue as a national security concern and "acted as if it were doing something about it" by imposing more restrictive measures and directing more resources to border controls, although it was clear, even then, that this did not stop the flows of Mexican migrants (Fagen, 1978: 226–227). García y Griego (1983b: 300) describes U.S. policy as a strategy "not to leave the door too open but not completely closed either" to guarantee the availability of labor for certain sectors but at the same time reassure the population of the government's capacity to control the border. Various initiatives to reform the INA and address the issue of undocumented migration and control of the border were presented in the U.S. Congress in the 1970s and 1980s, but it took almost fifteen years for Senator Peter Rodino's 1971 initial immigration reform proposal to be amended and passed in 1986 as the Simpson–Rodino or Immigration Reform and Control Act (IRCA; see Verea, 1982: 73–77).

The Relevance of Delinkage: Negotiating on Oil and Migration

The U.S.'s restrictive position on immigration changed temporarily in 1974 with the news about discoveries of oil reserves in southeast Mexico (Rico, 1992: 230).[23] The importance of the partnership with Mexico had become a priority during the 1973 oil crisis, given that Mexico was not a member of OPEC (Organization of Petroleum Exporting Countries),

---

[22] As Cornelius argued in 1977, every time the U.S. economy is running into difficulties, the undocumented worker is "rediscovered and blamed for all the possible or imaginary problems that the American society faces" (Cornelius, 1977). Evidence of this reaction has been identified throughout U.S. history. In the recent periods, particularly since the 1990s, this tendency of using immigrants as scapegoats during periods of recession or heightened security concerns (such as the context after 9/11) has been targeted in particular toward Hispanics.

[23] In October of 1974 the National Bank of Foreign Trade (*Banco Nacional de Comercio Exterior*) issued two reports with evidence of the oil reserves found in the Southeast and projections about the revenues expected from new oil exports (see Rico, 1991: 58, n. 76 and n. 79).

which had imposed an oil embargo on the United States. Thus, in the first presidential meeting between Echeverría and U.S. President Gerald Ford (1974–1977), the key issues were oil and, surprisingly, migration (Rico, 1991: 57–59). In this case, it was the U.S. president who used issue linkage as a negotiation strategy and gave positive signs about the possibility of discussing a renewal of the Bracero Program in exchange for oil. As during the Second World War, the United States considered Mexico's cooperation vital for its national security, and it was willing to offer agreements that could benefit Mexico's key interests (Fagen, 1978: 216–217; Ojeda, 1983: 123; García y Griego, 1990: 114; Rico, 1991: 67).

Mexico's negative response to this offer was unexpected, and even at the end of Echeverría's government, the question of why the outgoing president had not taken advantage of the newfound oil as an element for negotiation remained unanswered (Rico, 1991: 67). There are various interpretations of why the Mexican government decided not to negotiate in this case. On the one hand, this was due to the fact that Echeverría was confident that the so-called oil weapon could be used for domestic purposes to achieve economic development without creating further dependence on the special relationship with the United States (Meyer, 1985: 28–29).[24] On the other hand, the decision was influenced by scholars such as Ernesto Galarza, who argued that the Bracero Program had costly consequences for the country and weakened its international position. By then the government had realized that it no longer required a bilateral agreement for keeping the safety valve open and that it was more convenient to maintain the status quo rather than attempt a linkage between issues that could eventually become detrimental to its position and interests (Verea, 1982: 114–115; García y Griego, 1990: 115; Rico, 1992: 228). In addition, the nationalist discourse with regard to oil meant that it would have been very costly at the domestic level to negotiate this resource in exchange for something else, particularly if it was with the United States.[25]

[24] From the moment that the oil reserves were discovered, many analysts talked about the risks of relying on them as the solution to Mexico's economic problems, a warning that would prove to be right during the economic crises of the late 1970s and early 1980s (Pellicer, 1976: 42; Green, 1977b: 55; Ronfeldt and Sereseres, 1978: 252).
[25] As I discuss in Chapter 5, this issue reappeared for a short period in the United States–Mexico immigration debate in 2003, when the U.S. House of Representatives' Foreign Relations Commission proposed that Mexico could offer oil in exchange for a migration agreement (see Bustamante, 2003).

Emigration in a Context of Economic Changes

José López Portillo's administration (1976–1982) began with an economic crisis that led to two devaluations in 1976. Despite Echeverría's efforts to reduce Mexico's dependence on foreign markets and rely on the "oil promise," López Portillo faced a limited number of alternatives to reestablish domestic and international confidence in the country's political and economic situation. This led to measures "that diverged from the Mexican Revolution's most treasured ideals" and led to domestic criticism based on the idea that Mexico was sacrificing its sovereignty by expanding collaboration with the United States (Ojeda, 1977: 42; Rico, 1991: 69–70). However, one of López Portillo's main concerns was to regain U.S. support and promote a return to bilateralism, even if this created resentment from nationalist groups (Green, 1977b; Rico, 1991: 70).[26]

President Carter (1977–1981) was also interested in strengthening the relationship with Mexico. The concepts of interdependence and complementary and common interests were frequently used in reference to oil and problems of drug traffic and migration. Various joint groups dealing with bilateral issues such as border control and trade commissions were created and there were numerous conferences and seminars dealing with the United States–Mexico relationship (Bustamante, del Villar, and Ojeda, 1978: 303; Ronfeldt and Sereseres, 1978: 243). However, many congressmen and groups within the United States opposed Carter's position on these issues; most of his proposals and initiatives to improve Mexico–United States relations by supporting Mexico's exports and promoting a reform of the energy sector as well as a project to manage undocumented immigration were blocked by Congress (Pellicer, 1978: 203–205).

On the issue of immigration, Carter introduced the 1977 Alien Adjustment and Employment Act with the objective of reducing the number of undocumented workers and protecting Americans' jobs. President

---

[26] Based on the idea that sharing Mexico's oil with the U.S. would allow the country to negotiate as an equal with the U.S. and become interdependent, Mexico proposed to build a gas duct to the United States. There was great opposition from Mexican public opinion and the divisions between members of the administration and leftist groups on the issue of oil limited the government's capacity to use it as a solution to the country's problems. In the end, the project was suspended because the United States did not accept Mexico's gas prices, but it was evident that Mexico faced obstacles in trying to use oil as an element for negotiating (Pellicer, 1978: 211–215).

Carter's position reflected the opposing pressures that he faced from anti-immigrant groups and labor unions that favored measures to reduce the flow of undocumented workers and from employers who had a continuing demand for labor. He suggested increasing resources for the Border Patrol, issuing sanctions to employers who hired undocumented workers, granting special work permits, offering amnesty to migrants who had been in the United States for at least three years, and increasing cooperation with sending states. The so-called Carter Plan was not well received by Congress and many congressmen argued that the problem was a result of Mexico's economic and development problems and should not be solved by the United States. However, this proposal was used as a model for subsequent initiatives and it encouraged the creation of the Select Commission on Immigration and Refugee Policy, which was in charge of analyzing U.S. migration policies and issuing recommendations.

During the debates over the Carter Plan, Mexico expressed its concern regarding the fact that it was a unilateral policy and the Mexican government had not been consulted on the issue (Verea, 1982: 116–118). However, Mexico did not propose alternative policies (domestic or bilateral) in response to U.S. initiatives, arguing that it was waiting for data from the Mexican Department of Labor (*Secretaría del Trabajo*) in order to design adequate solutions to emigration (Bustamante, 1978: 522–530). Meanwhile, Carter and López Portillo did establish other areas for cooperation, particularly regarding smuggling networks and border control, and Mexico created a new department within the Foreign Ministry dedicated exclusively to the protection of workers residing abroad (Verea, 1982: 120). As documented by Riding (1977) and Iskander (2010: 208), one of the Mexican government's main concerns at the time was that a stronger position on this issue could strain the bilateral relationship.

In 1979, when favorable data regarding oil reserves were released, the Mexican government stopped concentrating its efforts on bilateral negotiations or getting U.S. support for economic development. The United States sought a closer relationship with Mexico regarding oil and gas agreements, but this was not extended to other areas. In 1979, Mexico decided not to join the General Agreement on Tariffs and Trade (GATT) in order to maintain its protectionist policies, and it took an active interest in its relation with Latin America and its participation in multilateral forums. As was the case during Echeverría's government, the "decline of the North American connection" and the confidence in oil reserves reinforced Mexico's efforts to broaden its foreign policy options, which contributed to the deterioration of the bilateral relationship (Rico, 1991: 109).

In 1981, the U.S. Select Commission on Immigration and Refugees presented its proposals and various initiatives for reform of the INA were introduced in the U.S. Congress. One of President Reagan's (1981–1989) ideas was to create another program to hire 50,000 temporary workers each year. López Portillo did not express an opinion on these measures; he just asked to be informed as the proposals developed (Verea, 1982: 123). Although the Republican Party had favored a temporary worker program, its position gradually became more restrictive in response to the economic recession of the 1980s and the high levels of unemployment, the so-called conservative wave, and pressures from anti-immigrant groups (García y Griego, 1982: 107). Mexico had a limited participation in this debate; it refused to take part in the congressional hearings to which it was reportedly invited, or to propose alternative solutions when there seemed to be a more flexible position from the United States. The Mexican government simply expressed its concern regarding the potential problems related to repatriations, unemployment, and a reduction in the flow of remittances, and it focused the need to promote bilateral studies on the issue (Asencio, 1990: 86–89; Rico, 1990b: 45). Some analysts argued that the Mexican government trusted that the United States had no political will to implement measures regarding migration that could have high political and economic costs and that it was a "secondary issue for U.S. interests"; therefore, there was no need to respond more forcefully (García y Griego and Giner de los Ríos, 1985: 271–272; Rico, 1992: 267).

Except for the 1980 Refugee Act, none of the immigration reform proposals introduced in 1981 were successful and there was a "political paralysis" on the issue, which for some was a "lost opportunity" to address migration issues with a long-term perspective (García y Griego, 1982: 123). It was not until 1983 that the Simpson–Mazzoli Bill won Congress' support and the debate on the issue resumed, leading to the passage of the IRCA in 1986.

Meanwhile, from the 1980s onward, there was more academic interest in emigration in Mexico and numerous research projects and conferences were launched (Verea, 1982: 22). In 1980, the first International Conference on the Rights of Undocumented Workers was held in Mexico with the participation of labor unions, political organizations, and social organizations that had not been previously involved in the discussion of the issue (Verea, 1982: 121). President López Portillo also commissioned the Center for Information and Work Statistics within the Department of Labor (*Centro Nacional de Información y Estadísticas del Trabajo*, or CENIET) to study the causes of emigration, which included the Survey on Emigration to the North and to the U.S. (*Encuesta Nacional de Emigración a la Frontera Norte del País y a los Estados Unidos*, or ENEFNEU) – a study that continues to produce key data on migration flows (Verea, 1982: 146). However, these studies were interpreted by some "as an excuse for the Executive not to risk any solution, maintain silence and wait to respond or react to U.S. measures" (Verea, 1982: 147).

When the price of oil fell in 1981, "the ace" of López Portillo's foreign policy was called into question (Rico, 1991: 111). In the absence of a substantive economic reform, it was impossible for the Mexican economy to avoid a crisis that had presented urgent symptoms for almost one decade. Foreign debt could not be paid, interest rates had gone up, Mexican exports and the tourism industry had lost competitiveness, agricultural production was insufficient, the peso was overvalued, and there were signs of a foreign currency flight. In 1982, Mexico had to devaluate and suspend the payment of foreign debt, beginning one of the worst economic crises in its history. Mexico's economic recovery depended fundamentally on U.S. financial support, which was negotiated in exchange for low-priced oil.

By 1980, there were 2.2 million Mexicans living in the United States (three times more than in 1970), but the 1982 crisis did not substantially affect the flow of workers to the United States, as many analysts feared. U.S. interest in satisfying employers' demand for labor determined its informal policy of maintaining control of the border while keeping an open door to undocumented migration. At the same time, President Reagan argued that "if they closed the escape valve, it could destabilize Mexico and would not be convenient for U.S. interests" (García y Griego, 1982: 106). Mexico tacitly agreed to the status quo by maintaining a passive position on emigration and avoiding sensitive linkages between this and other bilateral issues.

CONCLUSIONS

During the period from 1942 to 1964, the definition and implementation of Mexican policies for the bilateral management of Mexican migration to the United States through the Bracero Program were determined by the government's interest in promoting economic development, maintaining political stability in the country, and guaranteeing U.S. support for indus-trialization and commercial activity. The Mexican government's reactions to the problems faced by Mexican migrants and its position regarding the continuation of the Bracero Program were based on the perception of emigration as a safety valve to prevent domestic pressures resulting from unemployment. Although there were criticisms from some groups in Mexico regarding collaboration with the United States, the exploita-tion of Mexican braceros, and the problem of undocumented emigration, the government maintained a favorable position regarding the continu-ation of the Bracero Program. The complaints regarding emigration did not have a significant impact on the government's policies, although in certain periods the strong nationalist discourse regarding migrants' return reflected the need to respond to these issues at the domestic level.

The limited impact of domestic pressures in terms of policy imple-mentation can be explained by the fact that the Mexican regime generally operated as a closed system that did not provide institutional channels for organized groups to participate in decision-making processes as well as by the fact that Mexican public opinion in general was not interested or informed, or had an ambivalent position concerning emigration. Political tensions increased in the late 1960s and through the 1970s, following the repression of the 1968 student mobilizations and other social protests. Emigration was an escape valve to some of these problems, but gradu-ally it became more difficult for the Mexican government to avoid social unrest and pressures for democratization, which, as I discuss in the next chapter, extended to the Mexican community in the United States in the late 1980s.

At the transnational level, consular activity was not as prominent as before and relations between Mexican migrants and the government were not as dynamic as in previous decades, although they continued to develop as the Mexican community in the United States grew and formed new types of organizations. The Mexican government's ties to the popula-tion abroad mainly focused on Mexican Americans and Chicanos and were pursued actively during Echeverría's government, in part, with the objective of improving the country's image abroad. However, the govern-ment's relationship with these groups was mostly focused on educational and cultural activities; political involvement was considered risky because it could be interpreted as interventionism.

This period is exceptional in terms of Mexico's foreign policy considerations regarding the management of migration. For the first time, the Mexican government was presented with an opportunity to negotiate with the United States from a relatively stronger position, given U.S. vulnerability during the Second World War and the Korean War. Thus, Mexico temporarily abandoned the idea of preventing linkages between issues in the bilateral agenda by providing Mexican labor through the Bracero Program as well as military cooperation in exchange for U.S. support in commercial and financial areas. Nonetheless, Mexico's vulnerability in terms of ensuring compliance with this formal agreement and its limited capacity to renegotiate the rules to its advantage was soon made evident. Still, to preserve the status quo in the bilateral relationship, guarantee U.S. support in other areas, and ensure the continuation of migration flows, Mexico preferred to maintain a disadvantageous but familiar situation through the Bracero Program, even if its rules were not entirely convenient for Mexican migrants.

The Bracero Program exemplifies the limits of the sending state's vulnerability in an asymmetrical relationship in terms of negotiating and ensuring compliance of common rules for the management of migration. The lessons of this period are also crucial to an understanding of Mexico's shift to a policy of limited engagement in the following years. The policy of having no policy, as it is commonly known, can also be considered a return to the passive position that prevailed in the preceding periods. However, in this case the decision to limit Mexico's participation in the immigration debate and to avoid policies that implied changing the status quo was made more consciously and explicitly than in the past because of the precedents established by the Bracero Program.

From 1965 through 1982, Mexican migration grew significantly and its characteristics changed in response to more restrictive immigration laws in the United States. After almost ten years of insisting on a renewal of the Bracero Program, in 1974 Mexico decided to abandon this possibility and avoided bilateral negotiations on this issue. The logic behind this position was that by remaining passive, Mexico could ensure that the situation would continue as it was, with no conflicts with the United States that could prevent the continuation of the migration dynamic as a channel for the political and economic tensions in the country. The discovery of oil reserves in 1974 and 1979 also gave the Mexican government confidence that it would provide a solution for emigration that did not require U.S. collaboration, given the expected economic opportunities that the newfound oil would bring to the country. Moreover, given the experience with the Bracero Program, cooperation with the United States and linkage between issues was considered disadvantageous, both in terms of the government's vulnerability in negotiations with the

United States and its limited capacity to ensure the implementation of specific conditions for the benefit of migrants. This began to change in 1982 with Mexico's economic crisis and its dependence on U.S. support.

In the next section I will examine the changes in the bilateral relationship as a result of Mexico's new economic policies since the mid-1980s and the signing of NAFTA; the changes in national politics that led to greater participation from new actors regarding migration issues; and the development of transnational relationships between Mexican migrants and their communities of origin as well as their closer relationship with the Mexican government. I will analyze the extent to which they each influenced the transformation in Mexico's generally passive migration policies to a more proactive position based on the creation of national institutions for migration management and the development of specific programs and institutions to promote a closer relationship with Mexican migrants and Mexican Americans. These changes also involved a more comprehensive definition of consular activities, more flexible interpretations of nonintervention in U.S. internal affairs, and attempts to make linkages between migration and other issues in the bilateral agenda.

FROM LIMITED ENGAGEMENT TO ACTIVE
EMIGRATION POLICIES (1982–2006)

4

From a Policy of Having No Policy to a Nation beyond Mexico's Borders (1982–2000)

The 1982 economic crisis was the critical point of the structural and political problems in the Mexican growth model that had become apparent from the late 1960s and through the various crises in the 1970s. After Mexico announced a devaluation and the suspension of its debt payments, it began a process of profound reform of its economic model that implied direct and indirect support of the U.S. government as a crucial element to avoid a deepening crisis and the default of Mexico's international obligations (Meyer, 2003a: 12). Given the U.S. government's fear of a possible collapse of Mexico's political and economic systems, particularly in the context of instability in Central America during the Cold War, President Reagan gave a high priority to stabilizing the Mexican economy by providing lines of credit and other types of assistance (Kaufman Purcell, 1997).

The changes involved in the restructuring of Mexico's economy included opening the economy to foreign investment and imports, fiscal discipline, deregulation of key sectors of the economy, and privatization. This new model implied rejecting the statist policies of the past and a move toward accepting the liberal trading principles sponsored by the GATT and other international organizations. President Miguel de la Madrid (1982–1988) and the new political elite that he brought into his cabinet sought to abandon the nationalist discourse and protectionist models from previous decades and foster a closer economic relation with the United States. This change was strongly reflected in Mexico's decision to join the GATT in 1986 (which it had previously rejected in 1979) and the signing of the 1987 Framework Agreement on Procedures and Principles for Trade with the United States. Although they were not

framed as such at that time, de la Madrid's decisions for economic liberalization paved the way toward a closer association with the United
States that would later lead to the signing of NAFTA in 1993 (Mabire,
1994: 545–546).

As this closer bilateral relationship evolved, Mexico's dependency on
U.S. investments and trade increased. At the same time, the Mexican
government began to develop closer relationships with U.S. government
and nongovernment actors at multiple levels rather than focusing mainly
on negotiations at the Executive level. Throughout this process, Mexico
began to redefine the limits of nonintervention by introducing lobbying
activities and public relations campaigns to promote its interests in the
United States.

Although enhanced economic cooperation with the United States was
not directly linked with a political opening of Mexico's PRI-dominated
regime, the need to present an image of stability to foreign investors and
to acquire a more active role in multilateral forums gradually increased
the pressures for democratization in the country. By opening the country
to international scrutiny, foreign and domestic criticisms were no longer
contained and it became more costly to maintain past and present policies
that helped legitimize the regime at the expense of delaying economic and
political reforms. As the distinction between domestic and international
agendas was blurred, Mexico assumed a more proactive role on issues on
which it had traditionally tried to maintain a low profile, such as drug
traffic control, human rights, and migration, and it promoted significant
political reforms that provided an opportunity for opposition parties to
gain ground and finally win the presidential election in 2000.

These changes had a significant effect on the way in which Mexico developed its migration policies in the 1990s. As opposed to the
Mexican government's previous limited engagement with the Mexican
and Mexican-American communities, its restricted statements regarding
U.S. policies affecting Mexican migrants, and an emigration policy based
mainly on a traditional definition of consular protection activities, from
the 1990s onward, Mexico developed a more active strategy to engage
with the Mexican-origin population in the United States through specific programs and enhanced consular activities; it expressed more direct
opinions on U.S. laws and policies; and it participated actively in the
development of bilateral cooperation in this area through special commissions and working groups.

This move toward a more active policy and a greater attention to emigration issues, both domestically and bilaterally, was also a reaction to

the growth of the migrant population and its increasing participation in Mexican politics – through hometown associations, state federations, and other organizations – and in the economy – through remittances – which increased pressures for the Mexican government to take an active position on emigration. The salience of these issues in domestic and international media made it more costly to maintain a limited engagement in the face of discrimination, anti-immigrant backlash, and a growing number of deaths related to border crossings, as well as emigrants' demands for greater participation in Mexican politics. Nevertheless, the Mexican government's position was limited by the concern that defending its interests on migration could compromise other areas of the bilateral relationship. This is made evident in its continued use of the strategy of delinkage – for example, by not including immigration in the NAFTA negotiations – and a discourse of nonintervention as a premise in most of its activities and statements.

This chapter traces the process through which the Mexican government gradually began to change its position of maintaining the status quo through a limited engagement in the development of emigration policies, domestically, transnationally, and bilaterally. For the period from 1982 to 1988, I identify the beginning of Mexico's reformulation of its relationship with the United States in terms of economic integration and foreign policy objectives. The debates over immigration reform in the United States that led to the passage of the IRCA in 1986 reflect Mexico's continuing restraint regarding its possible participation in the discussions, given its fears of a change in the status quo, a possible linkage with other issues, and the persistence of a traditional interpretation of nonintervention. However, the IRCA implied a fundamental change in the migration dynamic by regularizing the status of more than 2 million Mexicans, which was one of the factors that determined the break of the cycle of circularity in migration patterns and lengthened migrants' periods of stay in the country. The IRCA also marked the beginning of the implementation of a more restrictive U.S. policy for border crossings, which was strengthened in the mid-1990s. This created new demands from the Mexican population in terms of consular protection, and it made the issue more salient in Mexico.

By 1988, the political and economic impact of migration and the problems faced by Mexican migrants in the United States could no longer be ignored by the Mexican government. From 1988 to 2000, the Carlos Salinas de Gortari and Ernesto Zedillo administrations developed a series of policies that assumed a greater responsibility for the management of emigration and for the development of a broader relationship with the Mexican and Mexican-American communities in the United States. In the context of economic integration and a formal change in Mexico's traditional policy of maintaining a distant position from the United States in order to protect its autonomy, the countries began to develop a series of formal mechanisms for collaboration over the management of migration flows, including, for example, memoranda of understanding and working groups for the development of a bilateral approach to migration issues. As I discuss here and in the following chapters, the precedents set in this period have had a significant effect on the redefinition of Mexico's strategies and objectives on migration management and its relations with its diaspora.

THE EFFECTS OF ECONOMIC LIBERALIZATION ON MEXICAN FOREIGN POLICY (1982–1988)

As Mexico's dependence on U.S. economic support became more evident, there was an obvious inconsistency with the nationalist foreign policy that emphasized Mexico's autonomy from its neighbor. Furthermore, with closer collaboration between the countries, the bilateral agenda became more complex, making it "increasingly difficult to delink the various bilateral issues from each other" and gradually forcing Mexico to address the need for domestic policy reforms (Kaufman Purcell, 1997: 137). In terms of emigration, the change in Mexico's economic policies did not immediately affect the government's objectives and interests regarding the management of the flows, and it continued trying to maintain the status quo. It was not until the effects of the passage of the Immigration Reform and Control Act of 1986 were felt that Mexico had to face the irreversible changes in the characteristics of Mexico–United States emigration that made its policy of laissez faire unsustainable.

Contrary to expectations, the 1982 crisis on its own did not have the substantial effect on migratory flows from Mexico to the United States that many had predicted.[1] While the debate over immigration reform begun in the 1970s continued in the U.S. Congress with the Simpson–Mazzoli Bills and other proposals, President Reagan insisted that changes in the law should take into account Mexico's interests in this

---

[1] Internal migration from rural to urban areas in Mexico did increase, particularly in border cities, which meant that the number of "potential migrants" also grew (García y Griego and Giner de los Ríos, 1985: 230; Verduzco, 1998).

issue. This reflected part of the effort that began in 1971 with the initial discussions over comprehensive immigration reform in the United States, which prompted Mexican and U.S. officials to create special study groups and commissions. However, as domestic pressures and anti-immigrant reactions increased, the president changed his position on the issue and focused mainly on U.S. interests in this issue based on a unilateral solution (Bagley, 1988; Domínguez, 1989).

By 1980 there were over 9 million people of Mexican origin living in the United States, including Mexican immigrants and Mexican Americans (almost doubling the 5.4 million estimated in 1970; see CONAPO, 2008c). Given the growing and more evident presence of Mexican and other Latin-American immigrants in the United States[2] and the increasing number of migrant apprehensions at the border (from 900,000 in 1982 to 1.7 million in 1985),[3] there was a perception of loss of control at the border (including both undocumented migration and drug traffic – a key concern at the time).

In this context, in 1986 the U.S. Congress finally reached consensus on a bill for immigration reform that included several of the initiatives presented throughout the past decade. The Immigration Reform and Control Act or IRCA, also known as the Simpson–Rodino Bill, included measures for the regularization of undocumented migrants who had arrived before 1982, a special program for agricultural workers, and a reinforcement of employer sanctions that repealed the 1953 Texas Proviso, described by Senator Alan Simpson as "the most stupefying law in the history of man . . . [as it] said it was legal to hire an illegal, but illegal for the illegal to work" (interview with Sobel, 2001: 31). The bill also allocated 50 percent more resources to the Border Patrol and the INS. Such a comprehensive reform tried to offer a compromise to each of the interest groups involved – businesses, agricultural employers, labor unions, civil rights organizations, religious groups, and restrictionist groups – but as a whole it did not satisfy anyone and did not achieve its objective of reducing undocumented migration. As Senator Simpson explained, "we had a

---

[2] Weintraub (1998) explains that the growth of the Mexican population was not necessarily due to an increase in migration flows. The perceptions of a substantial growth of the migrant population could be due to their longer periods of stay, their high fertility rates, and the concentration of the Mexican population in certain areas, which made it appear bigger than it was.

[3] This did not necessarily imply increasing migration but could have been due to stricter controls by the Border Patrol. Moreover, the data collected by the INS did not take into account multiple crossing attempts by the same person, which meant that they could be counted more than once (Weintraub, 1998).

three-legged stool: increased enforcement, amnesty and large sanctions. Couldn't have one without the other . . . We needed to do all that, and got hell for it" (interview with Sobel, 2001: 31). With its unfulfilled objectives and unintended consequences, the passage of this law had a permanent effect on the characteristics of Mexican migration to the United States and was a crucial factor determining changes in migration policies in both countries.

MEXICO'S REACTION TO THE IRCA: THE LOGIC
OF LIMITED ENGAGEMENT

Throughout the debates over the IRCA, U.S. and Mexican officials held various meetings in which they discussed the future of immigration reform. During these encounters (some of them in Mexico), the Mexican government argued that it was necessary to offer "bilateral solutions to a bilateral problem" and expressed its concerns about a possible deportation of migrants as a result of changes in the law (Asencio, 1990: 86–89, 90–100; Rico, 1990b: 45–46).

When Senator Simpson visited President López Portillo he expressed a positive response to the president's petitions regarding the protection of migrants' rights (Vernez, 1990). Even though U.S. officials were receptive to Mexico's position, "the Mexican authorities reacted to the IRCA's passage as they had to previous U.S. legislative and other U.S. responses to migration matters. They remained largely silent, treating the legislation as an internal matter of the United States about which it would be inappropriate to comment" (Weintraub, 1998: 1231). Thus, it has been argued that Mexico could have engaged more actively in the discussions about the content of the IRCA by enhancing its lobbying activities with congressmen, expressing direct opinions on the various issues being debated, or launching initiatives for enacting these proposed "bilateral solutions" (Rico, 1990b: 45).

There is a lack of consensus regarding whether the U.S. was actually trying to establish a mechanism for consultation with the Mexican government about the proposed legislation through these meetings. For example, Bernardo Sepúlveda, Secretary of Foreign Affairs during the de la Madrid administration (1982–1988), argues that Mexico was never invited to participate in the debate over the IRCA (personal interview, September 2, 2006). Meanwhile, Diego Asencio (1990) and Carlos Rico (1990b), who participated in various working groups and publications about the legislation, claim that Mexico rejected the opportunity to express its opinion on these issues when U.S. officials offered possibilities to do so.

Bernardo Sepúlveda explains that Mexico's main concern at the time was a possible deportation of Mexican migrants as a result of the new legislation (personal interview, September 2, 2006). To prevent this or any other negative consequences, during their conversations with Senator Alan Simpson and other congressmen, as well as with President Reagan, Mexican officials expressed the view that a unilateral measure would be insufficient to address the situation. In Sepúlveda's opinion, the strategy was successful because some of Mexico's concerns were incorporated into the law, such as the creation of a joint consultative committee that would analyze the consequences of the new law – although he recognizes that after the law was enacted this mechanism was considered unnecessary given that mass deportations did not occur (personal interview, September 2, 2006). However, the IRCA did mandate the creation of the Commission for the Study of International Migration and Cooperative Economic Development (also known as the Asencio Commission, named after its chairman, Diego Asencio), a U.S.-led effort to establish bilateral consultations with Mexico and other sending countries about the causes of migration and possible joint solutions to the situation (Weintraub et al., 1998: 448). As I will detail in the sections that follow, this initiative had an important influence on future bilateral collaboration over these issues.

During this period, Mexico limited its official declarations to suggesting that it was necessary to continue collaborating and developing joint studies on the issue; it stressed the fact that the Mexican government respected the sovereign right of the United States to legislate on these issues and would not intervene in the process of formulation of domestic laws (Rico, 1990b: 45–6, 54). In terms of Mexico's emigration policies, the government emphasized the continuation and strengthening of its traditional policies of consular protection and the defense of migrants' rights.

The government's limited participation in the debates over immigration reform is explained by the fact that government officials feared that by pressuring for a change in U.S. immigration laws, they would be forced to implement measures to curb undocumented migration from Mexico and that at the end of the day the resulting reforms would affect the dynamic of the safety valve (Asencio, 1990). Just as in the 1970s, the Mexican government considered that the status quo was preferable to any change. Rico (1992) also argues that Mexico considered a significant shift in policy to be unlikely, given how long it had taken to find consensus regarding necessary adjustments to immigration laws. Thus, it was not worthwhile for the Mexican government to invest its political capital on the issue. In addition, Mexico feared that by demanding certain policies for Mexican immigrants, the United States would propose a linkage between a favorable immigration policy and a negotiation for oil as it did in 1974. Finally, an active participation in the debate could represent an interventionist policy in U.S. internal affairs and create problems in the bilateral relationship. To some analysts, this position demonstrated the Mexican government's limited understanding of the U.S. legislative process and the way in which lobbying works (Asencio, 1990: 86; Rico, 1992: 265).

It is worth noting that during Sepúlveda's term as Secretary of Foreign Affairs there was a strong emphasis on a foreign policy based on principles and international law. In 1988, Article 89, Section X of the Mexican Constitution was reformed to formally include the foreign policy principles of self-determination, nonintervention, prohibition on the threat or the use of force, peaceful resolution of controversies, equality of states, international cooperation for development, peace, and international security as the basis for Mexican foreign policy (Sepúlveda, 1994, 1998). The fact that the normative elements of Mexican foreign policy had such priority illustrates part of the reasoning behind the cautious response to immigration matters affecting Mexicans in the United States.

After the IRCA was signed into law, Mexico and some Central American governments were concerned about the increase in border controls and employer sanctions, which could lead to massive deportations and an abrupt interruption of migratory flows and remittances. However, García y Griego and Giner de los Ríos (1985: 230) argue that these concerns were exaggerated because it was evident that the United States had neither the political will nor the capacity to enforce massive deportations as it had done in the past.

Indeed, in the following years, these fears proved to be unfounded, which is illustrated by Strickland's (1989) description of the IRCA as "the bomb that did not explode." Rather, the law had other unexpected negative effects that neither government was prepared to respond to. Most significantly, the circularity of migration flows was transformed into a more permanent migration when an unexpectedly high number of 2 million Mexican migrants were able to regularize their status and bring their families to the country (including other nationalities, the total number of immigrants whose status was regularized was close to 3 million). Furthermore, those who did not qualify for the program continued evading migration controls but gradually extended their periods of stay as it became more difficult to cross the border. Even though the Border Patrol had more resources and personnel, migrants continued crossing through unpatrolled areas and, as a result of the existence of social networks developed throughout the many decades of United States–Mexico migration, it was still easy to get a job in the United States with fraudulent documents or through an employer that did not require them.

Given the shift toward new crossing areas, and longer periods of stay of migrants, the number of apprehensions was reduced in the first years after the passage of the IRCA. Nonetheless, undocumented migration continued with the unabated demand from U.S. employers and the additional incentive of another amnesty or reunification with their families, which led to an increase in the number of migrant women and children, more emigration from urban areas in Mexico, and more emigrants with higher levels of education and prior employment (González Baker, 1997). At the same time, sending regions in Mexico were increasingly affected by the prolonged absence of working-age male citizens; many communities were left mostly with children, women, and seniors.

The Mexican foreign-born population in the United States increased from 2.2 million in 1980 to almost 4.4 million in 1990 (Gibson and Jung, 2006; CONAPO, 2008c). With the extension of periods of stay and the growth of emigration, remittances also increased and became a significant component in the total amount of foreign currency flows to Mexico. In 1980, remittances represented an inflow of $1.8 billion dollars a year (almost as much as the income from tourism). At this point, some scholars and government officials expressed their concern about helping families use remittances as a source for development rather than spending it all on basic goods, particularly given the prolonged absences of working-age male citizens, but no measures were implemented in this respect (Alba, 1985; Lozano Asencio, 1992: 70).

The regularization process not only attracted a greater number of immigrants, but also gave them access to new types of jobs that had not been available before because of their undocumented status, particularly in sectors such as construction, services, and manufacture. This implied that immigrants moved to new areas and communities, which was seen by some as a threat to the American way of life. Although there was no definite evidence about the negative effects of migration (i.e., depression of wages or increase in unemployment) the debate was – and continues to be – surrounded by taboos and inconsistent data that led to the public's negative perceptions.

One of the greatest criticisms against the IRCA is that the section on employers' sanctions was never enforced. On the contrary, employers used the new law as an excuse to impose harsher conditions on undocumented workers. Undocumented migrants took seventy-two-hour jobs so they wouldn't appear on the payroll, they had excessively long working days, and they accepted lower salaries with neither health or housing benefits nor compensations for accidents at work. In addition, some employers forced migrants to pay them "insurance" in case they faced an audit and sanctions from the INS (Verea, 1988: 41; Strickland, 1989: 210–211).

Although the Mexican government's interests were not seriously affected by the consequences of the law, given that the safety valve remained open and remittance flows continued – and even increased – the IRCA created new demands from the Mexican community that the government had to meet. On the one hand, there was an increase in petitions for consular protection for migrants who had not qualified for the amnesty and for families that were separated. On the other hand, there were more abuses against undocumented migrants at the workplace as employers took advantage of their vulnerability. Violence at the border and risks of crossings had also increased, given the strengthening of the Border Patrol with new resources.

In response to the new problems faced by Mexican emigrants, the government reinforced its consular activities through the Department for Consular Protection within the Mexican Foreign Ministry, but it neither elevated these issues as a concern in the bilateral agenda nor developed new policies to address the causes of emigration (Vernez, 1990: 40). Although the increasing problems of undocumented migrants in the United States could have created more pressures for the Mexican government to be more proactive, the issue was not a main concern for domestic public opinion and opposition to Mexico's policies was not prominent, particularly in a long-standing PRI-dominated Congress (García y Griego and Giner de los Ríos, 1985: 253).

In terms of the relationship with Mexican communities, Sepúlveda explains that during de la Madrid's administration there was not as much emphasis on this issue as there had been during Echeverría's government (personal interview, September 2, 2006). The existing cultural and education programs weakened, as did political ties with migrant organizations. This was partly a result of budgetary constraints but also a response to political pressures from members of the U.S. government who considered Mexico's engagement with Mexican Americans to be a threat that would potentially give rise to a separatist movement (Iskander, 2010: 212).

Although contact with Chicano and Mexican-American groups was limited, President de la Madrid continued to establish cooperation mechanisms with organizations such as LULAC, MALDEF, and the NCLR (González, 1999). De la Madrid also sought a closer connection with the business community through the *Proyecto de Acercamiento del Gobierno y el Pueblo de México con la Comunidad Mexico-Norteamericana* (Project for the Strengthening of Ties Between the Mexican Government, the Mexican Population and the Mexican-American Community), but these contacts were not pursued actively until the Salinas de Gortari administration. According to Sepúlveda, the Foreign Ministry perceived that many of these groups and leaders were mainly interested in establishing business relationships to obtain special concessions from the Mexican government, and therefore it was better to maintain a certain distance. In his view, expanding the relationship with these communities was not considered a useful instrument for promoting Mexico's policies in the United States or reinforcing the protection of their rights in the country (personal interview, September 2, 2006).

Regarding the bilateral agenda, Mexico's "passive attitude" is also explained by the fact that Mexico did not want to be submitted to pressures from the United States or create tensions in the relationship – particularly regarding commercial and financial activities – by expressing its disagreement with some of the IRCA's provisions (Rico, 1990a: 97, n. 14; Vernez, 1990: 40).[4] Mexico was content with the development of bilateral study groups and commissions, a type of solution that it had promoted since the 1970s, because these groups provided a forum for expressing its concerns on immigration issues without being perceived as interventionist. Some examples are The Mexico–U.S. Working Group on Migration

---

[4] Although there were differences and tensions between Mexico and the United States at the multilateral and regional levels, particularly given Mexico's diplomatic intervention in the political crisis in Central America, there was a clear rapprochement in the economic arena. Thus, Mexico–United States relations during the first half of the 1980s "were characterized by the coexistence of two different logics" with disagreements in some areas and convergence in others, which at times "made it difficult to manage the [bilateral] agenda coherently" (Rico, 1991: 124, 157).

and Consular Affairs (1987), The Bilateral Commission on the Future of
U.S.–Mexico Relations (1988), The Commission on the Study of International Migration and Cooperative Economic Development (1987–1990),
and the continuing work of the Binational Commissions inaugurated in
1981.

These joint ventures were also evidence of the expansion of contacts
between different levels of government and other actors as well as of a
growing consensus about the need to promote cooperation in certain issue
areas, a process that was partly a result of a closer economic relationship
between the countries. For example, the Asencio Commission held consultations with senior officials of the Mexican Foreign Ministry, the Ministry of the Interior, the Mexican Senate, and the Chamber of Deputies
as well as with the National Population Council (*Consejo Nacional de
Población*, or CONAPO) and academics; this "helped set in play a consultative process between Mexico and the United States that had not existed
earlier" (Weintraub, 1998: 1233).

Through these contacts between government institutions, academia,
and organizations involved in migration issues, information exchanges
increased; there was a greater conscience about the need to protect
migrants' rights; and new issues were included in the discussion, such
as migration from Central America to Mexico, and the linkage between
migration, trade, and foreign investment. The bilateral activities that were
developing in other areas, mainly economic, had an effect on the discussion and the management of migration – a process Rico (1990a: 99)
describes as "indirect bilateralism" – although at the time no specific
joint policies resulted from it.

In the early 1980s Cornelius argued that the United States was an
accomplice to Mexico's failed emigration policies because government
officials had never pressured their Mexican counterparts to take more
active measures to address the causes of emigration and thus "allowed
Mexican elites to export dissension and prevent popular pressures to
implement the necessary reforms that had been delayed for years" (1981:
105–106, 126). However, this indirect bilateralism that Rico describes as
a result of closer economic relationship with the United States was part of
the process that influenced the gradual opening of the Mexican political
system, which in turn led to a significant change in the way in which
migration was perceived in Mexico – by government officials, Congress,
the media, and nongovernment actors. Eventually this resulted in policy
changes and a more active debate about Mexico's emigration policies,
both at home and abroad.

ADAPTING MIGRATION POLICIES TO A NEW BILATERAL CONTEXT (1988–2000)

The end of the Cold War and bipolarity, the collapse of communist regimes, and regional tendencies toward economic integration increased the competition for foreign capital, and thus increased the pressures for Mexico to accelerate its economic reforms and seek a closer and formal economic partnership with the United States (González González, 2000: 18; Meyer, 2000: 126–127, 137–138). In 1988, when President Carlos Salinas de Gortari (1988–1994) came to power, he "recruited young, internationally oriented economists who strongly supported deepening Mexico's integration into the global economy" (Kaufman Purcell, 1997: 140).[5] Their knowledge of and experience in the United States made them more inclined to promote closer bilateral cooperation. This was facilitated by recent coincidences between the countries in economic policies and also by the fact that members of the George Bush Sr. administration (including him) had lived and worked close to the Mexican border and gave a higher importance to Mexico in their agenda (Kaufman Purcell, 1997). Resistance in Mexico to these economic reforms and the closer relationship to the United States "was easily neutralized by a still very powerful presidency" and resistance in the United States[6] "was overcome by clever diplomacy, negotiations, public relations campaigns and intensive lobbying" (Meyer, 2003a: 12).

[5] Similarly, during Ernesto Zedillo's government (1994–2000), many of the top positions in the cabinet were filled by young politicians with a strong economic background, many of them educated in the United States. Such was the case of the Mexican Ambassador to the United States, Jesús Silva-Herzog – graduate of Yale University (1960–1962) – and the Secretary of Foreign Affairs, José Angel Gurría – with postgraduate training at Harvard University (1975) and the University of Southern California (1977–1978). The latter was considered by some as "the least Mexican of the Mexicans," given his command of English and his understanding of the nuances of the U.S. financial sector (see Dresser, 1994; Camp, 1995; Rodríguez, 1997; and Godínez, 2000).

[6] Some U.S. labor unions and other critics were against NAFTA because they thought the U.S. government had no responsibility in terms of helping Mexico solve its economic problems. They argued that NAFTA would increase competition for local businesses, would lead to higher unemployment rates, and would have a negative effect on the economy. Anti-immigrant groups argued that economic integration would further encourage the so-called invasion of migrants in their country. Various business groups were concerned about losing government subsidies as well as the benefits from protectionism in certain areas. In the end, the Clinton administration managed to convince a majority of legislators that Mexico's growth and economic stability was beneficial for the country because it would create a potential market for U.S. exports and that forming a regional economic bloc would balance competition from the European Union, Japan, and Asia (Aguilar Zinser, 1990: 39; see also Eisenstadt, 2000a, 2000b).

Despite the progress in bilateral cooperation over economic issues, this process did not include the same level of formal collaboration on more sensitive political issues, such as migration. However, taking advantage of the greater exchange of information and dialogue between different levels of government and other actors, both governments engaged more actively in bilateral mechanisms for the management and discussion of aspects related to migration flows. As Domínguez and Fernández de Castro (2001: 154) explain, "NAFTA prompted a new attitude among Mexican officials to institutionalize bilateral affairs, that is, to engage the U.S. government, formalize bilateral dialogues, and create mechanisms to manage bilateral affairs."

Mexico's activism in the promotion of these bilateral mechanisms allowed the government to explore more possibilities for cooperation and channels for expressing its opinion more openly on certain issues. The Salinas de Gortari and Zedillo administrations also enhanced their activities regarding the promotion of relationships with the Mexican and Mexican-American communities in the United States through the *PACME: Programa de Atención a las Comunidades Mexicanas en el Exterior* (Program of Attention to the Mexican Communities Abroad), commonly referred to as *PCME, Programa para las Comunidades Mexicanas en el Exterior* (Program for the Mexican Communities Abroad) or simply as *Comunidades*. Zedillo also implemented the dual nationality constitutional reform. Both of these changes implied a shift in the government's interpretation of nonintervention in terms of the state's relationship with the diaspora as well as lobbying activities, particularly during the NAFTA negotiations. This was framed as a consistent position with Mexico's foreign policy principles, and the Mexican government continued emphasizing its respect for U.S. sovereignty when its new activism was called into question. Still, Mexico avoided linkages with other areas of the relationship and was careful in its statements and declarations that could be considered an intervention.

THE NAFTA NEGOTIATIONS: IMPLICATIONS FOR MEXICO'S FOREIGN POLICY

In 1990 Mexico and the United States began the negotiations for a free trade agreement. A few months later, the Canadian government expressed its interest in the initiative and thus began the trilateral discussions for the North American Free Trade Agreement, or

NAFTA.[7] Mexico's interests were not only to reduce the tariffs on trade (which were already below 10 percent) but to provide the mechanisms to solidify the economic reforms at home, prevent future protectionism from the United States, promote economic growth, reduce inflation, pay its foreign debt, and attract investments and foreign technology (Meyer, 1992: 73–75). In addition to lobbying for a free trade agreement, President Salinas de Gortari lowered tariffs and other barriers to free trade, changed the 1973 law on foreign investment, accelerated the privatization of state enterprises, and adopted an anti-inflation program with the objective of making Mexico more attractive as a trade partner to the United States (Chabat, 1991; Kaufman Purcell, 1997). Negotiations for the NAFTA were held between June 1991 and August 1992; the parallel agreements on environmental issues and labor[8] were included later on; and in 1993 the process for ratification of the treaty began.

Despite opposition in Mexico[9] to a closer relationship with the United States, which could increase the country's dependence on its neighbor, and to a free trade agreement that could seriously affect certain sectors of the economy, President Salinas de Gortari was convinced that his government's legitimacy and the country's economic situation would benefit from economic integration with North America (Mabire, 1994: 546). As Meyer (1992: 75) points out, "making neoliberalism the new ideology of the regime [required], among other things, a profound revolution of the nature of Mexico's post-revolutionary nationalism and, therefore, of

---

[7] Between 1985 and 1988 the Canadian and U.S. governments had negotiated a free trade agreement that entered into force in January 1989, which served as a model for NAFTA in certain aspects. Its objectives were similar to those proposed with NAFTA in 1990, mainly strengthening the regional economy and trade between the countries. However, the free trade agreement had excluded Mexico because of the economic disparity between the countries (Domínguez and Fernández de Castro, 2001: 67–74).

[8] It is important to clarify that the North American Agreement on Labor Cooperation (NAALC) refers solely to working conditions in each country and does not include any provisions specifically regarding migrant workers. Its main objectives are the protection of workers in each country, the improvement of labor conditions, control of child labor, and the promotion of higher levels of productivity; one of its long-term goals is to reach parity between salaries in all three countries (see http://www.naalc.org/naalc.htm; last viewed May 9, 2008).

[9] Some of the initial critiques against NAFTA are documented in publications with suggestive titles: *El TLCAN se come sin chile* (Medina, 1991); *El TLC: un callejón sin salida* (Conchello, 1992); and *Me lleva el TLC!* (Barajas, 1993). A number of news reports and editorials document the continuing debate in Mexico over the costs and benefits of NAFTA and the closer relationship with the United States (see, e.g., Quintana and Zamarripa, 2002).

Mexico's relationship with the United States." Salinas' acknowledgment
of these criticisms and of the implications of his agenda was reflected in
his ambiguous references to Mexican nationalism in his statements,[10] but
he did not abandon his main goal of achieving closer commercial and
financial cooperation with the United States and Canada.

To achieve this objective, Salinas de Gortari began an intense lobbying campaign with congressmen, Mexican-American business groups,
and think tanks. These activities were based on hiring a group of high-
level lobbyists to promote Mexico's interests among investors, Mexican-
American and Hispanic groups, think tanks, Latino officials and leaders,
as well as the president and his cabinet leaders. Although Eisenstadt
(2000a, 2000b) and de la Garza (2000) note that the limited number
of Mexican-American businesses and congressmen that lobbied in favor
of NAFTA was not a determining factor in the passage of the agreement, the change in Mexico's attitude regarding its participation in the
U.S. decision-making process through lobbying activities had important
implications because it strengthened contacts between different actors
in both countries, fostered a better understanding of the U.S. political
system at various levels of the Mexican bureaucracy, and encouraged a
closer relationship between the Mexican government and its emigrant
population in the United States.

NAFTA's entry into force on January 1, 1994 represented a turning
point in the economic and political relationship between Mexico and the
United States. Some scholars argue that NAFTA merely provided a structure to a dynamic that already existed and, regardless of the agreement,
economic and commercial ties between Mexico and the United States
would continue in the same way.[11] The main difference, though, was
that the agreement established a mechanism for formal cooperation with
explicit rules for transactions between the countries, which meant that

---

[10] Mabire (1994: 568–569) analyzes how, in his statements, Salinas tried to change the
     meaning of Mexican nationalism but without completely abandoning the "ghost" of the
     taboos he was trying to destroy "because they were still useful as a means to communicate
     with a population in which they were still embedded, and therefore they were useful to
     strengthen the state." Domínguez (1998: 44–46) also draws on the Secretary of Finance's
     statements to illustrate the different discourses used by the Mexican government in
     Mexico and in the United States to justify the financial rescue package in 1995. Using
     Putnam's two-level game model, Domínguez explains that this strategy was useful for
     Mexico in terms of achieving contradicting domestic and foreign objectives.

[11] García y Griego and Verea (1998: 126–127) mention more than forty bilateral agree-
     ments that existed since 1978 in areas other than commercial and financial to illustrate
     the high level of cooperation that existed between the countries before NAFTA (also see
     de Olloqui, 1997).

they accepted the conditions and costs implied in fulfilling the obligations. Moreover, as part of NAFTA – and also as a result of it – numerous bilateral and trilateral institutions were created for the management of other issues, even if these were not included in the original agreement.

The most controversial aspects of NAFTA negotiations had to do with oil, environmental issues, transportation, and labor migration. In the case of migration, Mexico agreed to avoid the issue in the negotiations in order to prevent complications in the process of negotiation and ratification of the free trade agreement. However, at the domestic level, Salinas de Gortari approached this issue as part of a traditional nationalist discourse by arguing that Mexico would "export goods, not people," following Lopez Portillo's rhetoric of the 1970s. He also argued that the issue of Mexican labor would not be discussed with the United States in order to prevent a trade-off for Mexican oil, which is an example of the persistence of the idea of delinkage as a strategy to protect Mexico from its disadvantages in an asymmetrical relationship (Bustamante, 2003; Granados Chapa, 2003; Rincón Gallardo, 2003).

At the bilateral level, both Clinton and Salinas de Gortari defended the view that the benefits of foreign investment and trade available through NAFTA would, in the long term, eliminate salary differentials (estimated at 10:1 or higher),[12] create jobs, and reduce the pressures for emigration. Thus, "NAFTA became an element of additional stabilization of the migratory system, tending to maintain the status quo for a time," and it allowed both countries to share a vision that "maintains implicit the idea of gaining time in order for an open and orthodox model for development to solve the migratory issue" (Alba, 1993: 170–171). However, the economic model on which this so-called natural solution is based takes into account the level of development of the institutions of both participating countries as a key factor for success, which was not considered in this case. Neither Mexico nor the United States addressed the need to establish certain conditions to make this long-term solution a real possibility (Cornelius, 2002). Moreover, this logic did not take into account the historical development of migration between the countries, the existing social networks, and the complex economic, social, demographic, and political factors that maintained this constant migration flow. Andrés Rozental, former Undersecretary for North America for

---

[12] In June 2009, the federal minimum wage in the United States was $6.55/hour (approximately $52/day), although in some states it was as high as $8.55. Meanwhile, in Mexico the average minimum wage was $4 dollars/day ($52 pesos).

the Mexican government, made this argument in a personal interview (2005):

One of the greatest mistakes was to sell NAFTA as a panacea for the migration issue. It was said both in the U.S. and in Mexico that NAFTA would reduce migration pressures. They are just the same. Much of the flow, though not all of it, is a result of social networks rather than the pressures of the labor market. The migration phenomenon would continue to exist even if Mexico were more developed than it is now.

Meanwhile, the demand for labor in the United States continued as a result of lower levels of fertility and the coming of age of the "baby boomer" generation, and a high level of economic growth in the United States at the beginning of the 1990s. NAFTA also had negative effects in Mexico, such as the loss of jobs, displacement of certain sectors (especially agriculture), and disparities in development in northern and southern regions, which increased pressures for emigration to the cities and to the United States, particularly during the 1994–1995 economic crisis (Cornelius, 2002: 7; Delgado Wise and Márquez Covarrubias, 2007, 2008).[13]

OPEN BORDERS TO COMMERCIAL FLOWS, CLOSED BORDERS TO IMMIGRATION

The growing population of Mexican migrants and the opening of the border to commercial flows worried certain sectors of the U.S. population – particularly in a period of economic recession at the beginning of the 1990s – and in some cases led to anti-immigrant mobilizations (García y Griego and Verea, 1998: 110–111). One of the most controversial

[13] Delgado Wise and Márquez Covarrubias (2007, 2008) explain that Mexican migration to the United States has increased since 1994, in part as a result of the effects of NAFTA on Mexican economic development; many sectors, particularly agriculture, have been displaced while few occupational alternatives have been created. In fact, a large component of the process of economic integration has been the de facto creation of a labor-export-led model that includes indirect labor exportation through the maquiladora sector and the direct exportation of migrant workers. This has led to a loss of human resources for Mexico and to the abandonment of productive activities. One-third of Mexican municipalities currently face depopulation and economic decline. In addition, salary differentials between the countries have deepened and the dependency on remittances as a mode of subsistence and as a poverty-alleviation mechanism for more than 1 million families has increased and effectively substituted a sustainable economic development model.

moments in the anti-immigrant campaign was the law initiative promoted by Pete Wilson, governor of California, in 1993. Wilson published a letter addressed to President Clinton in which he demanded the cancellation of rights for all the children of undocumented migrants present in the United States, including access to health and education services. He also declared a state of emergency in California because of the high number of undocumented migrants in the state. This initiated a series of protests throughout the state and had a climactic point with the campaign in favor of the citizen initiative known as Proposition 187 or Save Our State (SOS), in 1994. This initiative, based on Wilson's proposal, would eliminate migrants' rights to access public education, welfare, and nonemergency health services and increase measures for verification of their migratory status at the local level.[14]

In the United States, the Catholic Church, nongovernmental organizations, members of the Democratic Party (including President Clinton), civil rights organizations, local governments, justices, and Latino and Mexican-American groups expressed their opposition to this initiative. Some of their arguments against Proposition 187 were that it violated the constitutional right to privacy; it contradicted federal laws regarding the eligibility for health services, social services, and education, as well as the statutes regarding nondiscrimination and confidentiality; it challenged the federal government's jurisdiction over immigration law enforcement; and it implied that state employees would have responsibilities corresponding to the INS (Burgess and González Gutiérrez, 1998: 284–289; Green, 1998: 357–365).

Despite opposition, the initiative was approved by 59 percent of the electorate on November 8, 1994. Although a federal court ruled against the implementation of the law, Proposition 187 influenced the political debate over immigration and instigated a discussion of similar initiatives in other states as well as in Congress. Candidates up for election or reelection in 1996, including President Clinton, also hardened their positions on immigration (García y Griego and Verea; 1998: 110–119).

---

[14] Proposition 187 denied health services to undocumented migrants and their families except in emergency cases. It required hospitals, teachers in public schools, social workers, and police officers to report any person whom they suspected of being in the country illegally. Public schools were required to verify the migratory status of students and their parents. These types of measures are part of a continuing debate, which has recently resurfaced (particularly since 2005), over the responsibility of nongovernmental agencies as well as local authorities in enforcing immigration laws.

Even though President Clinton had initially opposed radical proposals
for the control of immigration such as Proposition 187, during his term in
office (1992–2000) he responded to the increasing pressures of the American public and to Republican opposition in Congress by signing into law
various bills directed toward allocating more resources to border controls
and supporting states that incurred greater costs as a result of the presence of migrants. Clinton's policy, which he called the "most aggressive
and broad against immigration" (quoted in García y Griego and Verea,
1998: 113–114), consisted of a "dissuasion" strategy based on preventing
illegal crossings through the border, deporting undocumented migrants
who were already in the United States, and reducing their incentives to
remain in U.S. territory by limiting their access to services and other state
benefits (Cornelius, 2000, 2001).

In 1993, the Clinton administration began a series of border control operations that sought to enhance the monitoring of illegal border
crossings twenty-four hours a day by building wire fences with infrared
lights and watchtowers equipped with video cameras, and reinforcing the
Border Patrol with new equipment, helicopters, vehicles, and a greater
number of agents. The names of these operations – Blockade, Hold the
Line, Gatekeeper, Safeguard and Rio Grande – reflected the tone and
direction of the policy debate at the time.[15] In addition, in 1996 the
U.S. Congress passed a number of laws that limited migrants' access
to public services, imposed more controls at the workplace and restrictions for family reunification, and allocated resources for border controls:
the Personal Responsibility and Work Opportunity Reconciliation Act
(PRWORA); the Antiterrorism and Effective Death Penalty Act (AEDPA),
and the Illegal Immigration Reform and Immigrant Responsibility Act
(IIRIRA).

The PRWORA (or Welfare Reform Act) made undocumented migrants
ineligible for services such as Medicaid, food stamp assistance, and Sup-
plemental Security Income (SSI). The AEDPA authorized state and local
police to arrest and detain persons with an irregular migratory status
who had previously been convicted of a felony. The AEDPA and the

---

[15] The first operation for control of the border, Operation Blockade, later named Hold the
Line, began on September 1993 in the border between El Paso, Texas and Ciudad Juárez,
Chihuahua (in January 1997 it was extended all the way to New Mexico). In October
1994 Operation Gatekeeper was implemented in the San Diego–Tijuana border crossing
(in October 1996 it was extended to cover most of the California border). Operation
Safeguard was launched in the Nogales, Arizona–Nogales, Sonora border in 1995 (in
1999 the areas of Douglas and Naco were included). Finally, Rio Grande has covered
the Southeast Texas area since August 1997 (Andreas, 2000; Cornelius, 2001).

IIRIRA also expanded the number of crimes under which an immigrant can be subject to mandatory deportation. The IIRIRA tightened the government's handling of asylum claims and increased the penalties for unauthorized migrants in the country – in addition to being deported, undocumented migrants would be barred from reentering the country for three or ten years, depending on the length of their illegal stay in the country. Under the IIRIRA, an immigrant convicted of an aggravated felony would be subject to mandatory deportation without a hearing. It also allowed state and local law enforcement agencies to participate in the enforcement of immigration laws through memoranda of agreement, now commonly referred to as the 287(g) Program based on the corresponding section of the INA.[16]

Finally, in 1997, Congress passed a measure to eliminate Section 245(i) (also known as LIFE Act or Legal Immigration Family Equity Act) of the Immigration and Nationality Act. This provision, incorporated into the INA in 1994, had allowed eligible migrants, particularly those related to a U.S. citizen or permanent resident, who did not have a valid immigration status in the United States to pay a $1,000 fine and apply for adjustment of status in the United States. Until it was eliminated, various anti-immigrant groups had campaigned against this measure, which they considered an amnesty.[17]

None of these actions reduced undocumented migration or the demand for foreign labor in the United States, although the number of detentions and crossings decreased in urban areas where the operations were implemented. However, these measures had negative consequences for immigrants by making it more difficult to obtain visas and filing for family reunification as well as limiting access to services in the United States. This legislation also contributed to increasing violations of undocumented workers' rights, and raising the human and financial costs of crossing the border. Smugglers increased their fees from an average of $300 at the beginning of the 1990s to between $2,000 and $3,000 dollars by 2000

---

[16] As of 2001, no requests had been made through the 287(g) Program but the number surged since 2005, together with the number of state and local legislation on immigration issues, partly as a result of frustration given the failure of comprehensive immigration reform efforts in Congress. As of January 2011 there were seventy-two active memoranda of agreement as part of this program (sixty-five of which were signed after 2006; see Capps et al., 2011). See also U.S. Immigration and Customs Enforcement (available at http://www.ice.gov/partners/287g/Section287_g.htm; last viewed June 9, 2009).

[17] Section 245(i) was temporarily reinstated for a limited period from December 21, 2000 to April 30, 2001.

(Cornelius, 2001, 2002, 2004). An estimated 96 percent of migrants used their services in 2005, compared with 78 percent in 1986 and 40 percent at the end of the Bracero Program (Tuirán and Ávila, 2010: 122). The border control operations also had the "unintended consequence" of increasing the number of deaths at the border to an average of 300 per year since 1994 as a result of a diversion of the flows to more dangerous areas (Cornelius, 2001; CONAPO, 2008b); by 2009 the total was estimated at 5,300 (Tuirán and Ávila, 2010: 122.).

These changes also contributed to reducing the circularity of the flows, leading to a more permanent migration caused by the increasing difficulties of crossing back and forth frequently. Thus, the immigrant population grew significantly in the mid-1990s, which was supposedly what these measures had tried to prevent (Cornelius, 2001, 2002). Despite evidence about the failure and unintended consequences of these measures, they were maintained and even amplified through the years. The argument that Andreas (2000: 10) makes that these policies are more about "recreating an image of the border and a symbolic reaffirmation of the State's territorial authority rather than a real dissuasion strategy to reduce the flows of drugs and migrants" is supported by continuing evidence of the unsatisfactory results of border control measures and the persistence of discourse and policies based on this approach.

The strengthening of U.S. border control policies and the increase in anti-immigrant campaigns against Mexican and Latino immigrants in the United States had a significant effect on the Mexican government's policies: "U.S. restrictionist policies led to a more salient presence of this issue in the media. The topic became more visible and important in Mexico. It became more costly and required a political response. As the repression of Mexicans and the number of deaths at the border increased, more memoranda of understanding were signed and the consulates became more active" (personal interview with Gustavo Mohar, Mexican Foreign Ministry Chief Negotiator for a Migration Agreement 2001–2003, January 10, 2005). The Mexican government's new approach to these issues also revealed a "perception of the political influence of Mexican migrants" (Mohar, personal interview, January 10, 2005). Thus, in a context of growing collaboration between the United States and Mexico as a result of NAFTA, the Mexican government gradually opened up new spaces for dialogue and activism, both with U.S. actors, including federal and local governments as well as nongovernmental actors, and with the Mexican communities in the United States.

REDEFINING "NONINTERVENTION" IN STATE–DIASPORA
RELATIONS

The growth of the Mexican community in the United States since the
passage of the IRCA was a rising concern for the Mexican public and
government. As well, the diaspora's potential influence in domestic politics, both in Mexico and in the United States, was increasingly evident. In
Mexico, although the prospective impact of migrants in national politics
had been signaled by various studies since the 1970s (Vásquez and García
y Griego, 1983), this was made particularly evident during the 1988 presidential election. For the first time, the sixty-year ruling PRI felt that its
control of the presidency was threatened by the support that the Mexican community abroad gave to an opposition party. The mobilization
of various migrant organizations in the United States in support of the
Frente Democrático Nacional's candidate, Cuauhtémoc Cárdenas, and
their protests outside some Mexican consulates against the controversial
result of the elections – which gave the victory to the PRI – not only
threatened the legitimacy of the regime but implied the risk of drawing
international attention to domestic problems in Mexico. This situation
led Salinas de Gortari to develop new strategies to legitimize his government at home and abroad. An important part of this strategy included a
more active relationship with this population, whose potential influence
in domestic politics could no longer be denied (Dresser, 1993; García-
Acevedo, 2003).

García y Griego's opinion, published in 1988, that the "bases that
allowed the sustenance of the policy of having no policy" were unraveling,
shed light on the developments during the Salinas de Gortari administration (García y Griego 1988: 147). The adjustments in Mexico's migration
policies from 1988 onward are explained partly as a result of transformations in the bilateral relationship that implied an adaptation of Mexico's
foreign policy strategies in order to justify and take full advantage of
having a closer relationship with the United States. These were also due
to changes at the national level; the gradual process of political opening
gave a voice to new actors and to opposition groups as increasing concerns about violations of migrants' human rights and the consequences
of border controls became significant issues among the Mexican public.
New developments at the transnational level were also important factors,
given growing political, economic, and social interactions between the
Mexican population abroad and actors in both countries.

In response to critiques about Mexico's failure to protect migrants and manage emigration, in 1989 Salinas de Gortari established the Paisano Program (*Programa Paisano*) and the Beta Groups for the Protection of Migrants (*Grupos Beta de Protección a Migrantes*),[18] and he founded the National Institute of Migration (INM) in 1993. The Paisano Program was directed toward guaranteeing, by the use of information, humanitarian protection, medical assistance, and legal advice, a safe and easy return for Mexicans coming back to Mexico. Various government departments are currently involved in this program, which seeks to improve services at the borders as well as in ports and airports. The Beta Groups are in charge of surveillance at the border to prevent abuses against migrants and to control violence, criminal activities, and smuggling of people. Some of the officials participating in these activities have received training from the U.S. Border Patrol through a joint initiative that seeks to coordinate actions between patrols on both sides of the border. The INM, incorporated to the Ministry of the Interior, was created with the mandate of "planning, executing, controlling, supervising and evaluating migratory services" and coordinating activities with other government offices dealing with migration issues. Its main activities focus on regulating entries and exits into and out of the country according with the *Ley General de Población* (Population Law), which establishes the basic rules for the management of immigration and emigration matters in Mexico.[19] The creation of the INM was an important step toward recognizing the government's responsibility in terms of managing migration into, out of, and through Mexico. However, it did not – and to date has not – played an active role in the debate about the redefinition the Mexican government's emigration policies, which is mostly led by the Foreign Ministry and the Executive.

The Salinas de Gortari administration also began a series of activities oriented toward developing a closer relationship with Mexicans living in the United States and enhancing consular protection. One of the main priorities of this strategy was the promotion of consular activities: New consular offices and Mexican cultural institutes were established,

---

[18] See "Programa Paisano" (available at http://www. paisano.gob.mx) and "Programas especiales: Programa de Protección a Migrantes" (available at http://www.inami.gob .mx; last viewed January 21, 2007).

[19] In current debates over Mexico's migration policies, one of the main considerations has been the need to update this law and bring it up to code with international standards (see Oficina del Alto Comisionado de las Naciones Unidas para los Derechos Humanos en México, 2003: 171–175; Farah Gebara, 2007).

constituting a consular network of forty-two offices in the United States – one of the largest in the world and by far the largest in the United States, now consisting of fifty consulates (see Map of Mexican Foreign-Born Population and Mexican Consulates by State, located in the front matter to this book). Existing consular services were modernized and prominent diplomats and specialized government personnel were appointed to key positions in the Mexican Embassy and consulates in the United States.

The strengthening of consular representations also reflected the importance of the bilateral relationship and the interest in collaborating with new actors in the United States (González Gutiérrez, 1997). Through these and other actions, the Mexican government sought a closer relationship with U.S. labor unions, nongovernmental organizations, human rights groups, and national Latino organizations to advance the protection of migrants' rights (González Gutiérrez, 1997; de la Garza, 2000). As Mexican Ambassador to the United States Arturo Sarukhan explains, these relationships were in large part a result of the rapprochement between the countries since the negotiations for a free trade agreement: "NAFTA is what has allowed us to develop these grassroots relationships with mayors, chambers of commerce, etc. Since NAFTA, a dynamic has been developed where the Mexican Embassy in Washington, D.C. is seen as an ally, and that is pure gold" (personal interview, December 4, 2009).

Salinas de Gortari's most innovative proposal in terms of the relationship with the emigrant population was the creation of the *Comunidades* Program (PCME) in February of 1990. This was considered an open recognition of the growing influence of the emigrant community in national politics, the expansion of nongovernmental actors on both sides of the border, and the need to strengthen the protection of migrants through a closer relationship with the organized community. It has also been argued that it was a response to Mexican-American organizations that asked the Mexican government to have an official counterpart that would maintain exclusive contact between Mexican officials and the Mexican-origin population in the United States (González Gutiérrez, 1997; Secretaría de Relaciones Exteriores, 2000).

Through the PCME, the Mexican government offered numerous projects in education, health, welfare, culture, sports, business, and tourism, most of which continue to date through the Institute of Mexicans Abroad (IME), established in 2003. Closer contacts were developed between the government and hometown associations, state federations, and other migrant organizations, and between these groups and their communities of origin, also enhanced by the development of new communication and transportation technologies (González Gutiérrez and Schumacher, 1998). The number of hometown associations and state federations grew significantly during the 1990s and reached more than 600 by 2004 (IME, 2004a; Rivera-Salgado, 2006: 7); by some estimates, there were as many as 3,000 Mexican hometown associations in 2007 (Orozco and Rouse, 2007).

As opposed to the traditional forms of interaction with the U.S. government, "the PCME's activities were not previously negotiated with U.S. counterparts at the federal level" (González Gutiérrez and Schumacher, 1998: 196). Rather, Mexican authorities worked with local and state officials, taking advantage of the decentralization of the decision-making process in the United States. These activities represented a significant change in the government's definition of the boundaries for promoting its interests through different actors in the United States (González Gutiérrez and Schumacher, 1998: 196). This was also interpreted as a break with the traditional idea that "states should deal directly with each other rather than through their societies"; Mexico was no longer constrained by the idea that nonintervention prevented it from "maintaining direct and active relationships" with the Mexican and Mexican-American population in the U.S. (Domínguez, 2000: 315).

The PCME was also considered part of a strategy to obtain Mexican and Mexican-American groups' political and economic support in various issues in the bilateral agenda – particularly NAFTA – in order to influence the U.S. position on issues related to Mexico and promote a closer relationship between the two countries (González Gutiérrez, 1993). Attempting to gain the community's trust and show its goodwill, in 1990 the Mexican government for the first time recognized distinguished Mexican-American leaders such as César Chavez (union leader), Américo Paredes (founder of Mexican-American studies, professor at the University of Texas, Austin) and Julián Samora (civil rights advocate and scholar in Mexican-American studies) with the Order of the Aztec Eagle, the highest decoration offered by the Mexican government to noncitizens that make positive contributions to Mexico. In 1991 it honored Antonia Hernández (president of MALDEF) and Blandina Cárdenas (professor, University of Texas, San Antonio) with the Order, and in 1993 it was awarded to Raúl Yzaguirre (president of NCLR).

Another aspect of the development of ties between the Mexican government and the emigrant community was the 3 × 1 Program. Originally established in 1992 between the Zacatecas State Federation in California and the government of that state (as the 2 × 1 Program), and dating back to the 1980s as a 1 × 1 Program, the 3 × 1 is a scheme through which federal, state, and local authorities match funds sent by hometown associations and state federations for development projects in their communities in Mexico.[20]

Lupe Gómez, former president of the Zacatecan Federation of Clubs of Southern California, which began the 1 × 1 scheme and then led the formalization of the project as the 3 × 1 Program, explains the evolution of the relationship with Mexican government authorities from mistrust to collaboration through this program (personal interview, August 19, 2009):

This Federation began the 3 × 1. The Program dates back to the 1960s with the Zacatecan clubs and the first Federation of clubs, with a Zacatecan as the president. But they did not trust the government. So at first they just organized events to collect funds directly with the communities. It was until 1986 that the governor of Zacatecas came to California and saw this effort and tried to participate. It worked as a 1 × 1 until 1992. In October of 1992 we signed the first collaboration agreement with the federal government. It was a 2 × 1 from 1993 to 1998. Under President Ernesto Zedillo the municipalities were included and the 3 × 1 was born there; but only in Zacatecas. In 2001, when I became the president of the Federation of Clubs of Southern California I invited the President and other state governments to sign the 3 × 1.

Beyond the changes in infrastructure and development that the program has contributed to, Lupe Gómez explains that its objectives are long term and far reaching, as the 3 × 1 Program has helped create solidarity among the Mexican communities in the United States and empower them (personal interview, August 19, 2009):

It was a vision not only about transforming the communities with potable water, etc. but a vehicle to unite us. Now the Federation of Zacatecan Clubs is the largest in the U.S., even though it's a state with a small population. So we thought the program would have the same effect for other states and we sought to expand it at the national level. And we were not wrong. Now there are more than 1,100 organizations as part of the 3 × 1 and we started with 40–50 Zacatecan clubs. Now it is a national program, even an international one as it has been presented at the UN. The Zacatecan government was opposed to the inclusion of other states

[20] Currently, participating migrant organizations in the United States submit their projects to the Mexican government. The government selects those eligible to obtain the matching funds. The criteria are available through the Ministry for Social Development (http://www.sedesol.gob.mx/index/index.php?sec=3001&len=1; last viewed June 1, 2007). In 2005, 1,696 projects were approved. Of these, 873 were submitted by hometown associations in California, 225 by those in Illinois, and 161 by those in Texas. The associations raised about $20 million, matched by $60 million from Mexican government (IME, 2006b).

at first because they thought we would lose control and resources. But I thought this position was a mistake. I don't regret the decision to expand the program because it helped unite the communities. The institutionalization of the program led to the creation and integration of more clubs.

In response to the increasing activism of Mexican organizations in the United States and their interest in funding development projects in Mexico, many local and state governments developed closer ties with these organizations. The federal government attempted to provide a structure for managing relationships between emigrants and local governments through the establishment of State Offices for Migration Affairs (known as OFAMs). As Ayón (2006b) explains, the establishment of OFAMs in most states throughout the 1990s, "often at the behest of the federal government's PCME," facilitated the expansion of the 3 × 1 Program in the late 1990s. The growing participation of emigrants in the improvement of conditions in their communities of origin, and the increasing amount of remittances sent to Mexico (by 1990 they were estimated at about $3 billion), gradually changed the perception of emigrants by Mexican public opinion.[21] The idea of emigrants as traitors or as Mexicans who had lost their identity was slowly, though not completely, replaced by the positive image of paisanos (countrymen or compatriots) that made important contributions to the country.

The promotion of relations between emigrants and their home country gradually created more demands from some Mexican organizations and leaders to participate in the Mexican political process and to obtain the government's support in defending their rights in the United States. In this context, President Ernesto Zedillo (1994–2000) introduced the Mexican Nation Program in his administration's National Development Plan. This program, based on the idea that "the Mexican nation is not confined to its territorial borders," recognized the need – and the constitutional mandate – to develop policies in support of the Mexican population living abroad (Secretaría de Relaciones Exteriores, 1996: 39). Foreign Minister José Ángel Gurría emphasized in his statements that "this was the first time that the Mexican government recognized the importance of the relationship with Mexican communities living abroad in its official policies" (Secretaría de Relaciones Exteriores, 1995: 34).

---

[21] As noted in Chapter 1, the reported increase in the amount of remittances to the country was also due to the fact that the central bank (*Banco de México*) improved its methods to calculate the amount of remittances sent to the country and made them public (Lozano Asencio, 2004).

Part of these policies included the 1996 constitutional reform to allow dual nationality as a crucial step in giving Mexican emigrants the possibility to participate actively in their country of residence and exercise their rights as citizens. It was also considered a response to the debate over Proposition 187, because its passage had proven that even though a large percentage of California's Latino population was against it, many of the permanent residents who had the possibility of becoming citizens, and therefore exercise their voting rights, preferred not to in order to preserve their home country citizenship. Thus, the Mexican Dual Nationality Law gave Mexicans the option of maintaining their allegiance to the home country and also exercise their rights in the host country.[22] Together with this reform, an initiative to allow for absentee voting was passed but it was not implemented until June 2005.[23] I will return to this aspect of the reform in Chapter 6.

In the context of the debate over the dual nationality reform and reactions from U.S. groups that thought that this would hinder Mexican immigrants' integration, raise issues of dual loyalty, and be used by the Mexican government for political gain in the United States, Foreign Minister José Ángel Gurría declared that this reform was not intended "to influence Mexico's relationship with the United States" but rather "so [Mexican immigrants] can organize to defend their own interests" (quoted in Dillon, 1995). However, President Zedillo was quoted as telling a group of Mexican-American politicians in Dallas that "he hoped the amendment would not only permit Mexican-Americans to better defend their rights at a time of rising anti-immigrant fervor, but also help create an ethnic lobby with political influence similar to that of American Jews" (quoted in Dillon, 1995). This was an exceptional break with Mexico's

---

[22] The Dual Nationality Law was passed on December 10, 1996 and entered into force on March 20, 1998. The law established a five-year deadline for Mexican residents in the United States to present their documents at Mexican consulates (this deadline was later eliminated). However, of the expected 7 million Mexicans who had a right to claim dual nationality, only 84,672 registered for it between 2000 and 2009 (the data for 1998 and 1999 were not found). See Secretaría de Relaciones Exteriores, "Nacionalidad y Naturalización," "Estadísticas de Documentos Art. 30 Constitucional" (available at http://www.sre.gob.mx/tramites/juridico/estadisticas.htm; last viewed June 24, 2010). De la Garza (2002) argues that this low interest in claiming dual nationality can be a reflection of Mexican Americans' lack of trust or interest in maintaining links with Mexico.

[23] The fact that the section on absentee voting took such a long time to be ratified by Congress was subject of a heated debate in Mexico and among certain Mexican and Mexican-American organizations in the United States (see Calderón Chelius and Martínez Saldaña, 2002: 270–274).

tradition of avoiding such statements, particularly coming from the president, considering potential negative reactions in the United States to the idea of Mexico's attempting to interfere in U.S. domestic politics through Mexican immigrants. Mexico has generally been cautious in handling the idea of a potential lobby in the United States given the reactions it could generate, both in terms of backlash against Mexican immigrants who are perceived as disloyal if they maintain political ties to their home country and in terms of criticisms regarding Mexico's intervention in the United States. Nevertheless, this statement can be used as evidence of Mexico's dual and not always transparent objectives in aiding emigrants and improving their livelihoods in the United States. Granting dual nationality was both a way to legitimize the Mexican government by responding to emigrants' demands and concerns and giving them tools to defend their rights in the United States, as well as a possible means toward aiding the future development of an organized Mexican-origin ethnic lobby group with influence in U.S. politics in favor of Mexico's interests.

Despite the potential risks involved in these new positions on emigration, the fact that Mexico pursued these new policies demonstrates the government's recognition of the need to redefine its position in response to new domestic, transnational, and international pressures and also as a realization of potential gains. To promote many of these policies, Mexico made use of new foreign policy tools by expanding relations with local authorities and communities and lobbying with congressmen, business groups, Mexican-American leaders, and Mexican migrant organizations. The active promotion of Mexico's image among different actors in the United States "represents a break from the traditional policy of abstention from engagement in the domestic politics of other countries and forging alliances with external actors" (González González, 2000: 17). Part of these activities implied a decentralization of Mexican foreign policy-making process – traditionally controlled by the President and Foreign Affairs Ministry – giving a more prominent role to other ministries and departments (González González, 2000: 16–20).

This activism to promote Mexico's interests in the United States not only represented a shift from the nationalist rhetoric regarding the relationship with the United States but also transformed the idea that Mexico's intervention in issues beyond its northern border could motivate U.S. interference in Mexico's domestic affairs (Dresser, 1993). Nonetheless, as I describe in the next section, Mexico was cautious in the way it described and conducted these activities and continued to emphasize its respect for

U.S. sovereignty and the preeminence of the principle of nonintervention, particularly regarding U.S. legislation and policies on immigration.

REDEFINING "NONINTERVENTION" IN RESPONSES TO U.S. POLICIES

The heightened tone and consequences of the immigration debate in the United States in the beginning of the 1990s increasingly drew the attention of the Mexican public and media in both countries, as well as that of the international press (García y Griego and Verea, 1998). In this context, Mexico's traditional attitude of preventing confrontation by not expressing official opinions on U.S. policies and avoiding formal positions on emigration had higher costs. The pressures from domestic groups in the face of an anti-immigrant wave in the United States resulted in a more active response from the Mexican government to U.S. policies that had a negative effect on Mexican migrants in terms of violations of human rights, discrimination, and deaths at the border. Still, the Mexican government was always cautious to shield its declarations and actions under the principle of nonintervention and respect for U.S. sovereignty.

At the same time, following the practice from previous administrations, President Zedillo's government emphasized cooperation through dialogue and bilateral institutions as an alternative to address migration issues without compromising Mexico's position of nonintervention (Alba, 1998). The main difference was that during this period, the existing "migration dialogue" was expanded to include specific areas for bilateral collaboration and it was "institutionalized" through a series of formal mechanisms (Alba, 1998, 2000). The use of these new strategies, which were previously considered costly or unacceptable for Mexico, had positive results in terms of broadening the number of political counterparts in the United States and drawing greater attention to the United States–Mexico border from international organizations, civil groups, media, and public opinion in general. NAFTA played a key role in this regard; as Demetrios Papademetriou, director of the Migration Policy Institute, explains, it "opened up a space for dialogue; it changed the Americans' view of Mexico and vice versa. There was a change in ideologies, an identification of common interests. As a result, new topics such as migration can be placed on the agenda although the result is not necessarily positive for both" (personal interview, 2002).

This diplomatic activity and the growing economic interaction between the countries "provided the basis for the Mexican government to modify

its relatively passive foreign policy" (García y Griego and Verea, 1998:
120). One of the most significant examples of this change was Mexico's reaction to Proposition 187, which was set to be on the ballot in
the California election of November 8, 1994. As opposed to Mexico's
traditional position against expressing its opinion on U.S. legislative proposals, it openly rejected this citizen initiative that would limit migrants'
access to public services and education. On August 13, 1994 at an event
in Los Angeles, the Undersecretary for North American Affairs, Andrés
Rozental, expressed the Mexican government's strong opposition to this
initiative, in a statement that has been widely quoted as a climactic point
of the change in Mexico's noninterventionist attitude toward these issues:

> [W]e recognize the domestic nature of Save Our State. We strongly adhere to the
> principle of non-intervention in the internal issues of other countries. But in this
> case, as Mexicans we feel directly affected and our government cannot restrain
> itself from clearly expressing its categorical rejection and its commitment to work
> very closely with all those who aim to defeat Proposition 187.[24]

This statement was remarkable not only because it clearly expressed
the Mexican government's disagreement on an issue concerning U.S. politics, but mainly because it was expressed publicly, in U.S. territory, and
it included a commitment from the Mexican government to participate
actively in the debate. This evidence supports García y Griego and Verea's
argument (1998: 23) that "Mexico had arrived at a different interpretation of what had until then been understood as the policy of nonintervention given that previously the government did not even express its
opinion on U.S. legislative projects on migration issues."

In his speech, Rozental explained that "perhaps Mexican diplomacy
had never reached these levels of protest because it had never faced such
attacks and racism against Mexican people" (Avilés Senés, 1994). Given
the salience and the implications of Proposition 187, the Mexican government had also faced increasing domestic pressures from Congress,
labor unions, civil rights organizations, and nongovernmental organizations that demanded a strong response to this initiative that was considered discriminatory and racist.[25] The Senate recognized that, after having

[24] Remarks by the Ambassador Andres Rozental on the occasion of the Ceremony Award-
ing the Aguila Azteca to Luis Valdez and Baldemar Velásquez, Los Angeles, August 13,
1994, quoted by García y Griego and Verea (1998: 123); also documented in Avilés
Senés (1994).
[25] In 1992 Americas Watch issued a report registering the violations to undocumented
migrants' human rights by U.S. authorities. Other nonprofit organizations for the protection of migrants in the United States such as Human Rights Watch, American Civil

neglected the issue for a long time, it had the responsibility to pressure the Ministry for Foreign Affairs into taking a strong position against this law initiative and bringing it up to international forums such as the Organization of American States (OAS) and the United Nations (UN; Lomas, 1994). The House also issued a statement against Proposition 187 and proposed that the Executive should organize a meeting with the Mexico–United States Binational Commission to discuss the issue. Student groups, labor unions, and human rights activists held protests in Mexico in support of Mexican migrants and against Proposition 187, while civil rights organizations, Latino leaders, the Catholic Church, businesses, and other groups participated in demonstrations and boycotts in California and other parts of the United States to pressure against the initiative.

The fact that President Clinton and other prominent members of the government (Vice President Al Gore, Ambassador to Mexico James Jones, George W. Bush as governor of Texas, Attorney General Janet Reno, Immigration Commissioner Doris Meissner, among others) had openly expressed their opposition to Proposition 187 meant that Mexico's actions did not imply a direct confrontation at the federal level. Still, the Mexican government repeatedly argued that this was an exceptional case that concerned the state of California and did not affect the bilateral relationship or the free trade agreement between the countries. Moreover, the Mexican government insisted in almost every one of its declarations that it respected the sovereignty of the United States and California and would not interfere in their domestic affairs beyond expressing its opinion on an initiative that was considered discriminatory and had the potential of violating migrants' human rights, as well as supporting the judicial means for impugnation of the proposition according to U.S. laws and regulations (Barrera, 1994; Pérez and Jiménez, 1994).

In accordance with this definition of its position, the Mexican government developed a series of actions against Proposition 187. The outgoing President Salinas de Gortari and the incoming President-elect Zedillo both condemned the initiative as xenophobic and racist; the Foreign Ministry launched a campaign to provide information about Mexican migrants' contributions to California and to the United States (Reforma, 1994a); and the Mexican Embassy in Washington sent diplomatic letters to the Department of State expressing its concern with Proposition 187 as well as the recently launched border operations (Hold the Line and

Liberties Union, National Immigration Law Center and Center for Human Rights and Constitutional Law protested against Proposition 187 (Green, 1998: 352–363).

Gatekeeper). Mexican diplomats also expressed their support to organizations that were campaigning against the initiatives "within the boundaries of U.S. laws" (Reforma, 1994b) and increased their presence in the United States through contacts with local congressmen, opinion leaders, and other groups.

In an unprecedented type of diplomatic action, Mexico also used multilateral forums to express its opposition to the initiative and increase pressure against it. In November of 1994, the Mexican Ambassador to the UN, Víctor Flores Olea, denounced Proposition 187 before the General Assembly of the UN, considering it a violation of international norms on human rights and a form of discrimination (Reforma, 1994c). In December, President Zedillo condemned the initiative at the Summit of the Americas, and the Central American presidents denounced it as unconstitutional before the Inter-American Commission for Human Rights of the OAS (Reforma, 1994d).

Although some groups expected a backlash and a possible effect on commercial relations as a result of Mexico's actions and allegedly aggressive declarations, the bilateral relationship was not strained (Riva Palacio, 1994). The only reactions against Mexico's position were letters and declarations from supporters of Proposition 187. Governor Pete Wilson complained about the government's "interventionist" activities, which he considered "a threat to our sovereignty which should not be tolerated,"[26] and he signaled that it should step back (de Alva, 1994a, 1994b).

President Salinas' statements in an interview with *The New York Times* illustrate the Mexican government's new understanding of possibilities and limits for action within the bilateral relationship, which allowed for a wider space for action on some issues affecting Mexican immigrants' rights in the United States. Salinas de Gortari explained that Mexico's protests and measured reactions to Proposition 187 reflected that, as a result of the NAFTA negotiations, "there is a better understanding that the attitude of the U.S. toward Mexico is not monolithic. As a consequence, the reaction in Mexico is not monolithic against the U.S. now. There is an enormous concern about 187 but at the same time, it is not a national antagonism of Mexicans against Americans" (Golden, 1994).

As a result of this experience, the Mexican government expanded its definition of the boundaries of what it could do to participate in the immigration debate without creating tensions in the bilateral relations or

---

[26] See the letter from one of the groups supporting this initiative, "Yes on 187," cited in García y Griego and Verea (1998: 123).

suffering political costs, and thus provide a more comprehensive response to the problems faced by Mexican migrants. In the years after the debate over Proposition 187, Mexico's concerns regarding the violation of migrants' human rights were actively displayed through diplomatic notes and official statements as well as requests for the opinion of international organizations or for bilateral consultation mechanisms. Ambassador Sarukhan describes these activities and the change they represent with regard to the type of governmental response that existed in the past: "[I]t is a type of lobbying in the trenches in terms of consular protection, building alliances and dialogue with grassroots groups; one that did not exist before. It used to be all at the Executive level. There was little of this work with governors and civil rights groups that we now have" (personal interview, December 4, 2009).

With the support of various labor unions, nongovernmental organizations, the Catholic Church, Mexican-American groups, community leaders, local and state officials, and media, Mexico criticized the border operations and Border Patrol activities as an aggression against Mexico and a violation against migrants' human rights. The Mexican government also requested consultative opinions from the Inter-American Court for Human Rights of the OAS regarding the protection of migrants' labor rights, the rulings of the U.S. Supreme Court of Justice in cases involving Mexican migrants, police abuses, and death penalty sentences, among other issues.

Despite taking this increasingly proactive position, Mexico's response to the growing number of incidents reporting violations to migrants' human rights was perceived by some groups in Mexico as insufficient. An example was its response to the Riverside Incident. On April 1, 1996, two undocumented migrants were severely beaten by police officers who were chasing a truck that was transporting twenty undocumented migrants. The incident was recorded by a local television channel and was widely broadcast, resulting in strong reactions – considered by some to be "overreactions" (Weintraub et al., 1998: 499) – from civil right groups and the media in both countries, as well as demonstrations in the United States and in Mexico.

The Mexican Foreign Ministry issued a diplomatic note and the Mexican Embassy in Washington, D.C. and the Mexican Consulate in Los Angeles sent letters to U.S. officials complaining about the incident and condemning the violation of human rights. The Mexican Consulate in Los Angeles established contact with various organizations in the United States, including the NCLR and the United States Hispanic Chamber of Commerce (USHCC), who sent letters to U.S. officials expressing their concern over the incident. Mexico also brought up the case to the Human Rights Commission at the UN and asked it to issue a statement condemning the violation of Mexican migrants' human rights as well as enhanced international commitments regarding the treatment of migrants. In Aguilar Zinser's view (1996), appealing to the UN set an important precedent in Mexican foreign policy but it was a timid and ambiguous response because Mexico did not raise the issue of responsibility at the U.S. federal level for this type of abuses.

At the domestic level, the Mexican Congress criticized President Zedillo and the Minister for Foreign Affairs, considering their "lack of consistency in defending the rights of illegal workers in the U.S. and for their weak response to the Riverside incident" (Fernández de Castro, 1998: 1238). It also issued a joint congressional resolution in which it demanded that President Zedillo make public the list of human rights violations against Mexicans in the United States in the past five years, which had been recorded by the consulates in the United States and had presumably been kept secret to avoid damaging the bilateral relationship (Fernández de Castro, 1998: 1238). On April 11, the list was published in a document titled "Protection of Mexican Citizens Living in the United States." Finally, on May 8, at the 13th Meeting of the Binational Commission, Mexican and U.S. officials signed the Memorandum of Understanding on the Protection of the Rights of Mexican Nationals.

This is an example of growing pressures on the Mexican government in terms of responding to migration issues in a context of gradual political opening and democratization, which resulted from "high sensitivity in Mexico – [from] the Executive, Congress, the opposition parties, and the media – to the violation of human rights of co-nationals in the United States" (Fernández de Castro, 1998: 1240). At the same time, Mexico's emphasis on seeking support from domestic groups in the United States, raising the issue as an international concern at the UN, and promoting a formal bilateral mechanism for collaboration on the protection of migrants' human rights provided evidence of the change in the government's response to emigration issues at the bilateral level, moving toward a more flexible definition of noninterference in U.S. domestic affairs.

However, the persisting ambiguity in the Mexican government's interpretation of the limits and possibilities of responding to U.S. immigration laws and specific incidents was evident in its reaction to the passage of the IIRIRA and PRWORA laws in 1996. As opposed to its condemnation of Proposition 187 and the Riverside Incident, the Mexican government

returned to moderate declarations expressing its concerns about the possible negative effects of the legislation, while emphasizing its respect for
U.S. sovereignty. In September 1996, the Secretary of Foreign Affairs,
José Angel Gurría, expressed his "grave concern" about the proposed
bill in terms of its possible impact on human rights and negative attitudes against migrants (Reforma, 1996). The Director of Protection and
Consular Services, Enrique Loaeza Tovar, argued that the passage of this
law "is an act of the legislative sovereignty of the U.S." and the Foreign
Ministry would "do what it has always done, be very attentive, very
alert, very watchful to make sure that regardless of terms under which
the law is passed, it is implemented in a way that does not violate the
rights and individual guarantees of our compatriots" (Ortiz, 1996). Critics of the government's position, such as Jorge Bustamante, argued that
"it is inconsistent to have made such a scandal against Proposition 187
and now, nobody says anything against this law that is worse than 187"
(quoted in Martínez McNaught, 1996).

Although Mexico's response in this case was limited in terms of declarations and opinions, citing concerns about respect for U.S. sovereignty,
the Zedillo administration pursued alternative responses to the situation. Its main strategy was to promote an open and consistent dialogue
with various levels of the U.S. government through consultation mechanisms and formal agreements as a way to develop common definitions of
the issues and an institutional framework to discuss the situation without abandoning the tradition of nonintervention or compromising the
delinkage strategy (Alba, 2006: 314).

Thus, during Zedillo's administration, the presidents of both countries
signed numerous Joint Declarations on Migration in which they committed "to strengthen bilateral cooperation in order to deal with the migration phenomenon" while emphasizing that each nation has "the sovereign
right ... to implement its migration laws however it deems most appropriate for its national interests, always in keeping with international law
and in a spirit of bilateral cooperation."[27] A number of bilateral research
projects were conducted; one of the most prominent was the Binational

[27] See "The President's News Conference With President Zedillo in Mexico City, May
6th, 1997" (available at http://www.presidency.ucsb.edu/ws/index.php?pid=54103;
last viewed January 22, 2007). See also "Declaración Conjunta adoptada por
el Presidente de México y El Presidente de los Estados Unidos (14 de noviem-
bre de 1997)" (available at http://zedillo.presidencia.gob.mx/pages/vocero/boletines/
declaracionusa97.html or http://www.migracioninternacional.com/docum/indice.html?
mundo=prsnov97.html; last viewed February 2, 2007).

Study, conducted by the Working Group on Migration and Consular Issues in 1997, which Mohar considers "the basis for Mexico's proposal for a migration agreement in 2000/2001" (personal interview, 2005).[28] As Rozental, who participated in the group on behalf of the Mexican government, explains, "it was a key event in the whole process because it was the first time that we were able to find a common basis to define the situation. Before it was just rhetoric. Now there were common definitions. There was recognition on the part of both governments. It set the stage for the Carnegie group that prepared a proposal in 2000" (personal interview, 2005).

There were also a number of meetings between personnel of the INS and the INM and between U.S. and Mexican authorities from border states.[29] The Liaison Mechanisms for Border Issues[30] established in 1992 continued developing, various memoranda of understanding were signed,[31] civil consultation committees were established to promote border security and to control crossings, and there was an active promotion of information exchange, consular protection, the defense of human rights, and development issues in border communities.

Mexico was also proactive at the multilateral level through the promotion of initiatives for the creation of working groups on migration and participated in the existing ones within the UN and the OECD. These include the Working Group of Experts on Migration and Human Rights of the UN Human Rights Commission (created in 1997 as a result of a Mexican initiative and presided over for one term by Jorge Bustamante, a distinguished Mexican scholar), the International Convention for the Protection of All Migrant Workers and their Families (adopted by the

---

[28] See Secretaría de Relaciones Exteriores, 1997 or U.S. Commission on Immigration Reform, 1997.

[29] These meetings include the Annual Conference for Governors in the Gulf of Mexico and the Annual Conference for Border Governors.

[30] These liaison mechanisms are constituted by joint commissions that work in border areas to manage relations between both governments and societies. They mainly address issues related to crimes, security, the environment, health, urban development, trade, tourism, education, cultural, judicial cases, and migration. From 1995 the mechanisms reinforced the participation of state and local governments in these activities, and later on included other federal authorities such as consulates (Domínguez and Fernández de Castro, 2001: 142–143).

[31] These include the Memorandum of Understanding on Consular Protection for Mexican and U.S. Nationals (1996), the Memorandum of Understanding on Internal Consulatation Mechanisms (1998), the Memorandum of Understanding between CONAPO and the INS (1998), and the Memorandum of Understanding Against Violence at the Border (1999).

UN in 1990 and ratified by Mexico in 1999), and the Working Group on Migration at the OECD (in which Mexico has participated in since 1995). Mexico also proposed the creation of the annual Regional Conferences on Migration, also known as the Puebla Process, with the participation of Central and North American countries. It hosted the first meeting in 1996.

As a result of these developments, by the mid-1990s, many analysts argued that the "migration dialogue was institutionalized" (Alba, 2004). Some were cautious to point out that the establishment of commissions, committees, working groups, and mechanisms of consultations was not guaranteed as a permanent mechanism or as a way to expand formal cooperation between the countries, particularly considering the asymmetrical relationship and the U.S. preference for unilateral policies (Domínguez, 1998: 25; García y Griego and Verea, 1998). The validity of these reservations regarding bilateral cooperation can be tested against the fact that in the following administrations the expansion of such mechanisms, the specific reference to them by both governments, and the information available on their results has been limited. Although other agreements for collaboration were created such as the Partnership for Prosperity (2001) and the 22-point United States–Mexico Border Partnership Action Plan (2002), these referred mainly to economic development and border controls, not specifically to the management of migration.

The possibility for expanding the mechanisms and commissions established in the mid-1990s was tested in 2000–2001, when a group of government officials and specialists in United States–Mexico relations considered that this institutionalization of mechanisms for cooperation over migration and the level of interdependence between the countries provided the bases for a proposal for a comprehensive migration agreement between Mexico and the United States. Gustavo Mohar, Chief Negotiator of the agreement on behalf of the Mexican Foreign Ministry, argues that without the progress made since the mid-1990s to strengthen collaboration between the U.S. and Mexican governments, the context that allowed them to discuss a possible bilateral agreement for migration management in 2001 would not have been possible (personal interview, January 10, 2005). The failure of these negotiations reveals the limits of the institutionalization of collaboration between Mexico and the United States on migration issues. Nonetheless, they are evidence of the gradual change of Mexico's position on emigration and on its relationship to the United States, from a passive and limited engagement to active and more comprehensive policies on these issues.

CONCLUSIONS

In the period from 1982 through the year 2000, Mexico's policies became more active, both in terms of developing closer ties to Mexican emigrants, in responding to U.S. immigration policies, and in seeking closer collaboration on these issues. This period is crucial in terms of understanding the context and motivations behind Mexico's move from a policy of having no policy or limited engagement to more active positions on emigration – though still restrained in some ways. The transition into more active engagement with Mexican emigrants and responses to U.S. policies is best explained through a multilevel analysis that takes into account changes at the domestic, transnational, and international levels.

Throughout this period, emigration was still considered de facto as a relief to economic pressures in the country, particularly in the context of the 1982 economic crisis. Though it may be argued that it was also a safety valve to political resistance in Mexico, it no longer served as a way to muffle opposition to the PRI regime as emigrants in the United States became increasingly engaged in Mexican politics, particularly in opposition to the PRI and its disputed electoral victory in 1988. In a context of political and economic opening, this opposition was seen as a threat not only to the continuation of the PRI regime but also to the perception of international public opinion and potential investors. Thus, the Mexican government's strategy to improve its consular services and create programs directly targeting this population was partly a way to legitimize the government, and at the same time control political dissidence abroad.

In the context of the NAFTA negotiations, Mexico also recognized the potential influence of Mexican Americans in furthering Mexico's economic interests; therefore it actively engaged in a lobbying campaign that involved Mexican-American businessmen and politicians that could have an impact on the passage of the agreement. At the same time, remittances increasingly became a significant source of income for many families, and Mexican emigrants' funding of development projects in Mexico was seen as a positive contribution. All of this influenced the Mexican public's perception of emigrants, leading to a more favorable opinion of their ties to the home country and increasing demands for the Mexican government to respond to their needs and enhance the protection of their rights.

These factors operating at the domestic and transnational levels were closely intertwined. As emigrants became a more active force in Mexican politics, the government tried to legitimize the regime and control their opposition to the PRI but at the same time it considered emigrants as a potential vehicle for furthering its interests in the United States, as exemplified by the dual nationality constitutional reform and the lobbying for NAFTA. Emigrants were also considered a valuable economic resource; the amount of remittances they sent was increasingly significant and they became more actively involved in development in Mexico through programs such as the 3 × 1. Furthermore, the backlash against Mexicans in the United States increased the salience of these issues both in Mexico and in international media and pressured the government to react more forcefully to U.S. policies and provide better services for the protection of emigrants.

A key element in the change of Mexico's strategies also has to do with developments in the United States–Mexico bilateral relationship. The process of economic liberalization in Mexico led to a closer relationship between the countries and a gradual move away from anti-American and nationalist rhetoric that emphasized Mexico's autonomy and independence from its northern neighbor. As part of this process, the Mexican governing elite gradually began to include cabinet members that had been educated in the United States and had experience in dealing with the U.S. government. This helped develop a better understanding of opportunities for collaboration between the countries and influenced the move away from traditional interpretations of Mexican foreign policy. Although sensitive issues such as immigration were not included in the NAFTA agreement, it set a precedent in terms of developing mechanisms for collaboration in areas of common interest, including commissions and agreements focused on sharing information and joint management of certain issues related to migration.

The NAFTA negotiations also set a precedent in terms of Mexico's lobbying efforts in the United States, which had never been exercised before. The Mexican government realized the opportunities for mobilizing its allies in the United States in favor of its interests without a negative impact in the bilateral relationship or leading to U.S. interference in its own affairs. Mexico continued testing the limits and possibilities for action and reaction to U.S. policies in the context of anti-immigrant legislation. These responses were still framed in the context of nonintervention and respect for U.S. sovereignty, but this principle was interpreted more flexibly than in the past.

Following Keohane and Nye's model of complex interdependence, in this case the contact between governments that was facilitated by NAFTA contributed to "creating, altering or reinforcing institutional memories" as the relevant groups internalized "the principles and norms of regimes."

According to this model, when these principles and norms "become part of the belief systems which filter information . . . regimes themselves provide information that alters the way key participants in the state see cause-and-effect relationships" (Keohane and Nye, 1984: 266). Through a gradual process of learning, Mexico realized that the expected costs of its reaction to U.S. policies that affected migrants or a more active relationship with the diaspora did not have a significant consequence in the general status of the bilateral relationship, especially given the institutionalization of collaboration on priority issues such as trade. Thus, Mexico "took advantage of spaces that began to open, even while recognizing the limits of U.S. domestic politics where it can't do more" (Carlos Rico, personal interview, 2002).

The next chapter describes further developments in Mexico's policies following from its new position on migration based on the changes that took place between the mid-1980s and through the 1990s. The next period, covering the Vicente Fox administration (2000–2006), focuses on Mexico's proposal for establishing a United States–Mexico migration agreement and making this issue a priority in the bilateral and the national agendas, as well as on its promotion of closer political and economic relations with Mexican emigrants. These policies cannot be explained without considering the gradual process of changes in policies and perceptions described in this chapter, although a main difference is that Mexico's migration policies were defined and pursued more openly and consistently. Thus, the following period allows for an in-depth analysis of the scope and limitations of this innovative position in Mexico's emigration policies, considering the asymmetry of power in the bilateral relationship and the reactions to these policies both in the United States and in Mexico.

5

The Migration Agreement (2000–2003)

Many people in Mexico still consider that the migration phenomenon contributes so much to Mexico (particularly through the astronomic amount of remittances) that it's better not to touch it. It is a source of income. It is a safety valve to unemployment. What are the costs of the deaths at the border in comparison to migrants' contributions to the country? A profound debate on these issues has not yet taken place in Mexico.

– Interview with Andrés Rozental, former Mexican Undersecretary for North American Affairs, February 12, 2005

One of the most significant and controversial changes promoted by Vicente Fox's government (2000–2006) was the reinterpretation of Mexico's foreign policy. At the beginning of 2001, the Secretary of Foreign Affairs, Jorge G. Castañeda, described the new "axes" on which Mexican foreign policy would be based in order to adapt to the most recent national and international transformations, including the democratization process in Mexico, economic integration with the United States, and the pressures of globalization. This new approach would entail a more active presence in multilateral forums, a consistent defense of human rights at the national and international levels, and deeper integration with the United States, including a more comprehensive bilateral agenda (Castañeda, 2001). In this context, one of the main issues that was actively and explicitly incorporated into the United States–Mexico agenda for the first time was the need to establish broader cooperation mechanisms, including a migration agreement, to face the challenges of a migratory flow of between 400,000 and 500,000 people a year, and the presence of nearly 10 million Mexican migrants in the United States in 2000 (of whom close to 5 million were undocumented migrants at the time; Grieco, 2003).

Raising migration as one of the highest priorities in the bilateral agenda represented a turning point in the Mexican government's traditional attitude of "having no policy" (García y Griego, 1988) on this issue, and the climactic point of changes that had been developed since the mid-1980s. Fox's promise to govern for 120 million Mexicans, including the migrant "heroes" (as he called them), and to implement policies to improve their situation can be explained as a result of the historical evolution of the relationship between the Mexican government and the Mexican community in the United States, particularly since the end of the 1980s. It also has to be considered in the context of the change of regime in the year 2000 and the fact that the Fox administration was taking advantage of its so-called democratic bonus, detaching itself from the responsibility implied in the failure of the previous regime's development and migration policies (Alba, 2004). It is also crucial to emphasize that this represented a fundamental shift in the government's interpretation of the foreign policy principle of nonintervention and the delinkage strategy, based on the perception that given the level of integration between both countries and the legitimacy of the regime, a more assertive attitude regarding the relationship with Mexican migrants and the policies to address their necessities and demands would not cause the United States to close the escape valve for migration or imply unacceptable costs for Mexico in the bilateral relationship.

This change was based on developments in the bilateral relationship since the late 1980s: a greater degree of collaboration and information exchange between the governments that led to a better understanding of the U.S. political system; the process of economic integration that was institutionalized through NAFTA; and, in the specific case of migration issues, the establishment of working groups, memoranda of understanding, binational studies, and other bilateral efforts that helped establish a dialogue whereby each country was better informed about the others' position on the issue, which led the way toward common definitions and further cooperation in this issue area.

REINTERPRETING MEXICO'S FOREIGN POLICY

The changes in Mexico's foreign policy discourse and activities since the year 2000 reflect a search for a new definition of foreign policy that would balance the country's interests in the face of a new international and domestic context (Covarrubias, 2006). The end of the Cold War and the advent of U.S. hegemony, the strengthening of regional blocs, and the increasing pressures of globalization, especially for developing countries, were part of the Fox government's considerations regarding a shift from a closed and distant foreign policy to a more active presence in multilateral forums and an explicit, closer relationship with the United States. At the national level, the process of democratization, particularly with the change of government in 2000, gave the Mexican political system a newfound legitimacy before the international community and a wider space for action regarding certain issues that had not been dealt with at the international level before (González González, 2001). As Castañeda (2002b) described it, "putting an end to the authoritarian regime had a double effect: it meant fully becoming a democracy and, at the same time, abandoning the defensive attitude of relative distance and evasion that Mexican governments had maintained in the past in areas as important as human rights and democratization."

Although Mexican foreign policy had begun a process of change since the late 1980s, and particularly after the signing of NAFTA in 1994, the main difference during the Fox administration was that the priority of Mexico's relationship with the United States was expressed "open and vehemently" and the change was made explicit in Mexico's foreign policy discourse (Meyer, 2002). The traditional foreign policy principles still remained an important component of policy making in this area and to a certain extent limited Fox's agenda, but the government considered it necessary to update their interpretation according to new realities. Mexico now had the will and the capacity to express its opinion and to be more proactive; it was an open and democratic country that no longer feared international scrutiny (Meyer, 2001).

In this context, at the suggestion of Secretary Castañeda and other close advisors to President Fox, the Mexican government changed course in terms of the traditional role assigned to migration issues in the national and bilateral agenda. Moving away from a passive and reactive attitude toward U.S. migration policies, Mexico decided to take the offensive, proposing an agenda for bilateral cooperation on these issues, mainly through a migration agreement. The Mexican government described this proposal as part of the process of economic integration and a move toward a "NAFTA-Plus," which represented a change in the strategy of delinkage of issues. This agenda for a migration agreement necessarily required a reform of U.S. immigration laws, which implied a change in the traditional interpretation of nonintervention in U.S. domestic issues. This attitude represents a key change in Mexico's perception of the limits imposed by the asymmetric relationship and its "resignation in advance" (Fernández de Castro, 2002b) to promoting an agenda favorable to its

interests under the assumption that Washington would ultimately impose
its own.

THE PROPOSAL FOR A MIGRATION AGREEMENT

The Mexican government's proposal for making migration a priority
issue in the bilateral agenda was based mainly on the United States–
Mexico Migration Panel's 2001 report "Mexico–U.S. Migration: A
Shared Responsibility." Some of President Fox's close advisors – includ-
ing Jorge G. Castañeda, who a few months later became Secretary of
Foreign Affairs, and Andrés Rozental, former Undersecretary for North
America – were part of this panel convened by the Carnegie Endowment
for International Peace and the Mexican University *Instituto Tecnológico
Autónomo de México* (ITAM) in the Spring of 2000 to analyze and make
recommendations on migration and border issues in the United States and
Mexico. On the U.S. side, the chair was Thomas "Mack" McLarty, a close
advisor to George W. Bush (and former Chief of Staff under President
Clinton). The study group included Mexican and U.S. academics, think
tanks, representatives of labor unions (SEIU and AFL-CIO), business
representatives, the U.S. Chamber of Commerce, and nonprofit groups
specialized in migration issues (such as MALDEF and Sin Fronteras).

The Migration Panel's report was mainly based on the findings of the
Binational Study Group (1995–1997), which provided the foundation for
common definitions and categories that enabled influential actors on both
sides to agree on the idea of a migration agreement (Rozental, personal
interview, 2005; Mohar, personal interview, 2005; also see Alba, 2003).
The main objective of the study was to call on the Mexican and U.S.
governments to engage in serious discussions on the need for a migration
agreement. According to the specialists who prepared this document, "if
properly crafted and implemented, both governments would be able to
shift from enforcing contestable unilateral priorities – with very mixed
results – to carrying out the terms of an agreement, and from asserting
absolute notions of sovereignty to affirming the provisions of a mutually beneficial negotiated deal" (United States–Mexico Migration Panel,
2001: 1).

The Migration Panel's proposal was based on the assumption that
bilateral cooperation for the management of migration issues was a natural and necessary step, given the extent of interdependence and integration
between the countries. According to the report, the current NAFTA context and the high levels of interdependence between the countries made

it necessary to expand cooperation to migration issues within the framework of integration: "If the U.S. and Mexico wish to reduce significantly the strain on their extraordinarily positive progress on integration, they must appreciate that it will be increasingly difficult to be partners on economic issues and antagonists on migration issues" (United States–Mexico Migration Panel, 2001: 1). Against the political and economic rhetoric that prevailed during the NAFTA negotiations and kept migration out of the agenda based on the argument that free trade would help reduce emigration pressures, the report claimed that out-migration would continue unless its economic and social fundamentals changed and thus it was necessary to establish a formal bilateral mechanism to manage the flows.

The Migration Panel also considered that existing institutions for the management of migration, particularly the exchange of information and collaboration in border controls, provided the necessary elements to expand cooperation. In addition, the development of various bilateral consultation mechanisms in the 1990s, including working groups, border liaison, training and consultation mechanisms, binational studies, and repatriation agreements, were considered an enormous improvement in terms of building a common understanding of the problem and the possible solutions. The report argued that it was timely to move beyond this framework and "create an orderly system of migration flows that maximizes the positive effects of these flows for each partner and for the participants in that process while minimizing their negative consequences" (United States–Mexico Migration Panel, 2001: 12). The timing, the context, and the structural factors were deemed favorable for a migration agreement.

In terms of structural factors, the Migration Panel explained that the desirability for Mexican labor in the United States was based on the fact that the "baby boom" generation in the United States would pass into retirement over the next fifteen years and immigrants would be needed to work and pay the taxes that fund their retirement. Moreover, the United States Bureau of Labor Statistics predicted that, by 2008, the United States would have over 5 million more jobs than people to fill them, and that most of them would require low- and medium-skilled workers. On the Mexican side, it was suggested that fertility rates would continue to decrease and migration flows would gradually recede in the next fifteen to twenty years. In this context, the report proposed matching U.S. demand with Mexico's supply of workers through a bilateral agreement, without experiencing the unintended consequences of creating more flows,

as happened with the Bracero Program. In terms of the political environment, it quoted Federal Reserve Chairman Alan Greenspan, business
associations, congressmen, and organized labor – particularly the AFL-
CIO[1] – who called on the U.S. government for an immigration reform
that recognized the importance of immigrants in sustaining the country's
economic growth. In the Migration Panel's view, this meant that there
was a coincidence between structural conditions and increasing domestic
support for a change in the approach to migration issues.

The report described that there had been a fundamental change in the
way major U.S. and Mexican societal institutions and the general public
expect their governments to act on human and labor rights and social
justice issues, and they hold government officials accountable in these
matters. It argued that respect for workers' rights "seems to be capturing
not only the imagination of ever broader segments of the U.S. society
but also to be energizing the creation of increasingly robust cross-border
civil society coalitions" (United States–Mexico Migration Panel, 2001:
10). As described in Chapter 4, U.S. and Mexican media and the public
in both countries had reacted strongly to a variety of extreme incidents
involving Mexican migrants and anti-immigrant legislation and policies
enacted in the 1990s. The Migration Panel considered that these costs as
well as public interest in the issue provided a positive context for creating
a new dialogue on migration and agreeing on a common set of goals with
more attention to the protection of human rights (United States–Mexico
Migration Panel, 2001: 9).

Finally, the panel saw the election of Presidents Fox and Bush as a
unique opportunity to address these issues because of the experience
of these individuals as governors of traditional migrant-sending and
migrant-receiving states (Guanajuato and Texas, respectively), the interest they manifested in migration issues during their election campaigns,
and the fact that they both defeated governing parties and could distance
themselves from previous policies. The election of President Fox was seen
as particularly opportune given the so-called democratic bonus that he
obtained after defeating the PRI in the 2000 election and the general

---

[1] In 2000, the Executive Council of the AFL-CIO renounced its long-standing position in
favor of employer sanctions and against any form of amnesty, and instead endorsed the
full legalization of undocumented immigrants. This change reflected the unions' dissatisfaction with the ineffective enforcement of employer sanctions and the continuing abuses
against undocumented migrant workers by employers, as well as the need to incorporate
migrant workers into unions in order to protect them (and native workers) and to increase
membership (National Immigration Law Center, 2000).

interest in Mexico's democratic transition at the international level. In addition, both presidents had highlighted the importance of the United States–Mexico relationship, which President Bush referred to as "the most important partnership" for the United States, and which President Fox portrayed as a step toward a NAFTA-Plus. The robust economic performance of both countries in the previous years and the success of NAFTA were also considered positive factors in this context.

Thus, the panel proposed a "grand bargain" based on the idea that migration from Mexico to the United States should be mutually beneficial; safe, legal, orderly, and predictable; and that in the long term the flows should naturally decrease and stabilize. This grand bargain later developed into the five points of Mexico's proposal: (1) providing regularization of undocumented workers who were already in the United States; (2) granting more visas for Mexican immigrants; (3) broadening the scope of temporary worker programs; (4) increasing border safety; and (5) targeting development initiatives to areas of high out-migration and strengthening the Mexican economy in order to reduce emigration pressures.

MEXICO'S INITIATIVE: A MOVE AWAY FROM DELINKAGE

At the initiative of Secretary Castañeda, the Mexican government adopted this agenda and presented it to its U.S. counterparts as one of the main issues to be addressed at the first presidential meeting between Bush and Fox in February of 2001. In January of 2001, Castañeda and Condoleezza Rice (as President Bush's National Security Advisor) had a "secret meeting" in which, according to Castañeda, they agreed that migration would be the central issue in the bilateral agenda, although Rice expressed her concern about the idea of an amnesty (Castañeda, personal interview, 2005; Castañeda, 2007: 73–78). The night before the Presidential summit in Guanajuato, an executive summary of the United States–Mexico Migration Panel's report was presented to President Fox by Andrés Rozental and Secretary Castañeda and to President Bush by Mack McLarty, as the "conceptual-empirical legitimation" of Mexico's proposal (Fernandez de Castro, 2002a: 117).

On February 16, 2001, the Mexican and U.S. presidents met at Vicente Fox's San Cristóbal Ranch in Guanajuato, Mexico to discuss their approach to the most pressing issues in the bilateral agenda. In their joint declaration, "Towards a Partnership for Prosperity: The Guanajuato Proposal," the presidents expressed their intention to strengthen the

North American economic community and expand their collaboration to address issues related to border control, drug traffic, energy resources, and, most importantly, migration. They recognized the need to create an orderly framework for migration "that ensures humane treatment, legal security, and dignifies labor conditions."[2] As a way to achieve this, they announced the creation of a high-level group of negotiators chaired by the Secretary of State and the U.S. Attorney General, Colin Powell and John Ashcroft, and by the Secretary of Foreign Affairs and the Secretary of the Interior of Mexico, Jorge G. Castañeda and Santiago Creel, respectively.

The fact that Mexico was willing and able to set the agenda on the issue was unprecedented. As Castañeda (2006) describes it, he "inserted" the agreement into the agenda, and "imposed it" on the United States against their will. According to Mohar, who was appointed Chief Negotiator on Migration Issues for the Mexican Foreign Ministry in 2001, the main reason why Mexico was able to push through this agenda was because, as a very rare circumstance, its negotiating group was better prepared than the U.S. team, at least at the beginning of the discussions (personal interview, 2005).

Another intervening variable was the fact that, at the time, Bush's foreign policy agenda was very weak and he was inexperienced in this area, but he felt comfortable dealing with issues related to Mexico, as it was "the one country where Bush, notoriously short on foreign policy experience, could demonstrate familiarity" (Leiken, 2002: 7). He was also familiar with immigration, given his experience as governor of Texas; therefore, he was favorable to the idea of including the issue in the bilateral agenda (Davidow, 2004: 204; Papademetriou, personal interview, 2005). In personal interviews, Castañeda and Frank Sharry, director of the National Immigration Forum at the time, also claimed that the United States was taken by surprise by this proposal and Mexico was able to impose its agenda because at the time Bush did not consider the domestic costs that these negotiations would entail (personal interviews, 2005). This is confirmed by Davidow's (2004: 216) assertion that, "the administration in Washington did little serious analysis of the issues before making the commitment. Little thought was given to the real possibility for success in an area that was so complex and politically volatile." In some analysts' view, rather than a shared belief in the expansion of

---

[2] See the Joint Statement by President George Bush and President Vicente Fox, "Towards a Partnership for Prosperity: The Guanajuato Proposal," Guanajuato, February 16, 2001 (available at http://www.presidency.ucsb.edu/ws/index.php?pid=45870; last viewed February 9, 2011).

NAFTA and the need to collaborate in order to minimize the costs of migration, Bush and his advisors saw the relationship with Fox as an opportunity to add a success in the foreign policy agenda, which could also help increase the number of Latino votes for the Republican Party in the next election.[3]

On the Mexican side, the ability to promote this agenda at the bilateral level reflects the learning process that the Mexican government elite had experienced since the 1990s, and particularly since the NAFTA negotiations, regarding the U.S. political system, lobbying, and negotiating with different actors involved in the political process. Although Fox and his team met with legislators from both parties and Fox gave a testimony at the U.S. Congress in September, one of the main criticisms at the national level was that the Mexican government had wrongly focused its efforts on negotiations at the Executive level instead of broadening the strategy and including other actors (Bustamante, 2006b; Green, 2006a).

The fact that the strategy focused on the Executive level during the first months of negotiations does not mean that the Mexican government did not recognize that any reform of immigration laws would necessarily go through Congress and require lobbying there. Castañeda and his team were well aware of it and understood the process, but they thought that, as was the case with NAFTA, having the Executive's support would offer a better opportunity for the passage of such a proposal (Fernández de Castro, 2002a: 125; Mohar, personal interview, 2005; Castañeda, 2007). Thus, according to personal interviews with Papademetriou and Castañeda, if Bush had been seriously interested in the issue, he could have invested the necessary resources and convinced the public and specific interest groups about the benefits of an agreement (Castañeda, personal interview, 2005; Papademetriou, personal interview, 2005). At the same time, the Mexican team, led by Mohar and Rodolfo Tuirán, then head of the National Population Council (CONAPO), had taken the necessary steps to "prepare the ground" by getting these groups' support (Papademetriou, personal interview, 2005). An example of this was Fox's testimony in Congress and the private meetings with legislators. Throughout the process of negotiations the Mexican team also met with

---

[3] The argument about whether the Latino vote was an important element in Bush's foreign policy agenda is subject to debate. For example, whereas Alba (2003) claims that the Latino vote had very little importance in the U.S. position, Massey and Durand (2001) argue that the U.S. initiatives for cooperation with Mexico had more to do with "wooing Latino voters."

Mexican-American leaders, business groups, the U.S. Chamber of Commerce, and labor unions as part of its strategy to build support and lobby for the agreement (Rozental, personal interview, 2005).

In the Mexican team's view, achieving a migration accord would be similar to the process that led to the passage of NAFTA. In Arturo Sarukhan's words (as Castañeda's Chief of Policy Planning Staff), it "does involve the same coalition building that was involved in NAFTA, that is grassroots, but you have one key component you didn't have in NAFTA, which is the trade unions" (quoted in Corchado and Sandoval, 2002). Castañeda also explained it as a similar situation to NAFTA, although in this case there was more support from the Democrats and the negotiations were more complex given the number of groups involved (the Church, Latinos, and labor unions on the Democrats' side, and businesses and employers[4] on the Republicans' side; Castañeda, personal interview, 2005).

The idea of a NAFTA-Plus was one of the main components of Mexico's justification for the need to sign a bilateral agreement related to migration. However, this implied a move away from the idea of delinkage that had kept migration issues out of the agenda in the initial NAFTA negotiations. In Castañeda's view, "based on his conversations with his U.S. counterparts," it was no longer feasible to compartmentalize issues in the agenda and separate economic, political, judicial, and security agendas to prevent "contaminating" each other, as Mexico used to believe. He argued that it was necessary to "inject" the economic agenda with political issues and vice versa.[5]

Even though it has been argued that the idea of NAFTA-Plus was not well received by the U.S. team who suggested that Fox should tone down the idea of a "North American economic community" (Rozental, personal interview, 2005), the Mexican government kept the NAFTA-Plus concept alive (even when the negotiations were stagnated after 9/11). An example is the following statement by Sarukhan in October of 2002: "NAFTA has taken North American integration to a new stage, but the big leap forward . . . is providing depth to that association and that depth

---

[4] Some of the most powerful businesses, whose labor force is composed of a large number of migrants, were involved in the Essential Worker Immigration Coalition (EWIC), which promoted an expansion of temporary worker programs but not necessarily tied to regularization. EWIC was also joined in 2002 by the CATO Institute, a conservative think tank close to the Bush administration.

[5] Interview with Sergio Sarmiento in "La entrevista con Sarmiento," *TV Azteca*, January 12, 2001.

will be provided basically, in a first step, by a labor agreement, and then by a number of initiatives which will deal with the socioeconomic, slow convergence of the economies and societies of the three countries" (quoted in Corchado, 2002).

This stance represented an important move away from the consensus during the NAFTA negotiations that linking migration with economic cooperation would be detrimental to Mexico's position. Given the development of NAFTA and other bilateral institutions, within sectors of the Mexican government there was a perception of stability in the relationship that would prevent changes in the status quo if Mexico introduced more sensitive issues into the agenda. González Gutiérrez confirms this view: "NAFTA had set a precedent and become a systemic part of the relationship; the institutionalization of the relationship opened new doors" (personal interview, 2004). In addition, Frank Sharry explains that "NAFTA forged relations between key actors who later participated in the process of negotiations on migration" (personal interview, 2005). On this basis, the Mexican government embarked in a "tactful but decisive" strategy (Meyer, 2003b) to pressure the United States into negotiating a migration agreement.

THE NEGOTIATION OF THE MIGRATION AGREEMENT

Throughout the following seven months (from February 16 to September 10, 2001), the high-level group held a series of formal and informal meetings in which it discussed the specific content of the bilateral agenda on migration and the possibilities for collaboration between the governments. As the discussions progressed, the U.S. team was consolidated and better prepared for the meetings, with an even better structure than the Mexican team, which at that point had limited resources and staff. This was perhaps due to the fact that it was seen as a high-level negotiation that only required a few experts at the initial stages, although it is likely that more resources would have been allocated if the discussions had moved further given the priority of the issue (Fernández de Castro, 2002a: 122; Mohar, personal interview, 2005). At the same time, conservative voices within the Bush administration began expressing their concerns about the possible consequences of an agreement. For example, they argued that it would be impossible to pass legislation on this issue with special conditions for Mexican nationals, because it would be necessary to grant the same rights to migrants from other countries. The voices against regularization (businesses as well as conservative groups in the Republican

Party) and against a temporary worker program (labor unions as well as members of the Democratic Party) began to grow stronger (Berruga, personal interview, 2005; Castañeda, personal interview, 2005).

Some of Bush's advisors were concerned about the risks of losing support from conservative Republicans such as the group led by Tom Tancredo, especially with a view toward the midterm elections (Davidow, 2004: 224). These groups were against any type of regularization or amnesty, under the argument that it would only generate additional undocumented migrants, as the 1986 IRCA reform did, and unfairly reward those who violated the law by entering the United States illegally. Although some of Bush's collaborators argued that the Latino vote could balance the costs, it was not completely evident that it could reap the electoral benefits expected. Even if pursuing a closer relationship with Mexico or a migration agreement could be seen as positive by Latinos – by 2003 the largest minority group in the United States with a population of 37 million, 66 percent of Mexican origin (Clemetson, 2003)[6] – migration has not been the highest priority for this group in terms of their voting preferences, and even Mexicans and Mexican Americans are greatly divided on this issue (Gimpel and Kaufmann, 2001; Bustamante, 2006a; Jacoby, 2006; López and Minushkin, 2008). Moreover, as Leiken (2002) argues, after 9/11 and particularly once the Iraq war began, Bush's popularity increased greatly and his administration no longer considered it a priority to seek the Latino vote.

In June of 2001 Secretary Castañeda made a controversial statement at the Convention of the Association of Hispanic Journalists (June 20–23, 2001 in Phoenix, Arizona), implying that Mexico would not accept any agreement that did not include both a regularization and a temporary worker agreement, which he notoriously nicknamed "the whole enchilada." Although labor unions and the Latino community who had conditioned their support on the inclusion of the regularization clause saw it positively, it was not well received by the U.S. government (Fernández de Castro, 2002a: 124). Members of the cabinet and legislators considered it a provocation from Castañeda: "It infuriated Republicans as well as lower and middle level officials as it came through as a demand for 'all or nothing' and was seen in Washington as if someone were telling them what to do"; presumably, Colin Powell later told Castañeda that "it was an ill-considered and arrogant statement" and that "he was getting

---

[6] By 2009, this figure had increased to 46.9 million (U.S. Census, 2009).

ahead of President Bush" (Papademetriou, personal interview, 2005; see also Castañeda, 2006; 2007: 82).

Mohar argues that this insistence on a "whole enchilada" became one of the main flaws of the Mexican strategy, because even though it garnered support from important groups in the short term, in the bigger picture it made the Bush government take distance from the negotiations given the politicization of the issues of temporary worker programs and regularization (personal interview, 2005). In hindsight, even if Mexico had avoided this terminology and been more cautious in presenting it as an all-or-nothing negotiation, it is likely that the Bush administration would have stepped back anyway, given the divisiveness of the issue. Both Rico and González Gutiérrez coincide in their assessment that, even before 9/11, the United States was already pulling back in terms of its commitment to an agreement and was concerned about Mexico's preparedness to manage it: "Even before 9/11, there was reticence in the U.S. bureaucracy regarding a migration agreement given the lack of infrastructure and institutions in Mexico to manage and control migration flows" (Carlos Rico, personal interview, October, 2002). This raised a key discussion about Mexico's assessment of the costs and benefits of a migration agreement and what its commitment would entail, but as González Gutiérrez explains (personal interview, December 2004), this question was not sufficiently debated in Mexico:

It was clear that we were on a path where the U.S. was pulling back, even if 9/11 hadn't happened. Mexico used it as a way to justify what happened instead of presenting a more clear strategy and publicly discussing its differences with the U.S., which would have been healthier. Instead, 9/11 helped mummify the myth of a grand agreement. This is hurtful for Mexico; it's equal or worse than having the topic at the center of the agenda. It does not allow for a discussion about the fact that perhaps an agreement is not in Mexico's best interest, or at least for a debate about the costs that it would have. Mexico is not prepared for such an agreement. It needs to educate Mexican public opinion about the fact that negotiating with the U.S. implies costs.

In the spirit of their "special relationship" and "authentic partnership," the presidents met in Washington, D.C. in early September. In their joint statement of September 6, 2001 they highlighted the progress made by the Joint Working Group on Migration, which they described as "the most fruitful and frank dialogue we have ever had on a subject so important to both nations." They recognized migration issues as "deeply felt by our publics and vital to our prosperity, well-being, and the kind of societies we want to build." The most important aspect of this statement was that they agreed on the framework within which the "new and realistic approach" to migration was to be based. This included "matching willing workers with willing employers; serving the social and economic needs of both countries; respecting the human dignity of all migrants, regardless of their status; recognizing the contribution migrants make to enriching both societies; and shared responsibility for ensuring migration takes place through safe and legal channels." The presidents requested that the working group provide specific proposals with respect to border safety, a temporary worker program, and the status of undocumented Mexicans in the United States. Finally, they agreed to form the Partnership for Prosperity, a public–private alliance to address some of the root causes of migration and foster economic growth in Mexico, particularly in areas where most migrants came from.[7]

However, one of the main setbacks of this meeting was that President Fox insisted on setting a deadline for reaching an agreement and declared this publicly during his first statement on September 5, 2001. In Fernández de Castro's view (2002a: 121), this was a result of Castañeda's idea that they needed to move fast before the democratic bonus expired and before the groups opposing the agreement became stronger. This announcement made the U.S. team take an even more cautious approach to the discussions with Mexico. After Fox's speech, National Security Advisor Condoleezza Rice declared that the United States was aware that Fox had this objective. She explained the U.S. government was also committed to moving the discussions as fast as possible but, more importantly, to "doing it right, not just quickly."[8] Rice emphasized that by September 5, 2001 there was still no clear definition of what the agreement actually meant or the details on how the governments would proceed; there was just a set of shared objectives and principles for dealing with the problem bilaterally. Nevertheless, she clearly stressed the fact that there was no conception of a general amnesty. To some, this was a sign that the president and his advisors were taking a very cautious stance on the issue. Thus, even without a drastic change of context, as happened after 9/11, this meant that the future of the negotiations on a bilateral deal was going to be very difficult for Mexico. Even if the Mexican

---

[7] See the "Joint Statement between the United States of America and the United Mexican States," Washington, D.C., September 6, 2001 (available at http://georgewbush-whitehouse.archives.gov/news/releases/2001/09/20010906-8.html; last viewed February 10, 2011).

[8] See "National Security Advisor Condoleezza Rice Discusses State Visit," Press Briefing, September 5, 2001 (available at http://georgewbush-whitehouse.archives.gov/news/releases/2001/09/20010905-15.html; last viewed February 10, 2011).

government had a successful strategy to gain support from certain groups and congressmen, without high-level backing it became almost impossible to reach an agreement.

Conventional wisdom is that the 9/11 attacks were the main reason for the shift from a bilateral to a unilateral approach to migration management on the part of the United States. In contrast to this view, Jeffrey Davidow, Ambassador to Mexico at the time, argues that, even before the terrorist attacks, domestic U.S. political concerns and intra-administration differences made a negotiation with Mexico almost impossible. Furthermore, Davidow (2004: 217) claims that real negotiations in the classic form of diplomatic bargaining never actually took place and the Mexican government overestimated the process. In his view, "the Mexicans insisted on calling the talks a negotiation, while the Americans preferred the more casual *conversations* or *discussions*." Mohar clarifies that Davidow may be right in the sense that by September 2001 the negotiators had not yet discussed the specific details of a bilateral agreement, particularly regarding what Mexico would offer, but the fact was that there were high-level meetings where the framework for possible agreements on the common management of these issues was seriously discussed (personal interview, 2005).[9]

On the basis of this evidence, it is likely that even if the events of 9/11 had not occurred, the Bush administration would have eventually taken a step back from the idea of a migration agreement because of the political costs that it entailed. Moreover, taking into account the differing positions between and within the Democratic and Republican parties, which were not only evident at that point but have always made the debate over immigration reform a very long and controversial process, it is hard to imagine that this migration accord would have been passed as such in the U.S. Congress.

BREAKDOWN OF THE DISCUSSIONS, YET MEXICO PERSEVERES

The fact is that after September 11, 2001 the course of this bilateral dialogue was altered as the U.S. government's foreign and domestic policy priorities changed. Although migration issues were not dropped completely from the agenda, they were addressed in a very different

---

9 Papademetriou argues that Davidow's assessment is derived from the fact that the negotiations were held at a very high level, which meant that at the time very few people had information about the actual process. In his view, there was definitely a real commitment on both sides to move forward in these negotiations (personal interview, 2005).

manner by the Bush administration. As Mohar (2004) explains, "the ability of the terrorists to elude the controls, regulations, and scrutiny aimed at foreigners arriving in the U.S. sparked a re-conceptualization of how to protect U.S. borders and prevent the entry of any foreign nationals who would pose a new threat." Thus, after 9/11, immigration was viewed through a security lens and cooperation with Mexico was limited to the control of the borders and related security issues.

Although U.S. officials declared that they were still interested in the proposal for a migration agreement, there was no progress in this regard at meetings between cabinet members or between the presidents in the following year. For example, in February of 2002, James Ziglar, director of the INS, declared that the proposal for a migration agreement between Mexico and the United States was still a key issue for both countries and a fundamental aspect of U.S. security: "[S]ome people think that the dialogue with Mexico ended after 9/11 but that's not the case; proof of it is the meetings we had last week with Undersecretary of State Mary Ryan, and Mexican officials, with whom we analyzed proposals to improve the possibilities of passing a migration agreement" (Unomásuno, 2002).·

At the Presidential meeting of March 22, 2002 in Monterrey, the presidents issued a joint statement in which they declared that they would continue the work begun on February 16, 2001 to create a framework for the management of migration, although they did not mention the idea of an agreement:

Slightly more than one year ago, in Guanajuato, we talked about migration as one of the major ties that join our societies. We launched then the frankest and most productive dialogue our countries have ever had on this important and challenging subject. Those talks have continued over the past year, and have yielded a clearer assessment of the scope and nature of this issue. This bond between our nations can render countless benefits to our respective economies and families. Over the past year, important progress has been made to enhance migrant safety and particularly in saving lives by discouraging and reducing illegal crossings in dangerous terrain. On September 7, 2001, during President Fox's historic State Visit to Washington, we issued a joint statement instructing our cabinet-level working group to provide us with specific proposals to forge a new and realistic framework that will ensure a safe, legal, orderly, and dignified migration flow between our countries. We have today agreed that our Cabinet level migration group should continue the work we charged it with in Guanajuato and Washington.[10]

[10] See "Joint Statement by the Presidents of the United States and Mexico," Monterrey, Mexico, March 22, 2002 (available at http://georgewbush-whitehouse.archives .gov/news/releases/2002/03/20020322-9.html; last viewed February 10, 2011).

Although there was no progress on the migration accord, Mexico and the United States continued to collaborate closely on the security front based on the 22-point Mexico–United States Border Partnership Action Plan, also known as the Smart Borders Initiative, signed at the meeting in Monterrey. This included agreements in areas of infrastructure and secure flow of people and goods. They also signed the Partnership for Prosperity initiative to promote foreign and domestic investment in Mexico's marginal areas, although it was considered a limited initiative that appeared "to stand little chance of raising Mexican living standards significantly, and thereby reducing pressures to migrate" (Alba, 2004). Migration-related initiatives were thus left out of the bilateral agenda, and in November 2002 Colin Powell declared that the political conditions did not exist in the United States to advance the migration discussions and Mexican officials should be patient (Mohar, 2004). From then on, and until the end of the Fox administration, the idea of a migration agreement was no longer formally discussed at the bilateral level. Nevertheless, the Mexican government maintained this proposal as a guideline for its position and activities on immigration.

Instead of retreating at the sign of the U.S. disinterest, as would have been expected given Mexico's traditional position on the issue and its concern about creating tensions in the bilateral relationship, the Mexican government continued insisting on the idea of a migration agreement. President Fox went as far as declaring that there would be no "special relationship between Mexico and the U.S. if they did not address the immigration issue in a comprehensive manner"; he stated that achieving a migration agreement would be the ultimate test ("*la prueba de fuego*") of their commitment to a new and closer relationship (Melgar, 2002). In September, 2002, Castañeda announced that after the midterm elections in the United States, Mexico would launch a "great offensive" targeting the parties in the U.S. Congress to promote Mexico's position, "using the lobbying companies that we have had for some time" as well as the consulates and the Embassy (Millán and Torre, 2002). In October, 2002, the Mexican government announced the hiring of ZEMI Communications, a high-priced consulting agency in New York, to promote Mexico's position in the United States. Alan Stoga, president of ZEMI, declared that they would aim to create a positive debate regarding key issues in the bilateral relations, such as immigration, through a coalition of Democratic and Republican legislators, labor unions, business leaders, and state and local governments (Armendáriz, 2002; Corchado and Sandoval, 2002).

CONTINUING TO LOBBY FOR IMMIGRATION REFORM

In January of 2003, Castañeda presented his resignation as Secretary of Foreign Affairs, reportedly out of frustration with the stalemate in relations with the United States, including the migration agreement (Weiner, 2003). Although the importance given to migration issues was mainly attributed to his own interests and personality, this agenda remained a priority during his successor's term. On January 27, 2003 Fox announced that Mexico would "continue with its proposal to achieve a migration agreement but would now diversify its strategy, working with local governments and with Congressmen in order to create a broader consensus that would lead to an agreement at the federal level at a faster pace" (Guerrero, 2003). Although Secretary of Foreign Affairs Luis Ernesto Derbez did not fully agree with the idea of a migration agreement and neither did Gerónimo Gutierrez, the Undersecretary for North American Affairs (González Gutiérrez, personal interview, 2004; Mohar, personal interview, 2005; Castañeda, 2007: 93), they maintained the issue as a priority in the agenda. According to Derbez (2003), they changed part of the strategy and the language, moving from the idea of "*the* migration agreement" to a broader framework of "agreements" and a more ambiguous concept of a "migration package":

The goals are clear: we want agreements that recognize in migration a regional phenomenon that should be addressed through objective, comprehensive and long-term criteria. We are looking for a negotiation with our northern neighbor for a comprehensive migration package that includes: a) the regularization of undocumented Mexicans living in that country; b) border security; c) increase in the number of visas for temporary workers, and d) economic development.

Still, this concept of a so-called package was not widely used, and President Fox kept insisting on the idea of a migration agreement, now also emphasizing the issue of border security.

Derbez also deemphasized the focus on the United States–Mexico relationship, responding to strong criticisms in Mexico regarding the concentration of the agenda on the United States and the alleged bad management of relationships with Latin America during Castañeda's tenure (Derbez, 2003). This reflects the fact that within conservative sectors of the government and members of the Foreign Service, there are groups that disagree with making the relationship with the United States the highest priority in the agenda (Green, 2006b; Sepúlveda, personal interview, 2006). As Jorge Lomonaco (2006), then Consul in Miami, explains, "the Foreign Service was one of the spaces of public service where there was greatest resistance to change when President Fox took office." Although some strategies changed in the second half of the Fox administration, in general the Mexican government's attitude toward migration issues since 2000 was consistent, beyond individual interests and beyond the context of Fox's democratic bonus in 2000. Undersecretary Gerónimo Gutiérrez (2005) recognized that "the issue has occupied a space in the public agenda that is hardly reversible" and that "the notion that the administration of the migration phenomenon requires a shared approach has gained terrain." As well, President Calderón's incoming administration in December of 2006 explained that it would not focus the whole foreign policy agenda on migration but "this does not mean that we will stop lobbying for immigration reform" (Ballinas and Becerril, 2007).

The fact that despite the lack of progress in the bilateral agenda the government no longer considered it feasible to return to the previously existing status quo was not only a result of the Fox administration's making it a priority in its agenda, but also reflects the development of a decade-long process of change in the government's attitude toward these issues, which provided a strong basis for this more proactive approach. At the same time, the problems faced by Mexican migrants in the United States in a context of heightened security concerns and anti-immigrant attitudes also implied a need for new responses from the Mexican government.

Considering that the U.S. agenda was focused on security issues after 9/11, the Mexican government adapted its proposal for a migration agreement, arguing that the shared management of migration flows through formal cooperation mechanisms and the regularization of undocumented immigrants in the United States would contribute to the country's security by "bringing them out of the shadows" (González, 2003). Mexico also focused on giving the United States guarantees of its commitment to enhancing security at the border. For example, on April 23, 2003, Secretary of Homeland Security Tom Ridge and Secretary of Government Santiago Creel issued a joint statement on enhanced bilateral cooperation to create a "smart border" that facilitates the transit of goods and people while protecting against crime and terrorism. On May 6, 2003, the day before a meeting with Secretary of State Colin Powell in Washington, D.C., Secretary Derbez indicated in a speech at the Centre for Strategic and International Studies that security was the number one priority for Mexico (Storrs, 2005: 6). On June 3, 2003, U.S. and Mexican officials announced the launch of Operation Desert Safeguard to save migrants' lives by deploying more and better-equipped Border Patrol agents west of Nogales, Arizona, increasing the number of warnings (in Spanish) of the dangers, and taking more forceful measures against smugglers (Storrs, 2005: 7). However, this did not render any results in terms of reviving the bilateral discussions over a migration agreement.

The only mention of a migration agreement was an unfortunate statement – which was mainly reported in Mexican media (Sarmiento, 2003) – by the House International Relations Committee in May of 2003 proposing that the U.S. government should negotiate a migration accord with Mexico that would include opening the Mexican petroleum monopoly to reform and investment by U.S. oil companies and address other issues such as extradition and law enforcement issues (Storrs, 2005: 6). Mexican officials and public intellectuals were outraged by this suggestion; they considered it an intrusion in Mexico's domestic affairs and argued that oil was not subject to any negotiation (Granados Chapa, 2003; Núñez and Salazar, 2003; Pineda, 2003; Sarmiento, 2003). The President's office issued a statement on May 11, 2003, acknowledging that the negotiation of a migration agreement was a priority for the Fox Administration, but pointing out that "negotiating such an agreement in exchange for opening up PEMEX to foreign investment would be wholly unacceptable" (Storrs, 2005: 6). This reflects one of the strong elements of nationalism that remain in Mexico regarding any U.S. negotiation, which was also evident in the 1970s when the U.S. indicated its interest in negotiating a new Bracero Program in exchange for oil.

This is also tied to the discussion of what Mexico was willing to offer in exchange for a migration agreement, which was never clear. Had the discussions for an agreement gone any further, this issue would have been very problematic, as Mexico had limited resources and infrastructure for the management of such a large temporary worker program or providing security at the borders (the situation at the southern border was particularly worrying); depending on the terms, this could have also led to an outcry from nationalist groups (Rubio, 2004; Berruga, personal interview, 2005; Mohar, personal interview, 2005).

FROM MIGRATION AGREEMENT TO COMPREHENSIVE IMMIGRATION REFORM

In January of 2004, President Bush presented a proposal for a temporary worker program based on the idea that the current U.S. immigration system "is not working" and "as a nation that values immigration, and depends on immigration, we should have immigration laws that work and make us proud." He called for a program that would "match willing foreign workers with willing American employers, when no Americans can be found to fill the jobs." It would also make U.S. immigration laws "more rational and more humane," without "jeopardizing the livelihoods of American citizens" and at the same time guarantee security, control of the borders, and meet the country's economic needs.[11] Although he did not introduce a formal bill, this proposal began a debate in Congress that led to various legislative proposals for immigration reform, particularly throughout 2005.[12]

In this scenario, the Mexican strategy gradually refocused and moved toward the idea of promoting a comprehensive immigration reform, including the five points on which the proposal for the migration agreement was based, and lobbying in favor of the bills that coincided with Mexico's position. In their statements, President Fox, the Secretary of Foreign Affairs, the Undersecretary for North American Affairs, the Ambassador to the United States, and various consuls strongly emphasized the government's support of certain bills such as the McCain–Kennedy initiative. This proposed legislation was closest to the Mexicans' position in terms of a flexible regularization process and a temporary worker program with an opportunity for adjustment of status. They also expressed their opposition regarding other bills such as the Cornyn–Kyl Bill, particularly the fact that it required immigrants to return to their home country before applying for a new status and did not allow for an adjustment of status after participating in a temporary worker program. Their greatest concern was the Sensenbrenner Bill, as it focused mainly on border security measures (such as extending existing fences at the United States–Mexico border) and criminalized undocumented immigration, and those who provided aid to immigrants under such status.

---

[11] See "President Bush Proposes New Temporary Worker Program," January 7, 2004 (available at http://georgewbush-whitehouse.archives.gov/news/releases/2004/01/20040107-3.html; last viewed February 10, 2011).
[12] Some examples of the various legislative proposals are as follows: Jackson–Lee (HR 2092), introduced on May 4, 2005; Kennedy–McCain (S. 1033), introduced on May 12, 2005; Tancredo (HR 3333), introduced on July 19, 2005; Cornyn–Kyl (S. 1438), introduced on July 20, 2005; Hagel (S. 1916–1919), introduced on October 25, 2005; Sensenbrenner (HR 4437), introduced on December 6, 2005 and passed in the House on December 15, 2005; Specter (S. 2611), introduced on April 7, 2006 and passed in the Senate on May 25, 2006; and the Secure Borders, Economic Opportunity and Immigration Reform Act of 2007 (S. 1348), introduced on May 9, 2007.

President Fox described the Sensenbrenner Bill and the proposal to extend the fence along the Mexico–United States border as "a 'shameful' setback in bilateral relations and as a troubling reflection of America's willingness to tolerate 'xenophobic groups that impose the law at will'" (quoted in Thompson, 2005). Secretary Derbez condemned it as "stupid" and "underhanded" (quoted in Weissert, 2005). In response to these statements, Sensenbrenner accused Mexico of intervening in U.S. domestic affairs, to which Secretary Derbez responded that the Mexican government would "do whatever is necessary to defend the human and labor rights of Mexicans who emigrate," stressing that this did not represent an intervention in the U.S.'s domestic politics (quoted in García, 2005). At a meeting in Mexico City on January 9, 2006, a group of Latin American Foreign Ministers and other officials issued a joint declaration that included a statement against "partial measures that only focus on reinforcing security" (IME, 2006a). Finally, Mexico declared that it would intensify its lobbying efforts, particularly with legislators in Congress, and also called on the immigrant leadership to organize and exercise pressure to promote a comprehensive immigration reform (García, 2006a; Gómez Quintero, 2006).

Despite these efforts, on October 26, 2006, President Bush signed Congress's Bill HR 6061 "to establish operational control over the international land and maritime borders of the United States," which included extending the fence along the United States–Mexico border and allocating more resources for Border Patrol operations. The Mexican government sent a diplomatic note to the United States that expressed its opposition to this initiative. In November of 2006, at the Ibero-American Summit, the presidents and government representatives of these countries issued a statement (*Declaración de Montevideo*) at the initiative of the Mexican delegation. In this statement, among other commitments to managing immigration with respect to human rights, they rejected any initiative to build fences and walls between borders.[13]

Although these reactions from the Mexican government can be likened to the statements and actions against Proposition 187 in California, in this case the Mexican government's actions were not a response to one event but rather a continuation of a consistent position throughout the Fox administration whereby the government openly expressed its opinion for or against federal and state law initiatives in the United States. Never before had the Mexican government been so vocal against U.S. proposed

[13] Mexican Foreign Ministry, Internal Communiqué, November 8, 2006.

federal legislation on immigration issues. This reaction was not limited to the Sensenbrenner Bill, the most extreme of the proposals.

In addition to these activities, the Mexican government also met with key legislators and with groups that could support its position. Carlos Félix, Minister for Migration Affairs at the Mexican Embassy in Washington, D.C., explained in a personal interview that the objective of this "diplomatic effort" (a term he says he prefers to "lobbying," because these activities were not publicized and could lead to accusations of interventionism) was to "sensitize" legislators to the Mexican government's concerns (personal interview, 2006). As part of this campaign, in December of 2005, the Foreign Ministry also announced the hiring of a Dallas-based consultant, Rob Allyn, to improve Mexico's image in the United States (Iliff, 2005). In Félix's view, the fact that cooperation on the management of migration with Mexico and other sending countries was included in the McCain–Kennedy Bill and recognized as an important component of immigration reform by other legislators was one of the main achievements of the Mexican strategy (personal interview, 2006).

MATRÍCULAS CONSULARES: BROADENING THE DEFINITION OF "CONSULAR PROTECTION"

In addition to these lobbying activities with regard to U.S. legislation on migration, the Mexican government also developed a broader interpretation of its traditional view of consular protection through activities that in the past could have been considered interventionist – and in some cases still lead to such criticism by conservative groups in the United States. In the absence of immigration reform and in a context of heightened security concerns and anti-immigrant backlash after 9/11, Castañeda and Derbez both emphasized that one of the government's main activities to support Mexican migrants was the issuance of consular IDs (*matrículas consulares*). To promote its acceptance as a valid form of ID in the United States, the government introduced new security features for the production of the card and lobbied financial institutions, cities, counties, and police departments to validate it (Castañeda, 2003; Derbez, 2003).

Although Mexican consulates have offered this form of ID since 1871 – based on a practice recognized by the Vienna Convention on Consular Relations – it was only after the terrorist attacks of September 11, 2001 and the increase in detentions, raids, and security measures that affected Mexican immigrants when the Mexican government considered it necessary to issue a new secure version and widely promote the acceptance of this form of ID by U.S. financial institutions, police departments, and government offices. It was mainly intended for Mexicans living abroad who could not obtain a Mexican passport or any form of official ID in the United States, or simply needed a more "portable" identification card that included their address in the United States (the *matrícula* does not provide any information on the person's migratory status and is mainly intended as a form of ID for daily activities). Contrary to Castañeda's (2007: 149) assertion that the *matrículas* were an instrument for "de facto legalization" or "backdoor amnesty," these consular IDs in no way affect the legal status of Mexicans in the United States; their main function is as a form of identification that, as a result of Mexico's lobbying efforts, is accepted by many police departments and financial institutions.

To update the document's design and adjust to U.S. security standards, in 2002 the Mexican government issued a new version of its consular IDs with improved security features. In addition, the Foreign Ministry updated its technology to create an up-to-date and secure database that would enable the government to contact the person or his or her family in case of an emergency, based on the information provided during the registration for a *matrícula consular*.[14] The advantages of the document were widely publicized and the government encouraged Mexican migrants to obtain it.

Against criticisms about whether foreign governments should be allowed to issue this type of identification in the United States, the Mexican government justified it as a document that can facilitate identification in case of an emergency as well as assist "law enforcement officials' communication with migrant communities by ensuring that people are not afraid to come forward as witnesses and report crimes" (IME, 2004c). As a result of the Mexican government's lobbying efforts, by the end of 2006 more than 400 financial institutions, 390 cities, 170 counties, and 1,200 police departments considered that the document was safe and facilitated the identification of residents in their localities (IME, 2006b). In 2006 it was estimated that more than 4 million Mexicans had a consular ID (González Gutiérrez, 2006b).

As part of this effort, the Mexican government organized a campaign through the consulates and the IME to promote consular IDs at

---

[14] The database has also been used to produce statistics about the characteristics of the Mexican population in the United States such as their state of origin and destination. See "Estadísticas de Mexicanos en el Exterior" (available at http://www .ime.gob.mx/ime2/index.php?option=com_content&task=view&id=158&Itemid=55; last viewed February 12, 2011).

financial institutions as one of the documents accepted in order to open a bank account. This became a key element in reducing the number of "unbanked" people among Mexican immigrants[15] and eliminating informal or illegal channels for transactions. It also reduced the cost of sending remittances to Mexico.[16] According to the Mexican government's estimates, between 2002 and 2004 "the increase in use of bank transfers as a means for sending remittances has led to savings of more than $700 million for migrants and their families" (IME, 2004c). As Gustavo Cano points out, an important aspect of the campaign to promote the *matrículas* was the fact that local U.S. officials were convinced of its importance and usefulness, which can be attributed to the Mexican government's development of a comprehensive strategy to justify the issuance and acceptance of the document: "The *matrícula* effort has triumphed not only because of Mexico's lobbying, but more important[ly], because U.S. community leaders strongly embrace the idea. The *matrícula consular* has opened a new communication channel between local communities and immigrants where none existed before" (quoted in Rozemberg, 2002). On the Mexican government's part, this reflects an enhanced use of the consular network and their contacts at the local level, which is also part of the process of developing a better understanding of U.S. politics and making a wider use of the channels available at various levels.

However, the active promotion of *matrículas*, and particularly their acceptance by financial institutions, also triggered a set of negative reactions from conservative groups. In response to a group of legislators' concerns, in July of 2003 the Treasury Department opened a period of

---

[15] According to the Foreign Ministry, "by July 2004, Wells Fargo estimated that it had over 200,000 new accounts since it began accepting the *matrículas consulares* in November 2001." In the Chicago area, eight surveyed banks reported that by June 2003, "12,978 new bank accounts had been opened, representing $50 million dollars in deposits"; see "Most Frequently Asked Questions Regarding the Matrícula Consular (MCAS)," Secretaría de Relaciones Exteriores, July 20, 2004 (available at http://bit.ly/hG1coB; last viewed February 12, 2011).

[16] As part of this effort, the Mexican government encouraged the reduction of transfer fees for remittances between financial institutions in Mexico and the United States. In 2001, the Bank of Mexico and the U.S. Federal Reserve signed the Directo a México initiative in 2001 in the context of the United States–Mexico Partnership for Prosperity. This initiative has helped reduce the transfer fees for remittances from an average of $20 dollars to $3 dollars (based on an average transfer of $350 dollars). By 2008, more than 340 banks in forty-two U.S. states were part of the initiative (Alberto Mendoza, Presentation on Directo a Mexico at the Annual Meeting of IME Personnel, Mexico City, March 10–12, 2008; see also www.directoamexico.com). As part of developments in this area, in October of 2005 the Bank of America began the Safe Send program, which offers money transfers at no additional cost (see Williams, 2005).

public comment on its bank rules regarding the acceptance of consular IDs. The consular network, the IME, and various Mexican-American, Hispanic, and pro-immigrant organizations widely publicized the survey and encouraged people to respond in favor of maintaining the current regulations. As reported by *The Wall Street Journal*, "behind the scenes, the Mexican government itself did a lot of work to support the card, mobilizing the Mexican immigrant community in the U.S. to push for a favorable decision. Those efforts – and the payoff – show how Mexico has developed considerable lobbying muscle by teaming up with the Mexican-American community" (Porter, 2003). Out of more than 24,000 participants, 83 percent approved the acceptance of the *matrículas* by financial institutions and the Treasury decided to maintain its existing regulations.

The Mexican government considers this as one of its main achievements in terms of lobbying activities in favor of the Mexican community and developing a common agenda with the communities abroad (González Gutiérrez, 2006b). Criticisms continue to date against the consulates' promotion of the *matrícula*, considered by some as a document that "encourages illegal immigration" (Sullivan, 2007), "is not a secure form of ID" (Dinan, 2006), and attempts "to 'document' the undocumented and make an end run around Congress" (Archibold, 2007).[17] In response, González Gutiérrez argues that as "long as we disseminate information in a frank and transparent manner we are acting like countless other players in the American political system.... We believe that nothing that we do is against the interests of the United States or against Mexico's interests" (quoted in Porter, 2003). This reflects the better understanding of U.S. system by the Mexican elite, which is part of the process of rapprochement between the countries that began in the late 1980s. It also provides evidence of the change in the government's interpretation of what is considered intervention regarding the protection of migrants' rights.

Nonetheless, there is still a lack of a clear definition of what the government is willing and able to do in this regard, particularly when it faces negative reactions from the United States. An example is the situation that arose after the Mexican government published a 2-million edition

---

[17] A noteworthy example of continued opposition to the *matrículas* is the HB 2460/SB 1236 Bill passed by the Congress in Arizona, which rejected the acceptance of consular IDs in the state. Governor Janet Napolitano vetoed the bill on May 8, 2007, under the consideration that without consular IDs, undocumented migrants would probably resort to obtaining fraudulent documents.

of the *Migrants' Guide* (*Guía del Migrante*) in December of 2004. The guide was actually a 32-page comic book that informed migrants about the risks of crossing the border through certain areas and of living in the United States without the necessary documents. It also gave advice regarding U.S. laws in order to prevent problems. However, in this case, at the signs of strong reactions from groups of legislators and anti-immigrant groups who argued that the Mexican government was promoting illegal immigration, it quietly retreated.

The Undersecretary for North America declared they would consider canceling the printing and distribution of the guides, and the issue was never mentioned again.[18] It is worth noting that, in this case, not only anti-immigrant groups but other sectors that would generally support the Mexican government's activities also considered that this went too far. For example, Randel Johnson, Vice-President for Labor, Immigration and Employer Benefits, U.S. Chamber of Commerce, who participated in the United States–Mexico Migration Panel, argued that "the *Guía del Migrante* was a big mistake" and it was a sign that "Mexico needs to be more cautious and conscious of tensions surrounding the issue" (personal interview, 2005). Perhaps it was the fact that, as opposed to the *matrícula*, there was no strong support of this idea from U.S. groups favorable to Mexico's position that made the Mexican government take a step back.

A similar initiative proposed in January of 2006 by Mexico's National Human Rights Commission to distribute maps of the Arizona desert at Mexican consulates to warn immigrants of the dangers of crossing through the area was dropped after the U.S. government expressed its opposition "in the strongest terms" (Gamboa, 2006). Reflecting a change in strategy, in 2008 the commission published two comic books attempting to dissuade immigration by disseminating stories about the horrors that migrants may face in crossing the border. As noted in a report by *USA Today*, "the tone is very different from previous government publications that focused more on travel and safety tips" (Hawley and Solache, 2008), which reflects Mexico's consideration of previous reactions to its publications for emigrants.

Regardless of the negative reactions in the United States, the initiative behind the 2004 *Guía del Migrante* was considered a positive sign by some groups in Mexico in terms of representing a new proactive

[18] The Ministry for Foreign Affairs later removed the guide from its Web site but an online version of it can still be found (see http://www.americanpatrol.com/AID_ABET/MEXICO/HOW-2-INVADE-GUIDE/01.html; last viewed, June 24, 2010).

attitude from the Mexican government regarding its responsibility toward Mexican immigrants and moving away from simply "masking its paralysis and disinterest with a verbosity that proclaimed its commitment to the *paisanos*" (Aguayo, 2005). Moreover, the fact that, despite opposition from certain groups in the United States *and* in Mexico, the Foreign Minsitry continued promoting the *matrículas consulares* – an initiative of much greater consequence than the *Guía del Migrante* – reveals that there is confidence on the possibilities for a wider room for action on the Mexican government's part.

Still, in Mexico there was concern about potential pressures from the United States in sensitive issues, such as the promotion of *matrículas consulares*, if the Mexican delegation voted against the U.S. intervention in Iraq in the Security Council. In response to these concerns, Adolfo Aguilar Zinser (Mexico's Ambassador to the UN at the time) argued that the debate over the consular IDs would follow its own destiny, which, in his view, was independent of Mexico's vote for or against the United States in the UN (see Aguayo, 2003). Carlos Rico also argued that "the vote regarding Iraq does not change the relationship in general: They'll use it against us whenever it is convenient, but the U.S. depends on the economic and security ties with Mexico" (personal interview, 2003). This supports Aguayo's (2003) view that the general stability in the United States–Mexico relationship, despite economic, diplomatic, or political crises (such as Mexico's position in the Security Council against the Iraq war), has shown that "the costs of disagreeing with the U.S. are manageable" and sharing a border with the United States is not an obstacle but rather provides an opportunity that can be used to Mexico's advantage.

Another significant example of Mexico's use of new tools to defend emigrants' rights, even in cases of strong disagreement with the United States, is the Avena Case, brought to the International Court of Justice (ICJ) in January of 2003. This case involves fifty-two Mexican emigrants who were charged with the death penalty in the United States. On March 31, 2004 the ICJ ruled in favor of the Mexican nationals, ordering the United States to revise each case and reconsider each verdict based on the alleged absence of due process and violation of the Vienna Convention on Consular Relations. By December of 2005, the death penalty sentence had been commuted in five cases (Román, 2005). By October 2007, one of the cases was being heard by the Supreme Court and forty-six cases were still pending; the death penalty had not been exercised in any of them (Olson, 2007). Although this was considered a significant victory for Mexico and an important precedent in terms of recourse to international institutions, on March 25, 2008 the U.S. Supreme Court rejected the ICJ's ruling, arguing that the judgment is binding on the United States in international law but that state courts did not have the obligation to carry it out (Biskupic, 2008). Mexico and groups such as Amnesty International protested the Supreme Court's decision, but by May of 2008 there was no sign of a change in the U.S. position. This is an example of the persisting obstacles that the Mexican state faces in pursuing its interests and defending migrants' rights vis-à-vis a host state with a greater capacity to undertake unilateral policies and to ignore the potential costs in bilateral or multilateral relations.

TOWARD AN EXPLICIT POSITION ON IMMIGRATION

Finally, toward the end of the Fox administration, for the first time Mexico made its own position on migration clear and explicit through the document "Mexico and the Migration Phenomenon" (published in English and Spanish). This document was the first serious attempt at reaching a consensus at the national level regarding Mexico's position on the management of migration and its response to an eventual immigration reform in the United States. The position document was the result of a working group convened by the Executive and the Senate, made up of Mexican government officials, legislators, academics, and experts on migration issues as well as representatives of nongovernmental and civil organizations. The main points of the report were that the current migration situation required a new approach from the Mexican government, assuming its responsibility as a sending, receiving, and transit country. It maintained and emphasized the idea of shared responsibility that served as the basis for the United States–Mexico Migration Panel's report and that underlay the proposal for a migration agreement. The document made no mention of a migration agreement but rather stressed the need for general collaboration between the countries as the only way to manage migration effectively and make any new U.S. legislation workable.[19]

The "Mexico and the Migration Phenomenon" document was made public in Mexico on October 24, 2005, and sent as a special bulletin

---

[19] The document is available in an online version (see http://www.sre.gob.mx/eventos/ fenomenomigratorio/docs/mexicofrentealfenommig.pdf; last viewed May 31, 2007). See also Gutiérrez (2005) and Derbez (2006).

through the newsletter service *Lazos*,[20] administered by the Institute of Mexicans Abroad (IME, 2005). The document was also sent by means of official notification from the Undersecretary for North America to all the Mexican Consulates in the United States.[21] Thus, it became the basis for Mexico's position on the issue and a great effort was made to disseminate it, particularly in the United States. The New York Consulate, for example, distributed the document widely among state and local legislators, think tanks, and academics.[22]

As a result of these efforts, on March 8, 2006 the House International Relations Committee sent out a "Dear Colleague" letter to bring other legislators' attention to the document, arguing that it represented "the first public acknowledgment that Mexico must accept responsibility for solving the immigration problem" and that it made a "very important contribution to the debate in both countries." They also considered that "these principles and the accompanying recommendations represent a sharp departure from past practices in Mexico."[23]

Finally, on March 20, 2006, Mexico paid for a full-page advertisement in three of the main U.S. newspapers – *The New York Times*, *The Washington Post*, and *The Los Angeles Times* – titled "A Message from Mexico about Migration." This summarized the key aspects of the "Mexico and the Migration Phenomenon" document and emphasized Mexico's obligation to promote development in Mexico in order to reduce emigration pressures, as well as its commitment to securing the border and fighting criminal organizations and smugglers (Reinert, 2006). The timing was probably not a coincidence; the ads were published just a few days before the 22nd United States–Mexico Binational Commission meeting in Washington, D.C. (March 24, 2006), a week before the U.S. Senate was due to reconvene and continue the debate on pending immigration legislation (March 27, 2006), and two weeks before a trilateral meeting between presidents Vicente Fox, George W. Bush, and Paul Martin, the Canadian Primer Minister, in Cancún, México (March 31, 2006).

---

[20] This newsletter service is aimed mainly at Mexican and Hispanic community leaders, businessmen, academics, students, and opinion leaders in the United States; in 2006, the IME reported having 11,400 subscribers (IME, 2006b).

[21] Mexican Foreign Ministry, Internal Communiqué, October 24, 2005.

[22] Personal observation at the Mexican Consulate in New York, October 2005.

[23] See "Mexican Congress Adopts Resolution to Address Illegal Immigration," Congress of the United States, Washington, D.C., March 8, 2006 (available at www.sandiego.edu/peacestudies/documents/tbi/kolbefinal.pdf; last viewed February 11, 2011).

This represented a fundamental shift from the position maintained in 1986 during the process leading to the passage of IRCA in which the Mexican government chose not to get involved in the debates over the content of the legislation and did not take an explicit position on the issue. It was also a much stronger position than the one assumed in 1996 when the government simply expressed its concern with the IIRIRA, AEDPA, and PRWORA laws once they were passed. These changes are significant in terms of the sending state's engagement with the host state's migration agenda, moving away from the passive attitude of the past. Clearly, the extent to which this has actually led to changes in U.S. migration policies or in Mexico's policies to address the causes of emigration is limited. However, on the Mexican side a significant change can be seen in consular protection activities and in the relationship with the migrant communities, which has long-term implications both in terms of migrants' integration into the host state and in terms of their economic and political influence in the home state. This will be discussed in greater detail in the next chapter.

CONCLUSIONS

Notwithstanding the unsuccessful results of the ground-breaking initiative for a migration agreement with the United States, the fact that Mexico formally promoted an agenda for collaboration on migration at the bilateral level and continued insisting on the guidelines for a comprehensive immigration reform, even after it was evident that there would be no agreement between the countries, signifies a fundamental change in its traditional position of limited engagement on these issues.

On the one hand, this represented a momentary shift in the Mexican government's strategy of delinkage, because cooperation on migration issues was included in a broader agenda for collaboration and as part of a move toward strengthening the North American economic community (or a NAFTA-Plus). On the other hand, Mexico's long-standing position of limited participation in the U.S. internal debate concerning immigration, based on the principle of nonintervention, was significantly modified. At first, it was an implicit change in Mexico's position, given that the Mexican government was promoting an agenda for a migration agreement that necessarily implied a reform of U.S. legislation on immigration. However, once the possibility of collaboration through a bilateral agreement collapsed, the Mexican government gradually turned toward an explicit promotion of immigration reform in the United States in favor of Mexican migrants. This included taking an open and more clearly defined position on certain proposals for immigration reform, lobbying activities, and continuous emphasis on the need for a comprehensive immigration reform based on the five aspects included in the initial discussions for a migration agreement and on the concept of shared responsibility. The Mexican government also took a step forward in terms of making its own position explicit, accepting its responsibility, and making commitments in terms of managing migration and creating job opportunities in Mexico to prevent further emigration.

At the domestic level, the change of regime in the year 2000 was a crucial factor determining the Fox administration's position on emigration, because it was believed that the democratic bonus offered an opportunity to obtain a favorable response from the United States in the proposal for a migration agreement. At the same time, the fact that a new party gained power after seventy years of PRI rule meant that it could detach itself from the responsibility implied in the failure of the previous regime's development and migration policies, thus leading to changes in discourse and strategies related to emigration.

The change in the perception of migrants by considering them to be heroes and emphasizing their contributions through remittances was significant in terms of giving more public attention to this issue and pressuring the government to actively defend the interests of migrants and their families. This was made evident particularly in the context after 9/11, given the rise in anti-immigrant reactions. At the same time, migrants became increasingly politicized in the United States and in Mexico and successfully carried forward some of their demands for more significant participation in Mexican politics, as will be discussed in the next chapter.

Gradually, a consensus is developing in Mexico about the need for a clear position on migration, although there is still an open debate about what this should be. More groups (civil society, Congress, political parties, and academics) are now participating actively and jointly in this discussion (as exemplified by the "Mexico and the Migration Phenomenon" document). Particularly with regard to the United States, whereas some members of the government and some public intellectuals are convinced of the need to move beyond a definition of Mexican nationalism as anti-Americanism, which is contradictory with the reality of the concentration of commercial and social exchanges between the countries, this novel approach to the bilateral relationship is disputed by more conservative groups within the governing elite, political parties, and public opinion

(Krauze, 2005). This debate has called into question what Mexico's foreign policy should consist of in the current bilateral, regional, and global context as well as the definition of its relationship with the United States and of its migration policies (Meyer, 2003b; 2005b).

At the international level, the fact that the stability of the bilateral relationship has not been significantly affected by any of the government's new activities in terms of reacting against U.S. legislation and lobbying for a specific agenda on immigration issues, or by its new consular protection activities, including the promotion of consular IDs, has allowed Mexico to take advantage of opportunities within the U.S. political system to promote its interests without fear of provoking U.S. interference in its own domestic affairs or creating tensions in the bilateral relationship, as was traditionally argued. On the one hand, Mexico has developed a better understanding of the United States and has identified groups that it can work with. This allows the government to design new strategies to support the Mexican migrant community that move away from traditional conceptions of nonintervention in consular protection (Rico in interview with Thelen, 1999). On the other hand, the level of integration and interdependence between the countries strengthens the idea that the United States will not exercise pressure in priority areas as a response to Mexico's activities, given that it is concerned with economic and political stability in the country (i.e., the precipice paradox) and that limiting commercial and labor flows also has high costs for the United States.

This obviously does not mean that the asymmetry of power between the countries has changed or that Mexico's relative autonomy could disappear if the U.S. government considers that its main interests are being affected by Mexico's position (Durand, 2004). However, this perception of the limits imposed by the asymmetry in the relationship is no longer an obstacle for the Mexican government to promote its own interests regarding Mexican migrants or actively engaging the diaspora, at least in the traditional understanding of these activities. In this sense, the existence of NAFTA and other mechanisms for dialogue, collaboration, and information exchanges between governments, academic institutions, bilateral commissions, nongovernmental organizations, businesses, and other actors developed since the late 1980s, and mainly in the 1990s, have contributed to a broader definition of the limits and possibilities of its policies in this issue area (Alba, 1993, 2000; Martin, 2001).

Notwithstanding these changes, legacies of the nonintervention principle are still present in the Mexican government's emigration policies and the potential linkage between issues in the bilateral agenda continues to be addressed with caution. These limitations are examined in greater detail in the next chapter, specifically considering the government's attempts to strengthen the relationship with migrant communities through social service provision, leadership development, and channels for their political participation in Mexico.

6

Institutionalizing State–Diaspora Relations (2003–2006)

> I am very proud to be Mexican and the opportunity to participate and learn how the Mexican government works [through the IME] makes me feel that they haven't forgotten about the people that they failed as a government many years ago . . . Maybe because of remittances or whatever, but they are there.
>
> – Member of the IME Advisory Council, Chicago, October 5, 2009

Beyond the proposal for a migration agreement, the change in Mexico's position of limited engagement since the year 2000 was also evident in its increasing activism regarding its relationship with the Mexican and Mexican-origin population. Through the creation of the Presidential Office for Mexicans Abroad and, later on, through the establishment of the Institute of Mexicans Abroad (*Instituto de los Mexicanos en el Exterior*, or IME), the Mexican government, particularly the Foreign Ministry, became more actively involved in promoting migrants' political participation in Mexico, empowering community leaders to promote the Mexican migrants' agenda both in their home country and in the United States, and expanding services available for migrants in the United States.

This was part of a broader interpretation of Mexico's traditional definition of consular protection. Rather than focusing merely on the customary practices regarding the defense of migrants' human rights (i.e., providing aid in legal affairs and repatriations, supporting migrant organizations, and promoting Mexican culture), the Mexican government adopted new policies to improve its consular protection services for migrants and it expanded programs in areas of health, education, and financial literacy. It also provided opportunities for the exercise of migrants' political rights in Mexico through the passage of the legislation regulating absentee voting at the federal level. Finally, it promoted the development of migrant leadership networks, offering them direct channels to communicate their views to the Mexican government through the creation of the CCIME (*Consejo Consultivo del IME*), an Advisory Council within the IME made up of migrant leaders.

The activism of the Mexican consulates in the United States and the creation of the IME and the CCIME are examples of a more substantive and energetic policy toward the diaspora with significant implications in the bilateral relationship. In addition to the continuous lobbying from the Mexican Foreign Ministry to keep alive the discussion over bilateral cooperation in the management of migration flows, described in the previous chapter, these activities represent a shift in the interpretation of foreign policy in relations with the Mexican-origin population in the United States and reflect the gradual development of a more proactive Mexican emigration policy since the late 1980s.

THE INSTITUTE OF MEXICANS ABROAD

President Fox's first effort toward institutionalizing a closer and more interactive relationship with the Mexican and Mexican-American communities in the United States was the creation of the Presidential Office for Mexicans Abroad, known as OPME (*Oficina Presidencial para los Mexicanos en el Exterior*). The appointment of a Mexican American, Juan Hernández, as its director was representative of the president's intention of establishing a direct communication with these groups. Between 2000 and 2002, Hernández focused most of his efforts on the promotion of Mexican products in the United States and on the investment of remittances in Mexico (which were calculated at about $10 billion per year in 2000). The Program for the Mexican Communities Abroad (PCME) – established in 1990 – continued to exist parallel to the OPME. However, as opposed to the PCME, "whose actions were instrumented through the consular network (in a deliberately discreet and non-interventionist fashion)," the OPME "sought the media's attention" with controversial statements and promoted its projects through Mr. Hernández's personal contacts rather than through the consulates and existing institutional channels (González Gutiérrez, 2003: 168). This situation created tensions within the Foreign Ministry because Hernández's agenda and strategies were at odds with Castañeda's and were considered to be overstepping the existing structure within the Foreign Ministry and the consulates. Moreover, the Presidential Office did not have the infrastructure or resources necessary to conduct these activities on a large scale.

The establishment of the IME on April 16, 2003 was a result of the Foreign Ministry's consideration that a new design was necessary, including both the existing programs operating through the PCME and the Presidential Office's goal of linking migrants more directly with the federal government. The IME incorporated and expanded the PCME's projects and objectives and tried to maintain the OPME's message of inclusion by appointing a migrant as its director. Moreover, it created an Advisory Council (the CCIME) made up of 125 migrant leaders in the United States and Canada.

The IME's objective, as officially described, is "to promote strategies, develop programs, gather proposals and recommendations of the communities, their members, their organizations and consultative bodies, with the goal of improving the quality of life of the Mexican communities abroad" (Diario Oficial, 2003). Its structure reflects this idea of gathering proposals and recommendations; it not only established an executive director and an office in Mexico City as an administratively independent department within the Foreign Ministry, but it also includes the CCIME and the National Council (CNCME, or *Consejo Nacional para las Comunidades en el Exterior*).

The CCIME is made up of an average of 125 community leaders in the United States and Canada[1] elected for a three-year period, whose role is to make recommendations to the Mexican government on issues related to the migrant communities through its various committees (politics, economics, education, health, legal affairs, border issues, and media and

---

[1] The first Advisory Council (2003–2005) included 105 Mexican immigrants, Mexican Americans and Mexican Canadians (elected by their communities or designated by the consulate or by a few community leaders, depending on each case), 10 members of Latino organizations in the United States, and 10 specialized consultants. In addition, 32 representatives of each of the states in Mexico can participate in the Advisory Council, although they cannot vote. The second Advisory Council (2006–2008) included 125 community leaders – 100 elected in the United States and Canada, 15 nominated in recognition of their career, and 10 consultants from Latino organizations. The third Advisory Council (2009–2011) includes 121 community leaders – 101 elected in the United States and Canada, 20 nominated in recognition of their career – and 7 consultants from Latino organizations. The distribution of the elected members of the Advisory Council per state or region is based on the population density of each consular district. However, during the first election of the Advisory Council the rules regarding the electoral process were not very clear. Thus, important sectors of the community were displeased with the election and argued that the CCIME was not a truly representative body and was controlled by the Mexican government. As a result, during the 2006 electoral process the IME and the CCIME developed a new framework that still offered a variety of methods for the election but under specific guidelines, and clearly established that the consulates would not participate in the process (see González Gutiérrez, 2006b). These guidelines are still in the process of being revised and improved.

communications).[2] Their participation is voluntary and the IME covers only some of their travel costs to the plenary meetings. The CCIME meets twice a year, generally in Mexico but on occasion in the United States, to make its recommendations to the Mexican government and meet with federal, state, and local officials. In recent years, some of the committees have also organized additional meetings and some *consejeros* have held regional meetings.

The CCIME is undoubtedly the most innovative component of this three-legged structure. Although other countries have similar migrant councils (see Agunias, 2009), the development of the CCIME did not purposely follow a specific model or a conceptual framework and it is distinct from existing migrant councils in other countries mainly because the members of the CCIME are elected by the Mexican communities in the United States and Canada (personal communication, González Gutiérrez, June 6, 2010). As Berruga, one of the main architects of the IME describes, "the CCIME was seen as a way to develop a mature and well-structured relationship with the Mexican communities, to improve communication with them, to learn what they expect from Mexico and to find out more about their needs as part of an early warning mechanism that would allow the Mexican government to respond to situations in which they needed its support" (personal interview, 2010). On the relevance of the CCIME, González Gutiérrez emphasizes its contribution to the empowerment of migrant leaders: "It gives a voice to a silent majority within the Mexican leadership. The challenge is to be able to have continuity, to have migrants make it their own and make sure that the leaders that become a part of it are the best of the best. It is important that the leaders themselves eventually recognize that without the CCIME, x, y and z would not have been possible" (personal interview, 2004).

The IME's National Council, a board that includes the heads of eleven Ministries in Mexico that deal with aspects related to migration[3] and is chaired by the president, has the mandate to bring together the heads of the main government offices dealing with issues related to migration to discuss the design and implementation of policies in these areas as well as the Advisory Council's recommendations. However, the National Council has not met consistently since its formation and the *consejeros*

---

[2] See "Consejo Consultivo" (available at http://www.ime.gob.mx/; last viewed February 11, 2011).
[3] The CNCME includes the Ministries of the Interior, Foreign Affairs, Treasury, Social Development, Economy, Agriculture, Education, Environment, Health, Tourism, and Labor.

report that communication with the ministries varies, depending on who is in charge as well as their personal interest in migration issues (Délano, 2010).

At the annual plenary meetings, the IME is supposed to report on the status of the CCIME's recommendations (340 were made between 2003 and 2008). However, as most of the *consejeros* interviewed report, there is a lot of frustration in this regard because many of their recommendations have not led to any specific policy changes. In some cases they recognize that it is due to their own inability to understand the limits of their role or to narrow down their agenda to a few items and follow up on them, but they also express distrust of Mexican authorities and criticize the IME's structure for these limitations (Délano, 2010). Nonetheless, in many cases, they do report significant changes as a result of the CCIME's activities, as noted in an interview with a CCIME member in New York, July 2009:

The advantage [of participating in the IME's Advisory Council] is that you can express your opinion directly and reach the highest authorities to solve the problems that we have here with regards to education, remittances, repatriation of bodies, passports. The clearest example is in the queues that we used to have outside the consulate with people waiting for hours in the cold. This has now been resolved. It wasn't us directly but we did have an influence.

The third component of the IME is its central office in Mexico City, which coordinates the relationship between the Advisory Council, the National Council, and the Foreign Ministry and manages the programs that are offered through the IME section at each consulate in the United States and Canada (some consulates still call this section "Comunidades," as it was known during the PCME period; the implementation of the programs also varies widely according to each consul's priorities). Symbolically, the Director of the IME is Cándido Morales, a Mexican migrant who spent most of his life in the United States. However, it is actually the Executive Director of the IME who designs the IME's objectives and strategies and coordinates the implementation of its programs. The first Executive Director of the IME was Carlos González Gutiérrez (2003–2009), a career diplomat and member of the Foreign Service, whose experience in the government and academic publications reflect a deep understanding of issues concerning the Mexican and Mexican-American communities in the United States as well as a clear vision of the potential of a closer relationship between the Mexican government and the diaspora, which greatly influenced the development of the IME's programs.

The fact that it is the Executive Director and not Mr. Morales who actually leads the IME is not lost on the migrant leaders. Although they have high respect for Mr. Morales, they recognize his symbolic role and associate this with the limits of the IME in terms of its true representativeness and inclusion of migrants: "Don Cándido just has the title. He has no power to make decisions. He doesn't have the place he deserves. He doesn't have the respect that he should have" (interview with member of the CCIME, Chicago, October 6, 2009).

Beyond its design and structure, the IME's main operational objectives are to strengthen independent leadership; develop and implement programs and services with a view toward improving the quality of life of Mexicans abroad; to generate synergies through collaboration with other agencies; and to disseminate information that may contribute to the development of the Mexican communities abroad (IME, 2006b). The IME provides education, health, business, and cultural services based on, but not limited to, the PCME's original structure.[4] It also strives to develop a network between community leaders, local officials, businessmen, and other prominent individuals in different sectors relevant to the Mexican-origin community in the United States, mainly through Information Seminars (*Jornadas Informativas*) that gather these leaders in Mexico,[5] and through knowledge transfer networks as part of the *Red de Talentos* program. As well, it disseminates information through the *Lazos* newsletter and other campaigns to publicize the Mexican government's agenda as well as its services for migrants and their families, in Mexico, in the United States, and in Canada.

Some of the IME's programs are inspired by initiatives in other countries, and at the same time they have influenced the development of similar models around the world, particularly in Latin America.[6] González Gutiérrez explains that the *Jornadas Informativas* "were

---

[4] The details of these programs are described in the IME's biannual reports (IME, 2004a, 2006b, 2008); also see www.ime.gob.mx and González Gutiérrez (2006b).

[5] Since its establishment in March, 2003 and until November, 2010, the IME had organized seventy-nine *Jornadas Informativas*, which every year bring approximately 400 community leaders (experts in health, education, media, politics, gastronomy, business, and other issues), mainly from the United States and Canada, to Mexico to meet their peers and learn about Mexico's services for migrants (IME, 2006b; also see http://www.ime.gob.mx/jornadas/jornadas.htm).

[6] Observers from Colombia, Uruguay, El Salvador, Guatemala, Honduras, Chile, and other countries have been present at *Jornadas Informativas* and CCIME plenary meetings as well as other IME conferences and events. Some of them have implemented similar initiatives in their countries (see IME, 2006b).

influenced by the American Jewish Committee and the American Israel Public Affairs Committee's work as well as Puerto Rico's and Israel's lobbying activities." Meanwhile, the financial education programs, particularly the establishment of agreements between banks and consulates, "originated through many conversations with the Inter-American Development Bank in Washington, D.C. as it began to focus on issues of remittances under Manuel Orozco's guidance" (personal communication, June 6, 2010).

González Gutiérrez also explains that, as Executive Director of the IME, he had the opportunity to travel and learn about other countries' experiences, which greatly influenced some of the IME programs: "I learned about what Colombians were doing and we began organizing housing fairs like they do (although our transborder mortgage programs already existed)" (personal communication, June 6, 2010). Mexico also organized three international conferences on diaspora issues (CIRED) in Mexico during González Gutiérrez's tenure, which allowed for the exchange of experiences and models between policy makers and academics from countries such as Morocco, Turkey, Philippines, India, Haiti, El Salvador, Argentina, and Uruguay, among others (see González Gutiérrez, 2006c, 2006d). The third of these conferences was focused on knowledge transfer networks based on the experiences of Chile, Colombia, Scotland, India, Ireland, New Zealand, and Mexico. In reference to this last conference, González Gutiérrez argues that "the IME program that benefitted the most from the contact with other countries was the *Red de Talentos*" (personal communication, June 6, 2010) because it has been developed with close reference to other countries' models and to meetings with the World Bank.

Considering this broad agenda of service provision, networking, and communication with the diaspora, González Gutiérrez argues that the IME represents "the ultimate example of the Mexican government's will to extend the channels for participation to 'the Mexico outside Mexico' [*Mexico de afuera*]" and that in the government's discourse, "disdain and indifference have made way for the explicit recognition of the multiple contributions that immigrants make to Mexico's development" (2006b: 200). In his various articles and statements describing the IME's objectives and activities, González Gutiérrez (2003, 2006b) has emphasized the idea of the institute as a way of "facilitating the synergy" and "developing bridges of communication and understanding" between the government and Mexican migrants' initiatives, as well as consolidating a network of Mexican migrant leadership in order to provide them with the necessary tools to effectively promote their interests, both in Mexico and in the United States.

This discourse represents a fundamental change on the Mexican government's understanding of and position regarding the relationship with the migrant community and the traditional idea of consular protection. The IME is conceived as part of the Foreign Ministry's responsibility to provide "support and protection to the Mexican population abroad," and its responsibilities include facilitating meetings between members of the Mexican communities abroad, promoting communication with them, and serving as a liaison (Diario Oficial, 2003). This mandate has been interpreted widely in terms of the breadth and scope of the IME's activities, which are not strictly limited by traditional conceptions of interference in another state's sovereignty as they were in the past, even though there is still caution in their promotion. The following examples provide evidence of the development of a new interpretation of the possibilities and advantages of engaging the Mexican diaspora, as well as some of its limits, based partly on reactions to these activities in the United States and, to a lesser extent, in Mexico.

THE IME'S SERVICES: IMPROVING MIGRANTS' LIVES — AND THEIR INTEGRATION IN THE UNITED STATES

The IME's decree describes the institute as part of the Foreign Ministry's responsibility to "improve the quality of life of Mexicans abroad," including activities dealing with "prevention, attention and support" and compiling proposals and recommendations geared toward "improving the social development of the Mexican communities abroad" introduced by "advisory councils constituted by representatives of those communities" (Diario Oficial, 2003). This agenda includes the promotion of education, health, leadership, and financial services for migrants in the United States that are provided through consulates and through partner agencies (schools, nonprofit groups, government offices, clinics and hospitals, banks and other financial institutions, and businesses).

"Improving the quality of life of Mexicans abroad" is a very broad idea that can and in practice does include programs that support immigrant integration in the United States with the collaboration of many U.S. institutions, agencies, and local, state, and federal government offices. This, in itself, is an innovative aspect of Mexico's policies because they were traditionally oriented, at least in the rhetoric used, to maintaining migrants' ties and loyalty to Mexico rather than in helping them integrate and remain in the United States. However, the focus on integration is not stated explicitly, in part because of Mexico's late understanding of the idea "that there is no contradiction between integration in the host country and maintaining contact with the home country" (González Gutiérrez, personal interview, 2009) but also due to concerns about potential reactions in the United States and in Mexico to the underlying assumptions of these programs and their costs. This also reflects Mexico's only recent development of an explicit migration policy and a slow recognition of the fact that the circularity of migration is no longer a main characteristic of the flows.

Considering the fact that the definition of "integration" is not clear or explicit in Mexico's emigration agenda, González Gutiérrez and other Mexican officials interviewed acknowledge that the quiet promotion of programs that implicitly support immigrant integration also has to do with how migration is viewed in Mexico. On the one hand, there is a serious implication that by promoting immigrant integration, the government is recognizing that the conditions for their return to Mexico (or even to prevent their emigration in the first place) do not exist, based on the traditional understanding of Mexico–United States migration as a circular phenomenon. On the other hand, the Mexican government is investing a large amount of resources in providing health and education services to the migrant population and improving their quality of life, when many of these are not available to a large percentage of the population in Mexico. Making these programs more explicit would probably generate such criticisms in Mexico, particularly among groups that do not have such a direct experience with migration or the benefits of remittances. This is even criticized by some Mexican migrants. For example, most of those interviewed in the context of the adult education *Plazas Comunitarias* program expressed gratitude for the availability of these programs and Mexican textbooks in the United States, but some of them explained that they would have preferred to have that support in Mexico so they would have had better opportunities to stay there, or that they would prefer for those resources to be invested in their communities back home for others who need them more (Délano, 2010).

Another reason why the Mexican and U.S. governments do not make these policies explicit is due to a persistent concern regarding the potential backlash in the United States. Critics have argued that the Mexican government's programs to promote adult education for Mexican migrants in the United States, and textbook donations to libraries and schools, create confusion for students in terms of their allegiances (MacDonald,

2005a, 2005b). They also argue that the Mexican government is promoting "multilingualism at the expense of English and help[ing] Mexicans and their children sponge off U.S. services ranging from schools to medical care" (Kent, 2006).

In the case of health programs, a recent article in the *Sacramento Bee* (Tong, 2009) reported on Mexico's health program (*Ventanillas de Salud* – Health Windows), which offers preventive health and referral services at the consulates with the support of community health centers, clinics, and hospitals. The article generated online comments such as the following (Warro, December 18, 2009):

This is insane. The Mexican Counselates [sic] are now funding a program to refer illegal immigrants to U.S. taxpayer funded free health care programs, and ensure that they have a place to go where they are not afraid of being deported. That sounds like they are openly aiding and abetting illegal immigration in the U.S. What ever happened to this country????? Maybe the U.S. is no longer a sovereign country.

A more direct example of this backlash was experienced in Oregon. A 2007 article published in *The Oregonian* reported that three state high schools adopted Mexico's public school curriculum "to help educate Spanish-speaking students with textbooks, an online Web site, DVDs and CDs provided free by Mexico to teach math, science and even U.S. history" and that conversations were under way to align the countries' curriculums, following similar initiatives in Yakima, WA; San Diego, CA; and Austin, TX (Bermudez, 2007). The article generated negative comments online with some postings arguing that those who supported the initiative were against assimilation.[7] There were also protests against participating schools, at least one of which was broken into. In response to such hostile reactions, one of the directors of these programs, a *Plaza Comunitaria* coordinator, argued in a personal interview (Portland, November 6, 2009) that they are helping address dropout rates, among other benefits:

If children or young adults come from another country and can't continue their studies in their native language we can't wait for them to learn English without teaching them other skills in the meantime. If they can continue to learn in Spanish, they will stay in school, make progress and eventually get into college and have better skills, whether or not they return to Mexico.... Even if they take some courses in Spanish, we are moving them toward the target language – English – both in terms of academic knowledge and skills.

[7] See 24Ahead.com: Illegal immigration, news, politics, media bias (available at http://24ahead.com/blog/archives/007076.html; last viewed December 18, 2009).

In this context, the Mexican government has opted for a discreet approach to the promotion of these programs, even if in some cases discretion gets in the way of efficiency. For example, the absence of a national communication strategy regarding the IME programs limits the government's ability to reach the target population (Délano, 2010). Another limitation is the uneven implementation of the programs, which is partly due to each consul's preferences but also to the different characteristics and needs of the population in each consular district. Nevertheless, an interesting development in recent years is that even if the Mexican government continues to *quietly* promote these programs (Wides-Muñoz, 2008), the IME, some Mexican consuls in the United States, and the Mexican Embassy in Washington increasingly present these programs as part of Mexico's commitment to a shared responsibility in the management of migration (IME, 2009a; Sarukhan, personal interview, 2009). The three examples examined in the following sections regarding IME's education, health, and leadership programs show that the Mexican government is making a contribution to the integration of migrants into the host country, which provides evidence of Mexico's broadening definition of its relationship with the diaspora and the limits and possibilities for these activities in the context of the United States–Mexico relationship. It also raises a key question regarding the allocation of costs and benefits of migration between sending and receiving countries and could eventually lead to a more positive assessment of the Mexican government's activities and more explicit and formal collaboration in some of these areas.[8]

Education

The IME's programs to promote education are based on the idea that the improvement of the lives of the Mexican-origin population in the United States should be addressed through collaboration between both countries. Among its initiatives are teacher exchange programs; textbook donations for schools, libraries, and community centers in the United States (about 1 million a year); adult literacy and education programs through *Plazas Comunitarias*; and a grants program, the IME Becas, begun in 2005 in partnership with the University of California, Berkeley to support community centers and institutions that provide education programs for Mexican students.

---

[8] I thank Alan Gamlen for his suggestions on this point. For a broader discussion on this issue, see Bhagwati's (2005) argument regarding the imposition of a tax on citizens abroad to compensate for sending countries' investments in their education.

By 2008 there were 373 *Plazas* throughout the United States. Some consulates have as many as 20 *Plazas* in their district operating through community centers, health clinics or hospitals, community colleges, hometown associations, schools, and jails. According to the Mexican Institute for Adult Education (INEA), in 2007 there were 16,758 students enrolled in these programs across thirty-five states in the United States (IME, 2008). The *Plazas* serve a population of students ranging from sixteen to eighty years of age. Although most of the students are Mexican, in almost every *Plaza* visited there were students and teachers from other Latin-American countries and in some cases even from non-Spanish-speaking countries.

Visits to thirty *Plazas Comunitarias*, in the Los Angeles, Atlanta, New York, Chicago, Houston, and Portland consular districts, included interviews with students, teachers, and coordinators of the programs (Délano, 2010). The interview questions were designed to assess participants' goals and the benefits they obtain from these programs in relation to the Mexican government's stated objectives (IME, 2006b, 2008). None of these objectives explicitly refer to the idea of promoting the integration of Mexican nationals to the United States, and particularly to learning English. However, the interview results reveal that the students' experiences in the *Plazas* do in fact provide the tools for a more successful interaction with U.S. institutions, particularly for adults who report a more active involvement in their children's schooling and better communication with their kids, as well as an improvement in their access to better jobs and higher levels of English proficiency. Although many students first come to the *Plazas* with the objective of learning English, the teachers and coordinators usually find that the students are also lacking basic education tools (in some cases they are illiterate). In those cases, the availability of textbooks in Spanish is essential. Most of the students enrolled in these programs (the majority of whom are women, at least in most of the *Plazas* visited) are motivated by the idea that an education in their own language will not only make it easier for them to learn to read and write or finish elementary or middle school, but will also allow them to learn English faster and, in some cases, get a GED and go to college in the United States. As one *Plaza* coordinator in New York City (personal interview June 24, 2009) said,

Many come with the idea of learning English. But their motivation changes when they realize they can learn to read and write in their own language. They want to help their children. Be productive. Some of them feel they can now socialize and be valued. They want to have a better job, a better salary, a better quality of life.

The fact that the *Plazas* in most cases are located inside schools, community centers, health clinics, churches, or colleges also helps immigrants become more familiar with these places and take advantage of a wider range of services available to them or their children. Many *Plazas* introduce their students to other programs and provide seminars or specialized training according to the resources available at each site, which provides immigrants with information and tools they can apply in their daily lives and improves their self-confidence. In this sense, one of the students explains, "I feel better in terms of being able to fill out an application, and I feel like a positive role model for my children. They have benefited as well because they see me study and they want to do the same" (personal interview, student, Houston, July 8, 2009). As described by one of the *Plaza* coordinators in Houston (personal interview, July 10, 2009), this is something that the collaborating agencies value, because in addition to the *Plaza* programs they can provide tools that help immigrants in their daily lives in the United States:

We are the lighthouse of their lives. They come here feeling lost. But here we are a light. They come here for the support, looking for a better life. Education gives them a better life. Their socioeconomic level improves. We are a site of hope. We not only give them education, but we give them orientation about the system, and they know it is a safe place. We guide them, we help them get services. But more importantly, we have changed their lives if we help them get an education.

Although most cities offer English as a Second Language (ESL) programs and adult education programs through the school system, many immigrants who need them sometimes are not informed or are afraid of participating in them because of their undocumented status or because their reading and writing skills are limited. In this context, the Mexican government programs play a key role in terms of serving as a bridge and connecting the students to institutions that they would not normally approach in the United States. The fact that most of the staff speaks Spanish and that the Mexican consulates advertise the programs gives migrants a sense that it is a safe place: "A community college near here has ESL classes but it is intimidating for some people. They'd rather come here. It is a more comfortable and homey setting" (interview with *Plaza* coordinator, Houston, July 9, 2009).

Finally, the *Plaza* coordinators argue that the program does not prevent the integration of their students into the United States and they do not consider that there is a tension between an education in Spanish or with Mexican textbooks in relation to their ability to learn English and set their roots in the country. In response to criticisms regarding the fact that the *Plazas* program comes from Mexico, one of the coordinators says that "people have to understand that the value of education is education itself; it doesn't matter where it comes from. The benefit of the *Plazas* program is mainly for the U.S. and it has produced great results" (coordinator, Los Angeles, August 22, 2009).

Health

The *Ventanillas de Salud* (or Health Windows) program is designed to provide information on preventive health to persons who visit the Mexican consulates. By December 2009, forty consulates in the United States had Health Windows and an estimated 2.5 million Mexicans had benefited from the service (Tong, 2009). The Health Windows (in some cases a full office, in others just a table with flyers) are usually located in the waiting rooms where between 100 and 500 Mexicans wait for their passports or consular IDs every day (the number varies, depending on the consular office and the season). Through the use of videos, talks, handbooks, flyers, and, in some cases, free diagnostic tests for HIV, high blood pressure, diabetes, and the like, the program coordinators and the collaborating institutions (hospitals, clinics, community health centers, and pharmacies) provide information about diseases that are common among the Mexican community. They also refer people to clinics and hospitals that can provide services at a low cost for those that are uninsured (an estimated 55 percent of the Mexican immigrants in the United States).

   The coordinators of the program in five cities and some of the participating health agencies interviewed explain that the program supports immigrants' interaction with U.S. health institutions by providing a safe space in the consulate that they can approach to ask questions about their or their children's health: "One of the greatest obstacles in reaching this community is to earn their trust.... The community sees [the services provided through the Health Windows] as something that the consulate offers... this gives them confidence. This opens a great opportunity to give people access to health, to help them learn about the resources available and the requirements. They can then disseminate this information among family members and friends" (interview with partner agency, Los Angeles, August 21, 2009). The Health Windows program also connects immigrants to U.S. institutions that they can have access to, regardless of their immigration status or access to insurance. An added benefit is that these preventive health services reduce the use of emergency care services (Giovine, 2008). For example, one of the agencies that provides free glucose tests in Los Angeles explains that 30–35 percent of those that receive the test are diabetic and do not know it (interview with partner agency, Los Angeles, August 14, 2009).

In terms of the target population, the service is still not widely known among Mexican migrants and the dissemination and implementation of the program varies in each consulate. However, interviews conducted in five consulates (Délano, 2010) reveal that those who do hear about or use the service report very positively on their experience and express their interest in learning more about health issues and programs that they or their family members can have access to, either at the consulate or with the partner health agencies or hospitals. In the context of the migration debate in the United States, these programs are significant because they help improve migrants' socioeconomic situation through preventive health and connections to organizations that support vulnerable groups; this contributes to dispelling myths about their abuse of public services.

Leadership Development

Beyond the local and federal government's relationships with hometown associations, which have developed more extensively since the 1990s, the Mexican government has established more direct linkages with Mexican and Mexican-American community leaders (in addition to hometown associations, community activists, academics, health workers, Mexican Americans in local and state governments and in the media, and Latino organizations). Since 2003, this relationship has been institutionalized through the IME's Advisory Council.

The stated objectives of the IME with regard to the Advisory Council are as follows: (a) to maintain a systematic, frank, and constructive dialogue with the leadership of the Mexican communities abroad; (b) incorporate them into the design of public policies that affect them; (c) create a forum for the exchange of ideas between Mexican and Mexican-American leaders; (d) identify the priority needs of the Mexican communities abroad and develop a shared agenda between them and the Mexican government; (e) provide a space for the free and frank expression of their ideas and concerns; (f) disseminate information about the Mexican government's programs; and (g) take advantage of the opportunity of the growing political and economic relevance of the migrant and Mexican-American leadership so these communities can develop to their full potential and serve as a bridge of understanding between Mexico and their host countries (IME, 2004a, 2006b, 2008).

The nature of this relationship is conflictual: Many migrants still feel resentment and mistrust toward the Mexican government, and some of them want more direct participation and representation in Mexico. Nevertheless, interviews with fifty former and current members of the Advisory Council reveal that they mostly see their participation in it as beneficial, in terms of their goals both in the United States and in Mexico. The main benefit that the majority of the *consejeros* identify is that their participation in the council has allowed them to learn about other Mexican community leaders in the United States and share experiences and knowledge. This has provided them with opportunities to develop a network of community leaders and collaborate on projects in their state of residence or of origin, and at the national level (in both countries). For many of the *consejeros* interviewed, the Advisory Council was essential for the success of the Spring 2006 migrant demonstrations against the Sensenbrenner Bill (HR 4437) and in favor of comprehensive immigration reform (see Bada et al., 2006), because it allowed them to develop a stronger network and communicate with each other. More recently, Mexican migrants formed a national coalition for immigration reform (known as the MX Coalition for Immigration Reform), and most of its members are former or current *consejeros*. In these interviews, most of them report that their participation in the Advisory Council was key to bringing them together and developing a common agenda. A *consejero* from New York (interviewed on June 17, 2009) explains these benefits as follows:

The advantages are great. You gain experience and relationships and you learn to communicate with those that represent us in the government. You learn a lot about the leaders who are professional leaders in California, Chicago and Texas, very professional people. You learn from them and you maintain a relationship with them. . . . Of course, you also meet those who just talk and do nothing.

Another *consejero* from Chicago (interviewed on October 6, 2009) highlights the importance of the Mexican government's role in promoting these networks and the dialogue within the immigrant community:

The connections, relationships and dialogue that are forming among migrants in the U.S. and the connection towards the issues and concerns of daily life, as well as the improvement of their home country . . . and the promise that we can have a direct impact, is what leads us to participate in the IME. The reality is that the greatest value is in that connection and in the relationships that are formed.

I think that as we mature as a community and continue to grow and have more power in this country [the U.S.], the investment that Mexico is making now on this dialogue, this conversation and developing relationships, is going to bear fruit.

Most hometown associations and their leaders maintain close ties with U.S. political authorities or are members of U.S.-based political or ethnic organizations while at the same time actively participating in development projects or political activities related to their hometown (see Portes, Escobar, and Arana, 2008). In most cases, they are more actively engaged in U.S.-based politics but they do not see their transnational connections as a limitation in terms of their integration in their host country. A *consejero* from Los Angeles (interviewed on August 14, 2009) explains the role of the IME in helping migrant leaders achieve their goals in both countries:

What is interesting and valuable about the IME is that they have put us to work in a way that we can work for both countries. We bring benefits to both sides, like health, investments there [in Mexico] so that people won't come here [the U.S.] and have jobs there. The IME helped us work with both governments and with foundations and clubs here and there. I feel great satisfaction by achieving so much thanks to this. My initiatives with the IME have allowed me to achieve a lot both nationally and binationally.

In the case of the IME's Advisory Council, 57 percent of current *consejeros* for the period 2009–2011 have their main political affiliation in the United States or Canada; only 30 percent belong to a hometown association (IME, 2009b). In terms of the effects of their participation in the Advisory Council and their activities in the United States, many report a positive result in terms of professionalization and transferring the skills of their interaction with Mexican authorities to local politics in the United States and vice versa. For example, a *consejero* from Houston (interviewed on July 8, 2009) explains that it helped him "give more seriousness" to his hometown association. Others have been elected for office in the United States or are planning to run for election as a result of their participation in the Advisory Council. Another *consejero* from Houston (interviewed on July 6, 2009) explains the importance of the CCIME in his political career in the United States: "I am going to run for public office in the U.S. If it hadn't been for the CCIME, I wouldn't have thought of it. I saw the potential of being a public servant in order to make a difference in your town." Others have seen a positive effect in terms of their relationship with local governments (in the

U.S.): "[Being a *consejero*] opened doors for me with local governments; they saw it as a bridge of communication with the Latino community. They [the local governments] want to learn about the Mexican government's programs and improve the relationship with the government and with the consulate" (Interview with CCIME member, Atlanta, July 28, 2009).

The majority of the interviewed Advisory Council members believe that the Mexican community has made significant progress in recent years in terms of solidifying its leadership and organizations, although the community is still divided and participation rates are low. For most of them, such as this *consejero* (interviewed in Chicago, October 1, 2009), the Mexican government's role has been positive, if not a key detonator, in this process of developing stronger leaders and organizations:

Much of this progress has been a result of the consulate's support, that keeps updating us with seminars, as well as the support from the local governments in Mexico. This has generated a more professional leadership, not so much a hometown club but a real organization with a board of directors, an NGO [nongovernmental organization]. Before they didn't even register; now they obtain their 501(c)(3) status, they obtain resources, and [they] can do a more professional job.

Although they are critical, the *consejeros* also see this relationship with the Mexican government as positive in terms of strengthening their own identity, interacting with Mexican government officials in constructive ways, having the opportunity to bring attention to the migrant communities' needs in the United States, and disseminating information about the Mexican government's services.

Bada et al. (2006: 8) reflect on the question of whether "there is a perception that Mexico's interest around these organizations is distinct from the interests that have been put forward today around more integration into U.S. society." Although there is an unstated objective and perhaps a long-term view of this relationship as something that might benefit Mexico if the Mexican and Mexican-American leadership represents the government's interests and lobbies in its favor, most of the emphasis in the official discourse has been on empowering them to defend their own interests and rights in the United States, which is also what most of the interviewed *consejeros* focus on. For Jorge G. Castañeda, this makes sense because "Mexican consulates cannot do enough to protect their rights and the Mexican government should provide them with the tools to defend themselves, not to act as a lobby group in Mexico's interests" (personal interview, October 30, 2009). Similarly, Ambassador Sarukhan argues that "even if the transnational relationship with the diaspora is important and commendable, the best way to help them and protect them is for them to learn English and, for those who can, to vote in the United States. We should not seek solely and primarily to have them represent the Mexican government's agenda in the United States" (personal interview, December 4, 2009). These statements, together with the community leaders' comments, affirm the idea that the Mexican government's programs are contributing to immigrants' civic participation and empowerment in the United States, perhaps with unstated objectives or unintended results but without contradicting the goal of Mexican immigrants' integration in the United States.

Although the existence of the programs discussed in this section is still not part of the mainstream discussion about Mexico's role in migration management or in the debate about immigration reform, there is growing attention to the Mexican consulates' role in promoting access to health, education, and other social services (Giovine, 2008; Gorman, 2009; Seder, 2009; Fuller, 2010). Most of this coverage is neutral or positive, even if some articles point out that these services are being used by "illegal aliens." Additionally, the Migration Policy Institute – a nonpartisan think thank in Washington, D.C. – recently released a report based on an analysis of the IME's programs, which they describe as "one of the most significant, if overlooked factors in U.S. immigrant integration policy" (Laglagaron, 2010).

Based on the reactions to the existing coverage and the position of anti-immigrant groups, the same type of backlash and accusations of interventionism would be expected if these programs were better known. Despite Mexico's fear of backlash and accusations of nonintervention, which in the past had been used as an excuse for inaction (and in some cases still is), the expansion of these programs and the strengthening of partnerships with U.S. institutions and governments at different levels throughout their implementation has allowed for the development of new spaces for action and new definitions of Mexico's objectives in relation to its migrant population. Still, some of these objectives are more explicit than others and are controversial in Mexico. Within the government offices involved, there is also a lack of consensus given the potential implications of these activities both for Mexican politics and for the bilateral relationship.

ABSENTEE VOTING RIGHTS: EMPOWERING MIGRANTS
AT HOME AND ABROAD

Another example of the Mexican government's interest in strengthening
the relationship between emigrants and the homeland, and extending
them political rights, was the passage of the legislation on absentee voting
rights after an almost ten-year delay. Although the constitutional reform
had been passed since August of 1996 (together with the reform on
dual nationality), it contained a clause that required Congress to reform
the Mexican Federal Elections secondary regulations (*Código Federal de
Instituciones y Procedimientos Electorales*, or COFIPE), which would
determine the rules on how this right would be exercised. It was not until
June of 2005 that Congress finally passed the legislation required for the
implementation of the constitutional right for absentee voting.

In 1998, the Mexican Federal Elections Institute (IFE, or *Instituto
Federal Electoral*) commissioned a group of experts to report on the
possible models for absentee voting, as well as their risks and costs,
considering other countries' experiences and the specific characteristics
of the Mexican case. The commission's report detailed certain technical
difficulties (e.g., high costs, issuance of voting cards abroad, establishment
of voting booths outside the country, limitations regarding regulations of
the campaigns and funding abroad, and irregularities in other experiences
with electronic voting). However, the main obstacle for the passage of the
reform was the lack of political consensus, which, to many observers, was
the result of the political parties' concerns regarding the potential (and
unpredictable) impact of migrants' vote in the elections (IME, 2004b:
3–4; González Gutiérrez, 2009).[9]

By 2004, more than fifteen initiatives regarding the regulation of
absentee voting had been introduced in Congress. This included initiatives from political parties and, remarkably, from migrant coalitions
such as the Federation of Michoacán Hometown Associations in Illinois

[9] Various studies were conducted to determine how many Mexicans would be able to
vote from abroad in the 2006 elections, with wide variations in their results. Cornelius
and Marcelli (2005) estimated that between 125,000 and 360,000 Mexicans could vote
from abroad in the 2006 election (although a previous version of their study presented
in 2003 calculated between 125,000 and 1.1 million – see IME, 2004b: 2–3). A study
conducted by El Colegio de la Frontera Norte calculated that close to 9 million Mexicans
residing abroad would be able to vote (98 percent living in the United States). Thus, it
was considered risky to support legislation whose effects had the potential of determining
the result of the elections.

(FEDECMI – *Federación de Clubes Michoacanos en Illinois*) and the Coalition for the Political Rights of Mexicans Abroad (CDPME – *Coalición por los Derechos Políticos de los Mexicanos en el Extranjero*). The IME's Advisory Council, the CCIME, was also actively involved in this campaign and made public its position on the initiatives presented. For example, regarding Congress's Political Agreement on Voting Rights, signed on April 6, 2004 (later integrated into the Initiative to Regulate the Vote of Mexicans Abroad, signed by President Fox on June 24, 2004), the CCIME published a statement in which it expressed its agreement with the main points but emphasized the immigrant communities' demand for obtaining voting cards in the United States and allowing them to vote for Senators (IME, 2004b: 5). The *consejeros* also participated in six consultation forums organized between January and February of 2004 in the United States and Canada together with the IME and the Ministry of the Interior. This represented an important development in terms of migrants' making wide use of channels available to participate in the discussion of policies in Mexico, and also of the government's willingness to provide these opportunities.

In light of the imminent passage of the reform, in April of 2004 the Foreign Ministry expressed its concerns about potential reactions in the United States to the Congress' Political Agreement on Voting Rights. Among some of its arguments, the Foreign Ministry claimed that even though the issue was not yet salient to U.S. public opinion, in the medium or long term, the exercise of voting rights abroad could reinforce the arguments of conservative groups such as those put forward in Samuel Huntington's controversial article "The Hispanic Challenge." In this article, and in his book *Who Are We: The Challenges to America's National Identity*, he maintained that Hispanics, particularly Mexicans, pose a threat to American values and ideals because they cannot be assimilated into "mainstream U.S. culture" and they reject "the Anglo-Protestant values that built the American dream" by forming their own political and linguistic enclaves (Huntington, 2004).[10] Based on examples of other countries' experiences and its own analysis of potential reactions in the United States, the Foreign Ministry warned that the establishment of voting booths or the issuance of voting cards in the United States could

---

[10] Similar arguments have been posed regarding dual nationality and absentee voting as an obstacle for migrants' integration in the United States (Fonte, 2005; Renshon, 2005); also see Buchanan (2006).

complicate the issue, making it more salient among general public opinion and possibly leading to accusations of dual loyalty.[11]

Finally, on June 28, 2005, the Mexican Congress passed the reform defining the rules, requirements, and procedures by which the absentee voting would be implemented. The legislation passed was considered the most restrictive version of the initiatives presented: There would be no voting booths in the United States, no voting cards would be issued outside of Mexico, there would be no campaigns or financing from abroad, the vote would be sent by post, and it would be limited to the presidential election (the 2006 election included Congress and some state and local elections; see Silva-Herzog Márquez, 2006; González Gutiérrez, 2009). This was not necessarily a direct response to concerns about potential reactions in the United States, but it was certainly a conservative approach aimed at preventing most of the risks signaled by the different groups involved in the debate, including the Foreign Ministry.

The fact that only 54,780 absentee registration cards were received (of which only 40,876 were valid) and only 32,621 of those registered individuals actually voted[12] was a source of great disappointment in Mexico. The whole exercise was considered by some as a waste of time and resources and proof of immigrants' indifference and mistrust of Mexican politics (Gaddis Smith, 2006; Silva-Herzog Márquez, 2006; Stevenson, 2006). However, it is also argued that strict requirements, insufficient information about registration procedures, and a limited amount of time for registering were also key factors explaining why only 0.5 percent of Mexicans in the United States sought absentee ballots for the presidential election (Suro and Escobar, 2006).[13]

Regardless of the limited participation and the restrictions of the law, it was considered a "historical milestone" by many Mexican immigrant organizations and proof of the Mexican government's willingness to recognize their political rights (Ayón, 2006b; Ross Pineda, 2006). Still, most Mexican migrant leaders argue that it is just a first step and that the

[11] "Observaciones de la cancillería al proyecto de iniciativa sobre el voto de los mexicanos en el exterior," internal document from the Mexican Foreign Ministry, April 16, 2004.
[12] Instituto Federal Electoral (2006), *Informe final sobre el Voto de los Mexicanos en el Exterior y Numeralia Electoral*, Mexico City (available at http://mxvoto6.ife.org.mx; last viewed February 12, 2011).
[13] According to the Pew Hispanic Center's survey, more than half (55 percent) of Mexicans in the United States were not aware that a presidential election was taking place in 2006. Only a few were familiar with the regulations and procedures and about one-third knew that the deadline for seeking an absentee ballot had just passed at the time of the survey (Suro and Escobar, 2006).

legislation is limited given the fact that most migrants do not have a voting ID and cannot obtain it in the United States or go back to Mexico to get it (Délano, 2010).

The debate over absentee voting rights and the activism of migrant leaders and organizations in this regard also translated into reforms of electoral regulations at the local level. The states of Zacatecas and Michoacán passed legislation in 2003 and 2007, respectively, to allow migrants living abroad to stand in state and local elections and, in the case of Michoacán, to vote from abroad.[14] These are seen as positive examples of migrants' motivations to participate in the political process in Mexico and, more importantly, of the government's interest in facilitating channels to do so. However, these local elections also reported an unexpectedly low number of absentee voters, which leads to questions regarding the representativeness of migrant leaders who have led the initiatives as well as migrants' real interest in maintaining political ties with Mexico (Martínez, 2008).

Beyond the issue of the limited participation of migrants in Mexican politics, in González Gutiérrez (2009) and Ayón's (2006a) view, the state's recent forms of engagement with the diaspora through the CCIME and the process leading to the passage of the regulations for absentee voting, as well as the strengthening of existing development projects such as the 3 × 1, has contributed to the empowerment of migrants, not only in terms of their political participation in Mexico but also in the United States. Through the CCIME, and the participation in other initiatives related to Mexico – be it development in their home communities or lobbying for voting rights – the migrant leadership has been able to develop strong networks and take advantage of channels through which they can promote their interests in both countries. González Gutiérrez (2009: 290) emphasizes the role of the Mexican government in this process:

Even if migrants' demands for exercising their political rights developed from the bottom-up, the Mexican state contributed in an important way to consolidate those incentives by creating structures with opportunities that the migrant leaders were able to capitalize in favor of their causes.

Although the Mexican government has played a role in helping Mexican organizations form and develop, within the Mexican government

---

14 The law in Zacatecas was passed in 2003. Many Zacatecan organizations and groups in the United States, mainly the *Frente Cívico Zacatecano* in Southern California, led an intense campaign in favor of this law. The law in Michoacán was passed in February of 2007 and was strongly supported by the *Frente Binacional Michoacano en Estados Unidos* (FREBIMICH; see Moctezuma, 2003a, 2003b).

it is not altogether clear what the long-term strategy and structure for engaging with the migrant communities is. At the same time, there are still concerns about the effects of reactions to these activities, both from Mexican migrants and from U.S. actors.

LIMITS: THE LEGACY OF NONINTERVENTION

One of the most controversial issues in the discussion about the Mexican state's relationship with its diaspora is whether the Mexican immigrant community will create its own lobby group (whether or not in favor of Mexican policies) and whether this is (or should be) encouraged by the Mexican government. According to Ayón (2006b), "there can be little doubt . . . of the Mexican government's interest in going beyond this relatively limited dynamic – to have the Mexican network develop into a pro-Mexico constituency and political force within the United States, i.e., a *Mexico lobby*." Fernández de Castro (2003a) claims that there is enough evidence about Mexicans and Mexican Americans' interests in "their new country – the U.S. – treating their *remote home* – Mexico – better," as well as of their willingness to "work politically for development in Mexico and for a better bilateral relationship"; therefore, in his view, it is probable that "eventually, even in a less than 10-years horizon, they will form an ethnic lobby that will promote Mexico's interests in the U.S.," especially as a result of the creation of the CCIME, "the embryo of that ethnic lobby."

Although the issue is not yet prominent in the general public debate over immigration in the United States, the fact that the IME and the CCIME, as bodies directly related to the Mexican government, are perceived as promoting (open or implicitly) the formation of a lobbying group in favor of Mexico's interests can trigger negative reactions in the United States. There is already criticism of the IME's and consulates' activities (Kent, 2006), which are perceived as being interventionist or stepping beyond consular duties:

The *Instituto de los Mexicanos en el Exterior* (Institute of Mexicans Abroad) has no respect for the internal affairs of our country. . . . Its vast computer database is used to deploy illegal and legal Mexicans to lobby state legislatures, city councils and county commissions to recognize worthless *matrícula consular* "identification" cards, support granting driver's licenses to illegals, promote multilingualism at the expense of English and help Mexicans and their children sponge off U.S. services ranging from schools to medical care.

The CCIME has also been accused of embodying "an attempt by Mexico to bypass U.S. sovereignty and set up a representative branch of the Mexican government on U.S. soil" (Dougherty, 2002).

Other notorious attacks against the Mexican government were often presented in the CNN program "Lou Dobbs Tonight." For example, on October 10, 2005 the "Broken Borders" segment discussed the role of Mexican consulates in the "illegal migration crisis" in the United States. Through interviews with public opinion leaders and members of migration policy think tanks, this program – which was known for its anti-immigrant position – criticized the Mexican government's use of its consular network to advance its political and economic interests in the United States, through practices that "violate the laws of the country." This argument, which has also been expressed in press articles and journals with a similar restrictionist position on immigration, suggests that Mexican consuls have "overstepped" their diplomatic duties and that the consulates have become political organizations or support centers by lobbying with local authorities and "opposing the implementation of migration laws" (FAIRUS, 2005; Fonte, 2005; MacDonald, 2005a, 2005b; Kent, 2006).[15]

Beyond the expected reactions from conservative groups, there have been scholars, members of immigration think tanks, and representatives of pro-immigrant groups who have also expressed reservations regarding the Mexican government's activities. Some of their arguments point out that Mexico will face great problems in the bilateral relationship if its activities imply a closer involvement – direct or indirect – in the organization of the Mexican and Mexican-American communities in the United States (Papademetriou, personal interview, 2005). For example, Randel Johnson argues that "the worst thing for Mexico would be to try to interfere with this community *behind the scenes*" (personal interview, 2005). Just as well, various groups in Mexico have argued that the government's activism on these issues can trigger U.S. reactions and imply more pressure in other issues in the bilateral agenda. This was considered to be the case in the context of Mexico's opposition to the Iraq war in 2003, as discussed in the previous chapter.

Finally, there is no consensus from immigrant groups themselves about whether creating a lobby group, or even maintaining close ties with the Mexican government, is in their interest. One of the reasons that explains

---

[15] See the Mexican government's response to some of these criticisms in *City Journal*, Letters to the Editor, "Diplomatic Impunity" (Vol. 16, No. 1, Winter 2006; available at http://www.city-journal.org/html/16_1_letters.html; last viewed February 12, 2011).

the absence of a lobbying group is that Mexican migrants fear that this could trigger accusations of dual loyalty, based on the idea that promoting issues in migrants' country of origin implies a subordination of their country of residence's interests (González Gutiérrez, 2002). Another obstacle for the development of a Mexican network, as described by Ayón (2006b), is "the entrenched position of the U.S. Latino network, its hold upon Mexican Americans, its determined focus on domestic affairs, and its capacity to continually absorb talented and politically inclined immigrants – especially younger, U.S.-educated immigrants."

Moreover, except for the interest in promoting education initiatives, it has been argued that there is little consensus within the Mexican community about what issues could unite Mexican migrants and Mexican Americans.[16] In recent years, though, many migrant leaders consider that the anti-immigrant discourse and the restrictionist policies against the community, particularly the raids, deportations, and 287(g) agreements that have been put in place, have helped bring them together and begin developing a consensus on a migration agenda. For example, one of the Atlanta *consejeros* (interviewed on July 27, 2009) argues,

Now there are more protests and the organizations that support migrants are well represented. This is mostly a reaction to the 287(g) agreements, the anti-immigrant legislation and the increasing discrimination against us.

A similar argument is made by a *consejero* from Los Angeles (interviewed on August 19, 2009), with an emphasis on what this means for the future political power of Latinos in the United States:

Something that has motivated us to organize is that they screw with us too much. The anti-immigrant groups that make proposals against us blame us for everything that is wrong with the country. They think that by chasing us away they are going to fix things . . . [meanwhile] we can't achieve an amnesty because we are still not at the level we should be. The way to fight this is to educate our children, to help the young ones be the next governors and eventually have a Latino President that understands people, that knows that we come here to work.

The Mexican community is characterized by the heterogeneity of its members and the diversity of interests and demands within it. Its relationship with the Mexican government through the IME, the consulates, or community organizations depends on each group and each issue. As

[16] This was one of the main preliminary conclusions of the binational study Focus Mexico/ Enfoque México, conducted in November 2003 (Fernández de Castro, 2003a).

in the past, the consuls' personality and ideology is also an intervening factor, although this could gradually change with the institutionalization of state–diaspora relationships through the IME and CCIME. Nevertheless, the level of participation of the communities in activities promoted by the government and the IME could even exacerbate the differences between Mexican community leaders and organizations in the United States, because not all of them agree with the IME or the CCIME as truly representative of the community's interests (Garrison, 2002; Mora and Ross Pineda, 2003; Avilés Senés, 2006; Ross Pineda, 2006).

Since the Spring of 2006, there has been an unprecedented effort from the Mexican community and other Hispanic groups to come together and express their views regarding immigration reform through public demonstrations. However, in the organization of these efforts, the divisions within the Mexican community as well as the absence of clear leadership are made evident. As Vertovec (2005) argues, most diasporas include "opposing factions and dissenting voices" that are often "muffled by better organized, networked, and financed actors, who are often the ones pushing nationalist or ethnic agendas" but do not necessarily represent the whole community. In the Mexican case, a single common agenda may divide instead of unite the migrant community, especially if this implies lobbying on issues on which there is limited consensus, as has traditionally been the case with the migration agenda. However, as pointed out earlier, a shift may be taking place in this regard; some migrant leaders do see the IME in a positive light in terms of helping them come together, develop networks, and overcome some of their differences. A *consejero* from Los Angeles (interviewed on August 14, 2009) makes this point:

Something that excited me about the IME is that before it I didn't see a strong organization among Mexicans. They were fighting each other or external forces were dividing them, as opposed to other groups like the Cubans. But now with the IME there is more unity and the organizations are longer-lasting. The IME put national leaders in touch and it helped us learn what there is in other states and now there is a relationship and we go to other states and we know each other; at least the most important leaders. More organizations for lobbying are now being formed. It is an amazing network. And all thanks to what the IME has done. It also started with the migrant demonstrations; these were movements that were born there. There is communication and very strong alliances that cannot be stopped now. This creates an identity and binds us together.

Although many academics, migrant leaders, and others criticize these efforts as attempts to co-opt or control Mexican migrant leaders, the

majority of fifty former and current *consejeros* interviewed consider that
the Mexican government does not try to influence their opinions and does
not restrict their right to express them, even when this does not reflect
the government's interests or opinions (Délano, 2010). Although they
recognize that the government often does push its agenda and projects,
most of them, as in this interview with a *consejero* from Houston (July 6,
2009), see it as a positive collaboration that in the long term will develop
into a true partnership:

Sometimes they say that the projects are ours, but in reality they come from
the IME itself and they just use us to launch the campaigns that they've already
planned. But I have faith that if we keep pushing and insisting we can really
achieve a 50/50 working relationship with the IME.

A *consejero* from New York (interviewed in June 24, 2009) emphasizes
that the government still plays a dominant role in the relationship but that
its presence has been key in the development of leadership networks given
the limited of experience of many migrant leaders and organizations,
particularly in areas of more recent migration:

They don't manipulate us. But the reality is that if the government didn't provide the leadership, we would not come together. If it [the Mexican government]
doesn't propose, nothing gets done. It is a father–son relationship. There's still
some way to go to achieve real autonomy. The community is still in its teenage
years. In Chicago and Los Angeles perhaps they already have that type of communication. But over here we're still a young community.

Through seven years of working with the migrant leaders as part of the
Advisory Council, Mexican government officials interviewed also argue
that the idea of co-opting the migrant leadership is far-fetched considering the communities' characteristics and interests. For example, Berruga
(personal interview, 2010) emphasizes the diversity within the community as part of the difficulties in developing a common agenda between
the government and migrant leaders:

If anyone ever tried this [to co-opt or control the migrants' agenda], it didn't
work. The community is very divided based on regionalisms, they each have their
own leaders and their interests are very varied. They don't all have the same
agenda and don't want the same things. What is clear is that the synergy between
"los de aquí y los de allá" (those of us here and the ones on the other side) is not
as good as we would like to imagine.

Meanwhile, at the CCIME plenary meeting in Mexico City on April
25, 2010, González Gutiérrez not only recognized but encouraged the

existence of multiple agendas within the Advisory Council as well as in its dealings with the IME and the Foreign Ministry:

> The CCIME is a big room with many doors for access. The government cannot control what happens there. Many agendas can be developed, regardless of what the government wants. This is a patrimony that is everyone's responsibility to protect – the migrants, the leaders, the Foreign Ministry, the consular network and the groups and offices with which we collaborate. We are mistaken if we try to control how the CCIME works and also if the government tries to use the CCIME for its own agenda and interests. The CCIME has an agenda that we cannot co-opt; it runs parallel to the IME's agenda and they don't necessarily have to converge.

Although it is true that many CCIME members want more direct spaces for political participation in Mexico, at the same time they increasingly defend this Advisory Council as their own, they recognize its limitations (particularly in the current model for electing *consejeros* and the ability to follow up on their recommendations) and want to continue to improve it. Although it is a young institution with only seven years in place, three generations of *consejeros* (i.e., more than 300 community leaders) have already been a part of it and most of them place a high value on this experience; in some areas, elections for a seat in the CCIME have become highly competitive.

A crucial question for the Mexican government is how far its responsibility goes in guiding these efforts, helping build and strengthen leaderships within the community, and trying to use their growing political power to its advantage. This could even turn out to be counterproductive if the communities' interests do not coincide with the government's (González Gutiérrez, 2006b). Moreover, as the Mexican immigrant community becomes a more active political force, the Mexican government recognizes that it has to be more cautious in how it promotes or relates to their activities. For example, during the immigrant demonstrations in the Spring of 2006, the Mexican government issued various statements clarifying that it was not involved in any way in the organization of the demonstrations and that it had instructed all the consulates "not to intervene," although it defended immigrants' democratic right to protest (*El Universal*, 2006; García, 2006b). It also called on the Mexican-origin community to conduct these demonstrations with respect to U.S. laws, authorities, and national symbols (mainly the American flag, which was widely used at the demonstrations; IME, 2006c).

The Foreign Ministry was also wary of potential reactions against members of the CCIME that were actively involved in the demonstrations, particularly in Chicago, Dallas, and Phoenix. A few days before the planned boycott on May 1, 2006, the IME and the Foreign Ministry flew more than thirty immigrant activists from the United States to Mexico City to discuss the recent mobilizations and advise them to avoid activities that could lead to negative reactions. The Mexican officials present at the meeting said they would neither support nor oppose the boycott and suggested the Mexican immigrant leadership should be cautious, because this type of action could be counterproductive to their interests. This approach from the Mexican government was interpreted as an indication that "it is heeding warnings that going too far – such as backing a boycott that proved harmful – could hurt efforts to get Congress to pass reforms" (Dellios, 2006).

This reaction, as well as the Mexican government's continuing use of nonintervention in most of its statements regarding migrants' actions and U.S. immigration policies, provide evidence of the government's persistent concern with creating adverse consequences in migration flows or in the situation of Mexican migrants by taking a position that could affect U.S. interests or prompt negative reactions from certain groups. The migrant leaders themselves recognize these limitations: "In the fight for immigration reform I don't see the IME playing an important role. We have organized events, demonstrations and lobbying but the opportunities through the IME are limited for fear that the Mexican government might be interfering in the U.S.'s issues" (interview with CCIME member, Los Angeles, August 19, 2009).

Nevertheless, the government's frame of action has significantly expanded since the 1990s, and particularly since 2000, in the context of changes in the bilateral relationship and Mexico's foreign policy strategies, as well as transformations in Mexico's political system and transnational relations with the diaspora. The scope and limits of these actions and the definition of the state's role regarding its population outside of its territorial borders are still in a process of development and will depend partly on reactions at the domestic, transnational, and international levels.

A telling fact regarding the need to develop a wider definition of Mexico's migration policies, including the relationship with the diaspora, is that up to 2006 the IME's activities had not been a key component of the Mexican government's general discourse on migration. For example, the Mexico and the Migration Phenomenon document did not mention the IME as an example of the government's assuming a shared responsibility or its commitment to improve Mexican immigrants' situation in the

United States. It is noteworthy, though, that President Felipe Calderón's 2007–2012 National Development Plan made an explicit reference to the IME as a "bridge of communication" with the Mexican communities abroad, "creating synergies" between the Mexican communities' initiatives and the government's objectives, and contributing to strengthening their own capacity to defend their rights (IME, 2007). This shows that there is a gradual development of a broader and more explicit definition of the government's position on these issues.

Although the institutionalization of relations between the Mexican government and its diaspora represents a turning-point in Mexico's traditional attitude toward these issues, the lack of a clear definition of Mexico's policies of engagement with migrants, including aspects of consular protection and their integration in the United States as part of a broader agenda on migration, reveals that there is a cautious approach and a limited understanding of these issues beyond the government elite within the Foreign Ministry that has promoted these policies. It also points to the fact that, despite significant progress in this regard, traditional conceptions of consular protection activities and the fear of provoking accusations of interventionism are still present.

CONCLUSIONS

This chapter provides examples of the interplay between domestic, transnational, and international pressures as the Mexican government has adapted its emigration policies in response to political changes in Mexico in a context of democratization, to the growing transnational activity of migrants, and to changes in the bilateral relationship with the United States. It has provided channels for participation for migrants, particularly through the IME and its Advisory Council as well as the absentee voting rights and dual nationality legislation, and it has expanded its consular activities and services in the United States. Nevertheless, Mexico's perceptions of the limits and possibilities of these activities are also informed and influenced by the responses (or lack thereof) to its policies from the U.S. government and other actors in the country.

The examples described in this chapter provide evidence of increasing contact between the Mexican government and various actors in the United States, which have been part of a process of learning and adapting its relationship with migrants and its position on U.S. immigration policies from limited engagement to more active policies, knowing that the general stability in the bilateral relationship is not significantly affected by disagreements or increased activism in these areas as was feared in the past. This supports institutionalist arguments that growing interactions between governments and other actors affect perceptions of interests and the limits of asymmetry of power in a relationship (Keohane and Nye, 1977).

This chapter also raises key questions regarding the role of sending states and their capacity to be proactive beyond traditional issues such as remittances or lobbying. In this case, the Mexican state's programs provide evidence of the potential for host and sending countries to share responsibility not only in the management of population flows and control of borders, but also in dealing with the effects of migration, particularly with regard to immigrant integration. In the Mexican case, the support that the sending state provides through health, education, leadership, and financial literacy programs, among others, can be seen as a bridge to reach out to vulnerable groups (particularly undocumented migrants) and support those that may not be eligible for some government programs or may not be willing to approach the institutions of the host state. This also implies a profound discussion of how a sending state views its emigrants and when and how it decides to engage with these groups considering the economic and political costs and benefits as well as the implications in the domestic, transnational, or international realms.

Although there has been an important evolution of the relationship between the state and Mexican immigrants in the United States, it is noteworthy that until the end of Fox's government this approach was not clearly defined in the Mexican government's general position on migration (as exemplified by the lack of reference to these activities or to the IME in the Mexico and the Migration Phenomenon document). Some aspects of the government's new policies in terms of rapprochement with the Mexican communities in the United States have also triggered negative reactions from anti-immigrant groups there and are not always received positively by the Mexican migrant community at large. Thus, this innovative aspect of Mexico's migration policies still requires a clear definition. The process of developing it will test the limits of the government's interpretation of nonintervention and its assessment of the advantages and disadvantages of a more proactive attitude with implications in the diaspora's activities in Mexico and in the United States.

Conclusions

Sending States' Emigration Policies in a Context of Asymmetric Interdependence: Limits and Possibilities (2006–2010)

Mexico's emigration policies, including the state's engagement with the diaspora, the discourse in relation to emigrants, the responses to U.S. policies and legislation affecting Mexican emigrants, as well as the priority given to the issue in the national and bilateral agendas, have undergone a significant change. This is particularly the case since the mid-1980s. From a history of generally limited engagement in terms of responding to U.S. policies and a traditional interpretation of consular protection activities, Mexico has gradually developed more active policies and has begun a process of redefining its position on migration. The argument developed here that these changes are tied to transformations taking place at the domestic, transnational, and international levels supports existing claims about the need to study states' emigration policies based on a multilevel analysis (Østergaard-Nielsen, 2003). Without disregarding the importance of the domestic and transnational processes, which have been more widely studied, in this analysis I have emphasized the influence of changes at the international level.

I have highlighted the importance of the process of economic liberalization that paved the way toward NAFTA and the learning process implied, which led the Mexican government to a more complex and multifaceted understanding of the U.S. system and to redefine its foreign policy discourse and strategies. This was reflected in Mexico's more active pursuit of its interests in relation the United States without being restrained by the fear of creating conflict in the relationship, as was traditionally thought. The modification in the use and interpretation of the foreign policy principle of nonintervention is exemplified by the Mexican government's active engagement with the Mexican diaspora, and its position in terms of expressing opinions and criticizing U.S. policies and legislation, or lobbying for specific policies within the country.

The strategy of delinkage of issues in the bilateral agenda – particularly sensitive issues such as migration – has also been modified, though it is still present as part of Mexico's general position on this issue. Examples of the move away from strict interpretations of delinkage include Mexico's willingness to place migration as a high priority in the bilateral agenda, its support for the establishment of bilateral cooperation mechanisms for the management of migration, and an attempted negotiation of a comprehensive agreement presented as a natural evolution of economic and regional integration. These changes are still in a process of development and are a matter of debate in Mexico (and they also generate negative reactions among some groups in the United States), but they have evolved in a similar direction through the past two decades, which is evidence of a profound and continuous shift in the Mexican state's position on emigration.

CHANGES IN MEXICO'S EMIGRATION POLICIES: THE VALUE OF A MULTILEVEL ANALYSIS

When the Mexican government decided to adopt a model of economic liberalization in the mid-1980s, its foreign policy discourse and priorities also began a process of gradual change. From a defensive and reactive attitude, particularly toward the United States, and a foreign policy discourse strongly based on principles of nonintervention and defense of sovereignty, Mexico's foreign policy evolved toward a more pragmatic model that involved a closer relationship with the United States, moving past the traditional anti-American and nationalist discourse. A climactic point in this process of the opening of the Mexican economy and rapprochement with the United States was the signing of NAFTA. The institutionalization of commercial and financial aspects of the bilateral relationship entailed the development of closer contacts between various actors at different levels within both governments, as well as nongovernmental actors. This implied a richer dialogue between the countries, led to an improved understanding of each other, and set the stage for the development of formal and informal bilateral institutions to address common interests and problems, beyond the issues included in the free trade agreement. Although there are limits, the development of institutional collaboration has expanded to other areas of the relationship – such as migration – as "wider political and security considerations have come to bear on NAFTA" (Serrano, 2003: 51).

In the case of emigration, abandoning the nationalist discourse and the traditional interpretations of foreign policy principles such as non-intervention led to a more proactive policy. This change implied a more comprehensive dialogue with the U.S. over these issues, a more active relationship with the Mexican emigrant community, and the development of institutions and programs targeting this population. It also included more consistent responses to U.S. policies affecting Mexican migrants, and innovative lobbying strategies to influence the debate on immigration in the country, as well as appeals to international institutions regarding the protection of migrant workers in the United States and violations of their human rights.

These actions, mostly developed since the 1990s, have not been exempt from contradictions and setbacks, given remaining concerns in Mexico about potential reactions in the United States and accusations of intervention in its domestic affairs as well as criticisms from the Mexican public and members of the government elite who consider these policies risky and unsuccessful. Nonetheless, a return to the traditional policy of limited engagement on migration issues or a justification of limited responses to U.S. policies that affect Mexican immigrants based on principles of non-intervention has higher political costs than in the past. The Mexican government faces growing pressures from domestic and transnational actors regarding the need to address the causes of emigration, provide adequate channels for the exercise of emigrants' political and economic rights in their home country, and effectively protect their rights in their host country. Although policies in Mexico are still greatly influenced by state elites, the costs of neglecting Mexican migrants and Mexican Americans' demands in the agenda have increased. This is reflected in constitutional reforms to grant them political rights and offer the possibility of political representation through the creation of institutions such as the IME, in which migrants are directly represented by the Advisory Council.

The change in Mexico's emigration policies is explained by political and economic developments at the domestic, transnational, and international levels, which are closely intertwined. At the domestic level, the gradual process of democratization beginning in the mid-1980s was accompanied by the opening of the economy, as Mexico saw the need "to improve its international image in order to attract foreign capital and avoid the internationalization of domestic security problems" (González González, 2000: 17). Within this process of political and economic opening, new actors demanded recognition of their political rights and became actively involved in the debate over Mexico's foreign and domestic policies. In the case of migration, Mexican migrant organizations and their leaders increasingly participated in political, economic, and social developments in their communities of origin. Gradually, they were able to mobilize their efforts toward exercising their influence at the federal level, demanding the recognition of their political rights – mainly their right to vote from abroad. Whether the Mexican government reacted directly to their pressures or saw it as an opportunity to gain legitimacy and co-opt these groups (or both), the fact is there was an acknowledgment of the need to respond to emigrants' needs and demands by passing constitutional reforms to allow dual nationality and absentee voting rights. The increasing recognition of the need (or convenience) to respond to these groups and channel their demands through government institutions not only influenced policies with effects at the domestic level but gradually developed into policies with consequences on both sides of the border. As a result of the increasing social and economic interaction between the United States and Mexico, "almost all of the issues on the official bilateral agenda between the two countries have also become intermestic – that is, they have both international and domestic components" (Selee, 2005: 2). In the case of migration, there is also a significant transnational component, given migrants' increasing political and economic activity in both countries.

The establishment of the PCME in 1990, and later of the IME in 2003, had significant implications in terms of the development of a more audacious and far-reaching definition of "consular protection," which is now interpreted as "defending *and promoting* the rights of Mexicans abroad" (Durand, 2005: 31).[1] These policies of rapprochement with the emigrant community have attracted the attention of and in some cases led to harsh criticisms from members of the U.S. government, anti-immigrant groups, and commentators. In the past, activities beyond providing documentation and legal assistance would have been considered (by Mexico) as interventionist. Today, in a context of growing integration between the countries, more salience of immigration issues, and growing demands from the migrant population, there is a recognized need to adapt foreign policy discourse and strategies and move beyond traditional perceptions of the limits imposed by the structural asymmetry in the bilateral relationship.

At the international level, the process of economic integration between Mexico and the United States, particularly since NAFTA, has

---

[1] The italics are mine.

influenced the development of additional processes of collaboration between the countries. Despite the fact that the costs and benefits of cooperation are asymmetric, the countries have established patterns of dialogue, information-sharing mechanisms, and joint programs for the management of common interests. Even in the case of sensitive issues, such as migration, there is collaboration at different levels, although it is limited in terms of establishing comprehensive agreements or institutions. The process of economic integration has also had an effect on Mexico's foreign policy: It has led to the governing elite's improved understanding of the United States and a change in discourse and strategies that emphasized the need to preserve Mexico's autonomy from its northern neighbor and prevent linkages between issues. In a context of interdependence it is more difficult to maintain a closed, defensive foreign policy agenda, as was traditionally the case in Mexico.

This is consistent with Kahler's argument (1997: 16) that economic liberalization and economic integration can influence profound changes in foreign policy preferences: "[T]his transformation can be a decline in ideologically driven or *passionate* foreign policies. . . . Ideology is replaced by a careful reckoning of economic costs and benefits, regardless of the regime type." As he notes, Mexico's "persistent anti-Americanism disappeared as the logic of economic liberalization reinforced Mexico's economic dependence on its northern neighbor" (Kahler, 1997: 302). Although ideology and nationalism still have a strong influence in Mexican and U.S. policies, particularly in relation to migration and other sensitive issues, this gradual change in Mexican foreign policy discourse had a definite effect on policies beyond NAFTA and the economic realm.

Notwithstanding these developments, there are limits to the success of Mexico's actions in terms of exerting pressure on the United States to change its unilateral policies or directly influencing policy reform. The push to establish formal institutions between the countries on issues of migration and expand the framework of regional integration to include the management of flows of people between the NAFTA countries has also found obstacles. This not only has to do with the differences in capabilities and vulnerabilities, but is also explained by the domestic context in each country as well as the particularity of the issue at hand. In the case of migration management, the limited development of frameworks for cooperation, not only in the United States–Mexico case but in other regions and also at the multilateral level, requires explanations that not only take into account state interests and power asymmetries but also consider the domestic context of sending and receiving countries as well as issues of identity and nationalism. In other words, to fully explain states' interests in the management of migration, it is necessary to take into account the economic, political, and ideological components and objectives of their policies at the domestic, international, and transnational levels. This is further complicated by the fact that these objectives are sometimes unstated or not necessarily made public (Castles, 2004a: 207).

THE UNITED STATES–MEXICO RELATIONSHIP: BEYOND POWER ASYMMETRY?

In the context of studies of the United States–Mexico relationship, these findings support claims regarding the idea that the concept or asymmetry of power has been used selectively by Mexican governments, in some cases as an excuse for inaction. Although the structure of power asymmetry does imply that Mexico is more vulnerable to changes in the dynamic of migration flows and to potential reactions from the United States that could affect this and other areas of the relationship, Mexican governments have gradually learned that the use of foreign policy strategies and tools, such as lobbying for policies and legislation that favor Mexico's interests, expressing official opinions on U.S. immigration policies, appealing to multilateral forums in defense of Mexican emigrants, and engaging the diaspora in activities related to their homeland, does not necessarily lead to conflict with the U.S. government or have negative effects in other areas of the relationship. Although there are reactions and criticisms from certain groups, these are manageable within the existing institutional framework of the bilateral relationship. Even if these initiatives are not always successful, Mexico has realized it has more to gain by engaging the diaspora, and increasingly more to lose by maintaining a limited response to U.S. policies.

Particularly in the context of NAFTA, Mexico has learned that conflict or disagreements in one area of the relationship do not affect the existing dynamic of economic cooperation and the general climate of stability in the relationship. As García y Griego and Verea (1998: 108) have pointed out, even at times when there is high tension regarding migration (e.g., strong anti-immigrant reactions in the United States, a growing number of deaths at the border, or an increasing number of migrant-smuggling networks), rather than cooling down, bilateral consultations on these issues have continued and even increased in frequency and reach.

In some cases, such as the Avena Case ruling, outcomes of situations that involve multilateral institutions – in this case, the International Court of Justice – have favored Mexico. Although the United States is still able to maintain unilateral policies and in April of 2008 rejected the validity of the ICJ's judgment, this case set an important precedent in terms of Mexico's use of multilateral forums to pressure the United States on issues related to Mexican migrants. Furthermore, Mexico maintained its position of opposing the U.S. legislation on the matter and reiterated its call on the United States to enforce the Vienna Convention, as stated in an opinion article by the Mexican Ambassador to the United States (Sarukhan, 2008):

Just as this nation has consistently invoked international obligations to protect U.S. citizens abroad, it should abide by that same rule of law when the treaty rights of Mexican citizens in the United States are at stake.

Since the NAFTA negotiations, Mexico has also learned that the relationship with the United States is multilevel and involves contacts not only with the Executive but also Congress, state and local officials, nongovernmental organizations, media, businesses, and other interest groups. As a result, Mexico has begun to develop more comprehensive policies and has taken advantage of opportunities to promote its interests and those of its nationals at many levels, without being limited by the traditional conception that this could be interpreted as interference in U.S. domestic issues and thus generate a similar intervention in its own affairs. Although the discourse of nonintervention is still present, it is no longer a stringent constraint. Neither is the idea that the asymmetry in the relationship makes it impossible for Mexico to promote a common migration agenda, cooperate in the management of migration flows, respond and criticize U.S. policies, or place the issue as a priority in the bilateral relationship.

Structural asymmetries such as the ones present in the United States–Mexico relationship make explicit cooperation extremely difficult, except during periods or in areas where underlying power capacities are relatively equal (Krasner, 1990: 51), as exemplified by the Bracero Program. The United States generally prefers to act unilaterally and Mexico is reluctant to enter into an agreement that it cannot adequately handle or that could increase its vulnerability in the long term, both in terms of resources and notions of national identity. Even though migration is determined by conditions existing in both countries (and can be considered an area of interdependence and mutual sensitivities where changes induced by policy or by external forces can affect the sending and receiving states), according to realists, policy in this area has mainly been conducted by U.S. preferences. High levels of asymmetry between the two countries are the basic constraint for cooperation (Krasner, 1990: 54).

In contrast to this argument, Keohane and Nye (1977: 19) claim that inequality between countries in terms of resources and power is not enough to understand bargaining outcomes in a context of interdependence and that it is necessary to take into account the domestic context and how it influences states' positions. Conditions of interdependence make states' choices harder because the multiple channels connecting societies at interstate and transnational levels make the distinction between domestic and foreign policy blurry and influence outcomes of political bargaining. Thus, it is important to examine the domestic context as part of the reasoning behind cooperation or lack thereof. In the United States–Mexico case, "the issues to be addressed, the nature of the approach to deal with them, the set of solutions to be considered, the modalities of joint work, even the language of diplomatic exchanges are determined by the interaction of the perceptions and misconceptions of the majority of the population in both nations" (Reyes Heroles, 2006: 45).

The increasing number of contacts and institutionalized forms of communication and information sharing between the United States and Mexico, particularly since the NAFTA negotiations, provide an example of changes in perceptions. This has facilitated dialogue and understanding, even if it has not been entirely consistent and has not expanded into formal institutions within NAFTA. To explain these developments and their limits, we must take into account how actors within states perceive each other and the effect of these conceptions in domestic and international politics, rather than viewing the state as a unitary and self-interested actor (Keohane and Nye, 1977: 34–35) or considering the asymmetry of power as an immutable concept based mainly on the distribution of capabilities.

This is not to say that the power asymmetries in the relationship are absent in policy considerations and outcomes. Considering recent developments in the bilateral management of immigration, Alba (2002) recognizes that "although the dialogue did much to enhance exchanges of information, institutionalize and increase the effectiveness of consular protection, and expand certain forms of cooperation at the border," it has not prevented the aggressive deployment of Border Patrol operations or the enactment of the restrictive laws. Some argue that "when cooperation has extended into new areas, it appears to result less from a substantive logic of spillover than from functionally-specific policy convergence or direct political pressures from the U.S." (González González and Haggard, 1998: 326).

Even if the United States is still able to implement unilateral initiatives and has a greater capacity to absorb the costs they may imply, it is important to recognize that the asymmetry in the relationship is not the only factor that limits bilateral cooperation over immigration issues. Furthermore, the traditional interpretation of the constraints within the structure of asymmetry does not explain the progress in establishing bilateral mechanisms for the management of certain aspects of the phenomenon and substantial information exchanges; neither does it explain the change in both governments' discourse toward shared definitions and responsibilities.

THE CURRENT CONTEXT (2006–2010)

During the Mexican government transition in 2006, one of the main questions was whether Mexico would maintain its position on migration as a priority in the domestic and bilateral agendas and renew its proposal for establishing a migration agreement with the United States. For many, this was a test of the "real" change in Mexico's position on emigration. The incoming Felipe Calderón administration has been criticized for attempting to remove migration issues from the bilateral agenda (*desmigratorizar la agenda*) as a way to prevent contaminating an already complex debate about U.S. immigration reform and arouse further anti-immigrant sentiments against Mexicans. Nevertheless, even if the "decibel level" of the Calderón administration is lower than Fox's (as described by Castañeda, 2007: xii), migration continues to be a priority on the national agenda and Mexico has persisted in its responses to U.S. policies and legislation. It has also continued collaborating with U.S. officials on various aspects related to migration, and promoting multilateral mechanisms on the issue. This shows that the changes developed in the past twenty years cannot be easily reversed, despite the costs of creating high expectations that are unmet (such as achieving a bilateral agreement with the United States) or the opposition from some members of the government elite and the Mexican public to taking a more proactive position on a sensitive issue in the bilateral agenda that could lead to negative reactions from the United States.

After a quiet start in its approach to migration issues, in October 2007 the Calderón government announced a campaign to strengthen the defense of Mexican emigrants. The response was framed in the context of a heightened anti-immigrant climate in the United States, with more than 3,500 state and municipal bills introduced between 2005 and 2007.[2] These mostly restrictive bills have proposed stronger enforcement of hiring laws to prevent the employment of undocumented workers, limiting undocumented immigrants' access to public services, English-only policies, and participation of local police in the enforcement of immigration laws. Added to this widespread anti-immigrant discourse throughout the fifty U.S. states, a number of raids at worksites and homes have led to an increasing number of deportations of undocumented workers and separated Mexican immigrant families living in the country (many of whose members are U.S. citizens or lawful permanent residents; see Capps et al., 2007).

Recognizing that "quiet diplomacy" had limited results, the Calderón government announced a set of new strategies. These included an increase in the consulates' budgets and the addition of two more consular representations to the existing forty-eight, as well as a media campaign aimed at promoting Mexican immigrants' image in the United States (Corchado and Solis, 2007). In the context of the U.S. presidential campaigns, President Felipe Calderón, Minister of Foreign Affairs Patricia Espinosa, and other high-level Mexican officials protested against the harsh discourse on immigration used by many presidential candidates and the lack of recognition of immigrants' contributions (Schwartz, 2007; The Associated Press, 2007). Taking a forceful position on Mexico's capacity to lobby in favor of Mexicans living in the United States, Calderón also instructed Mexican diplomats to participate more actively in public debates, liaise with nongovernmental organizations, and develop a strong, unified public position on immigration (López, 2007). In addition, Mexico has continued its efforts to expand the discussion of migration issues and the development of mechanisms for its management at the multilateral level.

One of the key issues that has arisen during the Calderón and Obama administrations is the passage of Arizona's Immigration, Law Enforcement and Safe Neighborhoods Bill (SB 1070) on April 23, 2010. Considered the strictest law passed at the local level so far, it requires officials and agencies of the state to fully comply with and assist in the enforcement of federal immigration laws. Opponents' main concerns about this

---

[2] In 2007 there were 1,562 bills introduced and in 2008 there were 1,305. It must be noted that not all these bills are considered restrictionist and that only a minority of them have been passed. See National Conference of State Legislatures, "State Laws Related to Immigrants and Immigration in 2008" (available at http://www.ncsl.org/default.aspx?tabid=13058; last viewed June 9, 2009).

legislation are that it gives the police broad power to detain anyone suspected of being in the country illegally and considers the failure to carry
immigration documents a crime, which could potentially lead to harass-
ment and discrimination against Latinos, regardless of their legal status.
A week before the passage of the law, the Mexican government expressed
its grave concern about the potential negative effects of this legislation
on Mexican migrants as well as in commercial, tourism, and friendly ties
between Arizona and Mexico. It reached out to all levels of government in
Arizona to discuss this matter (IME, 2010a; 2010b). Once the legislation
was approved, the Mexican Foreign Ministry issued a statement arguing
that "the Mexican government recognizes the sovereign right of every
country to decide on the public policies that should be applied in its territory. However, when a measure such as S.B. 1070 potentially affects the
human rights of thousands of Mexicans, it cannot remain indifferent."
Mexico also expressed that it would "revise the viability and usefulness
of existing cooperation mechanisms in place with Arizona" as a result of
the passage of this law (IME, 2010b).

The statement was very similar to those made in the context of Proposition 187 in California, but the actions that ensued were stronger than
in 1994 and reflect the learning process that has taken place since then in
terms of Mexico's capacity to respond to U.S. legislation through partnerships with nongovernmental groups as well as multilateral forums. For
example, on April 27 the Mexican government issued a travel warning
for Mexicans visiting, living, or studying in Arizona (IME, 2010c), and
on April 29 the Mexican Embassy declared its support to the advocacy
and civil rights groups that announced a coalition to present a lawsuit
against SB 1070. It later joined MALDEF, the NILC (National Immigration Law Center), and the ACLU (American Civil Liberties Union) in one
of the five lawsuits challenging the law by filing a legal brief as a "friend
of the court" (IME, 2010d). Governor Jan Brewer of Arizona expressed
her disappointment at the Mexican government, arguing that the brief
"distorts the truth about Arizona and the United States" and included
"false assertions and factual inaccuracies."[3]

These actions exemplify the changes in Mexico's strategies regarding
the responses to U.S. immigration legislation, as explained by Ambassador Sarukhan (personal interview, 2009): "Mexico's objectives are

[3] See "Gov. Jan Brewer on Mexico Joining Lawsuit against Arizona's Illegal Immigrant
Law," *Los Angeles Times*, June 22, 2010 (available at http://latimesblogs.latimes.com/
washington/2010/06/arizona-jan-brewer-illegal-immigrant-mexico.html; last viewed
February 14, 2011).

the same regarding comprehensive immigration reform and we continue implementing an intense lobbying effort. What has changed in relation to the previous administration is that we now avoid histrionics because that strategy Mexicanized the debate; it generated antibodies and made the path more difficult for those who support this agenda. What has changed is our public and media positioning on the issue." For example, he explains that an important shift has to do with the relationship with the largest Hispanic coalitions, such as MALDEF, NCLR, and LULAC: "[F]or the first time we are not asking them to follow us, but rather supporting their agenda."

In addition to the use of legal channels and the strengthening of consular protection activities in response to the Arizona legislation, during his state visit to Washington, D.C. in May 2010, President Calderón declared his government's strong opposition to it:

In Mexico, we are and will continue being respectful of the internal policies of the United States and its legitimate right to establish in accordance to its Constitution whatever laws it approves. But we will retain our firm rejection to criminalize migration so that people that work and provide things to this nation will be treated as criminals. And we oppose firmly the S.B. 1070 Arizona law given in fair principles that are partial and discriminatory.[4]

This led to critiques from various Republican U.S. Senators, who argued that Calderón had overstepped diplomatic boundaries by challenging U.S. legislation and commenting on U.S. domestic issues, which was considered interference (Hernández and Ramos, 2010). Despite these critiques, Mexico did not change its statements or its position on the issue and condemned Arizona's legislation at the UN Council on Human Rights, arguing that it endangered the universality of human rights. After the killing of an undocumented immigrant by U.S. Border Patrol agents in June 2010, President Calderón issued a strong statement expressing his concern about violence and abuse of human rights at the border, including the legislation in Arizona, arguing that it "opens a Pandora's box of the worst abuses in the history of humanity." Finally, the annual border governors meeting was canceled in response to a protest by Mexican governors who refused to hold the meeting in Arizona as previously scheduled.

---

[4] See "Remarks by President Obama and President Calderón of Mexico at Joint Press Availability," The White House, Office of the Press Secretary, May 19, 2010 (available at http://www.whitehouse.gov/the-press-office/remarks-president-obama-and-president-calder-n-mexico-joint-press-availability; last viewed February 14, 2011).

In addition to its active campaign against SB 1070 (and continuous though perhaps less visible efforts against similarly restrictive legislation and the local and state levels through the consulates), Mexico has also argued strongly against U.S. government plans to extend the existing fence along the border. These actions and statements have neither strained the overall relationship nor prevented continuing cooperation between both countries' border patrols and security agencies in border control operations. For example, in December 2007 the Mexican and U.S. governments established the International Transborder Police, which focuses on fighting organized crime and drug traffic, uncovering human smuggling networks, reducing violence at the border, and combating international terrorism (Fernández, 2007). In this regard, The Mérida Initiative, a three-year 1.4 billion dollar assistance package to Mexico and Central America to fight organized crime and drug trafficking, also contemplates increasing collaboration with the *Grupos Beta* (Martínez, 2008). Some of the officials participating in these activities have previously received training from the U.S. Border Patrol through a joint initiative that seeks to coordinate actions between patrols on both sides of the border.

As part of these efforts, the Mexican government has also continued strengthening its control of the southern border through plans such as using electronic chips to track Central American immigrants who cross the border regularly for work or tourism. In terms of updating domestic legislation to bring it up to international standards and respond to the critique that the Mexican government is hypocritical in asking for the protection of migrants' rights in the United States but not offering similar treatment to immigrants to Mexico, on April 29, 2008 the Mexican Congress passed legislation to remove criminal penalties for undocumented immigrants in Mexico. In February of 2011 Congress introduced a proposal for a (Migration Law), including the protection of migrants who are victims of crime in Mexico, and recognition of migrants' rights to education, emergency medical services, civil registration, and the administration of justice regardless of their immigration status.

As discussed in Chapter 6, it is noteworthy that Calderón's 2007–2012 National Development Plan (*Plan Nacional de Desarrollo*) makes an explicit reference to the IME as a way to expand channels of communication with the Mexican communities abroad and contribute to strengthening their own capacity to defend their rights. This shows that there is a gradual development of a broader and more explicit definition of the government's position on the relationship with the diaspora and migration issues in general.

These policies can be considered part of a fundamental change of Mexico's position on migration and evidence of a shift in foreign policy discourse and strategies. As Mexican historian Lorenzo Meyer describes it, "times are changing": "In the past, when Mexico's foreign policy was based on a principle of non-intervention, it was a taboo for Mexican leaders to talk about internal affairs of other countries, especially the United States" (quoted in Roig Franzia, 2008). Still, the extent to which Mexico should promote its migration agenda in the United States is a matter of controversy and the issue of nonintervention is strongly present in discussions about what Mexico can or should do. It is not yet clear whether Mexico has more to gain by being loud on these issues and lobbying for immigration reform, even though being quiet has not produced any positive results either (Castañeda, 2007: 160). Moreover, Mexico's position is vulnerable to changes in the international context, as was evident after 9/11. Even if U.S. laws do not prohibit homeland–diaspora relations, it is possible that in conditions of heightened security concerns, the U.S. government may take a stronger position on these issues (Chander, 2006: 88), which will certainly affect Mexico's objectives and strategies.

This discussion makes evident that it is necessary to promote a broader dialogue in Mexico (and possibly with other countries facing similar situations) about the challenges that host and sending states face in the management of migration as part of their bilateral agenda. This is also part of a wider and much needed debate about the general objectives in the United States–Mexico relationship, the current challenges and future goals of regional integration, the implications and potential of the institutionalization of relations between the Mexican government and the diaspora, and the possibilities and limits of Mexico's diplomatic activity regarding migration.

SENDING STATES: DEEPENING EXPLANATIONS
AT THE INTERNATIONAL LEVEL

The significance of these findings for migration studies, particularly for the literature on sending states' emigration policies, is first that they substantiate the argument on the importance of the international level of analysis and the influence of host state–sending state relations in the sending state's emigration policies (Østergaard-Nielsen, 2003). Beyond an obvious statement regarding the importance of the bilateral relationship for both countries' policy decisions on migration, this study explains how changes in the relationship have influenced Mexico's position on emigration throughout different historical periods. The most significant changes in Mexico's emigration policies in recent years are closely tied with a process of economic integration between the countries as well as redefinitions of Mexico's foreign policy strategies and discourse.

Second, the evidence presented here furthers the argument that, for a variety of political and economic reasons, sending states are interested in establishing relations with their diasporas and that the type of relationships they develop change over time, responding to changes at the domestic level, changes in the diaspora itself, and changes in the host state. Although this book does not approach the debate from a comparative perspective, the in-depth analysis of the Mexican case provides significant evidence for comparison with similar cases. Some examples are the influence of Morocco's relationships with Spain, France, or the European Union in its decisions to engage its diaspora (de Haas, 2007) or Turkey's interest in engaging its diaspora based on considerations about its role in bilateral and multilateral relations with European Union members (Østergaard-Nielsen, 2003: 220). Paoletti's (2010) analysis of Libyan migration to Italy and how these flows affect the bilateral relationship, particularly the bargaining power of the sending state, also provides a useful case to compare with the Mexico–United State case with regard to cooperation between states in an asymmetric relationship as well as the underestimated leverage of the sending state. Similarly to the conclusions reached here, Paoletti's work proposes that "new issues on the international agenda, such as migration, may partially reverse unequal North-South relations" as traditionally understood (2010: 16).

Østergaard-Nielsen (2003: 25, 220) mentions other cases in which sending state–host state relations have influenced migration policies, such as the priority given by the Philippines to relations with Saudi Arabia over considerations regarding the protection of Filipino workers in the country; South Korea's fear of a possible reaction from China if it offered dual nationality to Koreans living in the country; China's concerns about accusations of expansionist fifth-column policies in relation to its relationship with ethnic Chinese living in Southeast Asia; or India's history of limited relations with its diaspora after independence, considering potential effects in its diplomatic relations. Another related research agenda deals with the effects of the diaspora's activities in bilateral relations, such as Court's (2009) study of the current influence of Indian migrants in Canadian–Indian bilateral relations.

Mexico's emigration policies in particular can also be studied in comparison with other diasporas present in the United States (either from

Latin America or other regions), with the caveat that the Mexican case is significantly different because of the size of the Mexican and Mexican-American communities, the extent of the shared border between the countries, the history of immigration dating back as far as 160 years, the context of NAFTA, and the importance of the bilateral relationship in other areas.

Third, this analysis contributes to academic and policy debates on state–diaspora transnational relations and the obstacles that the sending state or the diaspora (or both) can face in developing a closer relation as a result of the host state's reactions (or expected reactions). The findings in this study support the argument by Østergaard-Nielsen (2003: 209) that "sending countries are certainly not pawns at the weaker end of asymmetric relationships with the host countries despite their usually peripheral position in the world economy." However, even though sending countries such as Mexico are more active in pursuing their objectives regarding emigration and can find a wider space for action, they still measure the potential costs of their policies vis-à-vis responses from the host state, together with the costs at the domestic and transnational levels.

Finally, it raises questions about the challenges the sending state faces in terms of engaging the diaspora. Not all the members of the diaspora participate in the same way or welcome the government's involvement in their affairs. On one hand, this is due to fears of accusations of dual loyalty within the host state and questions about their ability to integrate. On the other hand, it is a reflection of deep suspicion and mistrust of the home government's intentions. In the Mexican case, there is a growing interest from the Mexican and Mexican-American communities in channels opened by the Mexican government, such as dual nationality, absentee voting rights, and participation in the IME's Advisory Council. However, participation in these initiatives has not been widespread and in many cases is a divisive issue among members of the Mexican diaspora. The subject of transnational participation also raises the question of whether the Mexican government will welcome the diaspora's influence even in cases when it is against its own interests (Smith, 2008).

MIGRATION AND INTERNATIONAL RELATIONS

Although the development of migration studies in the field of international relations has been slow, particularly regarding sending states, the findings presented here demonstrate the relevance of the study of migration as a foreign policy issue. Evidence from the Mexican case shows that foreign policy interests, discourse, and traditions have an impact in emigration policies. This case also demonstrates that economic integration and the development of cooperation mechanisms in one area influence changes in foreign policy and can lead to further collaboration in other areas, such as migration.

From a theoretical perspective, these findings can further discussions about regional integration and the question of spillover. A relevant question arising from this discussion is whether Mexico and the United States will ever be able to develop a comprehensive bilateral agreement over the management of immigration or whether it will be developed within the NAFTA framework. Does regional integration imply a gradual convergence of policies on sensitive issues such as migration? Can the existing framework of cooperation between the countries spill over into a broad migration agreement?

This analysis also raises questions related to the implications of a process of regional integration in terms of changing the perceptions of limits and possibilities for action within a structure of power asymmetry. Of particular interest is the discussion of the United States–Mexico case in the framework of the debate in international relations about the development of cooperation between states in a situation of power asymmetry and the question of whether this context can fully explain migrant-sending states' position vis-à-vis receiving states.

Against realist and neorealist predictions about the inability to develop lasting relationships of cooperation or institutions between self-interested states in an anarchic international system, particularly in situations of great asymmetry of power, as is the case in the relationship between the United States and Mexico, since the 1980s and particularly since NAFTA, the countries have developed bilateral institutions and consultation mechanisms in different issue areas. There are also shared costs in terms of interrupting existing patterns of cooperation – albeit asymmetric – and there are changes in the discourse and the perceptions of each other, which have led to more collaboration between various actors at different levels. In a favorable atmosphere for dialogue, information exchanges between governments, academic institutions, and bilateral commissions have expanded in number and depth, including new actors (such as nongovernmental organizations, the media, or businesses) and issues not originally included in NAFTA, as is the case of migration. This leads to the question of whether, as Domínguez (1998: 33) argues, the realist paradigm has become insufficient in a bilateral context where cooperation prevails in most areas: While neorealism "would have predicted a distancing between U.S. and Mexico, as well as a renewed affirmation of independence of this country vis-à-vis its northern neighbor, the result was the opposite." There is evidence of convergence, dialogue, and formal instances of cooperation between the countries, beyond economic issues, which is not fully explained by realism. Still, there are limits to cooperation and to Mexico's capacity to pressure the United States to modify its position on priority issues for Mexico, which it recognizes and adapts to through strategies such as forming partnerships and alliances with groups within the United States that can have a more direct influence. In an informal sense, this is a spillover from an instance of regional cooperation through NAFTA; the institutionalization of relations at that level has been part of a process of learning and interaction with new sets of actors and groups that Mexico has used to promote its agenda on issues that are not included in NAFTA.

There are also political and ideological obstacles to establishing formal cooperation over migration issues. In the NAFTA case, for example, the importance of nationalism both in Canada and in Mexico has been a key factor in their governments' positions toward negotiating issues such as energy and cultural exchanges, and limiting the number and type of common institutions. In the case of Canada, there is a preference for bilateral negotiations with the United States on issues such as border security and migration, because including Mexico can complicate the process and dilute the existing special relationship between Canada and the United States (Hristoulas, 2003). The Mexican nationalist ideology, which in many cases was used to justify the state's limited responses to certain issues – as was usually the case in the management of emigration – is still used by many pressure groups to prevent the government from establishing a closer relationship with the United States. This demonstrates that historical and cultural factors can limit the scope of the institutions and the flexibility of the integration framework, as argued by constructivist theorists (Wendt, 1992). In the analysis of the United States–Mexico case, Richard Rodríguez (as quoted by Selee, 2005: 5) highlights the importance of this point: "[W]e have not yet developed the semantic or conceptual vocabulary that describes our proximity to one another and our shared destiny as part of the North American region. We have remained trapped in the limited economic conceptions of NAFTA without developing the corresponding political, social and cultural vision for the future."

Theories of cooperation argue that once a regime is established in one area, it is easier to link issues and extend the original agreement into new areas. However, in sensitive areas such as migration, energy, or secu- rity, there is little evidence that states are willing to make linkages to obtain concessions. Moreover, there are cases in which linkage between the issues can hinder further cooperation (George, 1988), so delinkage is generally considered a better strategy to protect an issue from being con- taminated. For example, in Baer's view (2004), one of the main reasons for the failure of the negotiations in 2001 was that Mexico tried to link the entire bilateral agenda to immigration. Although Castañeda (2007) argues against this point, explaining that the agenda was broader, Baer's argument reflects general perceptions of Mexico's position and explains domestic reactions to it. Much of the domestic criticism on Mexico's for- eign policy in this area was the fact that Mexico moved away from the strategy of delinkage used in the past by promoting the idea of a migra- tion agreement as part of the process of integration begun with NAFTA. As well, making a sensitive issue such as migration the main priority of the foreign policy agenda was considered risky because it put Mexico in a more vulnerable position vis-à-vis the United States and could have negative consequences in other areas of the relationship.

As exemplified by the Mexico–United States case, in a situation of interdependence it is not always clear if issues should be considered sep- arately or as a package and, if linkages are to be drawn, which issues should be included, on which areas concessions should be made, and how far a linkage should be pushed before it becomes counterproductive (Keohane and Nye, 1977: 31). It is noteworthy that Mexico is still very sensitive to the idea of a possible linkage of the management of migration with a negotiation over oil (as it was evident in 2003).

In such complex and sensitive areas, it is not always considered conve- nient to seek formal arrangements as opposed to settling for informal but less politically sensitive understandings. In emerging international issues in which states want to promote a common interest, it is necessary to ask first if they need an institution at all: "Perhaps their national capacities are more than adequate, or they are converging on tacit arrangements that require little elaboration. If they could benefit from explicit cooperation they would ask whether current institutions could be extended to cover the issue, in whole or in part" (Koremenos, Lipson, and Snidal, 2001: 769).

Mexico and the United States both face political, social, and economic costs by maintaining the status quo in the management of migration flows, and they have developed a certain level of collaboration to address these issues. Nevertheless, perhaps one of the obstacles to expanding this framework is that the perceived costs of creating a formal institution are higher than its potential benefits. As Hurrell (2006: 564) notes, bilateral cooperation between Mexico and the United States "worked best when it was tacit and *beneath the radar*," given domestic constraints that arise from the move toward more explicit institutions, which "disrupt the delicate political understandings on which implicit and often hidden cooperation had previously rested." This is made evident when we consider skeptical remarks from various government officials in the Fox administration regarding whether the proposed migration agreement could actually bring about more problems and pressures for the Mexican government, given its limited institutional capacity for the management of a temporary worker program of this size and to control its two borders according to U.S. standards (personal interviews with Mohar, 2005 and González Gutiérrez, 2004).

Beyond these considerations, even if top-level interests are to pursue further collaboration on sensitive issues such as migration, it is true that domestic circumstances are still an obstacle – in both countries. In the United States, vested interests from many different groups (employers of migrant labor, the Border Patrol and the Department of Homeland Security, labor unions, nongovernmental organizations, congressmen, and pro- and anti-immigrant advocacy groups), as well as public opinion pressures, lead to very contentious discussions over immigration. These make it difficult for a proponent of a reform or a bilateral agreement to see it as advantageous in political terms. At the same time, restrictive policies have negative consequences for employers of immigrant labor and represent a high cost for the U.S. economy in general, which explains part of the difficulty in reforming the legislation or even enforcing existing laws. In Mexico's case, although foreign policy is much more pragmatic than it was in the past, nationalist political forces within the country impose certain constraints in the government's actions because they still view close bilateral relations with the United States with mistrust, apprehension, and concern.

Whether the existing NAFTA framework will develop further in the future to include the free movement of labor, or at least a formal set of rules for the management of current flows, will depend not only on the international context but also on the political, social, and economic environment in each country as well as the evolution of questions of identity and nationalism. So far, the process of spillover is not reflected directly in the establishment of formal institutions or agreements on sensitive issues such as migration. However, the institutionalization of cooperation in many areas, beyond the commercial and financial, has led to changes in perceptions and strategies, promoting collaboration and dialogue where there was usually tension and passivity.

Furthermore, the context of interdependence and the framework of economic integration has allowed the weaker state, in this case the migrant-sending state, to find a wider space for action – both through bilateral collaboration and unilateral policies – on issues related to emigration that would have traditionally been considered controversial and risky in terms of increasing its vulnerability vis-à-vis the host state. Although these changes are intrinsically tied to domestic and transnational developments that influence the sending states' policy considerations, the international context – particularly the characteristics of the relationship with the host country – is key to understanding the sending state's position on migration and the extent of its engagement with the diaspora.

Bibliography

Interviews

Berruga, Enrique, Former Undersecretary for North America at the Mexican Foreign Ministry (2000–2003) and Former Permanent Representative of Mexico at the United Nations (2003–2006), New York City, March 4, 2005 and Mexico City, April 27, 2010.

Castañeda, Jorge G., Former Mexican Secretary of Foreign Affairs (2000–2003), Mexico City, January 11, 2005 and New York City, October 30, 2009.

Díaz de León, Javier, Director of Hispanic Affairs, Mexican Embassy to the U.S., Washington, D.C., December 4, 2009.

Félix, Carlos, Minister for Migration Affairs, Mexican Embassy to the U.S., Washington, D.C., January 10, 2005 and November 27, 2006 (both conducted by telephone).

Gómez, Lupe, Former President of the Zacatecan Federation of Clubs of Southern California, Los Angeles, August 19, 2009.

González Gutiérrez, Carlos, Executive Director of the Institute of Mexicans Abroad (2003–2009) and Consul General in Sacramento, CA (2009–present), Washington, D.C., April 6, 2003; Mexico City, December 26, 2004; October 30, 2009 (conducted by telephone); June 6, 2010 (personal communication).

Johnson, Randel, Vice-President for Labor, Immigration and Employer Benefits, US Chamber of Commerce, Washington, D.C., March 10, 2005.

Mohar, Gustavo, Former Chief Negotiator for Migration Issues, Mexican Foreign Ministry (2001–2002), Mexico City, January 10, 2005.

Papademetriou, Demetrios, Director of the Migration Policy Institute, Washington, D.C., March 11, 2005.

Rico, Carlos, Minister for Political Affairs at the Mexican Embassy in Washington, Washington, D.C., October 28, 2002 and April 6, 2003.

Rincón, Gabriel, Founder and President, Mixteca Organization, Inc., Sunset Park, Brooklyn, NY, November 21, 2009.

Rosenblum, Marc, Senior Policy Analyst, Migration Policy Institute, Washington, D.C., December 4, 2009.

Rozental, Andrés, Convenor of the United States–Mexico Migration Panel (2000–2001) and former Undersecretary for North America at the Mexican Foreign Ministry (1988–1994), London, February 12, 2005 (conducted by telephone).

Sarukhan, Arturo, Mexican Ambassador to the United States (2006–present), Washington, D.C., December 4, 2009.

Sepúlveda, Bernardo, Former Mexican Secretary of Foreign Affairs (1982–1988), Mexico City, September 2, 2006 (conducted by telephone).

Sharry, Frank, Executive Director of the National Immigration Forum, Washington, D.C., March 9, 2005.

Books and Articles

Aguayo, Sergio (2003). "México-Estados Unidos: el costo de disentir," *Reforma*, Op-Ed, February 19.

———— (2004). "Mexicanos en el exterior: la evasión," *Reforma*, Op-Ed, April 28.

———— (2005). "Lo que sí funciona: defender migrantes," *Reforma*, Op-Ed, January 19.

Águila, Jaime R. (2004). "Ayuda mutua mexicana: El origen de las Comisiones Honoríficas y las Brigadas de la Cruz Azul," in Fernando Saúl Alanís Enciso (coord.), *Labor consular mexicana en Estados Unidos, siglos XIX y XX. Cinco ensayos históricos* (pp. 95–120). Mexico City: Senado de la República.

Aguilar Zinser, Adolfo (1990). "Las debilidades del nuevo proyecto de negociación con Estados Unidos," in Lorenzo Meyer (comp.), *México-Estados Unidos, 1988–1989* (pp. 27–44). Mexico City: El Colegio de México.

———— (1996). "La diplomacia del equilibrista," *Reforma*, Op-Ed, April 19.

Agunias, Dovelyn (ed.) (2009). *Closing the Distance: How Governments Strengthen Ties with Their Diasporas*. Washington, D.C.: Migration Policy Institute.

Alanís Enciso, Fernando Saúl (1999). *El primer programa bracero y el gobierno de México*. San Luis Potosí: El Colegio de San Luis.

———— (2007). *Que se queden allá: El gobierno de México y la repatriación de mexicanos en Estados Unidos (1934–1940)*. Tijuana: El Colegio de la Frontera Norte.

Alarcón, Rafael (2006). "Hacia la construcción de una política de emigración en México," in Carlos González Gutiérrez (coord.), *Relaciones Estado-diáspora: aproximaciones desde cuatro continentes* (pp. 157–179). Mexico City: Miguel Ángel Porrúa.

Alba, Francisco (1976). "Éxodo silencioso: la emigración de trabajadores mexicanos a Estados Unidos," *Foro Internacional*, 17: 152–179.

———— (1985). "El patrón migratorio entre México y Estados Unidos: su relación con el mercado laboral y el flujo de remesas," in Manuel García y Griego and Gustavo Vega (comps.), *México–Estados Unidos, 1984* (pp. 201–220). Mexico City: El Colegio de México.

———— (1993). "El acuerdo comercial: ¿un paso hacia la convergencia sobre la cuestión migratoria?," in Gustavo Vega (ed.), *México–Estados Unidos-Canadá, 1991–1992* (pp. 161–175). Mexico City: El Colegio de México.

_____ (1998). "Diálogo y cooperación México-Estados Unidos en materia migratoria," in Olga Pellicer and Rafael Fernández de Castro (coords.), *México y Estados Unidos: las rutas de la cooperación* (pp. 59–83). México: ITAM/SRE.

_____ (2000). "Diálogo e incomprensión: el tema migratorio a cuatro años de vigencia del TLC," in Bernardo Mabire (ed.), *México- Estados Unidos–Canadá 1997–1998* (pp. 157–177). Mexico City: El Colegio de México.

_____ (2002). "Mexico: A Crucial Crossroads," *Migration Information Source* (July). Washington, D.C.: Migration Policy Institute (updated March 1, 2004).

_____ (2003). "Del diálogo de Zedillo y Clinton al entendimiento de Fox y Bush sobre migración," in Bernardo Mabire (ed.), *México- Estados Unidos–Canadá 1999–2000* (pp. 109–164). Mexico City: El Colegio de México.

_____ (2004). "Política migratoria: un corte de caja," *Nexos*, 317: 31–37.

_____ (2006). "Hacia una política migratoria integral: perspectivas y retos," in Elena Zúñiga Herrera, Jesús Arroyo Alejandre, Agustín Escobar Latapí, and Gustavo Verduzco Igartúa (coords.), *Migración México–Estados Unidos. Implicaciones y retos para ambos países* (pp. 311–327). Casa Juan Pablos, México: CONAPO/ Universidad de Guadalajara/ El Colegio de México/ CIESAS.

Amnesty International (2010). *Invisible Victims: Migrants on the Move in Mexico*. London: Amnesty International Publications.

Andreas, Peter (2000). *Border Games: Policing the U.S.–Mexico Divide*. Ithaca, NY: Cornell University Press.

_____ (2003). "A Tale of Two Borders: The U.S.–Canada and U.S.–Mexico Lines after 9–11," in Peter Andreas and Thomas J. Biersteker (eds.), *The Rebordering of North America: Integration and Exclusion in a New Security Context* (pp. 1–23). New York: Routledge.

_____ and Thomas J. Biersteker (eds.) (2003). *The Rebordering of North America: Integration and Exclusion in a New Security Context*. New York: Routledge.

Archibold, Randal C. (2007). "Debate Raging: Mexico Adds to Consulates in the U.S.," *The New York Times*, May 23.

Armendáriz, Alberto (2002). "Entrevista/ Alan Stoga/ Buscan revertir mala imagen," *Reforma*, December 26.

Asencio, Diego C. (1990). "The Anticipated Effects of IRCA on U.S. Relations with Mexico," in George Vernez (comp.), *Immigration and International Relations: Proceedings of a Conference on the International Effects of the 1986 Immigration Reform and Control Act (IRCA)* (pp. 86–89). Washington, D.C.: The Rand Corporation/The Urban Institute.

Avilés Senés, Alberto (1994). "Censura Rozental en EU racismo y xenofobia," *Reforma*, August 15.

_____ (2006). "México: La agenda migrante: ¿qué es?," *La Opinión Digital*, July 19.

Axelrod, Robert and Robert O. Keohane (1985). "Achieving Cooperation Under Anarchy: Strategies and Institutions," *World Politics*, 38(1): 226–254.

Ayón, David (2006a). "La política mexicana y la movilización de los migrantes mexicanos en Estados Unidos," in Carlos González Gutiérrez (coord.), *Relaciones Estado-diáspora: la perspectiva de América Latina y el Caribe* (pp. 113–144). Mexico City: Miguel Ángel Porrúa.

———— (2006b). "Latino & Mexican Leadership Networks in the U.S and the Role of the Mexican State," Paper prepared for the 2006 Meeting of the Latin American Studies Association, San Juan, Puerto Rico, March 15–18.

Bada, Xóchitl, Jonathan Fox, and Andrew Selee (eds.) (2006). "Invisible No More: Mexican Migrant Civic Participation in the United States," Washington, D.C.: Woodrow Wilson International Center for Scholars (available at http://www.wilsoncenter.org/news/docs/Invisible%20No%20More1.pdf; last viewed February 16, 2011).

Bagley, Bruce Michael (1988). "Interdependence and US Policy toward Mexico in the 1980s," in Riordan Roett (ed.), *Mexico and the United States: Managing the Relationship* (pp. 223–241). Boulder, CO: Westview Press.

Baer, Delal (2004). "Mexico at an Impasse," *Foreign Affairs*, 83(1): 101–113.

Balderrama, Francisco E. (1982). *In Defense of La Raza: The Los Angeles Mexican Consulate and the Mexican Community, 1929 to 1936*. Tucson: University of Arizona Press.

Ballinas, Víctor and Andrea Becerril (2007). "Ofrece Sarukhán cambiar la estrategia hacia EU," *La Jornada*, February 16.

Banco de México (2007). "Las Remesas Familiares en Mexico," February 2 (available at http://www.banxico.org.mx/publicadorFileDownload/download?documentId={A5443598–2DF0–815D-4077-A416D3429AA9}; last viewed August 23, 2007).

Barajas, Rafael (1993). *Me lleva el TLC!* Mexico City: Grijalbo.

Barrera, Jaime (1994). "Apelaría México validez jurídica," *Reforma*, October 25.

Barry, Kim (2006). "Home and Away: The Construction of Citizenship in an Emigration Context," *New York Law Review*, 81(1): 11–59.

Bermudez, Esmeralda (2007). "Mexican Lesson Plans Crossing the Border." *The Oregonian*, September 19.

Betts, Alexander (2009). *Protection by Persuasion: International Cooperation in the Refugee Regime*. Ithaca, NY: Cornell University Press.

———— (ed.) (2011). *Global Migration Governance*. Oxford: Oxford University Press.

Bhagwati, Jagdish (2003). "Borders beyond Control," *Foreign Affairs*, 82(1): 98–104.

———— (2005). "A Deeply Flawed Report on Global Migration," *Financial Times*, October 6.

Biskupic, Joan (2008). "Court Spurns Bush in Death Row Case," *USA Today*, March 25.

Boswell, Christina (2007). "Theorizing Migration Policy: Is There a Third Way?," *International Migration Review*, 41(1): 75–100.

Brand, Laurie A. (2006). *Citizens Abroad: Emigration and the State in the Middle East and North Africa*. New York: Cambridge University Press.

Brettell, Caroline B. and James F. Hollifield (eds.) (2000). *Migration Theory: Talking across Disciplines*. New York: Routledge.

Brinkerhoff, Jennifer M. (2008). *Diasporas and Development: Exploring the Potential*. Boulder, CO: Lynne Rienner.

Brubaker, Rogers (2005). "The 'diaspora' diaspora," *Ethnic and Racial Studies*, 28(1): 1–19.

Buchanan, Patrick J. (2006). *State of Emergency: The Third World Invasion and Conquest of America*. New York: Thomas Dunne Books.

Burgess, Katrina and Carlos González Gutiérrez (1998). "Socio renuente: California en las relaciones México-Estados Unidos," in Mónica Verea, Rafael Fernández de Castro, and Sidney Weintraub (coords.), *Nueva agenda bilateral en la relación México–Estados Unidos* (pp. 284–297). Mexico City: Fondo de Cultura Económica.

Bustamante, Jorge (1975). "El programa fronterizo de maquiladoras: observaciones para una evaluación," *Foro Internacional*, 16: 183–204.

_____ (1977). *La migración indocumentada en los debates del Congreso de los Estados Unidos*. Mexico City: El Colegio de México.

_____ (1978). "Las propuestas de política migratoria en los Estados Unidos y sus repercusiones en México," *Foro Internacional*, 18: 522–530.

_____ (1983). "Mexican Migration: The Political Dynamic of Perceptions," in Clark Reynolds and Carlos Tello (eds.), *U.S.–Mexico Relations: Economic and Social Aspects* (pp. 259–276). Palo Alto, CA: Stanford University Press.

_____ (2001). "SOPEMI Report for Mexico," Paris: OCDE, December (available at http://latinostudies.nd.edu/pubs/pubs/SOPEMI2.pdf.).

_____ (2002a). "Crónica de un debate," *Milenio*, Op-Ed, July 22.

_____ (2002b). "El costo de la indiferencia," *Milenio*, Op-Ed, September 9.

_____ (2002c). "Absurdos del centralismo," *Milenio*, Op-Ed, October 7.

_____ (2002d). "Los migrantes, antes y después del informe," *Milenio*, September 2.

_____ (2003). "Acuerdo migratorio, ¿en cuál versión?," *Milenio*, Op-Ed, May 12.

_____ (2006a). "El voto latino en EU," *Reforma*, Op-Ed, November 14.

_____ (2006b). "Muro igual a enemigo," *Reforma*, Op-Ed, October 3.

_____, Samuel del Villar, and Mario Ojeda (1978). "Cuestiones clave en las relaciones México–Estados Unidos," *Foro Internacional*, 19: 303–325.

Calavita, Kitty (1992). *Inside the State: The Bracero Program, Immigration, and the INS*. New York: Routledge.

Calderón Chelius, Leticia and Jesús Martínez Saldaña (2002). *La dimensión política de la migración mexicana*. Mexico City: Instituto Mora.

Camp, Roderic Ai (1995). *Mexican Political Biographies, 1935–1993* (3rd ed.). Austin: University of Texas Press.

Cano, Gustavo (1997). "From Social Movements to Coalition Politics: The Mexican American Interest Group Formation," New York: Columbia University, unpublished paper.

Capps, Randy, Rosa Maria Castañeda, Ajay Chaudry, and Robert Santos (2007). *Paying the Price: The Impact of Immigration Raids on America's Children*. Washington, D.C.: National Council of La Raza, The Urban Institute.

Capps, Randy, Marc Rosenblum, Cristina Rodríguez, and Muzaffar Chishti (2011). *Delegation and Divergence: A Study of 287(g) State and Local Immigration Enforcement*. Washington, D.C.: Migration Policy Institute.

Cardoso, Lawrence A. (1977). "La repatriación de braceros en época de Obregón, 1920–1923," *Historia Mexicana*, 104: 576–595.

—— (1979). "Labor Emigration to the Southwest, 1916–1920: Mexican Attitudes and Policy," in George C. Kiser and Martha Woody Kiser (eds.), *Mexican Workers in the United States: Historical and Political Perspectives* (pp. 16–32). Albuquerque: University of New Mexico Press.

—— (1982). *Mexican Immigration to the United States, 1897–1931.* Tucson: University of Arizona Press.

Carreras de Velasco, Mercedes (1974). *Los mexicanos que devolvió la crisis: 1929–1932.* Mexico City: Secretaría de Relaciones Exteriores.

Castañeda, Jorge G. (2001). "Los Ejes de la Política Exterior de Mexico," *Nexos*, 288: 66–74.

—— (2002a). "Prólogo," in Rafael Fernández de Castro (coord.), *Cambio y continuidad en la política exterior de México* (pp. 11–19). Mexico City: Ariel.

—— (2002b). "Politica exterior y cambio democrático a dos años del 2 de julio," *Reforma*, Op-Ed, July 12.

—— (2003). "La matrícula consular," *Reforma*, Op-Ed, August 13.

—— (2006). "Fox y Derbez priístas en política exterior," *Reforma*, Enfoque, February 19.

—— (2007). *ExMex: From Migrants to Immigrants.* New York: The New Press.

Castillo, Manuel Ángel (2006). "Mexico: Caught between the United States and Central America," *Migration Information Source* (April). Washington, D.C.: Migration Policy Institute.

Castillo, Manuel Ángel and Mónica Toussaint (2009). *Diagnóstico sobre las migraciones centroamericanas en el estado de Chiapas y sus impactos socioculturales.* Mexico City: Agencia Española de Cooperación Internacional para el Desarrollo (AECID).

—— (2010). "Seguridad y Migración en la frontera sur de México," in Arturo Alvarado and Mónica Serrano (coords.), *Los grandes problemas de México: Seguridad Nacional y Seguridad Interior*, Vol. XV (pp. 269–300). Mexico City: El Colegio de México.

Castles, Stephen (2004a). "Why Migration Policies Fail," *Ethnic and Racial Studies*, 27(2): 205–227.

—— (2004b). "Confronting the Realities of Forced Migration," *Migration Information Source* (May). Washington, D.C.: Migration Policy Institute.

—— (2004c). "The Factors that Make and Unmake Migration Policies," *International Migration Review*, 38(3): 852–884.

—— and Mark J. Miller (2003). *The Age of Migration* (3rd ed.). New York: Palgrave/Macmillan.

Chabat, Jorge (1986). "Condicionantes del activismo de la política exterior mexicana," in Humberto Garza (ed.), *Fundamentos y Prioridades de la Politica Exterior de México* (pp. 89–108). Mexico City: El Colegio de México.

—— (1991). "Mexico's Foreign Policy in 1990: Electoral Sovereignty and Integration with the US," *Journal of Inter-American Studies and World Affairs*, 33(4): 1–25.

—— (1996). "Mexican Foreign Policy in the 1990s: Learning to Live with Interdependence," in Heraldo Muñoz and Joseph S. Tulchin (eds.), *Latin American Nations in World Politics* (pp. 149–163). Boulder, CO: Westview Press.

Chander, Anupam (2006). "Homeward Bound," *New York Law Review*, 81(1): 60–89.

Choate, Mark I. (2007). "Sending States' Transnational Interventions in Politics, Culture and Economics: The Historical Example of Italy," *International Migration Review*, 41(3): 728–768.

Clemetson, Lynette (2003). "Hispanics Now Largest Minority, Census Shows," *The New York Times*, January 22.

Cohen, Robin (2008). *Global Diasporas: An Introduction* (2nd ed.) New York: Routledge.

Commission for the Study of International Migration and Cooperative Economic Development (1990). *Unauthorized Migration: An Economic Development Response*. Washington, D.C.: Commission for the Study of International Migration and Cooperative Economic Development.

Conchello, José Ángel (1992). *El TLC: un callejón sin salida*. Mexico City: Grijalbo.

Consejo Nacional de Población (National Population Council) (2007). "Comunicado de prensa 40/07," December 25, 2007 (available at http:// www.conapo.gob.mx/prensa/2007/prensa402007.pdf; last viewed February 5, 2008).

_____ (2008a). "Mexicanos, principal fuente de mano de obra en Estados Unidos," Comunicado de prensa 26/08, August 20, 2008 (available at http:// www.conapo.gob.mx/prensa/2008/bol2008_26.pdf; last viewed September 24, 2008).

_____ (2008b). "Cuadro IV.3.6. Muertes en la frontera México–Estados Unidos, 1995–2006" (available at www.conapo.gob.mx/MigrInternacional/Series/04_ 03_06.xls; last viewed July 21, 2010).

_____ (2008c). "Cuadro III.5.1. Población de origen mexicano residente en Estados Unidos, 1900–2007" (available at http://conapo.gob.mx/Migr Internacional/Series/03_05_01.xls; last viewed February 7, 2011).

_____ (2009). "Número total de hogares, número y monto de hogares que reciben remesas por año, según tamaño de localidad, 1992–2006" (available at http://www.conapo.gob.mx/MigrInternacional/Series/08_02_01.xls; last viewed June 9, 2009).

Corchado, Alfredo (2002). "Migration a la Mexicana: One Whole Enchilada," *Dallas Morning News*, October 27.

_____ and Ricardo Sandoval (2002). "Fox to Intensify Bid for Immigration Changes," *Dallas Morning News*, October 25.

_____ and Dianne Solis (2007). "Mexico to Bolster Immigrant Defense," *The Dallas Morning News*, October 3.

Cornelius, Wayne (1977). "Undocumented Immigration: A Critique of the Carter Administration Policy Proposals," *Migration Today*, 5(4): 5–8, 16–20.

_____ (1978). "Migración ilegal mexicana a los Estados Unidos: conclusiones de investigaciones recientes, implicaciones políticas y prioridades de investigación," *Foro Internacional*, 18 (1978): 399–429.

_____ (1981). "Immigration, Mexican Development Policy, and the Future of U.S.–Mexican Relations," in R. H. McBride (ed.), *Mexico and the United States* (pp. 104–127). Englewood Cliffs, N.J.: Prentice-Hall, for The American Assembly, Columbia University.

———— (1983). "America in the Era of Limits: Migrants, Nativists, and the Future of U.S.–Mexican Relations," in Carlos Vásquez and Manuel García y Griego (eds.), *Mexican–U.S. Relations: Conflict and Convergence* (pp. 371–396). Los Angeles: UCLA Chicano Studies Research Center Publications.

———— (2000). "Acogida ambivalente: economía, cultura y etnia en las políticas de inmigración de los Estados Unidos," *Foro Internacional*, 16: 41–63.

———— (2001). "The Efficacy and Unintended Consequences of U.S. Immigration Control Policy, 1993–2000," *Population and Development Review*, 27(4): 661–685.

———— (2002). "Impacts of NAFTA on Mexico–U.S. Migration," in *NAFTA in the New Millennium* (pp. 287–304). La Jolla: Center for U.S.–Mexican Studies, UCSD.

———— (2003). "Las lecciones equivocadas," *Reforma*, Op-Ed, June 9, 2003.

———— (2004). "Controlling 'Unwanted' Immigration: Lessons from the United States, 1993–2004," Working Paper No. 92, San Diego, Center for Comparative Immigration Studies, UCSD, December.

———— and Enrico A. Marcelli (2005). "Immigrant Voting in Home-Country Elections: Potential Consequences of Extending the Franchise to Expatriate Mexicans," *Mexican Studies/Estudios Mexicanos*, 21(2): 429–460.

Corwin, Arthur F. (1978a). "Early Mexican Labor Migration: A Frontier Sketch, 1848–1900," in Arthur F. Corwin (ed.), *Immigrants and Immigrants: Perspectives on Mexican Labor Migration to the United States* (pp. 25–37). Westport, CT: Greenwood Press.

———— (1978b). "A Story of Ad Hoc Exemptions: American Immigration Policy Toward Mexico," in *Immigrants and Immigrants: Perspectives on Mexican Labor Migration to the United States* (pp. 136–175). Westport, CT: Greenwood Press.

———— (1978c). "Mexican Policy and Ambivalence toward Labor Emigration to the United States," in Arthur F. Corwin (ed.), *Immigrants and Immigrants: Perspectives on Mexican Labor Migration to the United States* (pp. 176–219). Westport, CT: Greenwood Press.

———— and Lawrence A. Cardoso (1978). "Vamos al Norte: Causes of Mass Mexican Migration to the United States," in Arthur F. Corwin (ed.), *Immigrants and Immigrants: Perspectives on Mexican Labor Migration to the United States* (pp. 38–66). Westport, CT: Greenwood Press.

Court, Erin (2009). "Politics in Motion: Emigration and the Sending State," Poster Session, American Political Science Association Annual Meeting, Toronto, Canada, September 2–6.

Covarrubias, Ana (2006). "Los principios y los intereses de la política exterior de México," paper presented at the Bernardo Sepúlveda: Juez de la Corte Internacional de Justicia Conference, Mexico City, El Colegio de México, January 25.

Craig, Richard B. (1971). *The Bracero Program: Interest Groups and Foreign Policy*. Austin: University of Texas Press.

Davidow, Jeffrey (2004). *The US and Mexico: The Bear and the Porcupine*. Princeton, NJ: Markus Wiener.

de Alva, María (1994a). "No incumbe a mexicanos," *Reforma*, October 20.

_____ (1994b). "Defienden Propuesta 187," *Reforma*, November 8.

de Haas, Hein (2007). "Between Courting and Controlling: The Moroccan State and 'Its' Emigrants," COMPAS Working Paper No. 54, University of Oxford (available at http://www.compas.ox.ac.uk/publications/Working% 20papers/wp-07-54.shtml).

de la Garza, Rodolfo O. (1983). "Chicanos and U.S. Foreign Policy: The Future of Chicano–Mexican Relations," in Carlos Vásquez and Manuel García y Griego (eds.), *Mexican–U.S. Relations: Conflict and Convergence* (pp. 399–416). Los Angeles: UCLA Chicano Studies Research Center Publications.

_____ (2000). "La política exterior vuelve a casa: las consecuencias internas del programa para las comunidades mexicanas en el extranjero," in Rodolfo de la Garza and Jesús Velasco (coords.), *México y su interacción con el sistema político estadounidense* (pp. 125–158). Mexico City: Porrúa/CIDE.

_____ (2002). "The Political Role of Mexican Americans and the 2001 and 2002 Elections," Conference, International Center for Migration, Ethnicity and Citizenship [ICMEC], The New School, New York, December 6.

de Olloqui, José Juan (1997). "Algunas consecuencias del TLCAN en la política exterior de México," in Francisco Alba and Gustavo Vega (comps.), *México–Estados Unidos–Canadá* (pp. 175–192). Mexico City: El Colegio de México.

Délano, Alexandra (2010). *Diagnóstico del Instituto de los Mexicanos en el Exterior*. México: Banco Interamericano de Desarrollo y Fundación para la Productividad en el Campo, A.C. (mimeo).

Delgado Wise, Raúl and Humberto Márquez Covarrubias (2007). "Teoría y práctica de la relación dialéctica entre desarrollo y migración," *Migración y Desarrollo*, 9: 5–25.

_____ (2008). "The Mexico–United States Migratory System: Dilemmas of Regional Integration, Development and Emigration," in Stephen Castles and Raúl Delgado Wise (eds.), *Migration and Development: Perspectives from the South* (pp. 113–142). Geneva: International Organization for Migration.

Dellios, Hugh (2006). "Mexican Government Tries to Remain Neutral on Boycott," *Chicago Tribune*, April 30.

Derbez, Luis Ernesto (2003). "Estrategias de la nueva política exterior de México," *Reforma*, September 19.

_____ (2006). "México ante el fenómeno migratorio," *Reforma*, May 1.

Diario Oficial (2003). "DECRETO por el que se crea el Instituto de los Mexicanos en el Exterior, con el carácter de órgano administrativo desconcentrado de la Secretaría de Relaciones Exteriores," decree issued April 16 (available at www.ime.gob.mx; last viewed February 15, 2011).

Dillon, Sam (1995). "Mexico Woos U.S. Mexicans, Proposing Dual Nationality," *The New York Times*, December 10, Section 1, p. 16.

Dinan, Stephen (2006). "Homeland Security accepts fake ID," *The Washington Times*, June 12.

Domínguez, Jorge I. (1989). "Una dialéctica en las relaciones entre México y Estados Unidos: estructuras, individuos, opinión pública," in Gerardo M. Bueno and Lorenzo Meyer (comps.), *México–Estados Unidos, 1987* (pp. 27–43). Mexico City: El Colegio de México.

_____ (1998). "Ampliando horizontes: aproximaciones teóricas para el estudio de las relaciones México–Estados Unidos," in Mónica Verea, Rafael Fernández de Castro, and Sidney Weintraub (coords.), *Nueva agenda bilateral en la relación México–Estados Unidos* (pp. 25–56). Mexico City: Fondo de Cultura Económica.

———— (2000). "La nueva politica exterior de Mexico: Estados, sociedades e instituciones," in Rodolfo de la Garza and Jesús Velasco (coords.), *México y su interacción con el sistema político estadounidense* (pp. 301–325). Mexico City: Porrúa/CIDE.

———— and Rafael Fernández de Castro (2001). *The United States and Mexico: Between Partnership and Conflict*. New York: Routledge.

Dougherty, Jon (2002). "Coming to America: Mexico Bypassing U.S. Sovereignty?," WorldNetDaily.com, December 27.

Dresser, Denise (1993). "Exporting Conflict: Transboundary Consequences of Mexican Politics," in Abraham Lowenthal and Katrina Burgess (eds.), *The California–Mexico Connection* (pp. 82–112). Palo Alto, CA: Stanford University Press.

———— (1994). "Gurría: el canciller posmoderno," *Reforma*, Op-Ed, December 7.

Durand, Jorge (1994). *Más Allá de la Línea: Patrones Migratorios entre México y Estados Unidos*. Mexico City: CONACULTA.

———— (2004). "From Traitors to Heroes: 100 Years of Mexican Migration Policies," *Migration Information Source* (March). Washington, D.C.: Migration Policy Institute.

———— (2005). "De traidores a héroes: Políticas emigratorias en un contexto de asimetría de poder," in Raúl Delgado Wise and Beatriz Knerr (coords.), *Contribuciones al análisis de la migración internacional y el desarrollo regional en México* (pp. 15–38). Mexico City: Universidad Autónoma de Zacatecas/ Porrúa.

Eisenstadt, Todd A. (2000a). "El ascenso del cabildeo en Washington: todavía más lejos de Dios y aún más cerca de Estados Unidos," in Rodolfo de la Garza and Jesús Velasco (coords.), *México y su interacción con el sistema político estadounidense* (pp. 159–218). Mexico City: Porrúa/CIDE.

———— (2000b). "El auge del cabildeo mexicano en Washington: más lejos del cielo y más cerca de Estados Unidos," in Bernardo Mabire (comp.), *México– Estados Unidos–Canadá, 1997–1998* (pp. 61–119). Mexico City: El Colegio de México.

El Universal (2006). "Instruye Presidencia a consulados no intervenir en marchas," April 17.

FAIRUS (2005). "Mexico's Defense of Illegal Immigrants," July (available at http://www.fairus.org/site/PageServer?pagename=iic_immigrationissuecenters_ defense; last viewed March 1, 2011).

Fagen, Richard (1978). "El petróleo mexicano y la seguridad nacional de Estados Unidos," *Foro Internacional*, 19: 216–230.

Farah Gebara, Mauricio (2007). "México, víctima y victimario," *Reforma*, Enfoque, January 7.

Fernández, Hilda (2007). "México y EU concentran policía transfronteriza," *El Universal*, December 2.

Fernández de Castro, Rafael (1997). "Perspectivas teóricas en los estudios de la relación México–Estados Unidos: el caso de la cooperación intergubernamental," in *La política exterior de México: enfoques para su análisis* (pp. 45–67). Mexico City: El Colegio de México.

_____ (1998). "The Riverside Incident," in *Migration between Mexico and the United States: Binational Study* (Vol. 3, pp. 1235–1240). Austin: Morgan Printing (available at http://www.utexas.edu/lbj/uscir/binpapers/v3c-4fernandez .pdf; last viewed February 7, 2007).

_____ (2002a). "La migración sobre la mesa de negociación," in Rafael Fernández de Castro (coord.), *Cambio y continuidad en la política exterior de México* (pp. 111–129). Mexico City: Ariel/ITAM.

_____ (2002b). "La hora de Tlateloco en Washington," *Reforma*, Op-Ed, September 16.

_____ (2003a). "La nación mexicana en Estados Unidos," *Reforma*, Op-Ed, November 10.

_____ (2003b). "El crecimiento latino: ventana de oportunidad," *Reforma*, Op-Ed, February 3.

_____ (2005). "Los Estados-nación Frente a la realidad trasnacional," *Reforma*, Op-Ed, October 9.

Fitzgerald, David (2005). "State and Emigration: A Century of Emigration Policy in Mexico," Working Paper No. 123, San Diego, Center for Comparative Immigration Studies, UCSD, September.

_____ (2006a). "Inside the Sending State: The Politics of Mexican Emigration Control," *International Migration Review*, 40(2): 259–293.

_____ (2006b). "Rethinking Emigrant Citizenship, *New York Law Review*, 81(1): 90–116.

_____ (2009). *A Nation of Emigrants: How Mexico Manages Its Migration*. Berkeley: University of California Press.

Fonte, John (2005). "Dual Allegiance: A Challenge to Immigration Reform and Patriotic Assimilation." Washington, D.C., Center for Immigration Studies (available at http://www.cis.org/articles/2005/back1205.html; last viewed March 1, 2011).

Fuller, Ruth (2010). "Literacy Program in Spanish Helps Immigrants Continue their Education Dreams," *Chicago Tribune*, February 26.

Gaddis Smith, David (2006). "Many Reasons Mexicans Abroad Didn't Register to Vote," *San Diego Union-Tribune*, February 5.

Galarza, Ernesto (1964). *Merchants of Labor: The Mexican Bracero Story. An Account of Managed Migration of Mexican Farm Workers in California (1942–1960)*. Charlotte, NC: McNally & Loftin.

Gamboa, Suzanne (2006). "Chertoff: No Maps for Mexico Migrants," The Associated Press, January 25.

Gamlen, Alan (2006). "Diaspora Engagement Policies: What Are They, and What Kind of States Use Them?," COMPAS Working Paper No. 32, University of Oxford.

García, Ariadna (2005). "Niega Derbez interferir en política interna de EU," *Reforma*, December 28.

264   Bibliography

——— (2006a). "Fortalece SRE cabildeo migratorio," *Reforma*, April 24.

——— (2006b). "Toman consulados distancia por marchas," *Reforma*, April 14.

García, J. R. (1996). *Mexicans in the Midwest, 1900–1932*. Tucson: University of Arizona Press.

García, María Rosa and David R. Maciel (1986). "El México de Afuera: Políticas mexicanas de protección en Estados Unidos," *Revista Mexicana de Política Exterior*, 12: 14–32.

García-Acevedo, María Rosa (2003). "Politics across Borders: Mexico's Policies toward Mexicans in the US." *Journal of the Southwest*, 45(4): 533–555.

García y Griego, Manuel (1981). "The Importation of Mexican Contract Laborers to the United States, 1942–1964: Antecedents, Operation, and Legacy," Working Paper in US-Mexican Studies No. 11, Programme in US–Mexican Studies, San Diego, UCSD; also in Peter Brown and Henry Shue (eds.) (1983), *The Border that Joins: Mexican Migrants and U.S. Responsibility* (pp. 49–98). Lanham, MD: Rowman & Littlefield.

——— (1982). "La comisión selecta, la administración Reagan y la política norteamericana sobre indocumentados: un debate en transición," in Lorenzo Meyer, (comp.), *México–Estados Unidos, 1982* (pp. 97–130). Mexico City: El Colegio de México.

——— (1983a). "The Importation of Mexican Contract Laborers to the United States, 1942–1964: Antecedents, Operation, and Legacy," in Peter Brown and Henry Shue (eds.), *The Border that Joins: Mexican Migrants and U.S. Responsibility* (pp. 49–98). Lanham, MD: Rowman & Littlefield.

——— (1983b). "Comments on Bustamante and Sanderson Papers and on Research Project ENEFNEU," in Clark Reynolds and Carlos Tello (eds.), *US-Mexico Relations: Economic and Social Aspects* (pp. 299–314). Palo Alto, CA: Stanford University Press.

——— (1988). "Hacia una nueva visión del problema de los indocumentados en Estados Unidos," in Manuel García y Griego and Mónica Verea, *México y Estados Unidos frente a la migración de los indocumentados* (pp. 123–152). Mexico City: UNAM/Porrúa.

——— (1989). "Interdependence and Power Asymmetries: International Migration and Bargaining Outcomes, 1942–1974," paper presented at the Interdependencia: un enfoque útil para el análisis de las relaciones México–Estados Unidos? Conference, Mexico City, El Colegio de México, April 20–22.

——— (1990). "El comienzo y el final: la interdependencia estructural y dos negociaciones sobre braceros," in Blanca Torres (ed.), *Interdependencia ¿un enfoque útil para el análisis de las relaciones México–Estados Unidos?* (pp. 87–117). Mexico City: El Colegio de México.

——— (1992). "Policymaking at the Apex: International Migration, State Autonomy and Societal Constraints," in Jorge A. Bustamante, Clark W. Reynolds, and Raul A. Hinojosa Ojeda (eds.), *US–Mexico Relations: Labor Market Interdependence* (pp. 75–110). Palo Alto, CA: Stanford University Press.

——— (2008). "La política exterior de México y la emigración a Estados Unidos: intereses y resultados," in Ana Covarrubias (coord.), *Temas de política exterior* (pp. 271–300). Mexico City: El Colegio de México.

_____ and Mónica Verea (1988). "Migración de trabajadores mexicanos a Estados Unidos," in Manuel García y Griego and Mónica Verea, *México y Estados Unidos frente a la migración de los indocumentados* (pp. 49–122). Mexico City: UNAM/Porrúa.

_____ and Mónica Verea (1998). "Colaboración sin concordancia: la migración en la nueva agenda bilateral México–Estados Unidos," in Mónica Verea, Rafael Fernández de Castro and Sidney Weintraub (coords.), *Nueva agenda bilateral en la relación México–Estados Unidos* (pp. 107–134). Mexico City: Fondo de Cultura Económica.

_____ and Francisco Giner de los Ríos (1985). "¿Es vulnerable la economía mexicana a la aplicación de políticas migratorias estadounidenses?," in Manuel García y Griego and Gustavo Vega (comps.), *México–Estados Unidos, 1984* (pp. 221–272). Mexico City: El Colegio de México, 1985.

Garrison, Jessica (2002). "Enfrenta Morales difícil camino," *Reforma*, December 21.

George, Alexander (1988). "Strategies for Facilitating Cooperation," in Alexander George, Philip J. Farly, and Alexander Dallin (eds.), *US–Soviet Security Cooperation: Achievements, Failures, Lessons* (pp. 692–711). New York: Oxford University Press.

Gibson, Campbell and Kay Jung (2006). "Historical Census Statistics on the Foreign-Born Population of the United States: 1850 to 2000," U.S. Census Bureau Working Paper No. 81, Washington, D.C., February.

Gimpel, James G. and James R. Edwards (1999). *The Congressional Politics of Immigration Reform*. Boston: Allyn & Bacon.

_____ and Karen Kaufmann (2001). "Impossible Dream or Distant Reality? Republican Efforts to Attract Latino Voters," Center for Immigration Studies Backgrounder, Washington, D.C., August.

Giovine, Patricia (2008). "Mexico Consulate Gives Free Health Care to Illegal Aliens in Texas Vaccinations and AIDS Tests," *The Latin American Herald Tribune*, December 23.

Global Commission on International Migration (2005). *Migration in an Interconnected World: New Directions for Action*. October (available at www.gcim.org/attachements/gcim-complete-report-2005.pdf; last viewed February 15, 2011).

Godínez, Víctor M. (2000). "Las negociaciones del gobierno mexicano con la comunidad financiera estadounidense: una nueva interpretación," in Rodolfo de la Garza and Jesús Velasco (coords.), *México y su interacción con el sistema político estadounidense* (pp. 255–269). Mexico City: Porrúa/CIDE.

Golden, Tim (1994). "Mexican Chief Urges Talks on Freer Flow of Migrants," *The New York Times*, November 14, p. A11.

Goldring, Luin (1998). "From Market Membership to Transnational Citizenship? The Changing Politization of Transnational Social Spaces," *L'Ordinaire Latino-Americain*, 173–174: 167–172.

_____ (2002). "The Mexican State and Transmigrant Organizations: Negotiating the Boundaries of Membership and Participation," *Latin American Research Review*, 37(3): 55–99.

_____ (2005). "Implicaciones sociales y políticas de las remesas familiares y colectivas," in Raúl Delgado Wise and Beatrice Knerr (coords.), *Contribuciones al análisis de la migración internacional y el desarrollo regional en México* (pp. 67–93). Mexico City: Universidad Autónoma de Zacatecas/Porrúa.

Gómez Quintero, Natalia (2006). "Derbez pide cabildeo en EU para reforma migratoria," *El Universal*, June 28.

Gómez-Quiñones, Juan (1976). "Piedras contra la luna, México en Aztlán y Aztlán en México: Chicano–Mexican relations and the Mexican consulates, 1900–1920," in J. W. Wilkie, M. C. Meyer, and E. Monzón de Wilkie (eds.), *Contemporary Mexico: Papers of the IV International Congress of Mexican History* (pp. 494–527). Berkeley: University of California Press.

_____ (1981). "Mexican Immigration to the U.S. and the Internationalization of Labor, 1848–1980: An Overview," in Antonio Ríos-Bustamante (ed.), *Mexican Immigrant Workers* (Anthology Series, no. 2, pp. 13–34). Los Angeles: UCLA Chicano Studies Research Center Publications.

_____ (1983). "Notes on an Interpretation of the Relations between the Mexican Community in the U.S. and Mexico," in Carlos Vásquez and Manuel García y Griego (eds.), *Mexican–U.S. Relations: Conflict and Convergence* (pp. 417–439). Los Angeles: UCLA Chicano Studies Research Center Publications.

_____ (1994). *Roots of Chicano Politics, 1600–1940*. Albuquerque: University of New Mexico Press.

Gonzáles, Manuel G. (1999). *Mexicanos: A History of Mexicans in the United States*. Indianapolis: Indiana University Press.

González, Gilbert G. (1994). *Labor and Community: Mexican Citrus Worker Villages in a Southern California County, 1900–1950*. Chicago: University of Illinois Press.

_____ (1999). *Mexican Consuls and Labor Organizing: Imperial Politics in the American Southwest*. Austin: University of Texas Press.

_____ (2004). "¿El amigo ambivalente de los trabajadores?: Los cónsules mexicanos y las huelgas agrícolas californianas de 1933 y 1934," in Fernando Saúl Alanís Enciso (coord.), *Labor consular mexicana en Estados Unidos, siglos XIX y XX. Cinco ensayos históricos* (pp. 121–172). Mexico City: Senado de la República.

González, Maribel (2003). "Ofrece Creel seguridad por migración," *Reforma*, July 11.

González Baker, Susan (1997). "The *Amnesty* Aftermath: Current Policy Issues Stemming from the Legalization Programs of the 1986 Immigration Reform and Control Act," *International Migration Review*, 31(1): 5–27.

González González, Guadalupe (2000). "Foreign Policy Strategies in a Globalized World: The Case of Mexico," *Documentos de Trabajo del CIDE No. 63*, Mexico City: CIDE.

_____ (2001). "Acciones en materia de politica exterior," interview with Gloria Abella, Radio UNAM, December 11 (available at www.sre.gob.mx/imred/difyext/transcripciones/radio001/ggonzalez.htm).

_____ and Stephen Haggard (1998). "The United States and Mexico: A Pluralistic Security Community?," in Emanuel Adler and Michael Barnett (eds.), *Security Communities* (pp. 295–332). Cambridge: Cambridge University Press.

González Gutiérrez, Carlos (1993). "The Mexican Diaspora in California: Limits and Possibilities for the Mexican Government," in Abraham Lowenthal and Katrina Burgess (eds.), *The California–Mexico Connection* (pp. 221–235). Palo Alto, CA: Stanford University Press.

_____ (1997). "Decentralized Diplomacy: the Role of Consular Offices in Mexico's Relations with its Diaspora," in Rodolfo De la Garza and Jesús Velasco (eds.), *Bridging the Border* (pp. 49–67). Lanham, MD: Rowman & Littlefield.

_____ (1999). "Fostering Identities: Mexico's Relations with Its Diaspora," *Journal of American History*, 86(2) 545–567.

_____ (2002). "Los latinos y la política exterior de Estados Unidos," *Foreign Affairs en Español*, 2(3): 113–122.

_____ (2003). "La diplomacia de México ante su diáspora," in Fernández de Castro, Rafael (coord.), *En la frontera del imperio* (pp. 165–175). Mexico City: Ariel.

_____ (2006a). "Introducción," in Carlos González Gutiérrez (coord.), *Relaciones Estado-diáspora: aproximaciones desde cuatro continentes* (pp. 11–21). Mexico City: Miguel Ángel Porrúa.

_____ (2006b). "Del acercamiento a la inclusión institucional: la experiencia del Instituto de los Mexicanos en el Exterior," in Carlos González Gutiérrez (coord.), *Relaciones Estado-diáspora: aproximaciones desde cuatro continentes* (pp. 181–220). Mexico City: Miguel Ángel Porrúa.

_____ (2006c) (coord.). *Relaciones Estado-diáspora: aproximaciones desde cuatro continentes*. Mexico City: Miguel Ángel Porrúa.

_____ (2006d) (coord.). *Relaciones Estado-diáspora: perspectivas de América Latina y el Caribe*. Mexico City: Miguel Ángel Porrúa.

_____ (2009). "La agenda politica de los mexicanos en el exterior: lecciones recientes," in Luis Herrera-Lasso (coord.), *México: país de migración* (pp. 278–300). Mexico City: Siglo XXI.

_____ and Ma. Esther Schumacher (1998). "El acercamiento de México a las comunidades mexicanas en Estados Unidos: el caso del PCME," in Olga Pellicer and Rafael Fernández de Castro (coords.), *México y Estados Unidos: las rutas de la cooperación* (pp. 189–212). Mexico City: SRE/IMRED/ITAM.

Gorman, Anna (2009). "Mexican Consulate in LA Takes Proactive Role in Guiding Immigrants to Social Services," *The Los Angeles Times*, July 22.

Granados Chapa, Miguel Ángel (2003). "Migración y Petróleo," *Reforma*, Op-Ed, May 13.

Grant, Stephanie (2005). "Migrants' Human Rights: From the Margins to the Mainstream," *Migration Information Source* (March). Washington, D.C.: Migration Policy Institute.

Green, Rosario (1977a). "México: la política exterior del nuevo régimen," *Foro Internacional*, 18: 1–9.

_____ (1977b). "Deuda externa y política exterior: la vuelta a la bilateralidad en las relaciones internacionales de México," *Foro Internacional*, 18: 54–80.

_____ (1998). "Las ONG y la defensa de los derechos humanos de los trabajadores migratorios mexicanos," in Mónica Verea, Rafael Fernández de Castro, and Sidney Weintraub (coords.), *Nueva agenda bilateral en la relación México–Estados Unidos* (pp. 342–365). Mexico City: Fondo de Cultura Económica.

———— (2006a). "Endurecimiento migratorio," *El Universal* (Op-Ed), September 28.

———— (2006b). "Historias de una pérdida de rumbo: el antes y el ahora de nuestra política exterior," paper presented at the Bernardo Sepúlveda: Juez de la Corte Internacional de Justicia Conference, Mexico City, El Colegio de México, January 25.

Grieco, Elizabeth (2003). "The Foreign Born from Mexico in the United States," *Migration Information Source* (October). Washington, D.C.: Migration Policy Institute.

Guarnizo, Luis Eduardo (1998). "The Rise of Transnational Social Formations: Mexican and Dominican State Responses to Transnational Migration," *Political Power and Social Theory*, 12: 45–94.

Guerrero, Claudia (2003). "Anuncia Fox un cambio en estrategia migratoria," *Reforma*, January 27.

Guiraudon, Virgine (2001). "Denationalizing Control: Analyzing State Responses to Constraints on Migration Control," in Virgine Guiraudon and Christian Joppke (eds.), *Controlling a New Migration World* (pp. 29–64). New York: Routledge.

Gutiérrez, David G. (1995). *Walls and Mirrors: Mexican Americans, Mexican Immigrants, and the Politics of Ethnicity*. Berkeley: University of California Press.

———— (1999). "Migration, Emergent Ethnicity, and the 'Third Space': The Shifting Politics of Nationalism in Greater Mexico," *The Journal of American History*, 86(2): 481–517.

Gutiérrez, Gerónimo (2005). "El debate migratorio," *Reforma*, Enfoque, December 4.

Haus, Leah (1995). "Openings in the Wall: Transnational Migrants, Labor Unions, and US Immigration Policy," *International Organization*, 49(2): 285–313.

Hawley, Chris and Sergio Solache (2008). "Mexico Draws Dire Picture for Migrants," *USA Today*, April 21.

Hawley, Ellis (1979). "The Politics of the Mexican Labor Issue, 1950–1965," in George Kiser and Martha Woody Kiser (eds.), *Mexican Workers in the US: Historical and Political Perspectives* (pp. 97–120). Albuquerque: University of New Mexico Press.

Heisler, Martin O. (1992). "Migration, International Relations and the New Europe: Theoretical Perspectives from Institutional Political Sociology," *International Migration Review*, 26 (2): 596–622.

Heller, Claude (2002). "Los principios de la política exterior a la luz del nuevo contexto internacional," in Rafael Fernández de Castro (coord.), *Cambio y continuidad en la política exterior de México* (pp. 77–93). Mexico City: Ariel.

Hernández-López, Ernesto (2008). "Sovereignty Migrates in U.S. and Mexican Law: Transnational Influences in Plenary Power and Non-Intervention," *Vanderbilt Journal of Transnational Law*, 40: 1345–1424.

Hernández, J. Jaime and Jorge Ramos (2010). "Calderón se pasó de la raya," *El Universal*, May 21.

Hoefer, Michael, Nancy Rytina, and Bryan C. Baker (2011). "Estimates of the Unauthorized Immigrant Population Residing in the United States: January

2011," Office of Immigration Statistics, Department of Homeland Security, January.

Hollifield, James F. (2000). "The Politics of International Migration: How Can We 'Bring the State Back In'?," in Caroline B. Brettell and James F. Hollifield (eds.), *Migration Theory: Talking across Disciplines* (pp. 137–185). New York: Routledge.

_____ (2004). "The Emerging Migration State," *International Migration Review*, 38(3): 885–912.

Hristoulas, Athanasios (2003). "Trading Places: Canada, Mexico, and North American Security," in Peter Andreas and Thomas J. Biersteker (eds.), *The Rebordering of North America: Integration and Exclusion in a New Security Context* (pp. 24–45). New York: Routledge.

Huntington, Samuel P. (2004). "The Hispanic Challenge," *Foreign Policy*, March/April (available at http://www.foreignpolicy.com/articles/2004/03/01/the_hispanic_challenge; last viewed February 15, 2011).

Hurrell, Andrew (2006). "Hegemony in a Region that Dares not Speak its Name," *International Journal*, 60(3): 545–566.

Iliff, Laurence (2005). "PR Guy Aims to Rebrand Mexico," *The Dallas Morning News*, December 23.

Instituto de los Mexicanos en el Exterior (2004a). *Reporte Bienal de Actividades (2003–2004)*. Mexico City: SRE/IME.

_____ (2004b). "Voto de los mexicanos en el exterior," *Boletín Temático*, 1(9), November (available at http://www.ime.gob.mx/noticias/boletines_tematicos/bol9.doc; last viewed February 12, 2011).

_____ (2004c). "Matrícula Consular de Alta Seguridad (MCAS)," *Boletín Temático*, 1(10), September (available at http://www.ime.gob.mx/noticias/boletines_tematicos/bol10.doc; last viewed February 12, 2011).

_____ (2005). "México frente al fenómeno migratorio," *Boletín Especial Lazos*, 354, October 25.

_____ (2006a). "Declaración Conjunta de Países Mesoamericanos," *Boletín Especial Lazos*, 381, January 10.

_____ (2006b). *Reporte Bienal de Actividades (2005–2006)*. Mexico City: SRE/IME.

_____ (2006c). "Inaceptables los actos de provocación contra símbolos patrios," *Boletín Especial Lazos*, 426, April 10.

_____ (2007). "Prioridad a los Migrantes Mexicanos en el Plan Nacional de Desarrollo 2007–2012," *Boletín Especial Lazos*, 571, June 4.

_____ (2008). *Reporte Bienal de Actividades (2007–2008)*. Mexico City: SRE/IME.

_____ (2009a). "La Universidad Estatal de Minnesota, Mankato, trabaja en colaboración con el Consulado de México en St. Paul para ayudar a inmigrantes mexicanos y latinos a continuar con su educación," *Boletín Especial Lazos*, 862, October 15.

_____ (2009b). "Perfil del Consejo Consultivo del IME (2009-2011)," September 21 (available at http://www.ime.gob.mx/ime2/images/ccime/reporte_ccime1.pdf; last viewed February 11, 2011).

_____ (2010a). "Declaración de la Embajada de México en Estados Unidos," *Boletín Especial Lazos*, 922, April 21.

———— (2010b). "Comunicado de la Secretaría de Relaciones Exteriores sobre la firma de la Ley SB1070 en el estado de Arizona," *Boletín Especial Lazos*, 924, April 23.

———— (2010c). "La SRE emite alerta de viaje a los mexicanos que visiten, residan o estudien en el estado de Arizona," *Boletín Especial Lazos*, 925, April 28.

———— (2010d). "La Embajada de México apoya esfuerzos de organizaciones civiles en defensa de los derechos de nacionales mexicanos en Arizona," *Boletín Especial Lazos*, 926, April 29.

———— (2011). "El IME entrega recursos para que 300 mexicanos realicen estudios de educacion superior en EEUU," *Boletín Especial Lazos*, 1055, February 3.

International Fund for Agricultural Development (2007). "Sending Money Home: Worldwide Remittance Flows to Developing Countries" (available at http://www.ifad.org/events/remittances/maps/; last viewed September 8, 2008).

Itzigsohn, José (2000). "Immigration and the Boundaries of Citizenship: The Institutions of Immigrants' Political Transnationalism," *International Migration Review*, 34(4): 1126–1154.

Iskander, Natasha (2010). *Creative State: Forty Years of Migration and Development Policy in Morocco and Mexico*. Ithaca, NY: Cornell University Press.

Jacoby, Tamar (2006). "GOP Can't Lose Latinos," *Los Angeles Times*, Op-Ed, November 17.

Kahler, Miles (ed.) (1997). *Liberalization and Foreign Policy*. New York: Columbia University Press.

Kaufman Purcell, Susan (1997). "The Changing Nature of US–Mexican Relations," *Journal of Inter-American Studies and World Affairs*, 39(1; Special Issue: US–Latin American Relations): 137–152.

Kent, Phil (2006). "Mexican Manipulations," *The Washington Times*, Op-Ed, March 28.

Keohane, Robert O. and Joseph S. Nye (1977). *Power and Interdependence: World Politics in Transition*. Boston: Little, Brown and Company.

———— (1984). *Power and Interdependence: World Politics in Transition* (2nd ed.). Boston: Little, Brown and Company.

Kiser, George and Martha Woody Kiser (eds.) (1979). *Mexican Workers in the U.S.: Historical and Political Perspectives*. Albuquerque: University of New Mexico Press.

Knerr, Beatrice (2005). "Dinámicas económicas regionales frente a la migración laboral internacional. Teorías y experiencias globales," in Raúl Delgado Wise and Beatrice Knerr (coords.), *Contribuciones al análisis de la migración internacional y el desarrollo regional en México* (pp. 137–170). Mexico City: Universidad Autónoma de Zacatecas/Porrúa.

Koremenos, Barbara, Charles Lipson, and Duncan Snidal (2001). "The Rational Design of International Institutions," *International Organization*, 55(4): 761–799.

Koslowski, Rey (ed.) (2005). *International Migration and the Globalization of Domestic Politics*. New York: Routledge.

Krasner, Stephen (ed.) (1990). "Interdependencia simple y obstáculos para la cooperación entre México y Estados Unidos," in Blanca Torres (ed.),

Interdependencia ¿un enfoque útil para el análisis de las relaciones México-Estados Unidos? (pp. 45–61). Mexico City: El Colegio de México.

Krauze, Enrique (2005). "You and Us," in Andrew Selee (ed.), *Perceptions and Misconceptions in US–Mexico Relations* (pp. 9–15). Washington, D.C.: Woodrow Wilson Center for International Scholars/Letras Libres.

Kritz, Mary M. (ed.) (1983). *US Immigration and Refugee Policy: Global and Domestic Issues.* Lexington, MA: Heath.

Laglagaron, Laureen (2010). *Protection through Integration: An Overview of Mexican Government Efforts to Build the Social and Human Capital of its Migrants in the United States.* Washington, D.C.: Migration Policy Institute.

Lajous, Roberta (1990). *México y el Mundo: Historia de sus Relaciones Exteriores* (Vol. 4). Mexico City: Senado de la República.

Leiken, Robert S. (2002). "Enchilada Lite: A Post-9/11 Mexican Migration Agreement," Center for Immigration Studies Backgrounder, Washington, D.C.

Levitt, Peggy and Rafael de la Dehesa (2003). "Transnational Migration and the Redefinition of the State: Variations and Explanations," *Ethnic and Racial Studies,* 26(4): 587–611.

Levitt, Peggy and Nina Glick-Schiller (2004). "Conceptualizing Simultaneity: A Transnational Social Field Perspective on Society," *International Migration Review,* 38(3): 1002–1039.

Loaeza, Soledad (1985). "Las clases medias mexicanas y la coyuntura económica actual," in *México ante la crisis* (Vol. 2). Mexico City: Siglo XXI.

Lomas, Enrique (1994). "Persistirá el Senado contra Propuesta 187," *Reforma,* December 5.

Lomonaco, Jorge (2006). "La diplomacia frente al cambio," *Reforma,* Enfoque, June 25.

López, Mark Hugo and Susan Minushkin (2008). "2008 National Survey of Latinos: Hispanic Voter Attitudes" (July 24). Washington, D.C.: Pew Hispanic Center, July 24 (available at http://pewhispanic.org/reports/report.php?ReportID=90; last viewed February 16, 2011).

López, Mayolo (2007). "Instruye FCH diálogo con EU," *Reforma,* December 8.

Loyo Brambilla, Aurora (1975). *El movimiento magisterial de 1958 en México.* Mexico City: Era.

Lozano Asencio, Fernando (1992). "Las remesas enviadas por los trabajadores mexicanos en 1990: reflexiones sobre su monto y significado económico y social," in Gustavo Vega (ed.), *Mexico–Estados Unidos–Canadá, 1990* (pp. 55–72). Mexico City: El Colegio de México.

_____ (2004). "Tendencias recientes de las remesas de los migrantes mexicanos en Estados Unidos," Working Paper 99, San Diego, Center for Comparative Immigration Studies, UCSD, April.

_____ (2005). "De excluidos sociales a héroes sexenales. Discurso oficial y remesas en México," in Raúl Delgado Wise and Beatrice Knerr (coords.), *Contribuciones al análisis de la migración internacional y el desarrollo regional en México* (pp. 41–65). Mexico City: Universidad Autónoma de Zacatecas/Porrúa.

Mabire, Bernardo (1994). "El fantasma de la antigua ideología y su resistencia al cambio de la política exterior en el sexenio de Carlos Salinas de Gortari," *Foro Internacional*, 34: 545–571.

MacDonald, Heather (2005a). "Mexico's Undiplomatic Diplomats," *City Journal*, Fall.

——— (2005b). "Mexico, the Meddling Neighbor," *Los Angeles Times*, Op-Ed, November 8.

Martin, Philip L. (2002). "Economic Integration and Migration: The Mexico–US Case," paper presented for the UN University World Institute for Development Economic Research (WIDER), Conference on Poverty, International Migration and Asylum, Helsinki, September 27–28.

Martin, Susan (2001). "Migration and Foreign Policy: Emerging Bilateral and Regional Approaches in the Americas," in Myron Weiner and Sharon Stanton Russell (eds.), *Demography and National Security* (pp. 177–196). New York: Berghahn Books.

Martínez, Alejandro (2008). "Inmigrantes desconocen la labor del IME," *Al Día*, April 22.

Martínez, Fabiola (2008). "El INM recibirá 20% de los recursos de la Iniciativa Mérida," *La Jornada*, December 12.

Martínez McNaught, Hugo (1996). "Ley de Asistencia Pública, peor que la 187," *Reforma*, November 10.

Martínez-Saldaña, Jesús (2003). "Los Olvidados Become Heroes: The Evolution of Mexico's Policies Towards Citizens Abroad," in Eva Østergaard-Nielsen (ed.), *International Migration and Sending Countries: Perceptions, Policies and Transnational Relations* (pp. 33–56). New York: Palgrave.

Massey, Douglas S. (1999). "International Migration at the Dawn of the 21st Century: The Role of the State," *Population and Development Review*, 25(2): 303–322.

——— and Jorge Durand (2001). "Borderline Sanity," *The American Prospect*, 12(17) (available at http://www.prospect.org/cs/articles?article=borderline_sanity; last viewed February 16, 2011).

———, Jorge Durand, and Nolan J. Malone (2002). *Beyond Smoke and Mirrors: Mexican Immigration in an Era of Economic Integration*. New York: Russell Sage Foundation.

Medina, Rodolfo (1991). *El TLCAN se come sin chile*. Mexico City: Grupo 7.

Melgar, Ivonne (2002). "Exige Fox a Estados Unidos avances reales en migración," *Reforma*, May 10.

Meyer, Lorenzo (1985). "México–Estados Unidos: lo especial de una relación," in Manuel García y Griego y Gustavo Vega (comps.), *México–Estados Unidos, 1984* (pp. 15–30). Mexico City: El Colegio de México.

——— (1992). "La crisis de la élite mexicana y su relación con Estados Unidos: raíces históricas del Tratado de Libre Comercio," in Gustavo Vega (comp.), *México–Estados Unidos–Canadá, 1990* (pp. 73–93). Mexico City: El Colegio de México.

——— (2000). "México en un triángulo. México, Estados Unidos y Europa," in *Diplomacia y Revolución: Homenaje a Berta Ulloa* (pp. 123–140). Mexico City: El Colegio de México.

_____ (2001). Comments on the United States–Mexico relationship after 9/11, at the Entender al Islam Conference, Mexico City, El Colegio de México, October 15.

_____ (2002). Comments on Mexico's foreign policy since 2000, at the La política exterior de Vicente Fox Conference, Mexico City, El Colegio de México, June 12.

_____ (2003a). "Focusing on Differences: The Historical Structure of U.S.–Mexican Relations," in *Congressional Program* (Vol. 18, No. 6, pp. 7–12). Washington, D.C.: The Aspen Institute.

_____ (2003b). "La salida de un canciller posmoderno," *Reforma*, Op-Ed, January 16.

_____ (2005a). "Hartazgo de presente y hambre de futuro," *Reforma*, Op-Ed, October 20.

_____ (2005b). "¿Y qué hacer con Estados Unidos?," *Reforma*, Op-Ed, January 24.

Meyer, Eytan (2000). "Theories of International Immigration Policy – A Comparative Analysis," *International Migration Review*, 34(4): 1245–1282.

_____ (2002). "Multilateral Cooperation, Integration and Regimes: The Case of International Labor Mobility," Working Paper No. 61, San Diego, Center for Comparative Immigration Studies, UCSD, November.

_____ (2004). *International Immigration Policy: A Theoretical and Comparative Analysis*. New York: Palgrave/Macmillan.

Millán, Daniel and Wilbert Torre (2002). "Anuncia SRE campaña para lograr pacto migratorio," *Reforma*, September 10.

Mitchell, Christopher (1989). "International Migration, International Relations and Foreign Policy," *International Migration Review*, 23(3): 681–708.

_____ (ed.) (1992). *Western Hemisphere Immigration and United States Foreign Policy*. University Park, PA: Pennsylvania State University Press.

Migration Information Source (2006). "UN High-Level Dialogue on International Migration and Development" (December). Washington, D.C.: Migration Policy Institute.

Moctezuma Longoria, Miguel (2003a). "La voz de los actores sobre la ley migrante y Zacatecas," *Migración y Desarrollo*, 1: 100–103.

_____ (2003b). "Territorialidad de los clubes zacatecanos en Estados Unidos," *Migración y Desarrollo*, 1: 49–73.

Mohar, Gustavo (2004). "Mexico–United States Migration: A Long Way To Go," *Migration Information Source* (March). Washington, D.C.: Migration Policy Institute.

Monto, Alexander (1994). *The Roots of Mexican Labor Migration*, Westport, CT: Praeger.

Mora, Juan Andrés and Raúl Ross Pineda (2003). *Instituto de los Mexicanos en el Exterior: notas para una discusión*. Chicago: Ediciones MX Sin Fronteras.

Morales, Patricia (1989). *Indocumentados mexicanos*. Mexico City: Grijalbo.

Moravcsik, Andrew (1997). "Taking Preferences Seriously: A Liberal Theory of International Politics," *International Organization*, 51(4): 513–553.

National Immigration Law Center (2000). "AFL-CIO Calls for Repeal of Employer Sanctions and Enactment of a New Legalization Program," February

16 (available at http://www.nilc.org/immsemplymnt/ircaempverif/ircao18.htm; last viewed November 19, 2010).

Newland, Katherine (2005). "Migration's Unrealized Potential: The Report of the Global Commission on International Migration," *Migration Information Source* (November). Washington, D.C.: Migration Policy Institute.

Núñez, Ernesto and Claudia Salazar (2003). "Rechazan el trueque migración por Pemex: Cuestionan condiciones al acuerdo." *Reforma*, May 11.

Oficina del Alto Comisionado de las Naciones Unidas para los Derechos Humanos en México (2003). *Diagnóstico sobre la situación de los derechos humanos en México*. Mexico City: MundiPrensa.

Ojeda, Mario (1974). "Las relaciones de México con el régimen revolucionario cubano," *Foro Internacional*, 14: 474–506.

——— (1976a). *Alcances y límites de la política exterior de México*. Mexico City: El Colegio de México.

——— (1976b): "La realidad geopolítica de México," *Foro Internacional*, 17: 1–9.

——— (1977). "México ante los Estados Unidos en la coyuntura actual," *Foro Internacional*, 18: 32–53.

——— (1983). "Mexico and United States Relations: Interdependence or Mexico's Dependence?," in Carlos Vásquez and Manuel García y Griego (eds.), *Mexican–U.S. Relations: Conflict and Convergence* (pp. 109–126). Los Angeles: UCLA Chicano Studies Research Center Publications.

Olson, Georgina (2007). "Confían salvar a 46 de pena capital," *Excélsior*, October 1.

Organización Regional Interamericana de Trabajadores (1953). "La ORIT y el problema de los braceros mexicanos," Conferencia de Sindicatos Mexicanos y Estadounidenses, Mexico City, December 14–16.

Orozco, Manuel and Rebecca Rouse (2007), "Migrant Hometown Associations and Opportunities for Development: A Global Perspective," *Migration Information Source* (February). Washington, D.C.: Migration Policy Institute.

Ortiz, Alicia (1996). "Vigilará México impacto de nueva ley migratoria," *Reforma*, May 4.

Østergaard-Nielsen, Eva (ed.) (2003). *International Migration and Sending Countries: Perceptions, Policies and Transnational Relations*. New York: Palgrave.

Paoletti, Emanuela (2010). *The Migration of Power and North–South Inequalities: The Case of Italy and Libya*. Basingstoke, England: Palgrave Macmillan.

Paz, Octavio (1993). *El laberinto de la soledad, Postdata y Vuelta al laberinto de la soledad* (2nd ed.). Mexico City: Fondo de Cultura Económica.

Pellicer, Olga (1968). "La revolución cubana in México," *Foro Internacional*, 8: 374–395.

——— (1972). *México y la revolución cubana*. Mexico City: El Colegio de México.

——— (1976). "Las relaciones comerciales de México: una prueba para la nueva política exterior," *Foro Internacional*, 17: 37–50.

——— (1978). "La política de Estados Unidos hacia México: la nueva perspectiva," *Foro Internacional*, 19: 193–215.

Pérez, Miguel and Norma Jiménez (1994). "Reclamará Zedillo por Propuesta 187," *Reforma*, November 11.

Pfeiffer, David (1979). "The Bracero Program in Mexico," in George Kiser and Martha Woody Kiser (eds.), *Mexican Workers in the U.S.: Historical and Political Perspectives* (pp. 71–84). Albuquerque: University of New Mexico Press.

Pineda, Octavio (2003). "Responde Derbez: Pemex no se vende," *Reforma*, May 11.

Porter, Eduardo (2003). "Mexico Adds Lobbying Muscle with Mexican-Americans' Help," *The Wall Street Journal*, October 3.

Portes, Alejandro (1997). "Immigration Theory for a New Century: Some Problems and Opportunities," *International Migration Review*, 31(4): 799–825.

———, Cristina Escobar, and Renelinda Arana (2008). "Bridging the Gap: Transnational and Ethnic Organizations in the Political Incorporation of Immigrants in the United States," *Ethnic and Racial Studies*, 31(6): 1056–1090.

Pozas Horcasitas, Ricardo (1993). *La democracia en blanco: el movimiento médico en México, 1964–1965.* Mexico City: Siglo XXI.

Putnam, Robert D. (1988). "Diplomacy and Domestic Politics: The Logic of Two-Level Games," *International Organization*, 42 (3): 427–460.

Quintana, Enrique and Roberto Zamarripa (2002). "Entrevista/ Carlos Salinas de Gortari/ Cargan al TLC culpas que no tiene," *Reforma*, December 9.

Reforma (1994a). "Combaten iniciativa SOS," *Reforma*, October 11.

——— (1994b). "Descarta Rozental deportación masiva," *Reforma*, October 31.

——— (1994c). "Denuncia México en la ONU," *Reforma*, November 12.

——— (1994d). "Año de antiinmigración en EU," *Reforma*, December 28.

——— (1996). "Manifiesta México 'grave inquietud'," *Reforma*, September 26.

——— (2010). "Condena México ley de Arizona ante ONU," *Reforma*, June 1.

Reinert, Patty (2006). "Mexico seeks migration deal," *Houston Chronicle*, March 21.

Renshon, Stanley (2005). "The 50% American: Immigration and National Identity in an Age of Terror," Panel Discussion Transcript, National Press Club, October 24.

Reyes Heroles, Jesús. "Changing Perceptions," in Andrew Selee (ed.), *Perceptions and Misconceptions in US–Mexico Relations* (pp. 45–51). Washington, D.C.: Woodrow Wilson Center for International Scholars/Letras Libres.

Reynolds, Clark and Carlos Tello (eds.) (1983). *U.S.–Mexico Relations: Economic and Social Aspects.* Palo Alto, CA: Stanford University Press.

Rico, Carlos (1986). "Relaciones México–Estados Unidos y la *Paradoja del Precipicio*," in Humberto Garza (comp.), *Fundamentos y prioridades de la política exterior de México* (pp. 59–72). Mexico City: El Colegio de México.

——— (1990a). "The Immigration Reform and Control Act of 1986 and Mexican Perceptions of Bilateral Approaches to Immigration Issues," in George Vernez (comp.), *Immigration and International Relations: Proceedings of a Conference on the International Effects of the 1986 Immigration Reform and Control Act (IRCA)* (pp. 90–100). Washington, D.C.: The Rand Corporation/The Urban Institute.

——— (1990b). "La Ley de Reforma y Control de la Inmigración de 1986 y las percepciones mexicanas de un enfoque bilateral del problema," in Lorenzo Meyer (comp.), *México–Estados Unidos, 1988–1989* (pp. 45–64). Mexico City: El Colegio de México.

——— (1991). *México y el mundo. Historia de sus relaciones exteriores: Hacia la globalización* (Vol. 8). Mexico City: Senado de la República.

——— (1992). "Migration and U.S.–Mexico Relations, 1966–1986," in Christopher Mitchell (ed.), *Western Hemisphere Immigration and U.S. Foreign Policy* (pp. 222–283). University Park, PA: Pennsylvania State University Press.

Riding, Alan (1977). "Mexicans Are Vexed by U.S. Migrant Plan," *The New York Times*, August 28.

Rincón Gallardo, Gilberto (2003). "El adiós del canciller," *Reforma*, January 11.

Risse-Kappen, Thomas (1991). "Did 'Peace through Strength' End the Cold War? Lessons from INF," *International Security*, 16(1): 162–188.

Riva Palacio, Raymundo (1994). "Estrictamente Personal: Oh Zedillo, Zedillo," *Reforma*, November 23.

Rivera-Salgado, Gaspar (2000). "Transnational Political Strategies: The Case of Mexican Indigenous Migrants," in Nancy Foner, Rubén G. Rumbaut, and Steven J. Gold (eds.), *Immigration Research for a New Century: Multidisciplinary Perspectives* (pp. 134–156). New York: Russell Sage Foundation.

——— (2006). "Mexican Migrant Organizations," in Xóchitl Bada, Jonathan Fox, and Andrew Selee (eds.), *Invisible No More: Mexican Migrant Civic Participation in the United States* (pp. 5–8). Washington, D.C.: Woodrow Wilson International Center for Scholars (available at http://www.wilsoncenter.org/news/docs/Invisible%20No%20More1.pdf; last viewed February 16, 2011).

Rodríguez, Esteban David (1997). "La difícil diplomacia," *Reforma*, Enfoque, April 13.

Rodríguez, Richard (2005). "The New Geography of North America," in Andrew Selee (ed.), *Perceptions and Misconceptions in US–Mexico Relations* (pp. 19–26). Washington, D.C.: Woodrow Wilson Center for International Scholars/ Letras Libres.

Roig Franzia, Manuel (2008). "Mexico Rebukes U.S. Candidates on Migrant Issues," *The Washington Post*, January 8.

Román, José Antonio (2005). "En la revisión de los procesos a cinco se les conmutó la pena: Sepúlveda Amor," *La Jornada*, December 1.

Ronfeldt, David and Caesar D. Sereseres (1978). "Un nuevo marco político para las relaciones de México con Estados Unidos," *Foro Internacional*, 19: 231–255.

——— (1983). "The Management of U.S.–Mexico Interdependence: Drift Toward Failure?," in Carlos Vásquez and Manuel García y Griego (eds.), *Mexican–U.S. Relations: Conflict and Convergence* (pp. 43–107). Los Angeles: UCLA Chicano Studies Research Center Publications.

Rosenblum, Marc R. (2004). "Beyond the Policy of No Policy: Emigration from Mexico and Central America," *Latin American Politics and Society*, 4(1): 91–125.

Ross Pineda, Raúl (2006). "El foxismo y los migrantes," *Diario La Estrella*, Op-Ed, November 14.

Rozemberg, Hernan (2002). "*Matrículas* gain acceptance," *The Arizona Republic*, October 31.
Rubio, Luis (2004). "El dilema de la integración," *Reforma*, Op-Ed, September 19.
Rudolph, Christopher (2004). "Homeland Security and International Migration: Toward a North American Security Perimeter?," paper prepared for the Conference on North American Integration: Migration, Trade, and Security, Château Laurier, Ottawa, Canada, April 1–2.
Russell, Sharon Stanton (1989). "Politics and Ideology in Migration Policy Formulation: The Case of Kuwait," *International Migration Review*, 23(1): 24–47.
Samora, Julián (1971). *Los Mojados: The Wetback Story*. Notre Dame: University of Notre Dame Press.
Sarmiento, Sergio (2003). "Petróleo nuestro," *Reforma*, May 13.
Sarukhan, Arturo (2008). "Why Enforcing the Vienna Convention Makes Sense," *Dallas Morning News*, May 7.
Schmitter-Heisler, Barbara (1985). "Sending Countries and the Politics of Emigration and Destination," *International Migration Review* 19(3): 469–484.
_____ (1992). "The Future of Immigrant Incorporation: Which Models? Which Concepts?," *International Migration Review*, 26(2): 623–645.
_____ (2000). "The Sociology of Immigration: From Assimilation to Segmented Integration, from the American Experience to the Global Arena," in Caroline B. Brettell and James F. Hollifield (eds.), *Migration Theory: Talking across Disciplines* (pp. 77–96). New York: Routledge.
Schwartz, Jeremy (2007). "Mexico's Frustration with U.S. Immigration Policy Builds," *Austin American Statesman*, November 17.
Secretaría de Relaciones Exteriores (1928). *La migración y protección de mexicanos en el extranjero: Labor de la Secretaría de Relaciones Exteriores en los Estados Unidos de América y Guatemala*. Mexico City: Secretaría de Relaciones Exteriores.
_____ (1995). *Discursos del Secretario de Relaciones Exteriores, Ángel Gurría, mayo-junio 1995*. Mexico City: Secretaría de Relaciones Exteriores.
_____ (1996). *Discursos del Secretario de Relaciones Exteriores, Ángel Gurría, marzo-abril 1996*. Mexico City: Secretaría de Relaciones Exteriores.
_____ (1997). *Informe del Estudio Binacional México–Estados Unidos sobre Migración*. Mexico City: Secretaría de Relaciones Exteriores.
_____ (2000). *Programa para las Comunidades Mexicanas en el Exterior (PCME) 1990–2000*. Mexico City: Secretaría de Relaciones Exteriores.
Seder, Andrew M. (2009). "King's Outreach Targets Hispanics: Immigrants to Benefit from Education Program, which also Is Sponsored by Mexican Gov't," *The Times Leader*, January 23.
Selee, Andrew (ed.) (2005). "Growing Closer, Remaining Apart," in Andrew Selee, *Perceptions and Misconceptions in US–Mexico Relations* (pp. 1–8). Washington, D.C.: Woodrow Wilson Center for International Scholars/Letras Libres.
Sepúlveda Amor, Bernardo (1984). "Reflexiones sobre la política exterior de México," *Foro Internacional*, 24(4): 407–414.

――― (1994). "Los intereses de la política exterior," in César Sepúlveda (comp.), *La política internacional de México en el decenio de los ochenta* (pp. 17–99). Mexico City: Fondo de Cultura Económica.

――― (1998). "Objetivos e intereses de la política exterior mexicana," in Ilán Bizberg (comp.), *México ante el fin de la Guerra Fría* (pp. 49–76). Mexico City: El Colegio de México.

Serrano, Mónica (2003). "Bordering the Impossible: U.S.–Mexico Security Relations after 9-11," in Peter Andreas and Thomas J. Biersteker (eds.), *The Rebordering of North America: Integration and Exclusion in a New Security Context* (pp. 46–67). New York: Routledge.

Shain, Yossi (1994–1995). "Ethnic Diasporas and US Foreign Policy," *Political Science Quarterly*, 109(5): 811–841.

――― (1999–2000). "The Mexican-American Diaspora's Impact on Mexico," *Political Science Quarterly*, 114(4): 661–691.

――― and Aharon Barth (2003). "Diasporas and International Relations Theory," *International Organization*, 57: 449–479.

Shapira, Yoram (1978). "La política exterior de México bajo el régimen de Echeverría: retrospectiva," *Foro Internacional*, 19: 62–91.

Sheffer, Gabriel (ed.) (1986). *Modern Diasporas in International Politics*. London: Croom Helm.

Sherman, Rachel (1999). "From State Introversion to State Extension in Mexico: Modes of Emigrant Incorporation, 1900–1997," *Theory and Society*, 28(6): 835–878.

Silva-Herzog Márquez, Jesús (2006). "Voto en el extranjero," *Reforma*, Op-Ed, April 17.

Smith, Robert C. (2003a). "Diasporic Memberships in Historical Perspective: Comparative Insights from the Mexican, Italian and Polish Cases," *International Migration Review*, 37(3): 724–759.

――― (2003b). "Migrant Membership as an Instituted Process: Migration, the State and the Extra-Territorial Conduct of Mexican Politics," *International Migration Review*, 37(2): 297–343.

――― (2008). "Contradictions of Diasporic Institutionalization in Mexican Politics: The 2006 Migrant Vote and other Forms of Inclusion and Control," *Ethnic and Racial Studies*, 31(4): 708–741.

Sobel, Richard (2001). "Immigration and Identification: Interviews with Alan Simpson," *Migration World*, 29(3): 30–36.

Stevenson, Mark (2006). "Few Mexican Migrants Seek Absentee Ballots," The Associated Press, February 16.

Storrs, K. Larry (2005). "Mexico–United States Dialogue on Migration and Border Issues, 2001–2005," Report for Congress, Congressional Research Service (CRS), June 2 (available at http://www.fas.org/sgp/crs/row/RL32735.pdf; last viewed February 16, 2011).

――― (2006). "Mexico's Importance and Multiple Relationships with the United States," Report for Congress, Congressional Research Service (CRS), January 18 (available at http://fpc.state.gov/documents/organization/60778.pdf; last viewed February 16, 2011).

Strickland, Barbara K. (1989). "Simpson–Rodino, 1987–1988: ¿bomba que no estalló?," in Gerardo M. Bueno and Lorenzo Meyer (comps.), *México-Estados Unidos, 1987* (pp. 175–213). Mexico City: El Colegio de México.

Sullivan, Bartholomew (2007). "Mexican ID Controversy on the Way Here," *The Commercial Appeal*, March 9.

Suro, Roberto and Gabriel Escobar (2006). "Pew Hispanic Center Survey of Mexicans Living in the U.S. on Absentee Voting in Mexican Elections" (February 22). Washington, D.C.: Pew Hispanic Center (available at http://pewhispanic.org/reports/report.php?ReportID=60; last viewed February 16, 2011).

Tamayo, Jesús and Fernando Lozano Asencio (1991), "Mexican Perceptions on Rural Development and Migration of Workers to the United States and Actions Taken, 1970–1988," in Sergio Díaz Briquets and Sidney Weintraub (eds.), *Regional and Sectoral Development in Mexico as Alternatives to Migration*, Series on Development and International Migration in Mexico, Central America, and the Caribbean Basin. Boulder, CO: Westview Press.

Taylor, Lawrence Douglas (2004). "En defensa de la patria: el papel de los cónsules mexicanos del sur de California durante la revuelta agonista de 1911," in Fernando Saúl Alanís Enciso (coord.), *Labor consular mexicana en Estados Unidos, siglos XIX y XX. Cinco ensayos históricos* (pp. 41–93). Mexico City: Senado de la República.

Teitelbaum, Michael S. (1984). "Immigration, Refugees, and Foreign Policy," *International Organization*, 38(3): 429–450.

Terrazas y Basante, Marcela (2004). "Joaquín José Castillo y Cos, Cónsul mexicano en Brownsville, y los problemas fronterizos durante 1851–1853," in Fernando Saúl Alanís Enciso (coord.), *Labor consular mexicana en Estados Unidos, siglos XIX y XX. Cinco ensayos históricos* (pp. 15–39). Mexico City: Senado de la República.

The Associated Press (2007). "Mexican President Accuses U.S. Candidates of Being *Anti-Mexican*," December 5.

_____ (2010). "Mexico's President Calls Stun Gun Death of Migrant at US Border Near San Diego *Unacceptable*," June 7.

Thelen, David (1999). "Mexico, the Latin North American Nation: A Conversation with Carlos Rico Ferrat," *The Journal of American History*, 86(2): 467–480.

Thompson, Ginger (2005). "Mexican Leader Condemns U.S. for Migrant Bill Passed by House," *The New York Times*, December 20.

Tong, Anna (2009). "Mexican Consulate in Sacramento Launches Health Care Program," *Sacramento Bee*, 18 December.

Torres, Blanca (1991). *México y el mundo. Historia de sus relaciones exteriores: De la guerra al mundo bipolar* (Vol. 7). Mexico City: Senado de la República.

Tuirán, Rodolfo and José Luis Ávila (2010). "La migración México–Estados Unidos, 1940–2010," in Francisco Alba, Manuel Ángel Castillo, and Gustavo Verduzco, *Los grandes problemas de México: Migraciones Internacionales* (Vol. 3, pp. 93–134). Mexico City: El Colegio de México.

Unomásuno (2002). "Vigente la discusión sobre inmigrantes con México: SIN," February 2.

Urquidi, Víctor I. and Sofía Méndez Villarreal (1975). "Importancia económica de la zona fronteriza del norte de México," *Foro Internacional*, 16: 149–174.

U.S. Census Bureau (2006). "Nation's Population One-Third Minority," News Release, May 10 (available at http://www.census.gov/Press-Release/www/releases/archives/population/006808.html; last viewed March 20, 2008).

——— (2009). "Hispanic Heritage Month 2009: Sept. 15–Oct. 15," News Release, updated September 14, 2009 (available at http://www.census.gov/newsroom/releases/archives/facts_for_features_special_editions/cb09-ff17.html; last viewed September 30, 2009).

——— (2010). 2009 American Community Survey. Data sets: "Selected Characteristics of the Foreign-Born Population by Region of Birth: Latin America" and "Hispanic or Latino Origin by Specific Origin" (accessed online at http://www.census.gov/acs/www/).

U.S. Commission on Immigration Reform (1997). *Binational Study: Migration Between Mexico and the United States* (available at http://www.utexas.edu/lbj/uscir/binational.html; last viewed February 6, 2007).

United States–Mexico Migration Panel (2001). *Mexico–U.S. Migration: A Shared Responsibility*. Washington, D.C.: Carnegie Endowment for International Peace/ITAM, February.

Vásquez, Carlos and Manuel García y Griego (eds.) (1983). *Mexican–U.S. Relations: Conflict and Convergence*. Los Angeles: UCLA Chicano Studies Research Center Publications.

Velasco, Jesús (2000). "Vender ideas y comprar influencias: México y los *think tanks* estadounidenses en la promoción del TLCAN," in Rodolfo de la Garza and Jesús Velasco (coords.), *México y su interacción con el sistema político estadounidense* (pp. 159–218). Mexico City: Porrúa/CIDE.

Verduzco, Gustavo (1998). "Economía, demografía y políticas migratorias en la migración mexicana a Estados Unidos," in Ilán Bizberg (comp.), *México ante el fin de la guerra fría* (pp. 375–397). Mexico City: El Colegio de México.

Verea, Mónica (1982). *Entre México y Estados Unidos: los indocumentados*. Mexico City: El Caballito.

——— (1988). "Contradicciones de la Ley Simpson Rodino," in Manuel García y Griego and Mónica Verea, *México y estados Unidos frente a la migración de los indocumentados* (pp. 13–48). Mexico City: UNAM/Porrúa.

Vernez, George (1990). *Immigration and International Relations: Proceedings of a Conference on the International Effects of the 1986 Immigration Reform and Control Act (IRCA)*. Washington, D.C.: The Rand Corporation/The Urban Institute.

Vertovec, Steven (2005). "The Political Importance of Diasporas," *Migration Information Source* (June). Washington, D.C.: Migration Policy Institute.

Walsh, Casey (2000). "Demobilizing the Revolution: Migration, Repatriation and Colonization in Mexico, 1911–1940," Working Paper No. 26, San Diego, Center For Comparative Immigration Studies, UCSD.

Weiner, Myron (1995). *The Global Migration Crisis: Challenge to States and to Human Rights*. New York: HarperCollins.

Weiner, Tim (2003). "Foreign Minister in Mexico Will Quit, Frustrated by the U.S.," *The New York Times*, January 9.

Wendt, Alexander (1992). "Anarchy Is What States Make of It: The Social Construction of Power Politics," *International Organization*, 46(2): 391–425.

Weintraub, Sidney (1998). "Responses to Migration: IRCA and the Facilitation of U.S.–Mexico Migration Dialogue," in *Migration between Mexico and the United States: Binational Study* (Vol. 3, pp. 1229–1233). Austin: Morgan Printing (available at http://www.utexas.edu/lbj/uscir/binpapers/v3c-3weintraub .pdf; last viewed February 7, 2007).

Weintraub, Sidney, Francisco Alba, Rafael Fernández de Castro, and Manuel García y Griego (1998). "Responses to Migration Issues," in *Migration between Mexico and the United States: Binational Study* (Vol. 1, pp. 437–509). Austin: Morgan Printing (available at http://www.utexas.edu/lbj/uscir/binpapers/v1-5weintraub.pdf; last viewed February 7, 2007).

Weissert, Will (2005). "Mexican Official Calls Fence Plan 'Stupid'," The Associated Press, December 19.

Wides-Muñoz, Laura (2008). "In Twist to Immigration Debate, Mexico Quietly Helps Teach Citizens Who Have Emigrated to U.S.," The Associated Press, September 24.

Williams, Krissah (2005). "U.S. Banks Hope Money Transfers Attract Hispanics," *Washington Post*, October 6.

Zazueta, Carlos H. (1983). "Mexican Political Actors in the US and Mexico: Historical and Political Contexts of a Dialogue Renewed," in Carlos Vázquez and Manuel García y Griego (eds.), *Mexican–US Relations: Conflict and Convergence* (pp. 441–482). Los Angeles: University of California.

Zolberg, Aristide (2006). *A Nation by Design: Immigration Policy in the Fashioning of America*. Cambridge, MA: Harvard University Press.

Zoraida Vázquez, Josefina (1990). *México y el mundo: Historia de sus relaciones exteriores* (Vol. 1). Mexico City: Senado de la República.

_____ and Lorenzo Meyer (1994). *México frente a Estados Unidos: Un ensayo histórico (1776–1993)*. Mexico City: Fondo de Cultura Económica.

Index

287(g) program, 143, 224
3 × 1 Program, 40, 148–150, 221
   Zacatecas, 40, 149
9/11, 29, 50, 174, 176, 177–180, 183, 187,
   196, 244

absentee voting rights, 39, 47, 48, 52, 151,
   217–221, 222, 229, 234, 246
   IFE–Mexican Federal Elections Institute,
   218
   Mexican Foreign Ministry opinion,
   219–220
   Michoacán, 221
   voting cards, 218, 221
   Zacatecas, 221
ACLU, 241
AEDPA, 51, 142, 195
AFL-CIO, 97, 168, 170
Aguilar Zinser, Adolfo, 192
Alemán, Miguel, 92, 94
American G.I. Forum,
American Jewish Committee, 205
amnesty. *See* regularization
Amnesty International, 193
anti-immigrant groups, 95, 110, 115, 135,
   143, 191, 217, 224, 234
Arizona, 240–242
   Jan Brewer, 241
   S.B. 1070, 240–243
Asencio Commission. *See* Commission for
   the Study of International Migration
   and Cooperative Economic
   Development
Asencio, Diego, 128–129

asymmetry of power, 28, 29, 30, 48, 50,
   54, 81, 83, 86, 139, 161, 164, 168,
   197, 230, 234–239, 246, 247
   precipice paradox, 29
Avena Case, 53, 192–193, 237
   International Court of Justice, 53, 237
   Vienna Convention on Consular
   Relations, 53, 237
Ávila Camacho, Manuel, 86

Banco de México. *See* Remittances
Becas de Aztlán. See Chicano Movement
Berruga, Enrique, 3, 27, 176, 202
Beta Groups. *See Grupos Beta*
bilateral agreement. *See* migration
   agreement
Binational Commission, 36, 134, 155, 158,
   194
Binational Outreach Commission. *See*
   Comisión Mixta de Enlace
Binational Study Group, 168
Binational Study on Migration, 36, 160
border control, 92, 111, 114, 130, 142,
   144, 161, 169, 172, 230, 243
   decentralization of, 92
   Mexico's southern border, 184, 243
   operations, 142, 156
      Blockade, 142
      Gatekeeper, 142, 156
      Hold the Line, 142, 156
      Rio Grande, 142
      Safeguard, 142
border fence, 186, 243
Border Liaison Mechanisms, 36

283